The ORACLE of
DelphAI

//

The ORACLE of DelphAI

Arturo Martinini

R

revelore press
Olympia WA
2023

Book design and typography by Jenn Zahrt.
Illustrations and cover art designed between
July 2nd and December 1st 2022 by Arturo Martinini
with the help of Midjourney versions 1–4.

ISBN: 978-1-947544-50-5
Printed worldwide through Ingram.

Revelore Press
1910 4th AVE E PMB141
Olympia WA 98506
United States
www.revelore.press

First printed in 2023.

Contents

//

/Mission

THIS BOOK is my contribution to the living tradition of astrological magic. The images you're about to interact with emerged from my exploration with the relationship between technology and the occult. I created these talismanic images wanting to emphasize the Greek root of the word technology, techne, which simply means making, or doing. I worked in collaboration with the artificial intelligence network known as Midjourney in its versions 1–4 to generate images inspired by the collected aesthetics of medieval and classical paintings, as well as the mysterious pages of ancient compendiums of alchemy and magic.

In following the traditional instructions to create magical images in grimoires, I found myself participating in the continuum of talismanic ekphrasis that animates this deep spiritual practice. The digital nature of the tool I utilized to create the elements of each talismanic image did not feel like a distraction or a sacrilegious shortcut, but a completely integrated mechanical process moved by all the principles found in the worldview based on the Anima Mundi. The neural network, with its "hidden layers" mysteriously at work, crystalizes potent images out of noise, drawing in the sense of awe and summoning the forces of inspiration we seek when performing magical ritual. With these images printed and physically in your hands, I openly invite you to participate in keeping the practice of creative divination alive and iterating.

On the left page, you'll see the codex; on the right, a talismanic image. The image sources appear below the codex page, with the most central works being the /Picatrix/ (Ghāyat al-Hakīm), and the /Three Books of Occult Philosophy/ written and compiled by H. C. Agrippa. I consulted various translations of each text as I crafted my prompts.*

Work with this book in the spirit of techne. Copy its pages. Write on their blank spaces and on the images. Rip them and burn them if appropriate for your talismanic rituals. The tradition hungers for us to wrestle with it, using our own compulsive and idiosyncratic methods. I hope this collection can serve as one arena to engage that confrontation.

/Ad maiora.

Arturo Martinini
Portland, OR
2023

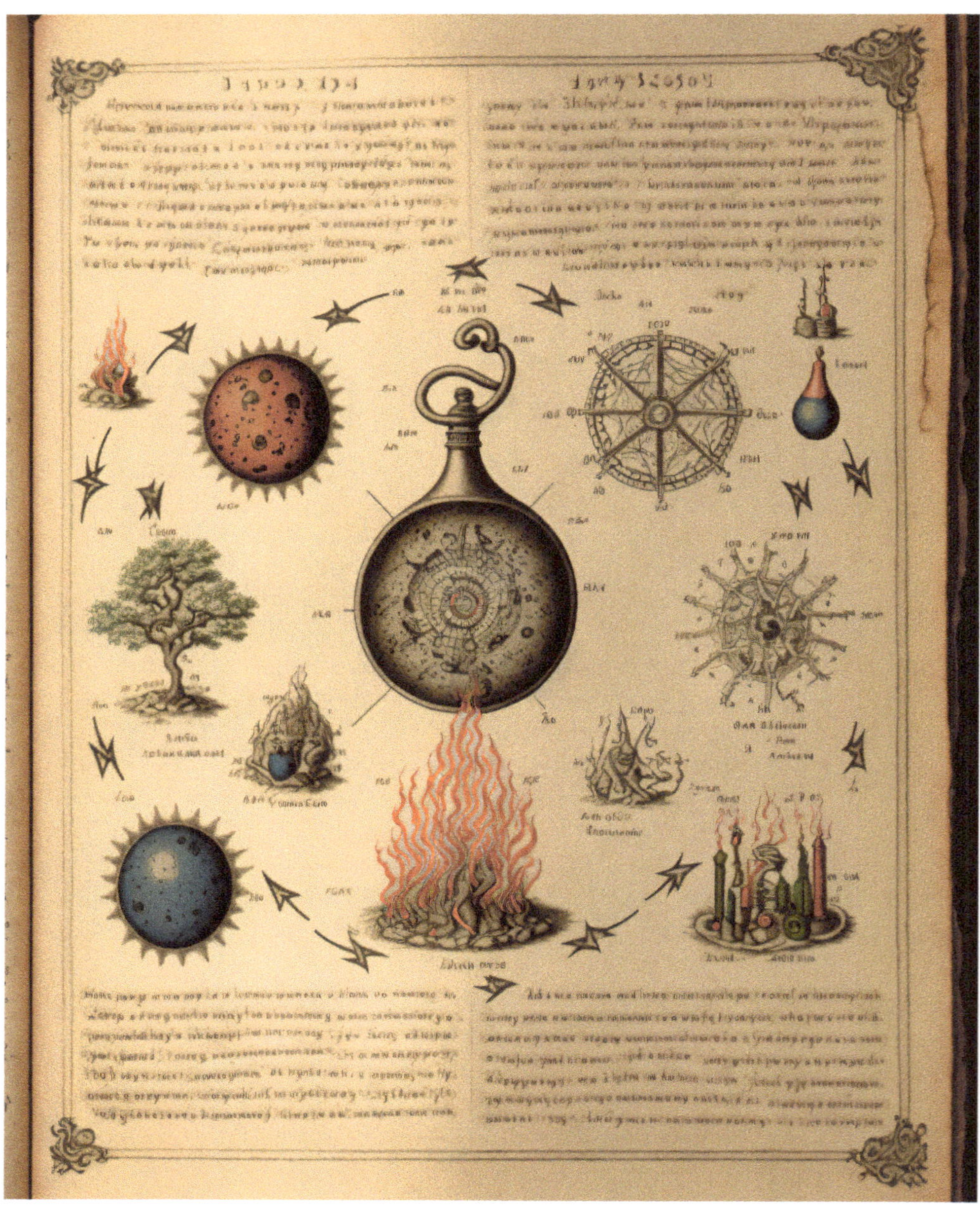

I.I: Mars ... according to the opinion of other sages, is the shape of a man riding a lion, holding a sword in his right hand and brandishing the head of a man in his left; his clothes are of iron and mail. (Picatrix‡2.X§21)

/Oracle of DelphΛI

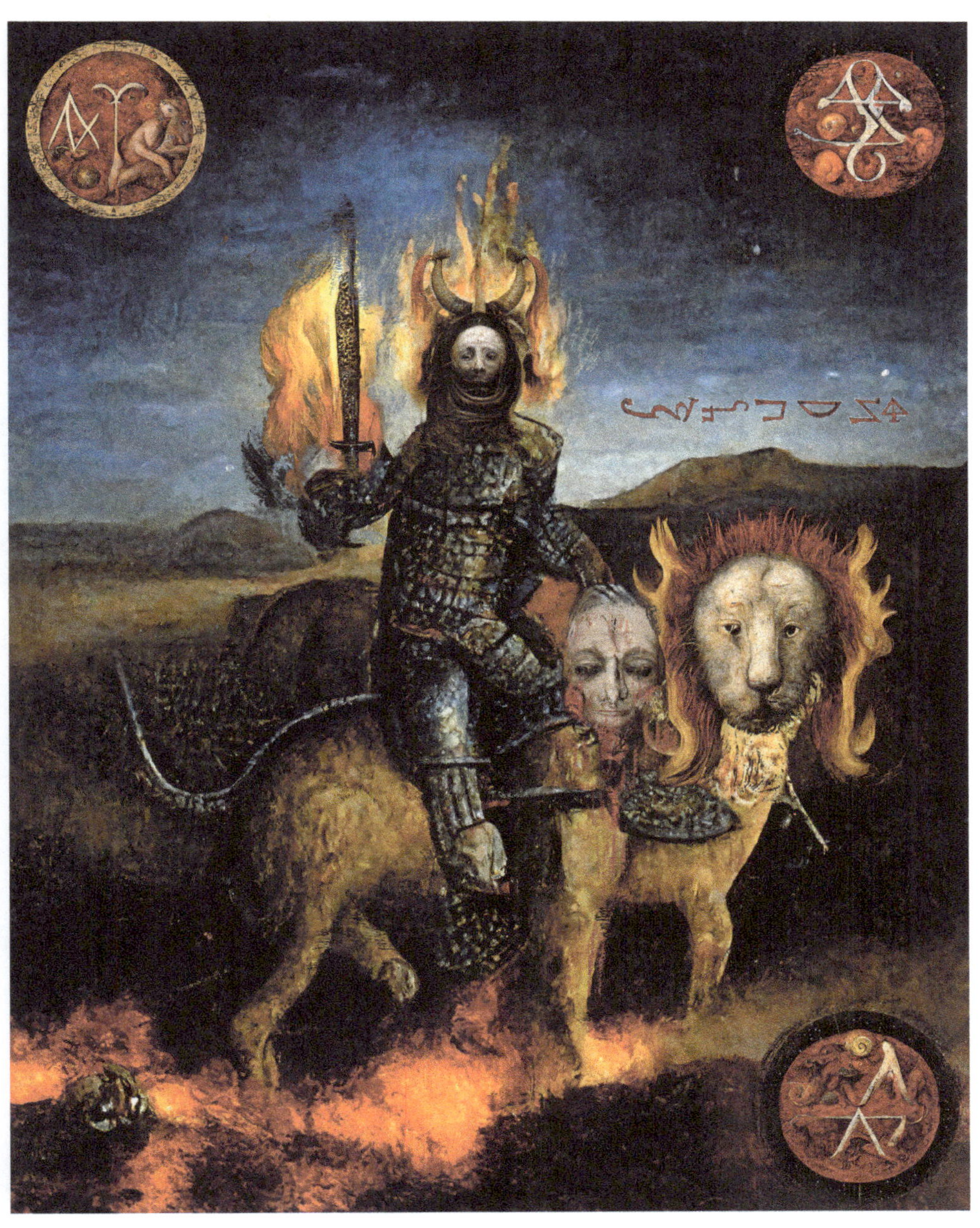

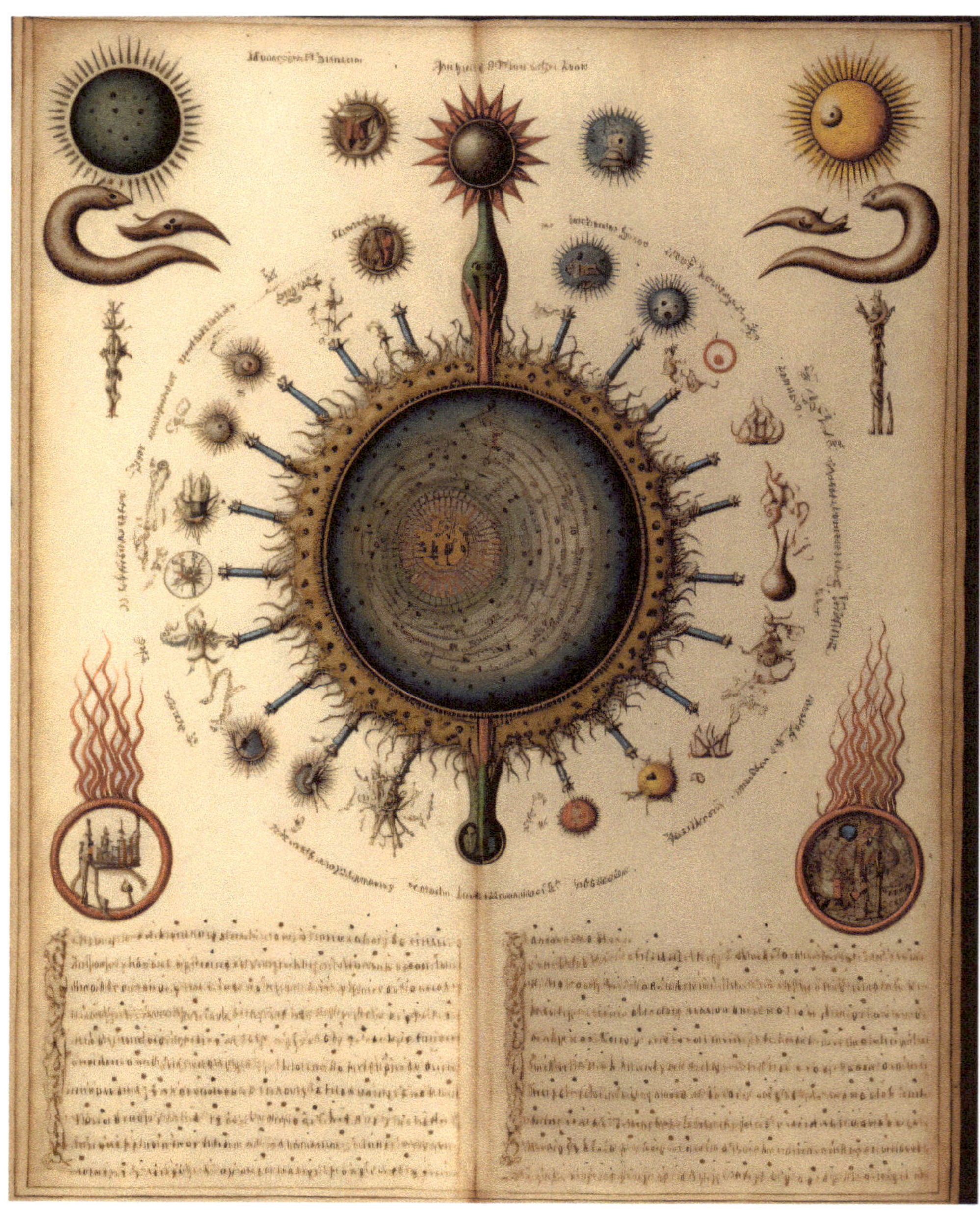

1.2: Sun ... the image of a woman sitting in a chariot drawn by four horses, holding in her right hand a mirror and in her left hand a scepter with a seven branched candelabra over her head. (Picatrix†2.X§22)

/Oracle of DelphΛI

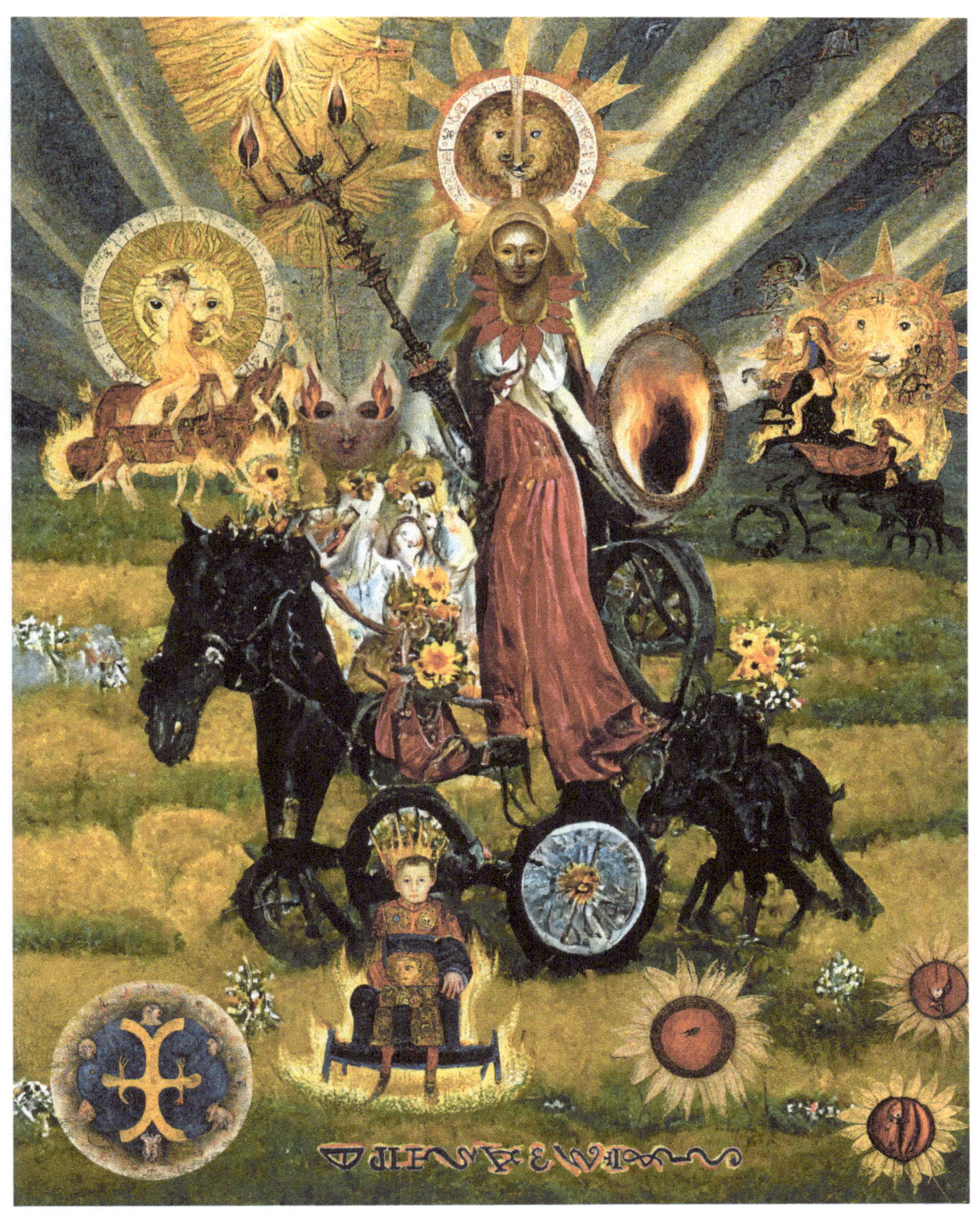

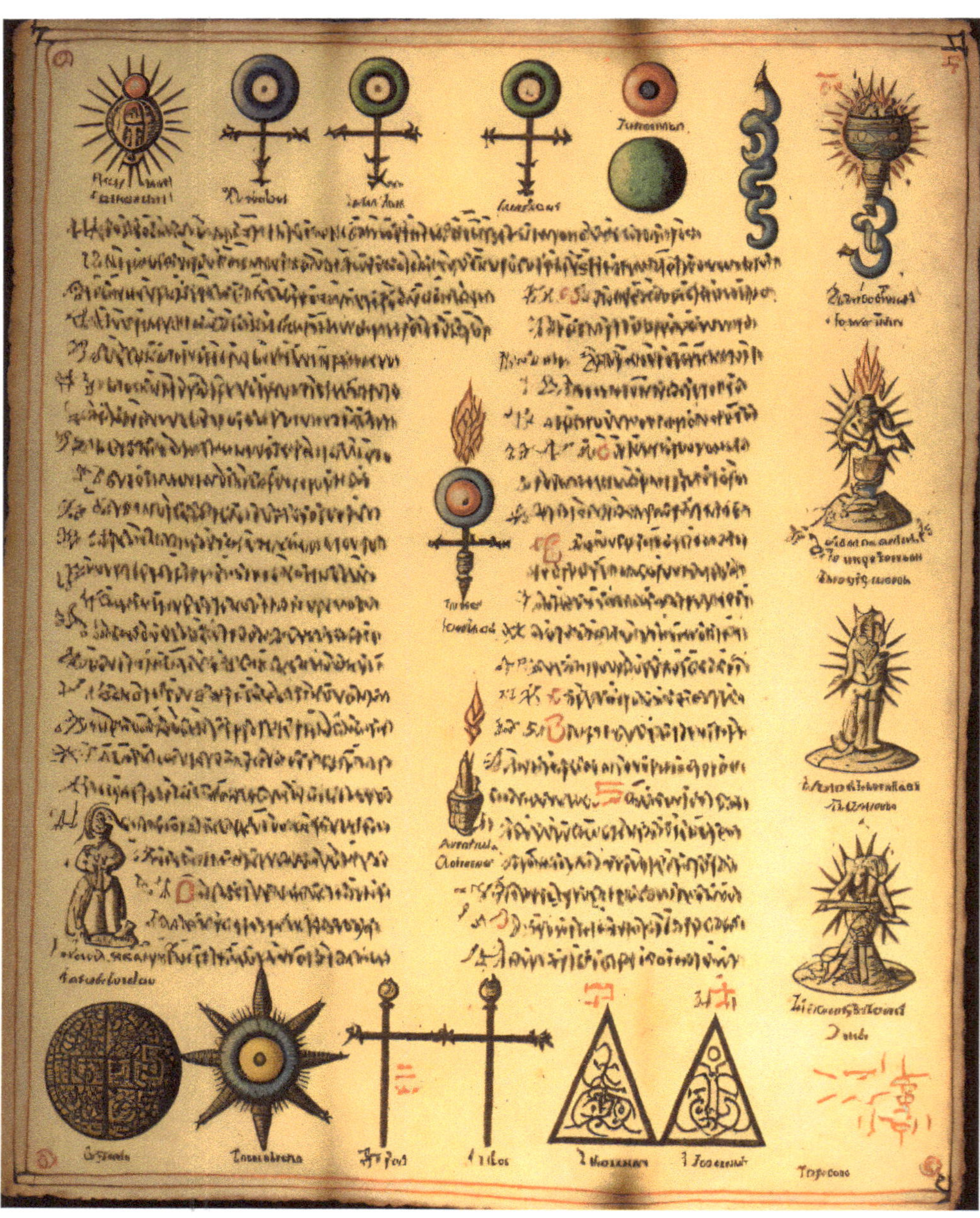

1.3: Venus ... the image of a woman whose body is human with the head of a bird and the feet of an eagle, in her right hand an apple and in her left hand a wooden comb. (Picatrix†2.X§§26–30)

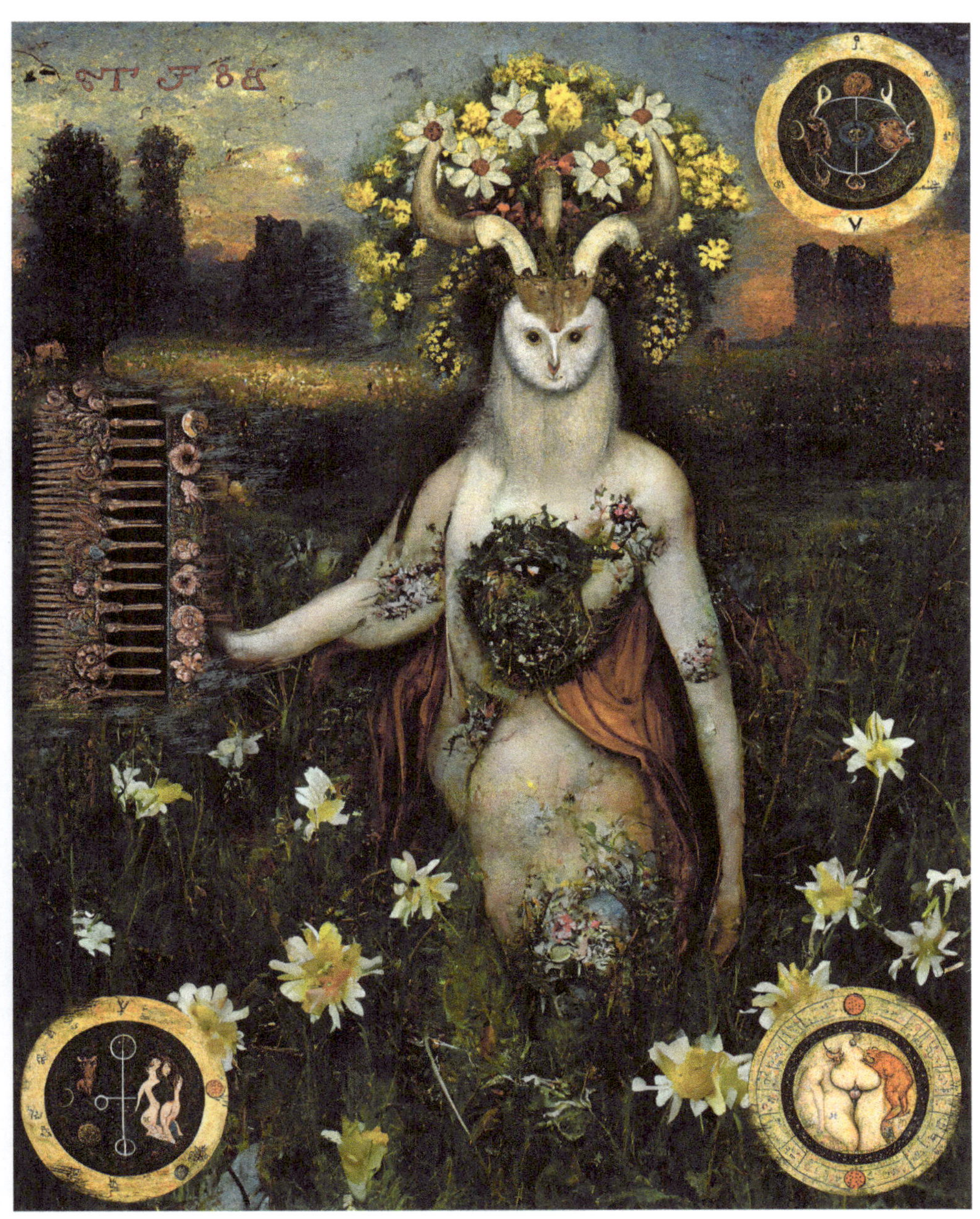

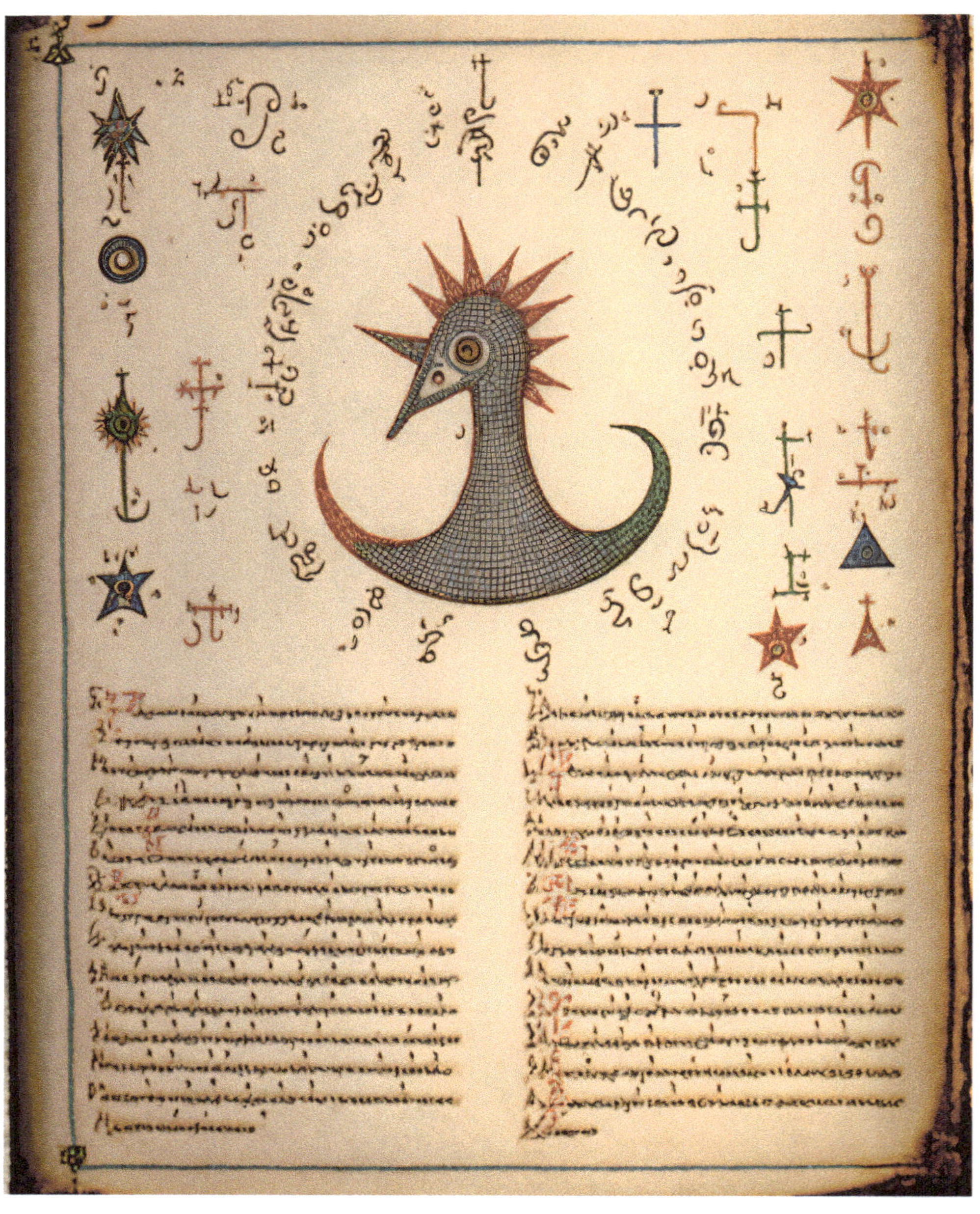

I.4: Mercury ... the image of a nobleman seated on a chair with the head of a rooster and the feet of an eagle, and in his left hand fire. (Picatrix[†] 2.X§§31–34)

/Oracle of DelphΛl

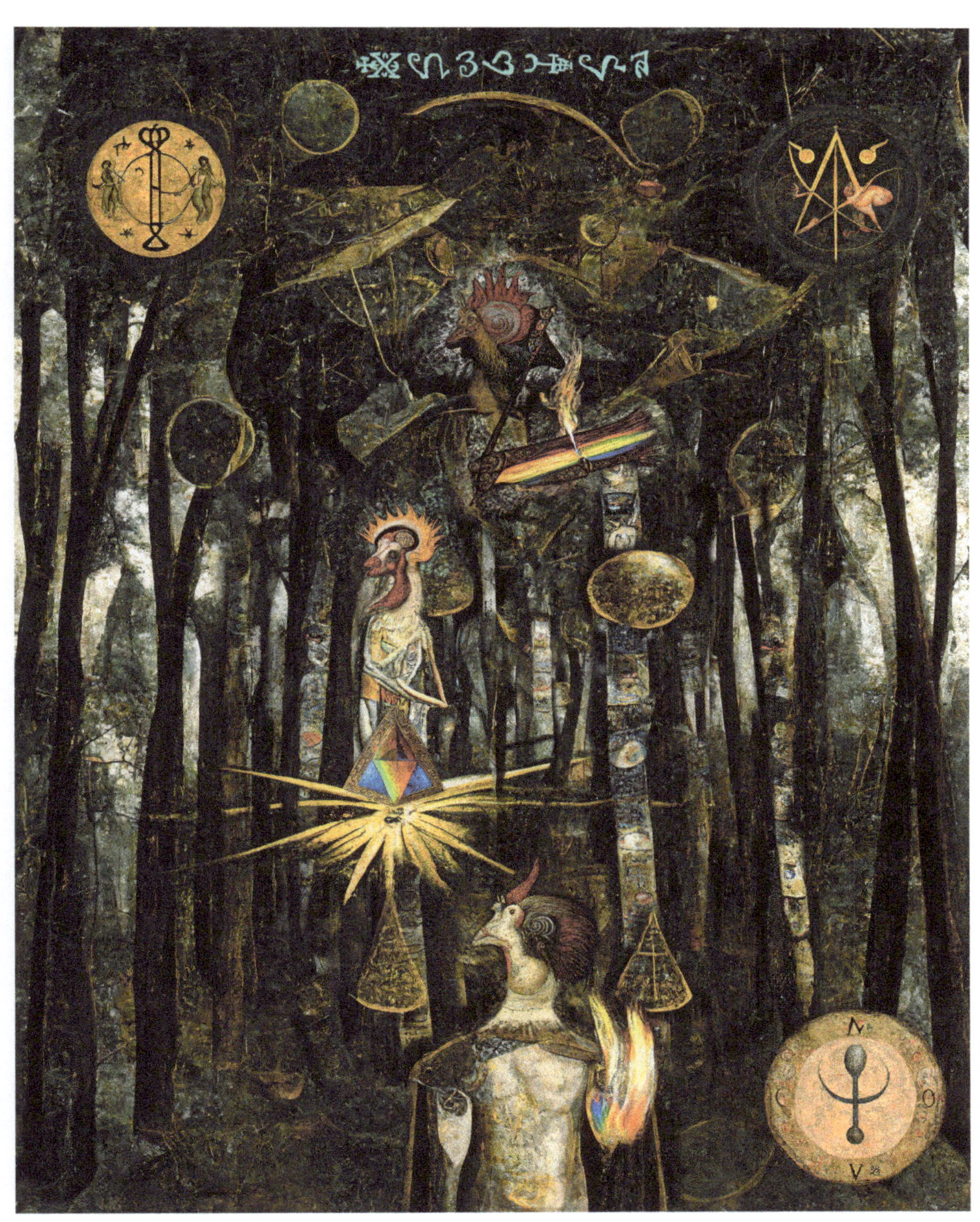

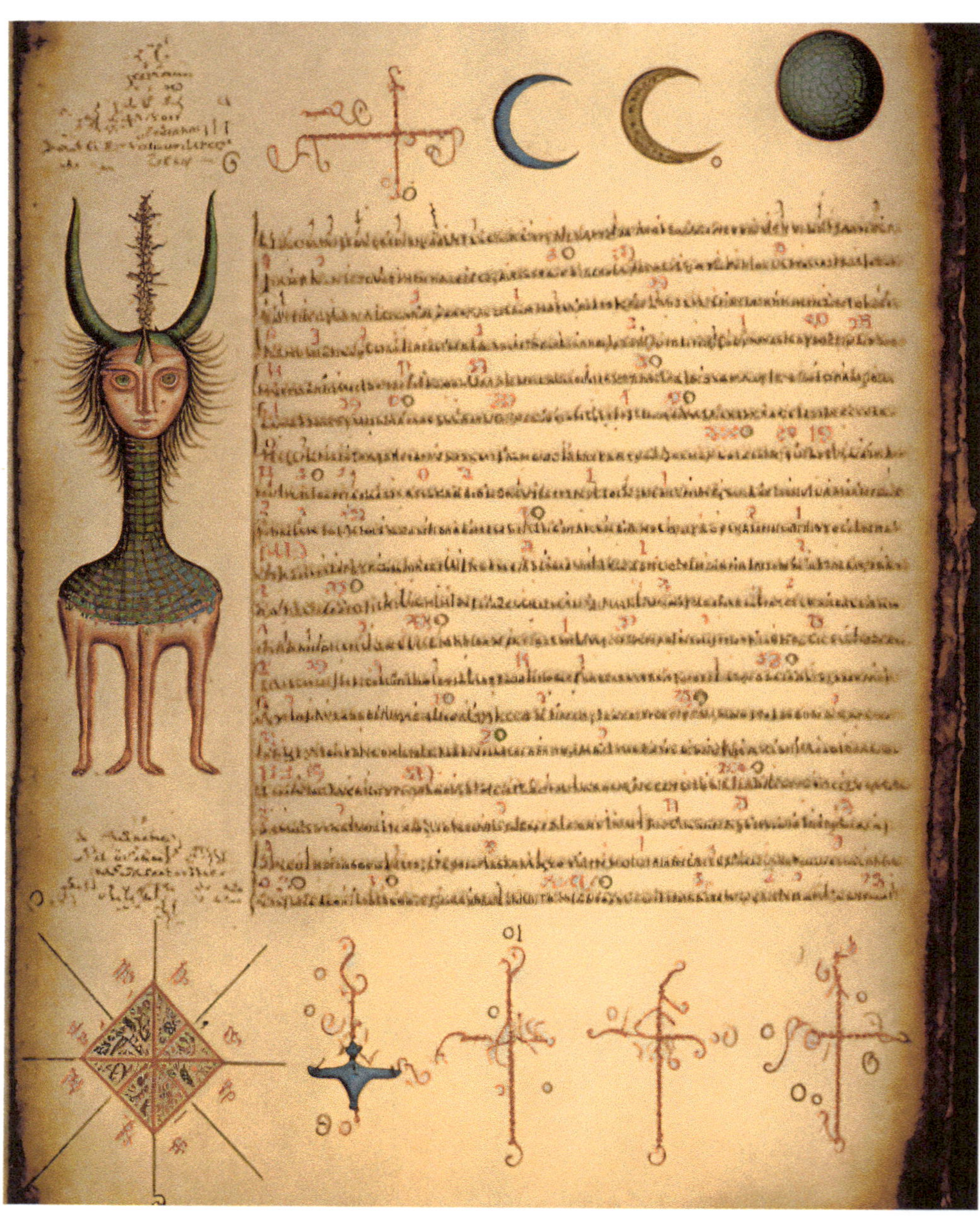

I.5: Moon ... the shape of a woman with a beautiful face, encircled by a dragon, with horns on her head, encircled by two snakes (on her head there are two snakes and on each arm a snake is entwined); above her head there is one dragon and another beneath her feet; each of these dragons has seven heads. (Picatrix‡2.X§35)

/Oracle of DelphΛI

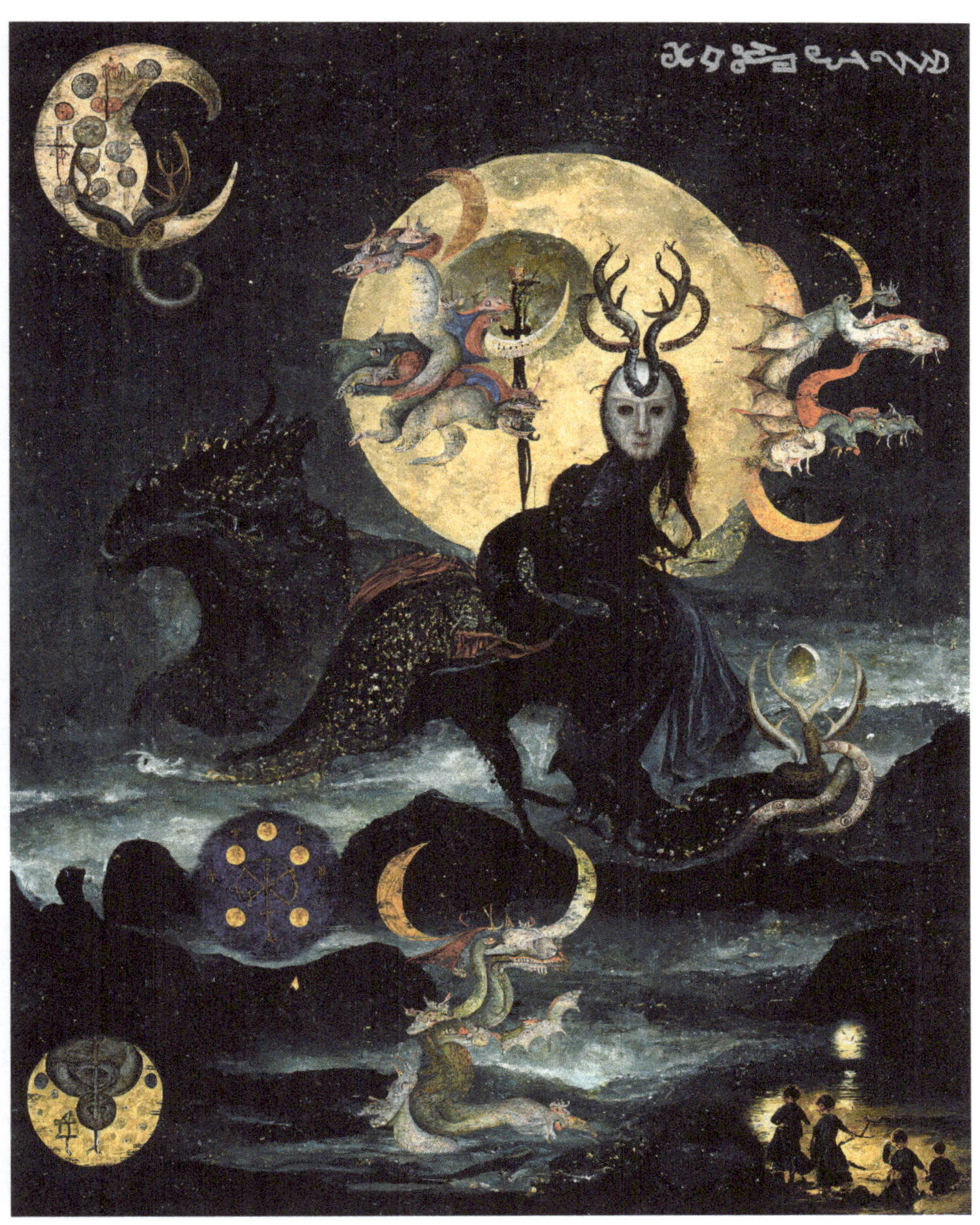

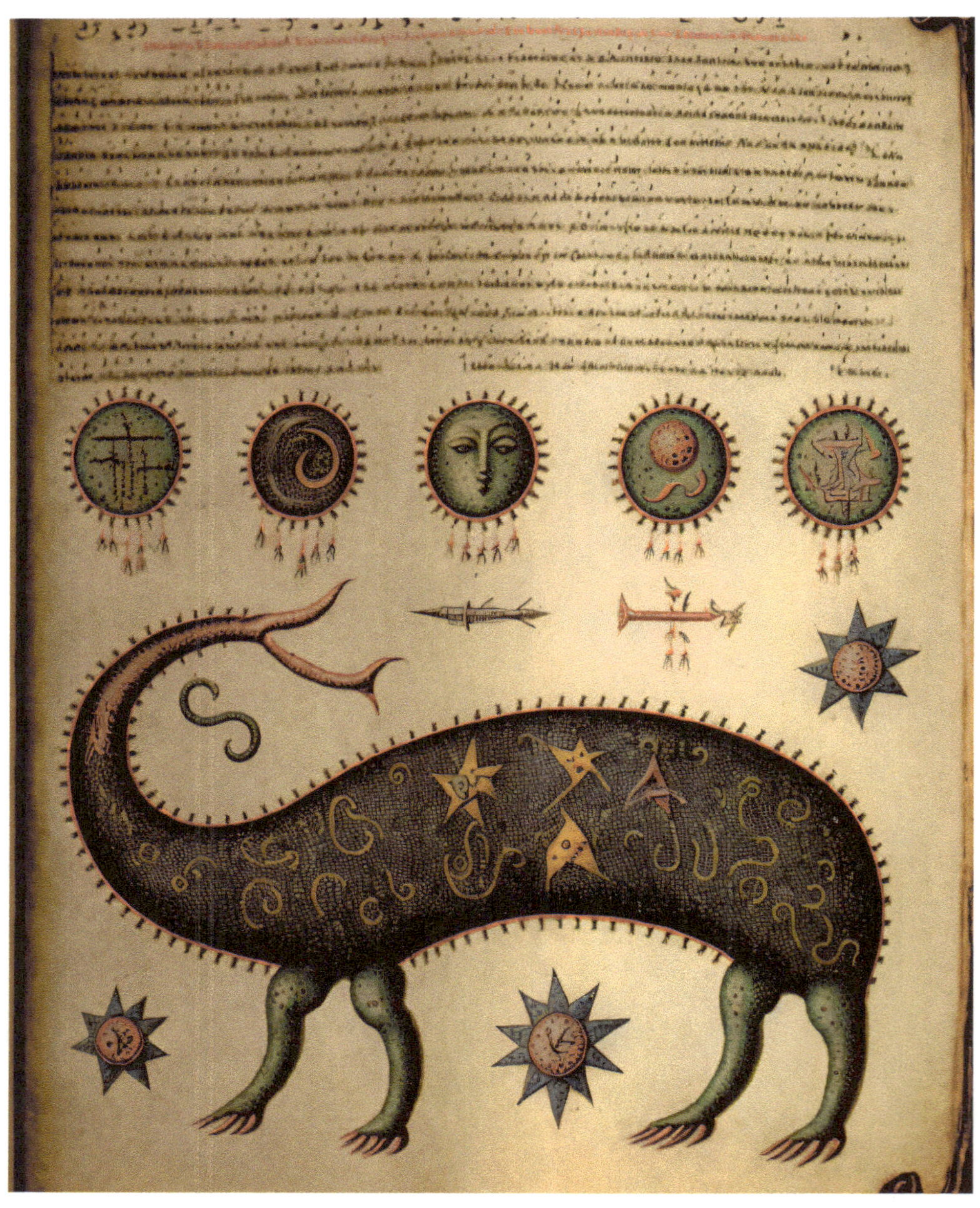

I.6: Saturn ... the image of a man with the face of a deer and the feet of a camel, sitting on a chair or dragon, his right hand holding a sickle, in his left an arrow. (Agrippa, TBOP II§38)

/Oracle of DelphAI

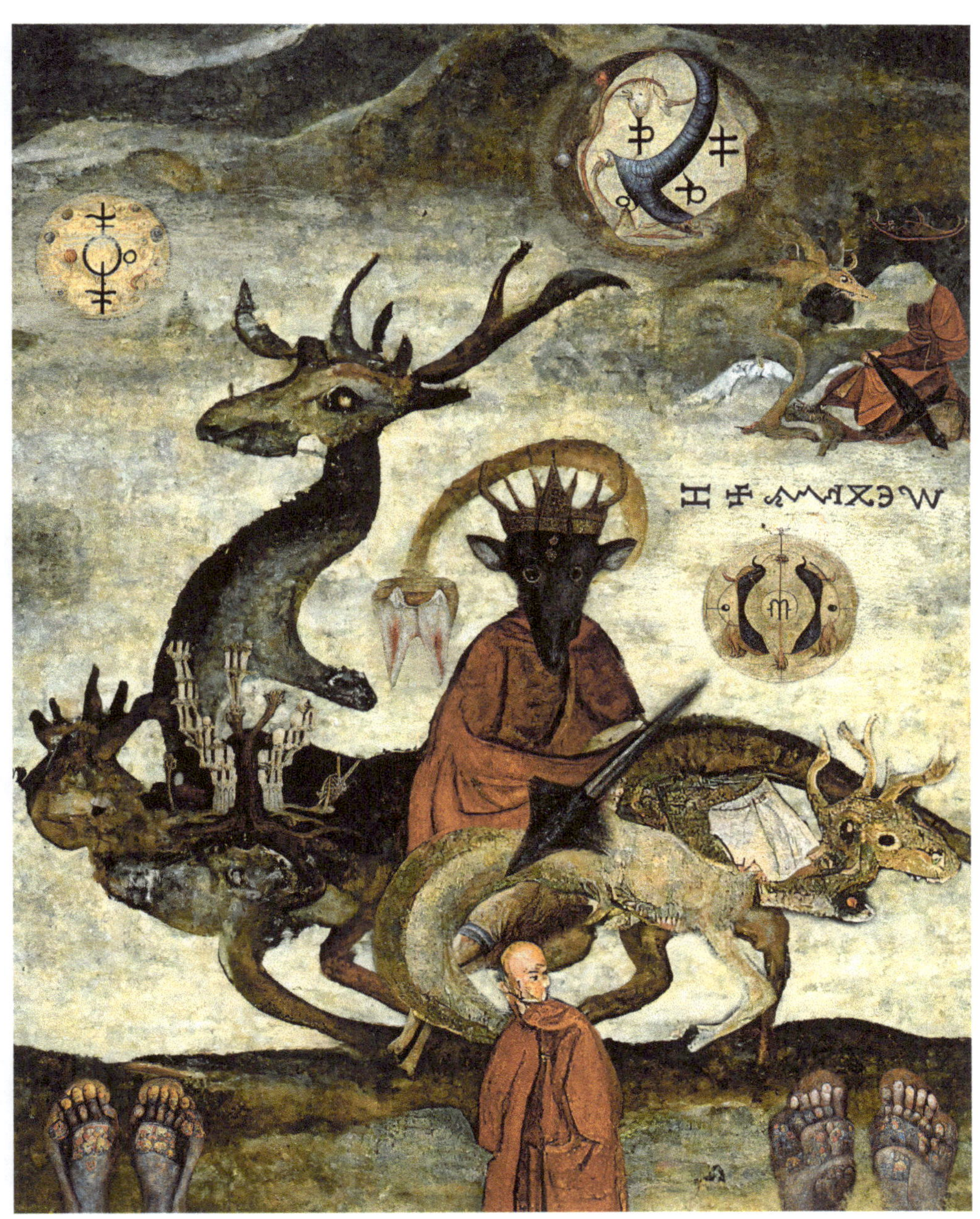

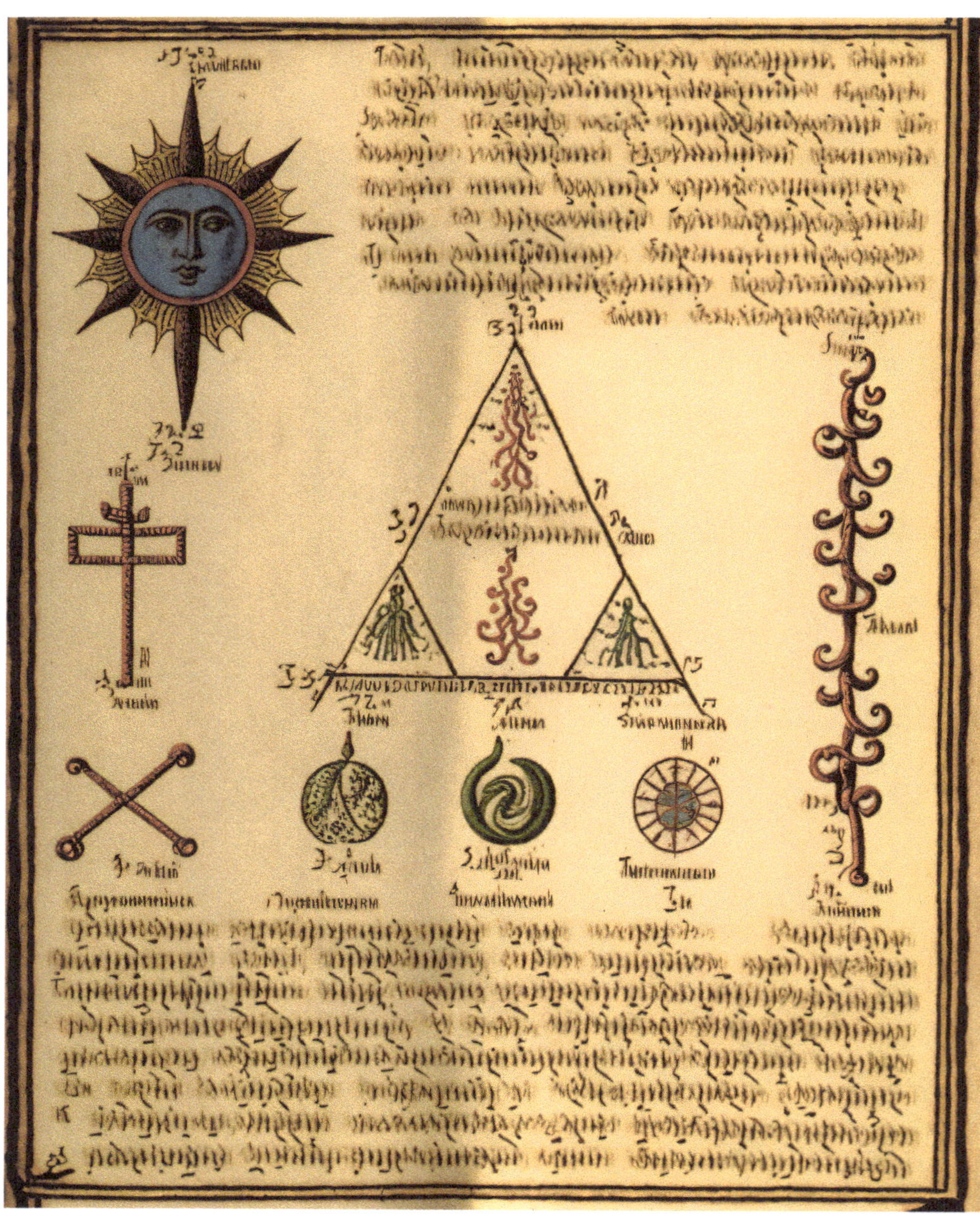

I.7: Jupiter ... is the image of a man riding on an eagle, carrying cloth in his right hand and holding nuts in his left hand, and all of his clothing is saffron clothed. (Picatrix[†]2.X§18)

/Oracle of DelphΛI

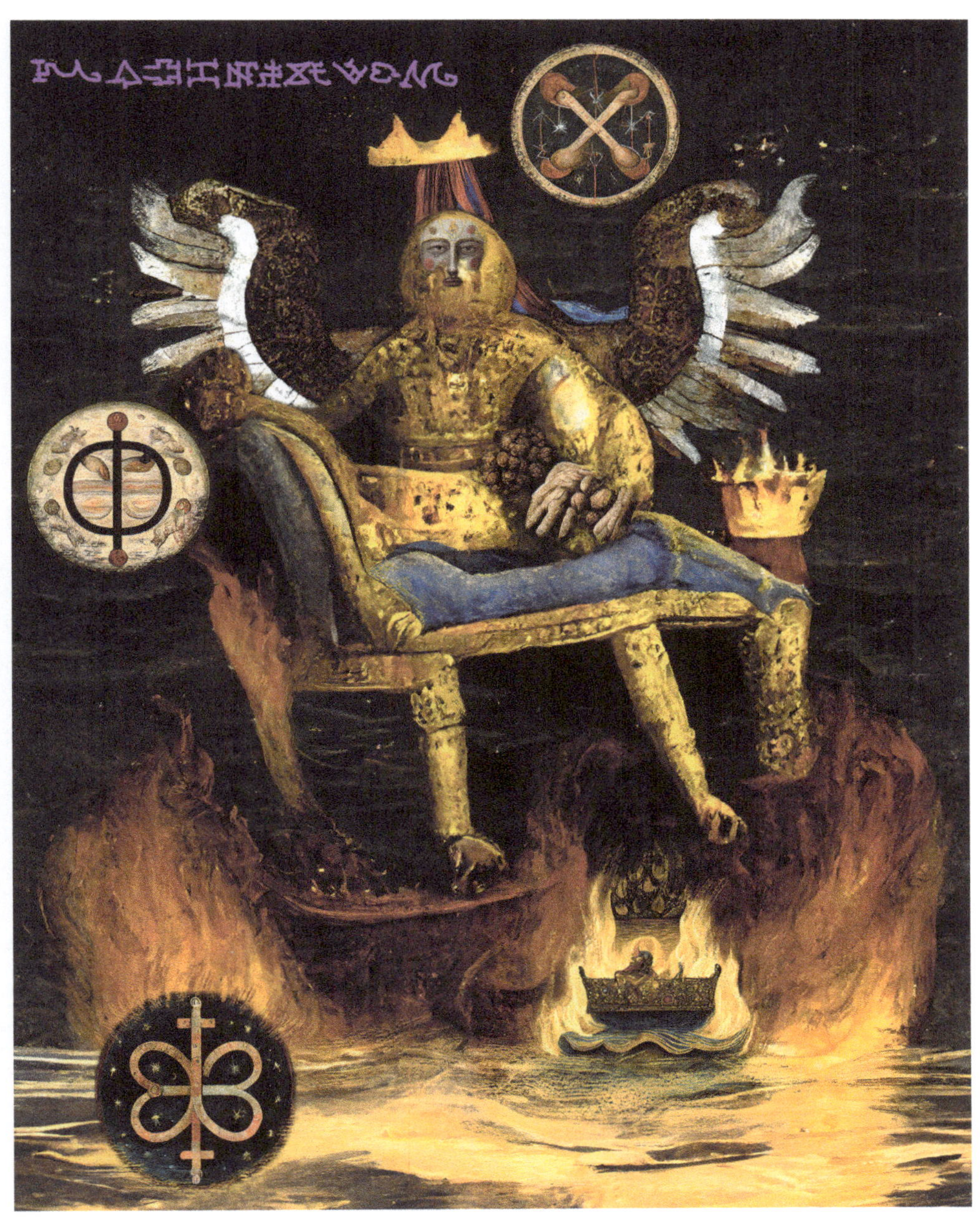

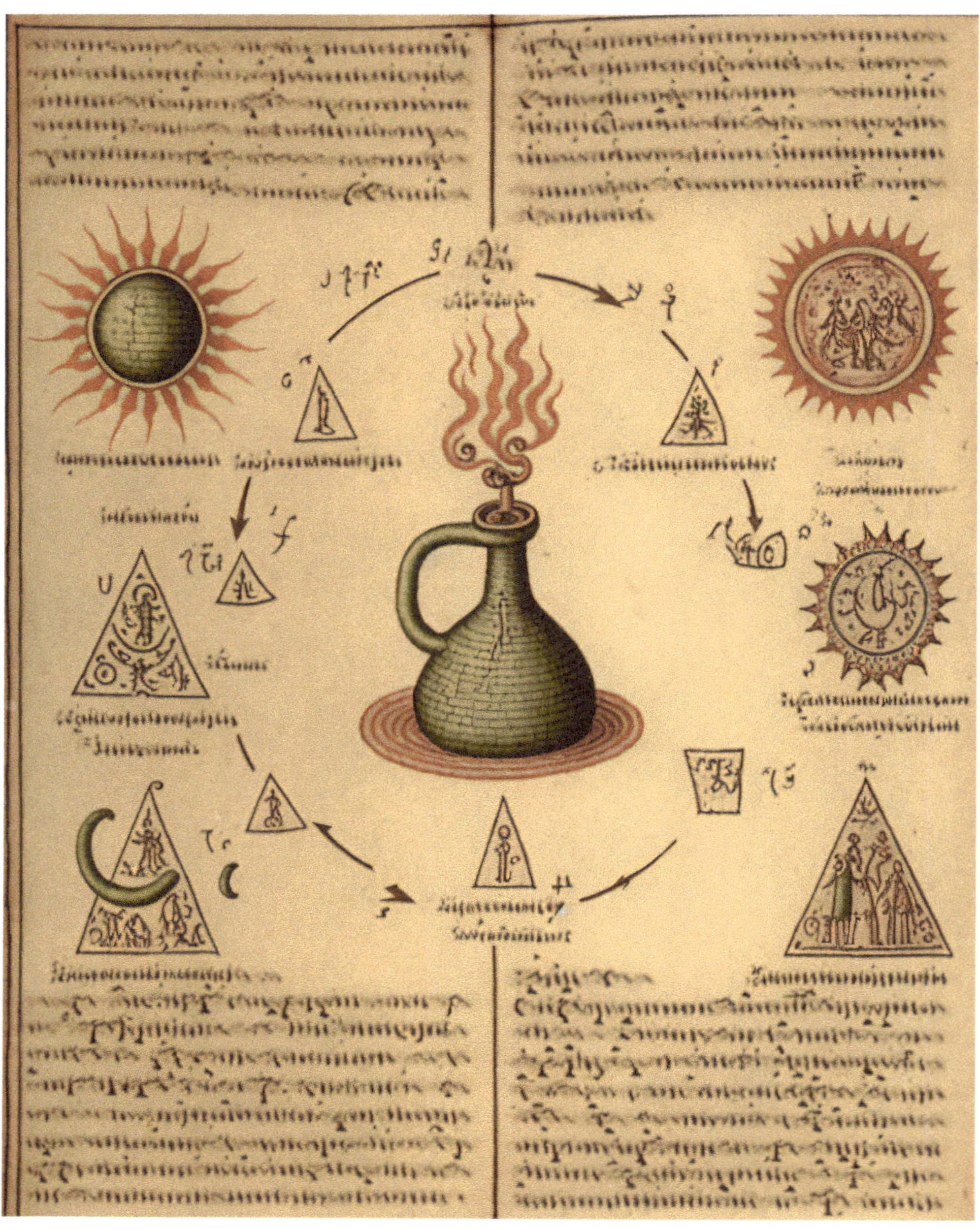

II.I: "Under **Aldebaran** they made images according to the likeness of God or a flying man: it gathers wealth and honor." (Agrippa, TBOP II§47)

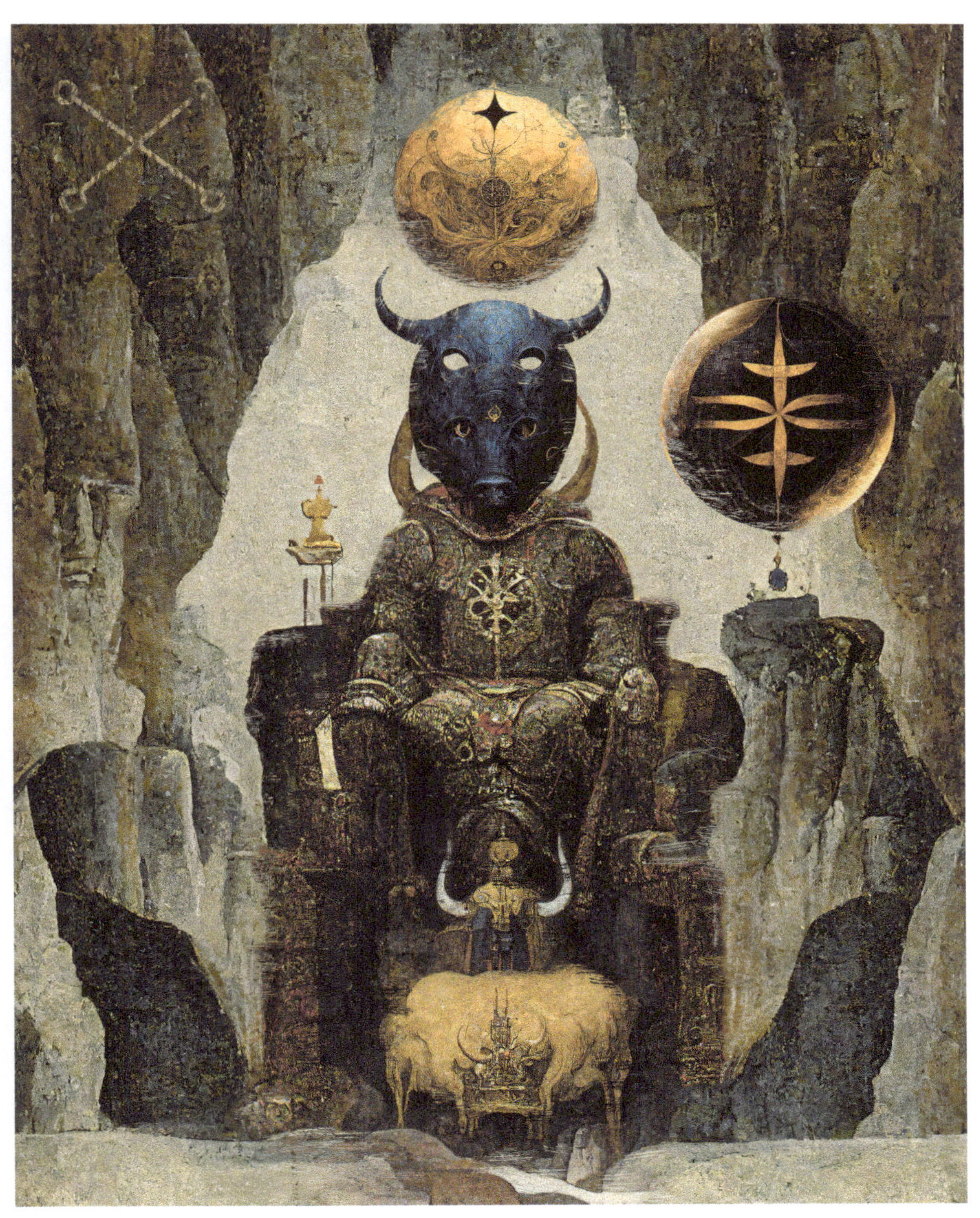

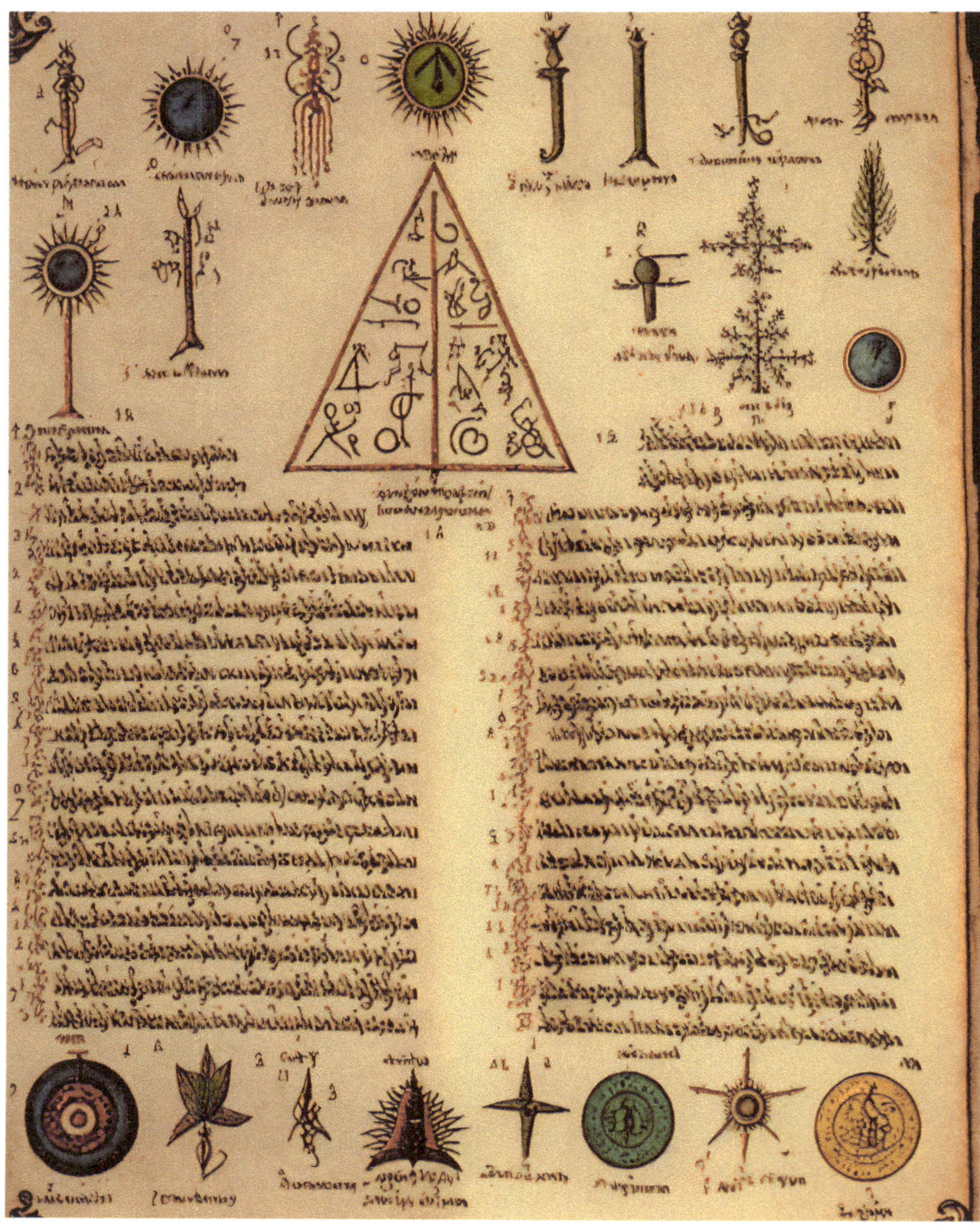

II.2: "Under the constellation of the **Pleiades**, they made an image of a virgin girl or the figure of a torch: [this image] brings an increase of light to the eyes, collects daemons, promotes winds, and reveals secrets and hidden things." (Agrippa, TBOP II§47)

/Oracle of DelphAI

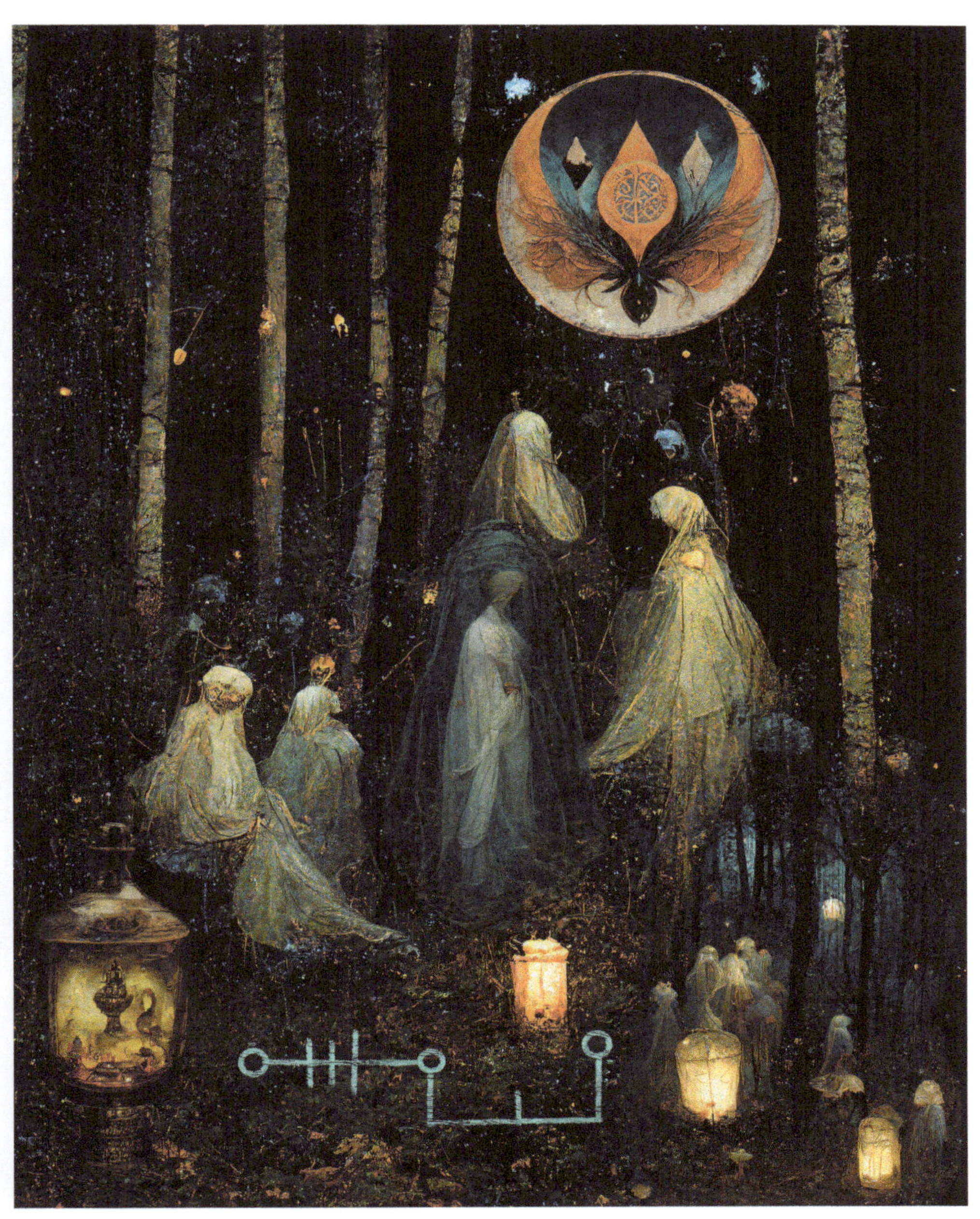

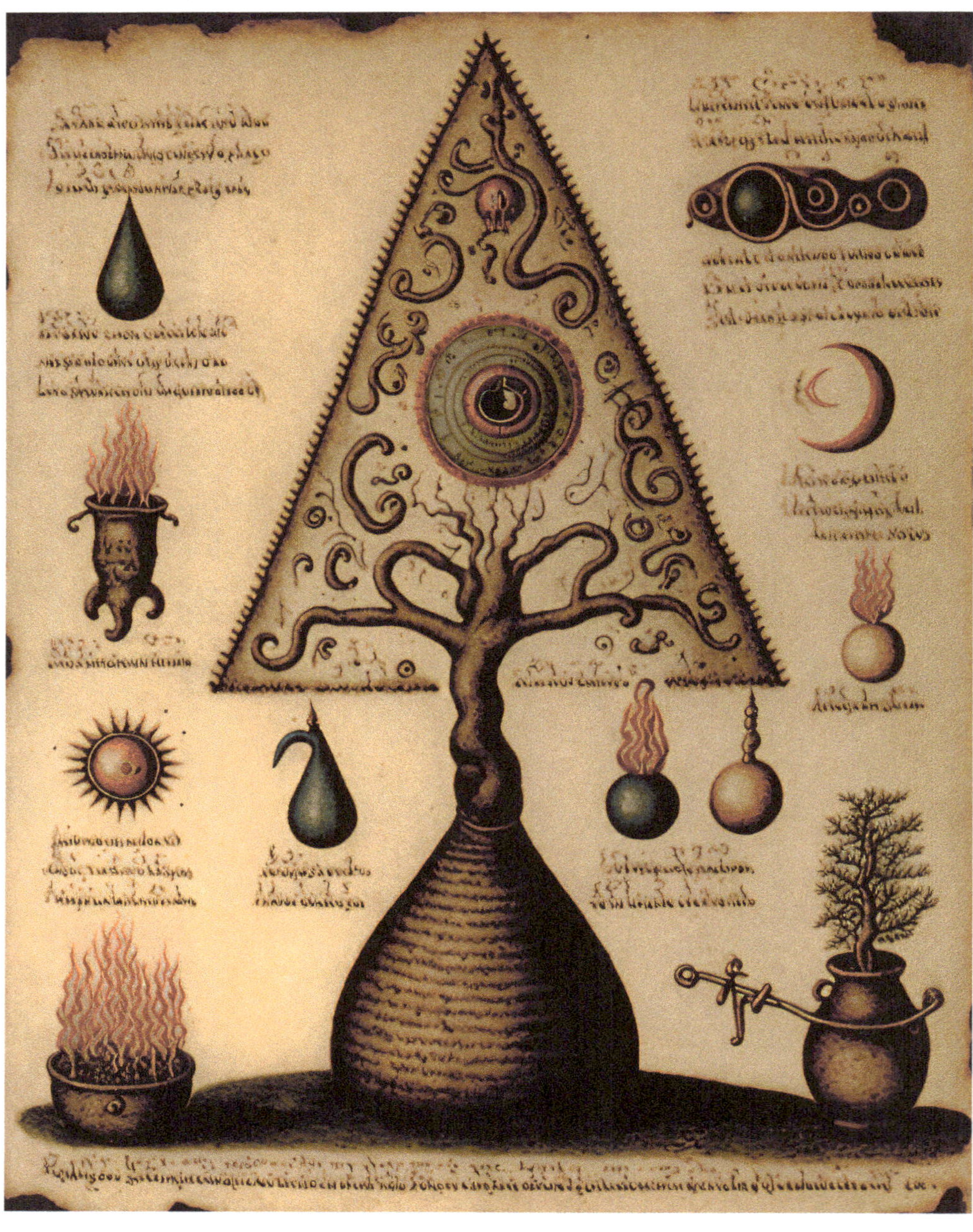

II.3: "Under **Caput Algol**, they made an image whose figure was the head of a man with a long beard, having a bloody neck. This brought the good outcome of petitions, gave the bearer boldness and nobility, preserved members of the body from injury, helped against sorceries, and reflected evil attempts and evil incantations from enemies." (Agrippa, TBOP II§47)

/Oracle of DelphAI

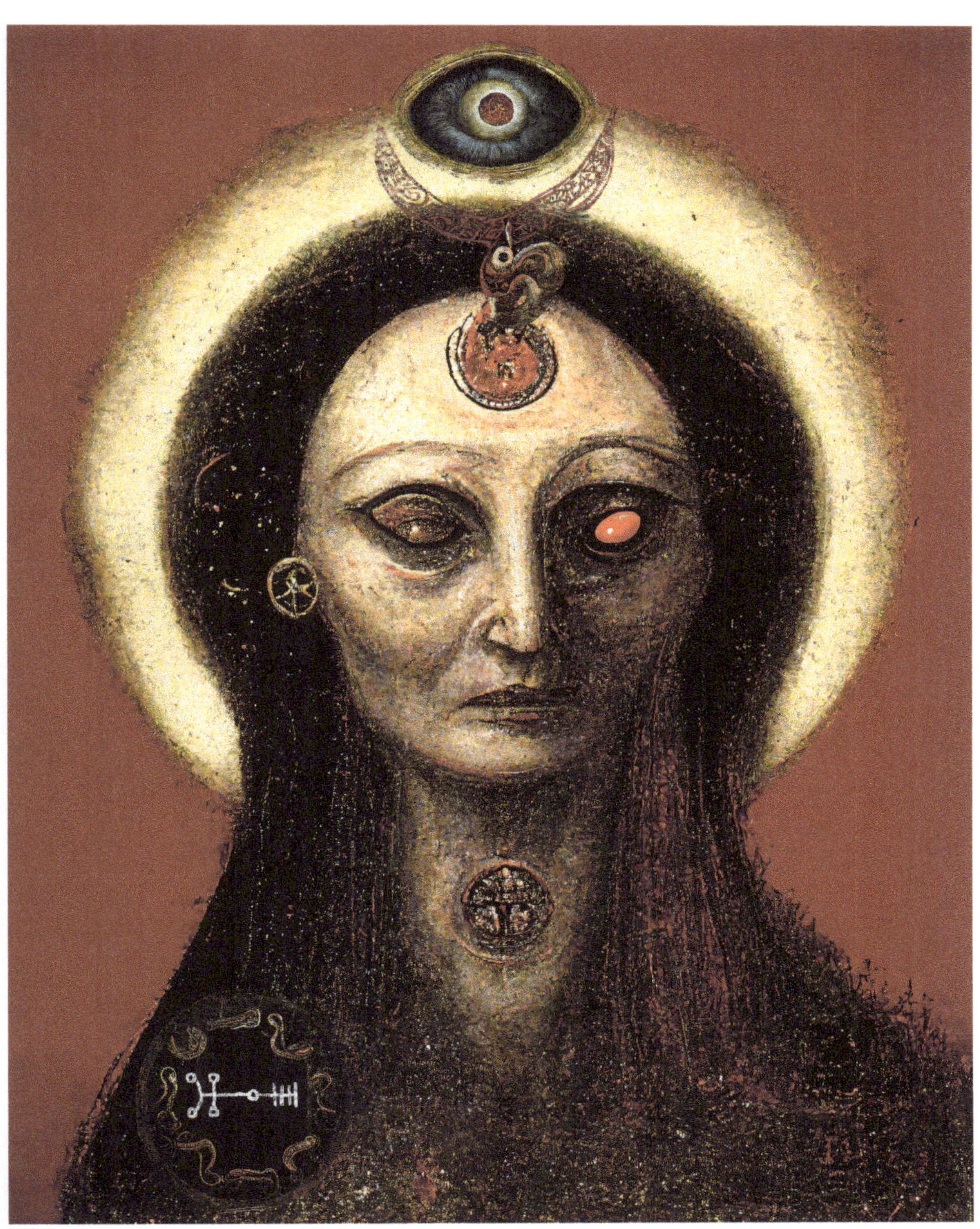

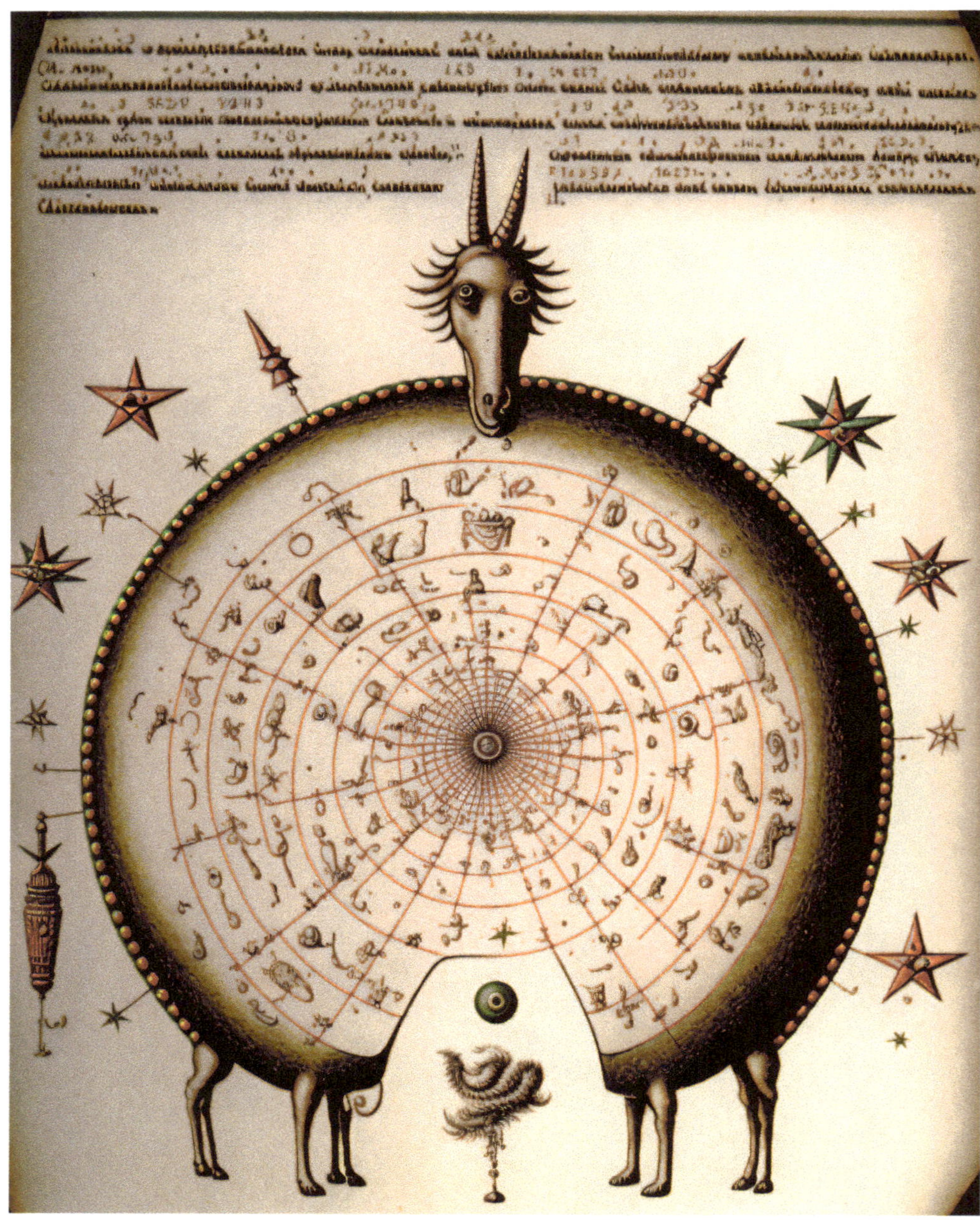

II.4: "Under **Capella,** they made an image whose figure was a man as if he wished to rejoice in musical instruments: this image affects the bearer with grace and honor, the public exaltation of kings and princes, and helps against dental pain." (Agrippa, TBOP II§47)

/Oracle of DelphAI

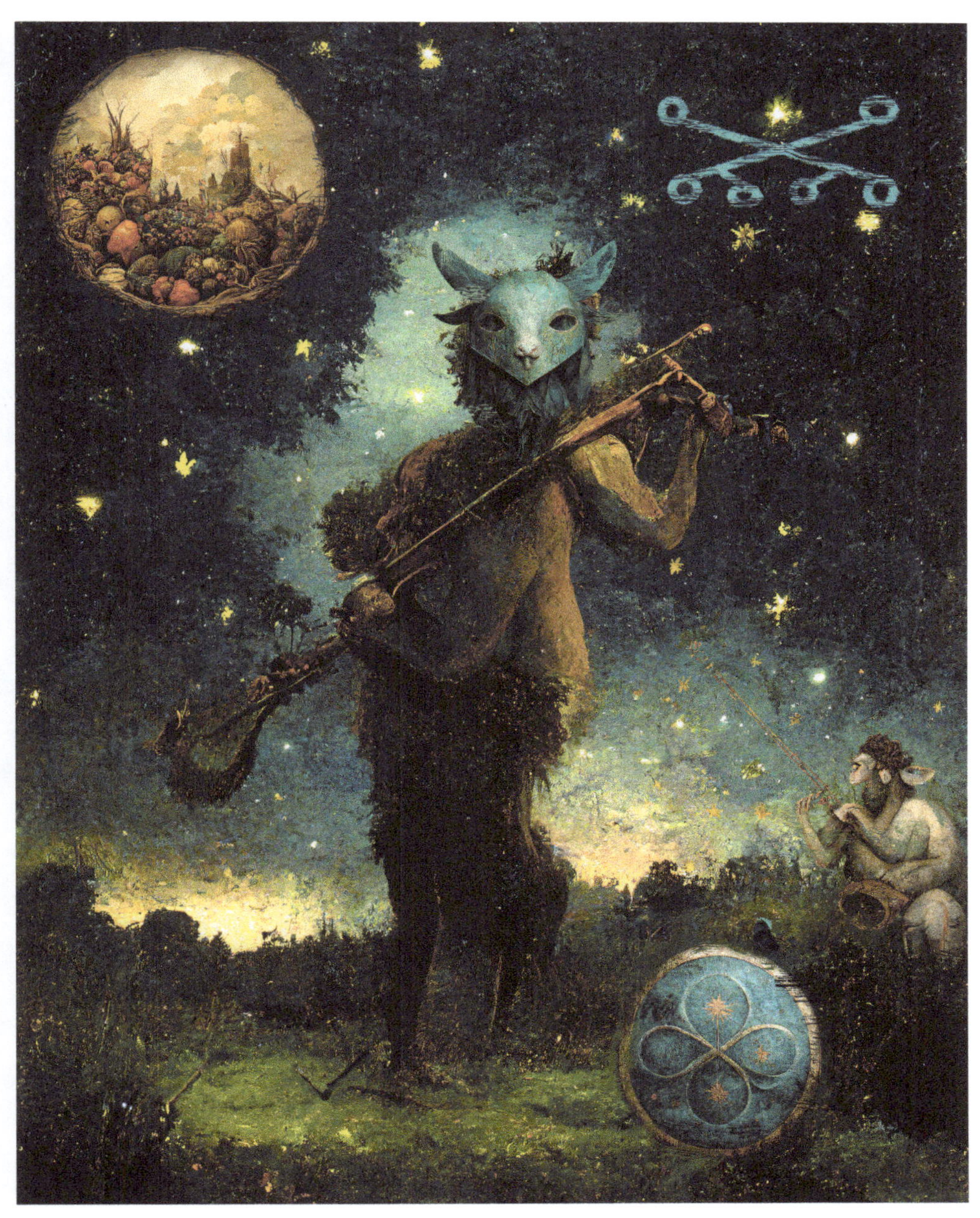

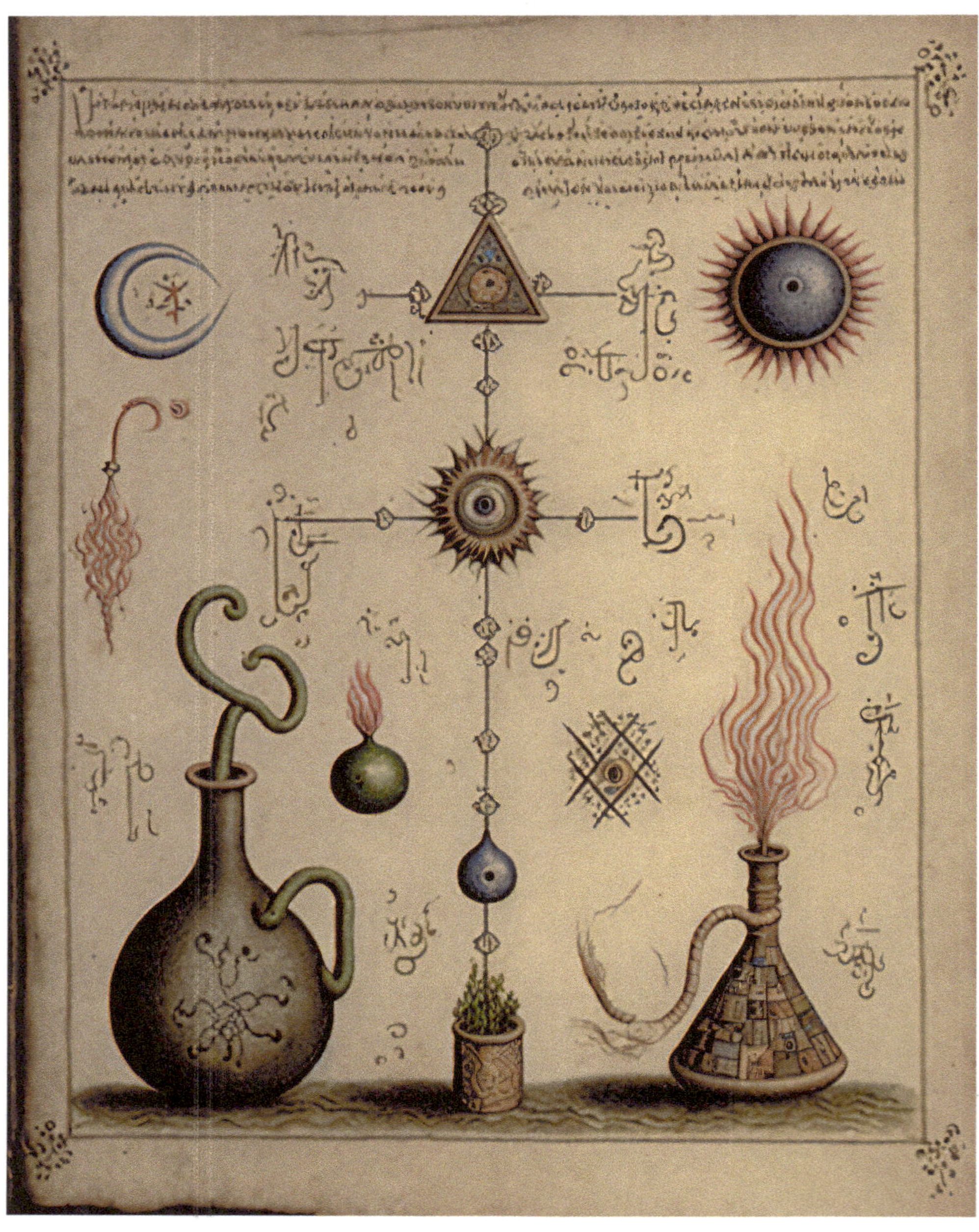

II.5: Sirius "Under Canis Major they made images of a dog, hare, or virgin girl: these bring honor, benevolence, and grace from men and airy spirits, and give the power to pacify and harmonize with kings and princes and other men." (Agrippa, TBOP II§47)

/Oracle of DelphAI

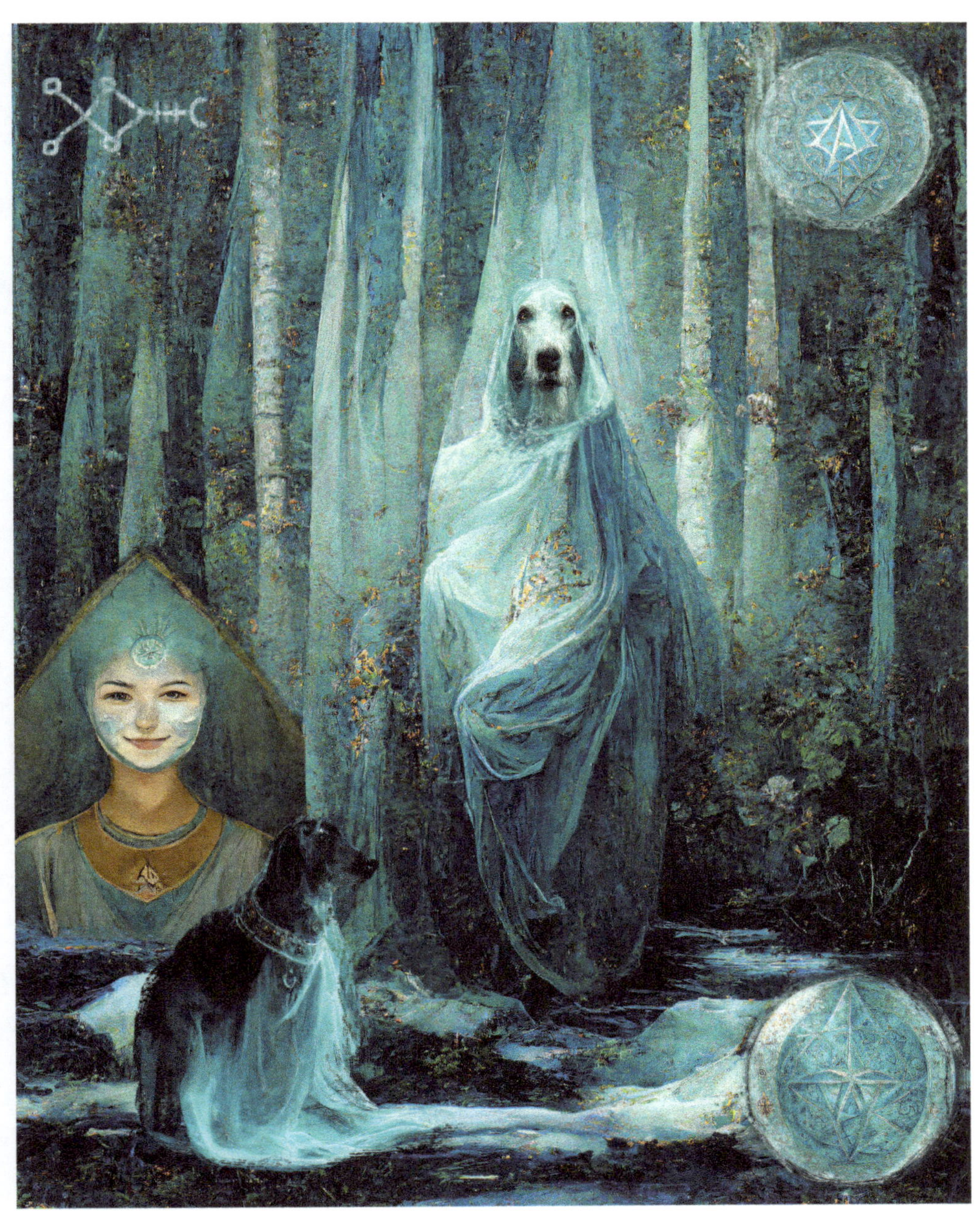

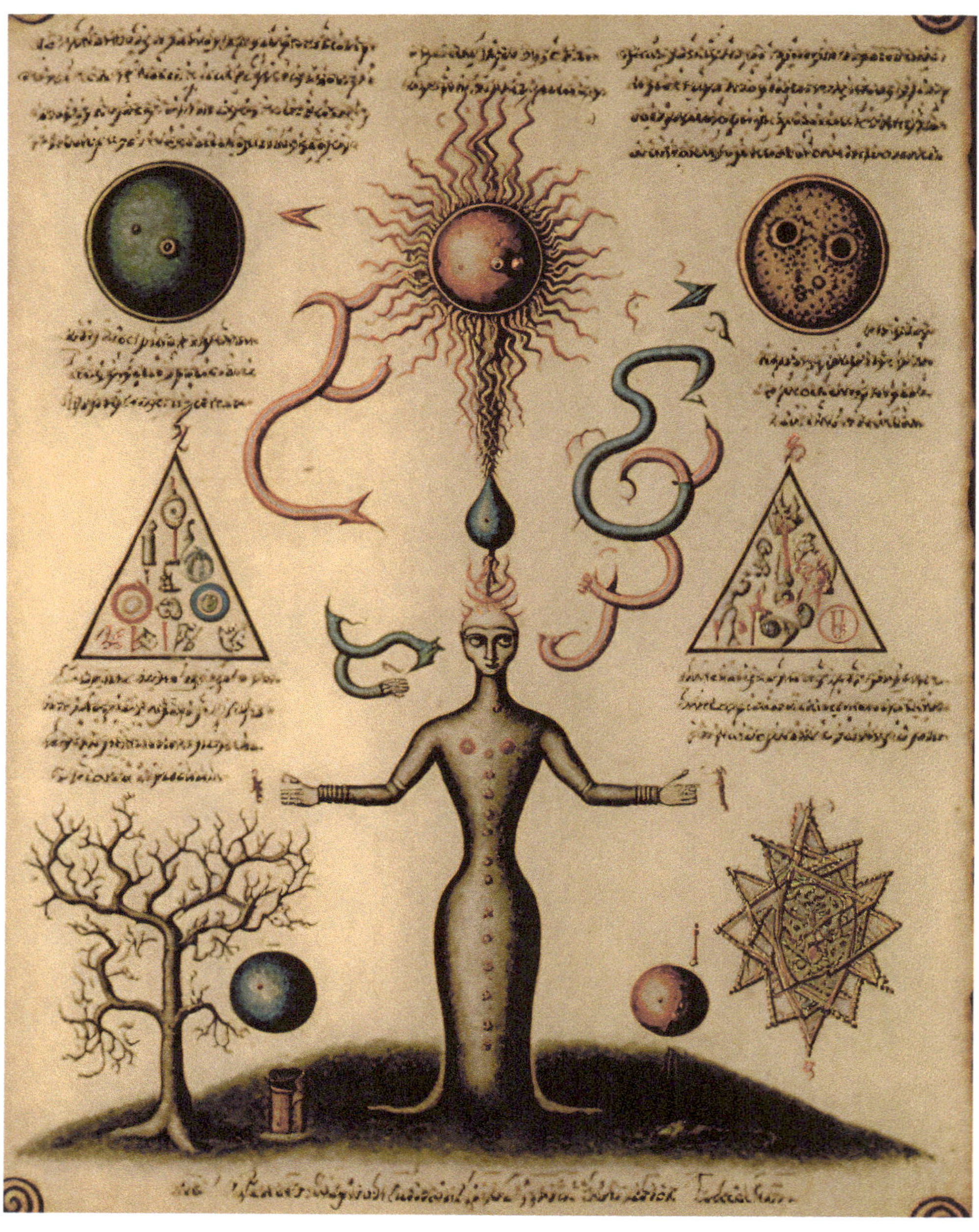

II.6: Procyon "Under Canis Minor, they made an image of a rooster or three girls: these bring the grace of God, spirits, and men, grant the ability to counter sorceries, and preserves health." (Agrippa, TBOP II§47)

/Oracle of DelphAI

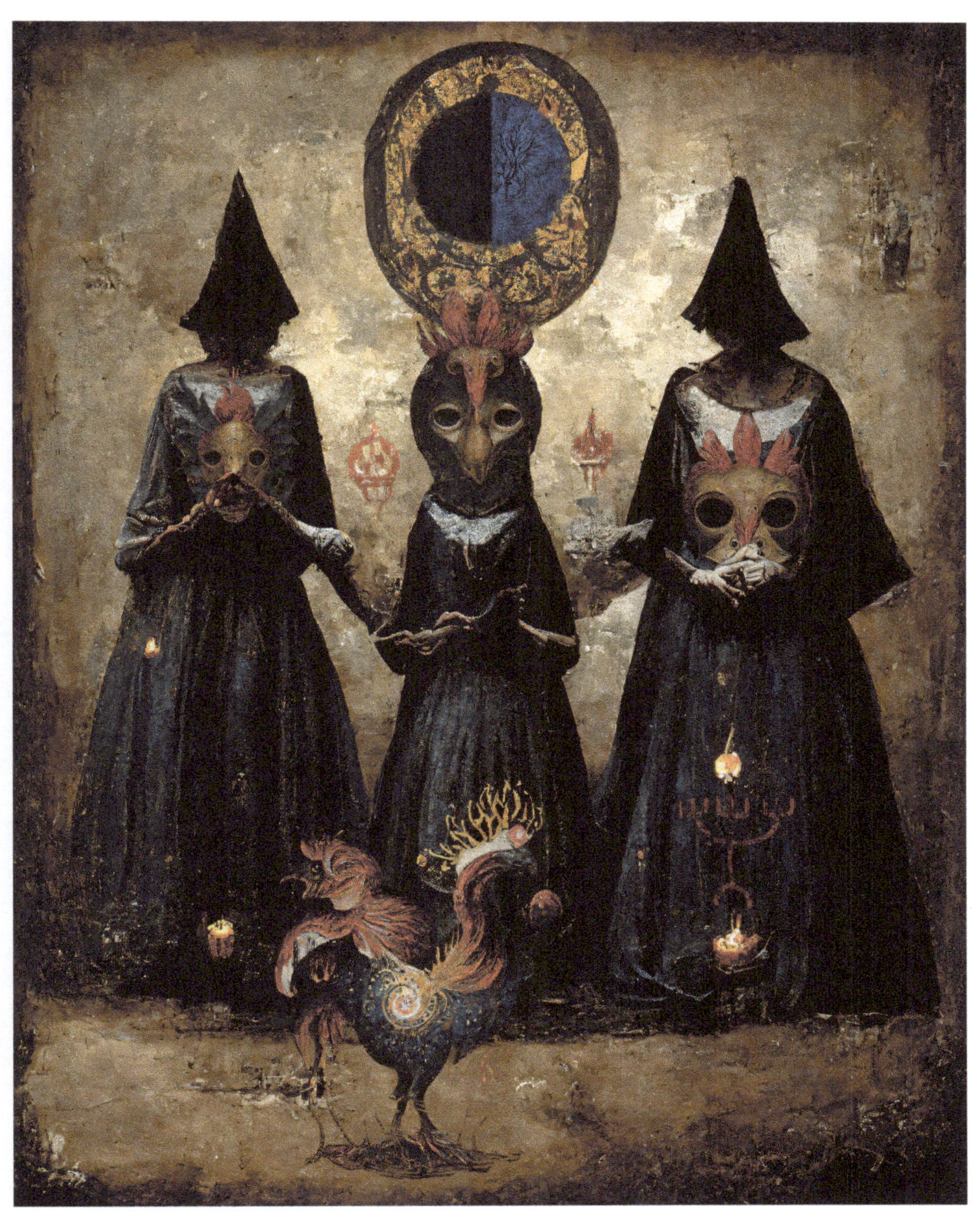

/33

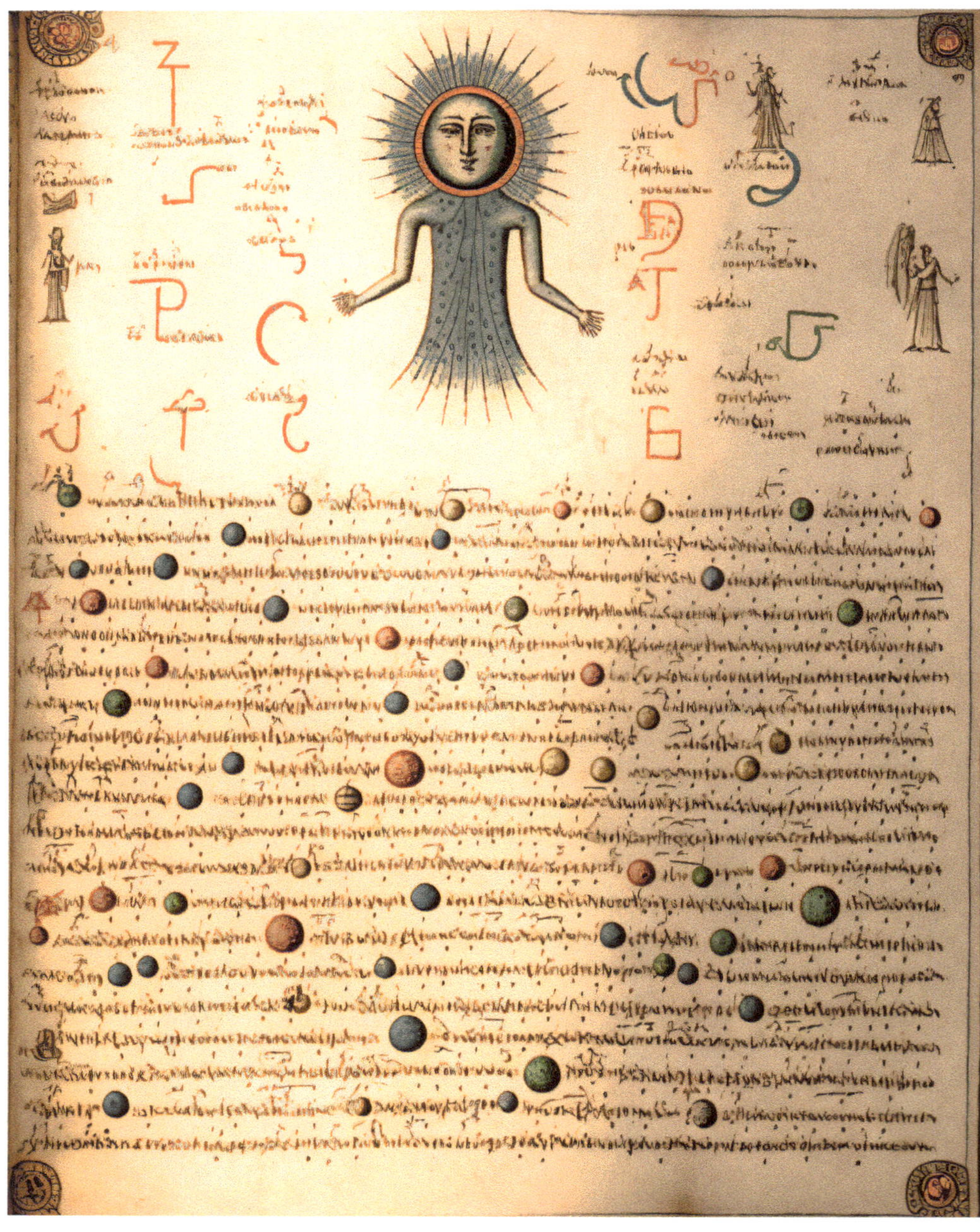

II.7: Regulus "Under Cor Leonis, they made an image of a lion, cat, or the figure of a respected man sitting in a chair: these make a man temperate, keep anger away, and give grace." (Agrippa, TBOP II§47)

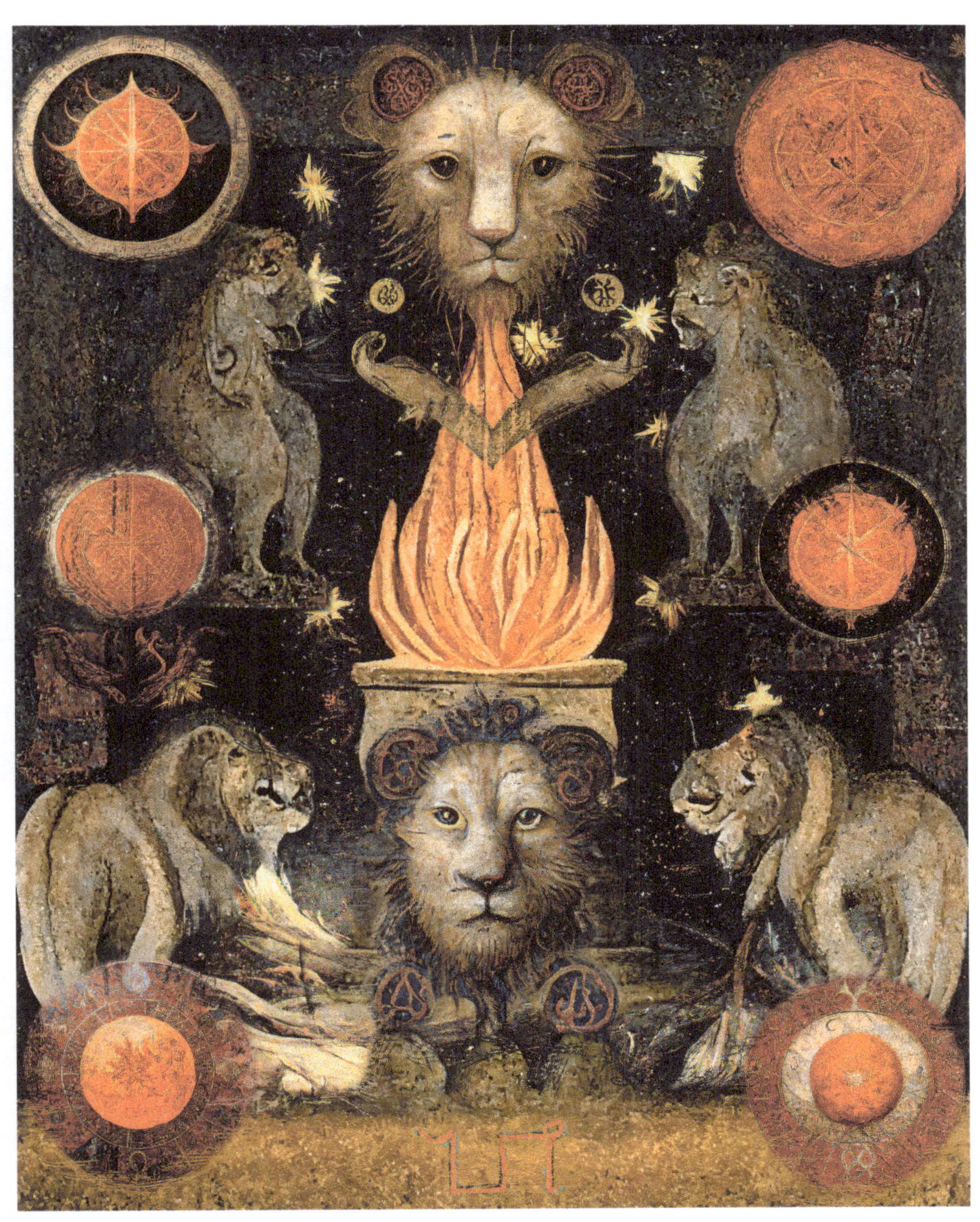

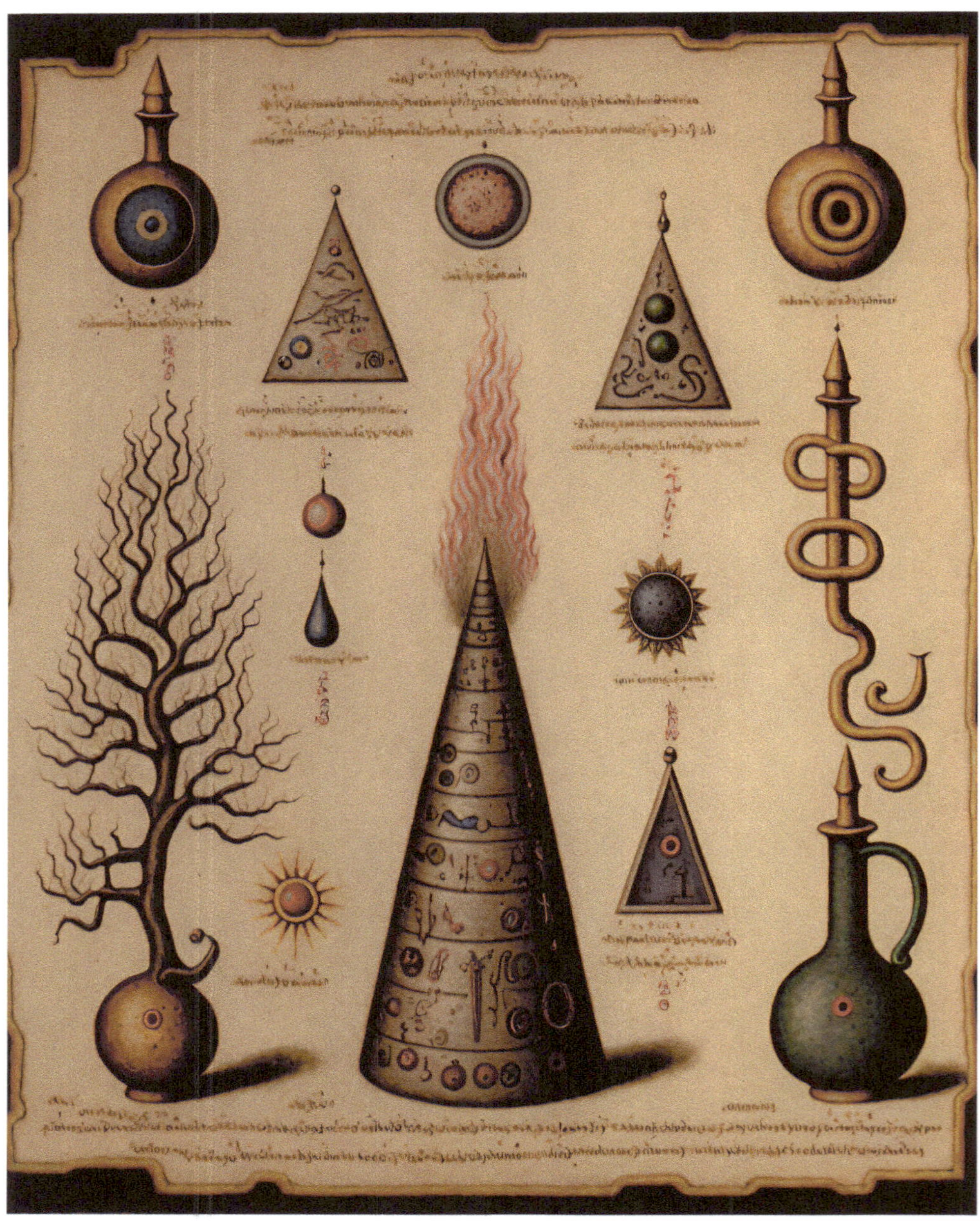

II.8: Algorab "Under the Wing of the Raven they made images of a raven, serpent, or a black man dressed in black garments: these make men angry, bold, courageous, thoughtful, a slanderer, and give evil dreams. They also give the ability to make daemons flee and gather. They are useful against wicked men, daemons, and winds." (Agrippa, TBOP II§47)

/Oracle of DelphAI

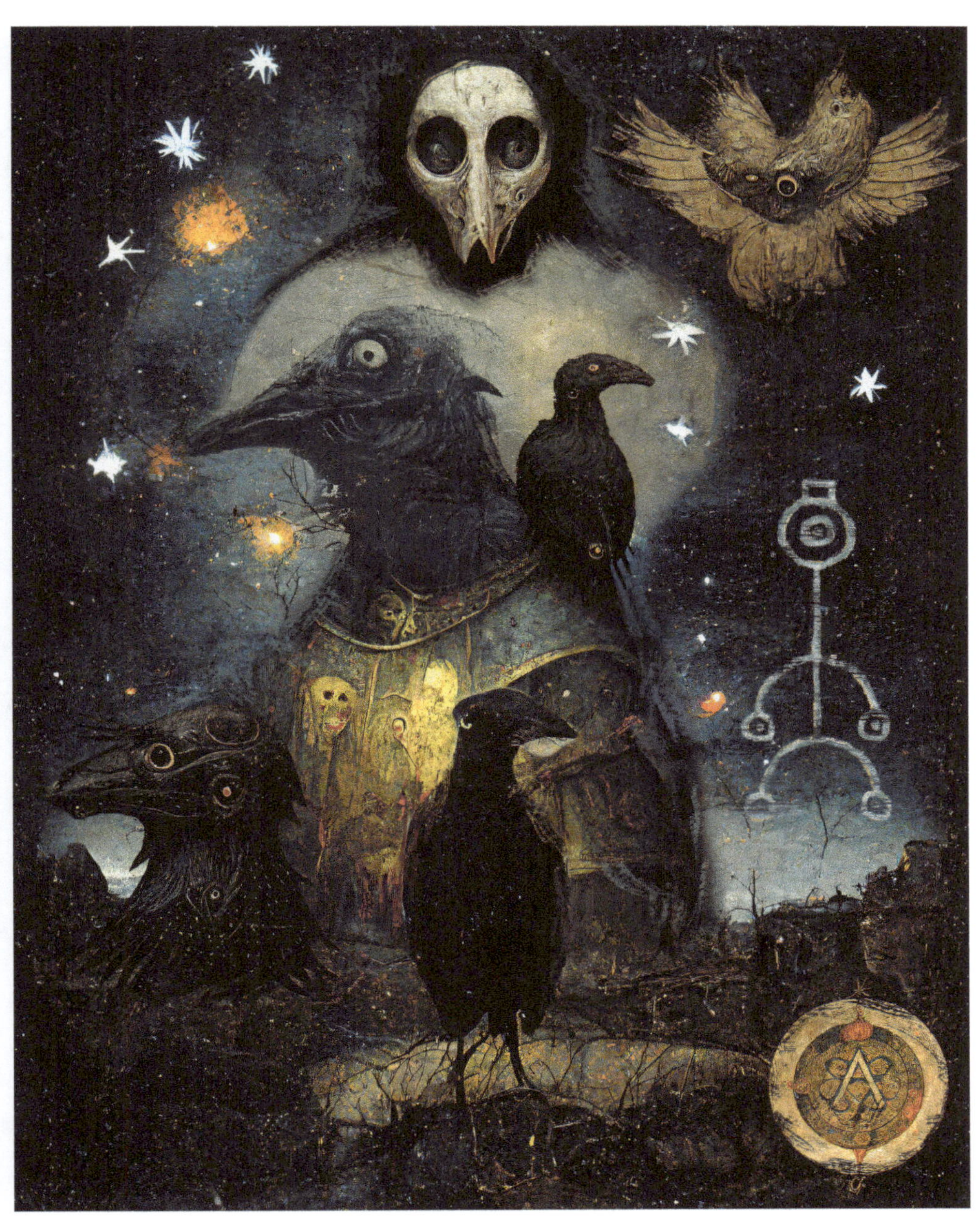

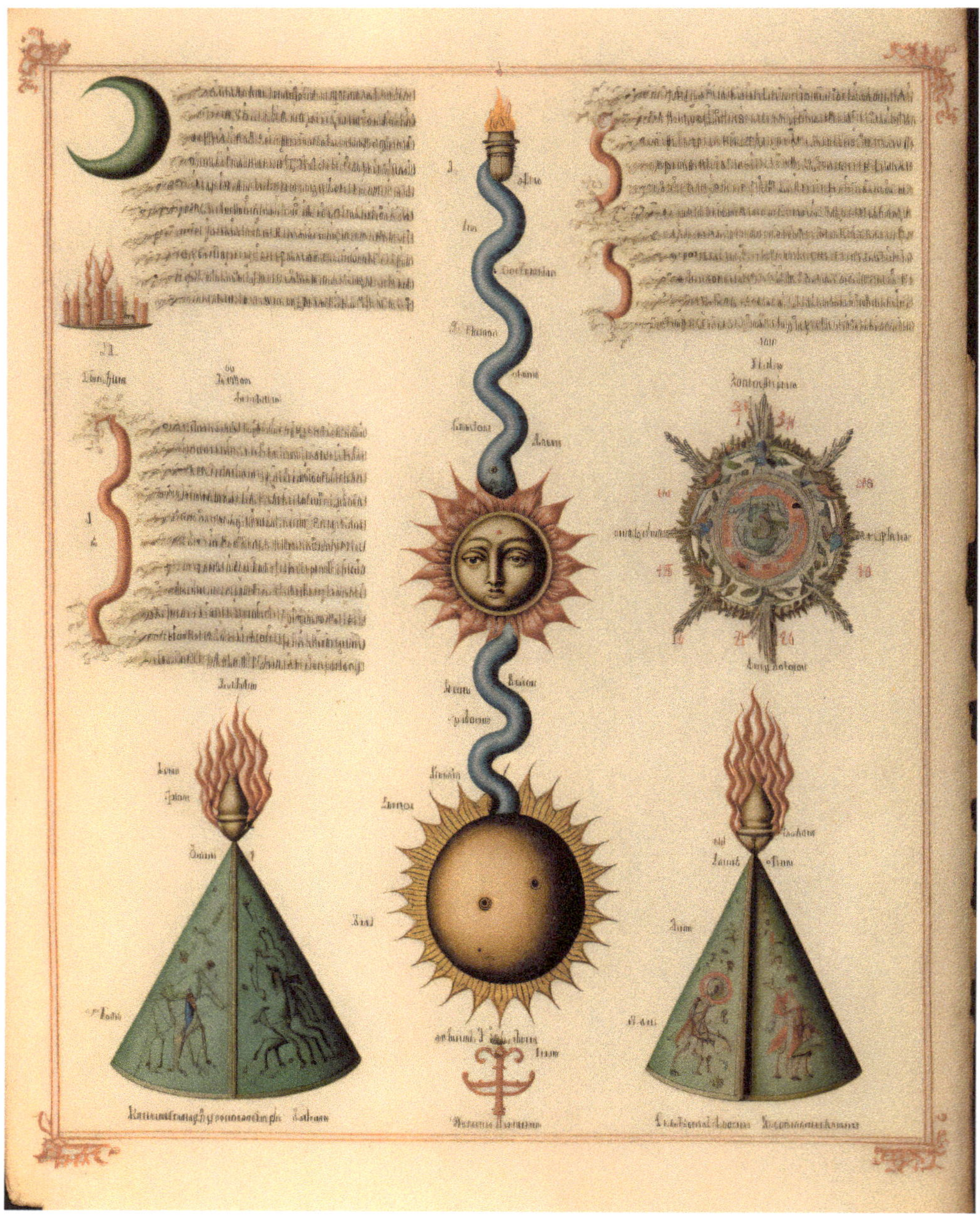

II.9: "Under **Spica** they made an image of a bird or a man laden with merchandise: these give wealth, make one conquer lawsuits; it takes away difficulties and evil." (Agrippa, TBOP II§47)

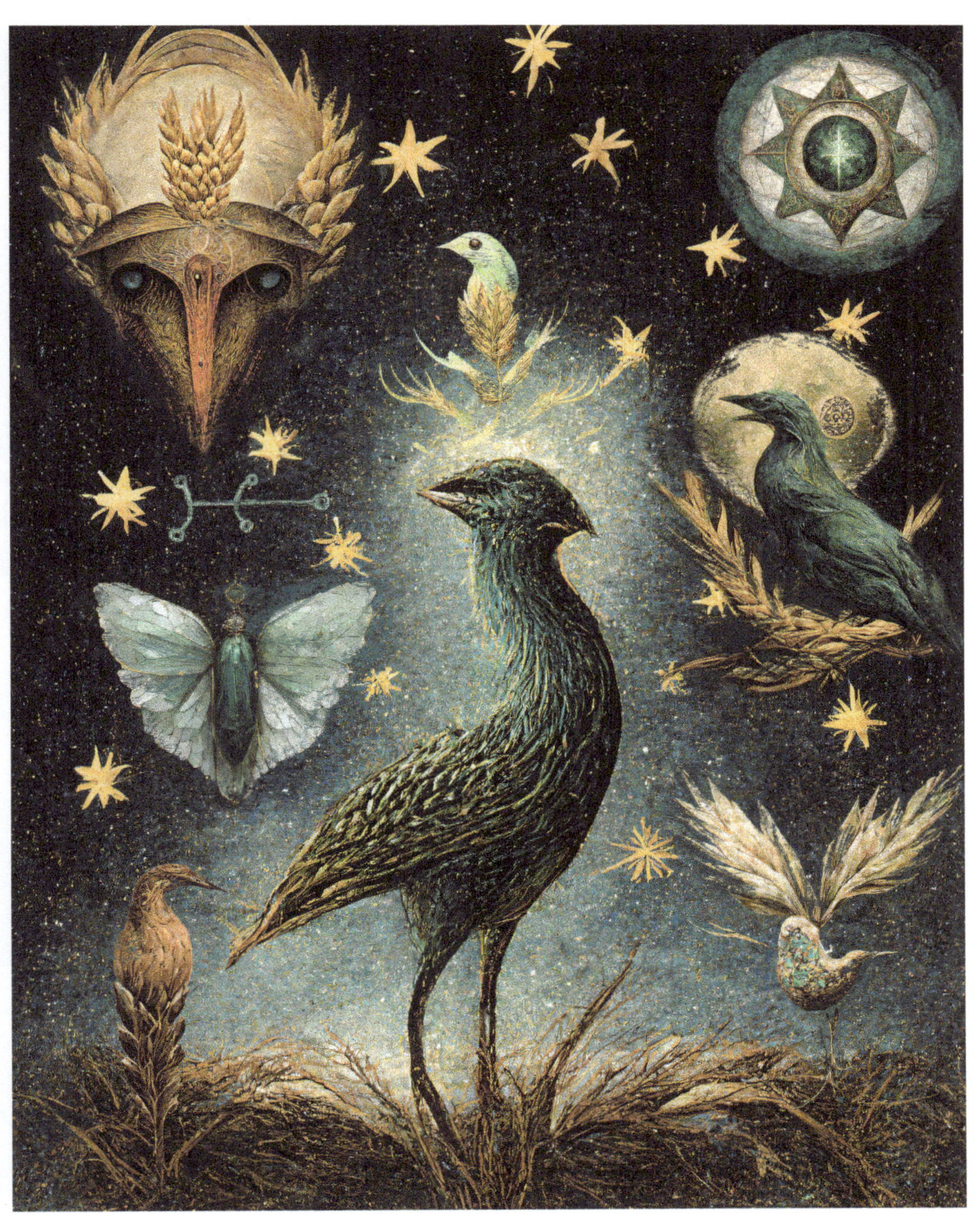

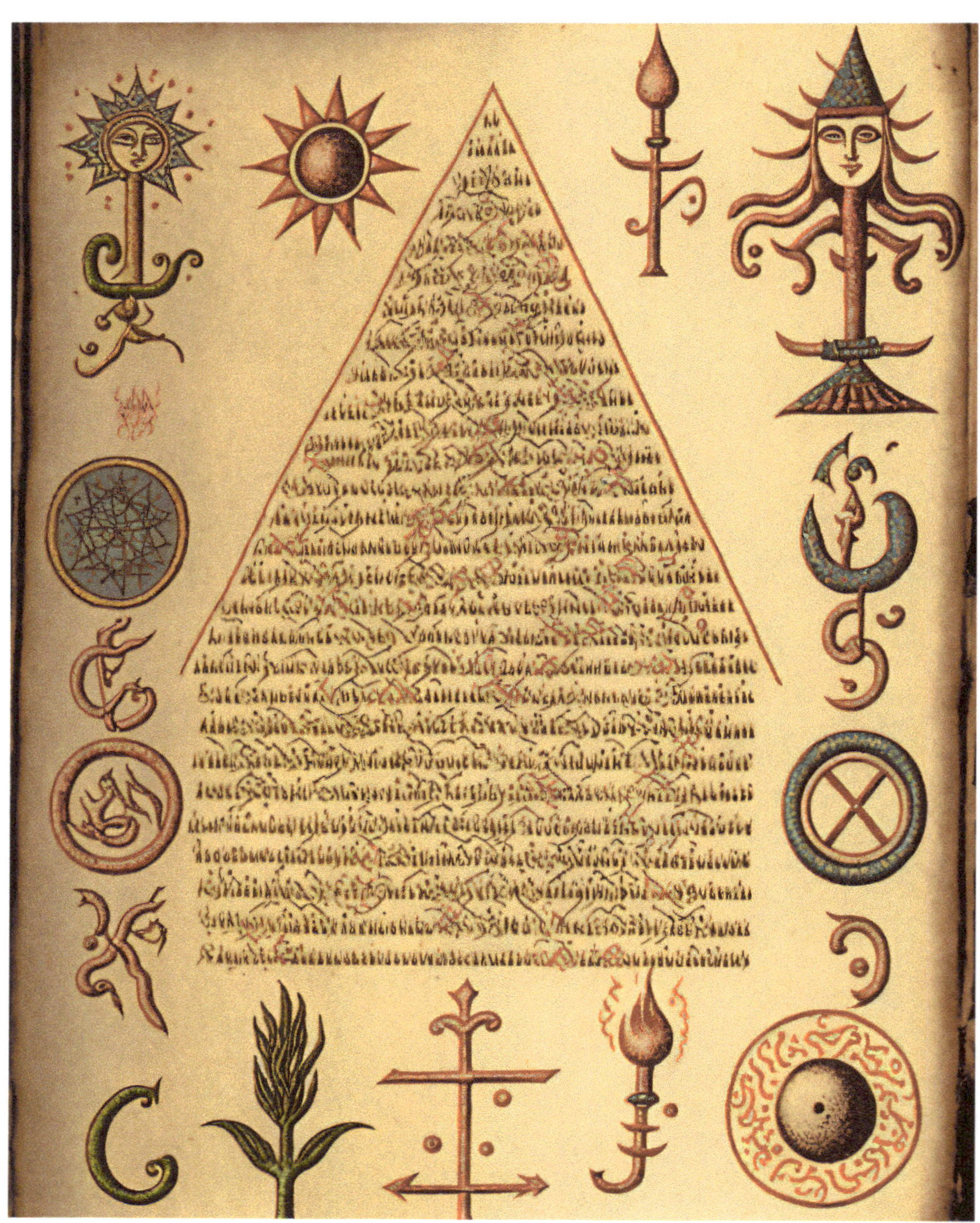

11.10: "Under **Arcturus** they made an image of a horse, wolf, or the figure of a man dancing: these help against fevers. [They] also astringe and restrain blood." (Agrippa, TBOP II§47)

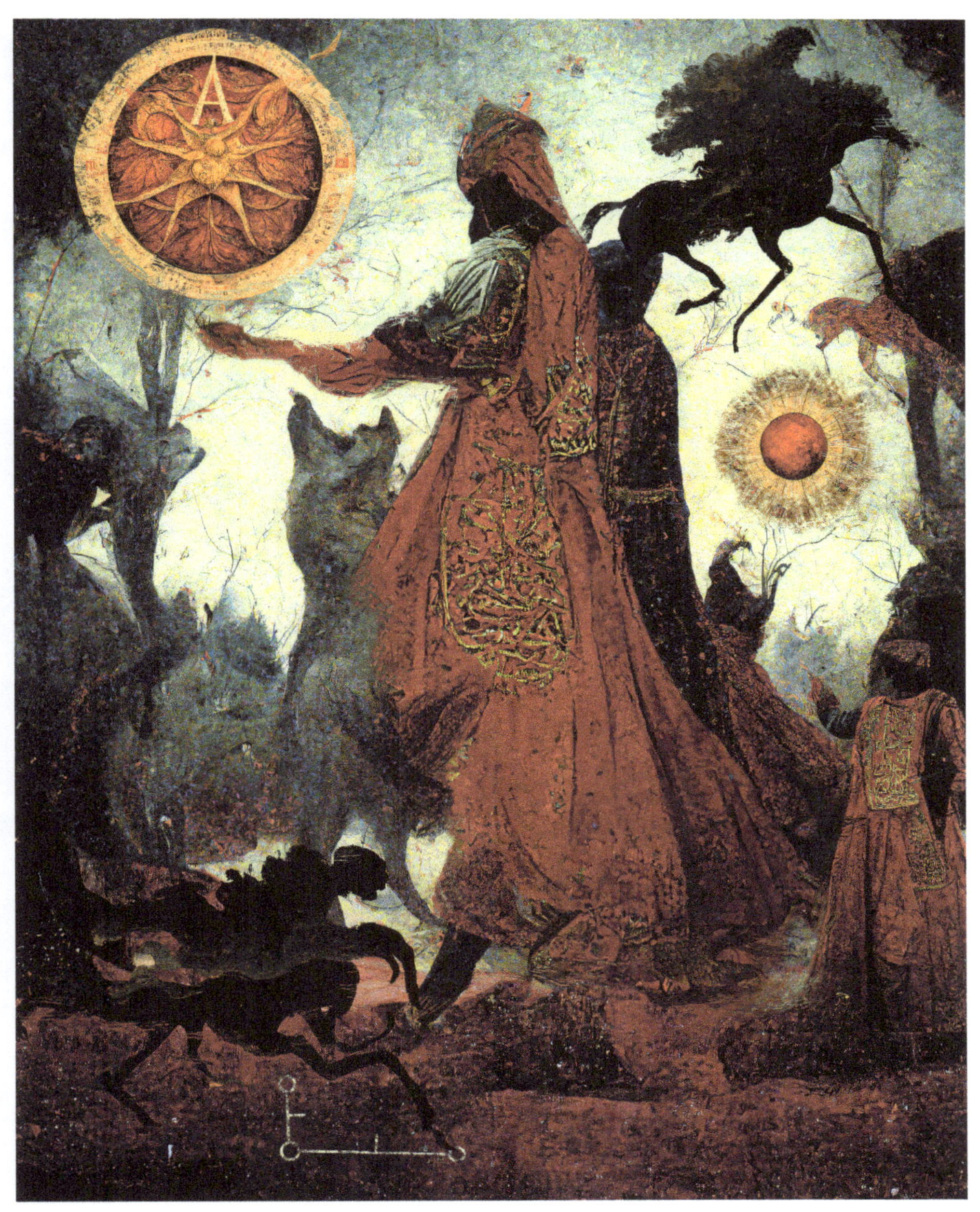

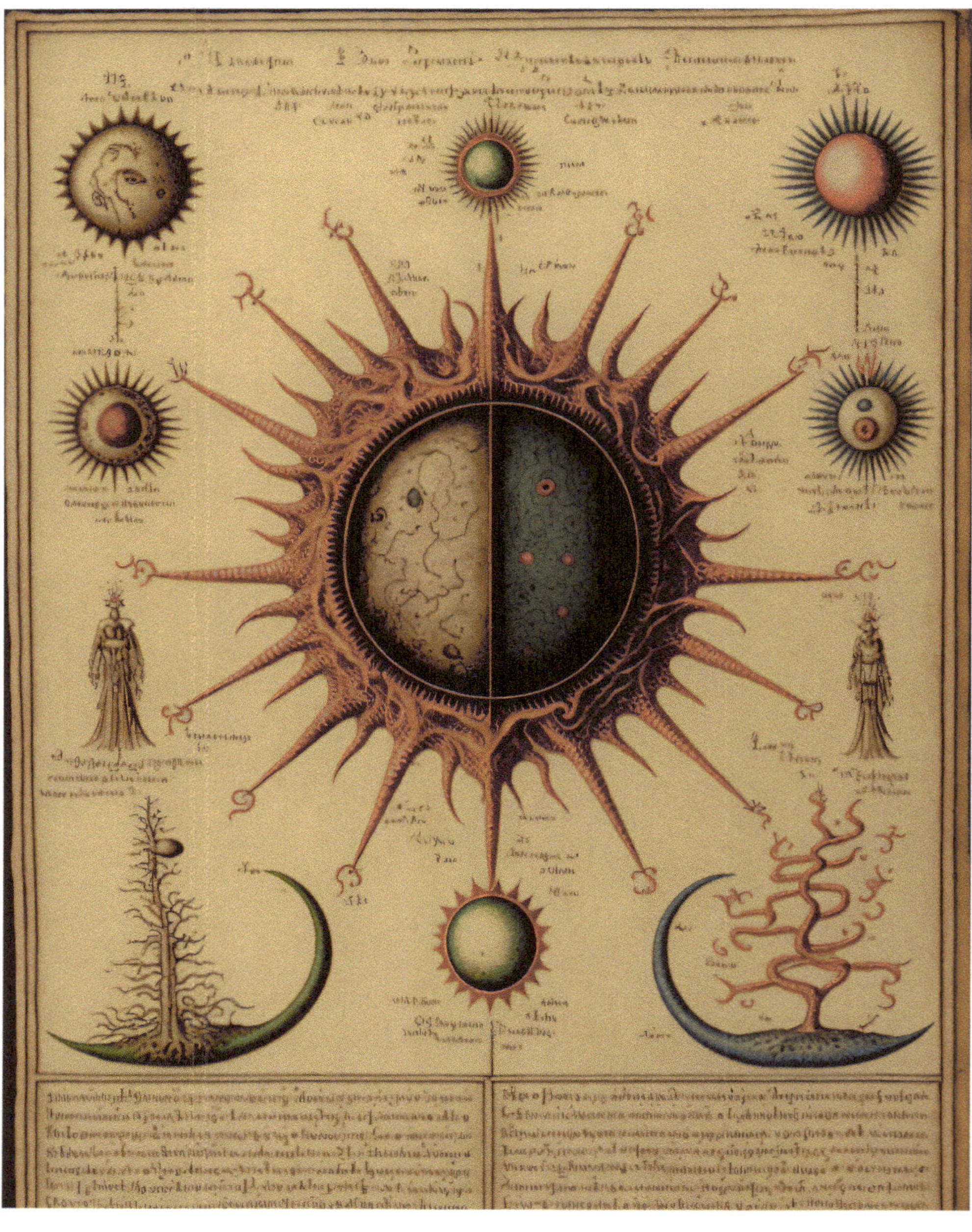

II.II: Alkaid "Under the Tail of Ursa Major, they made an image of a man wrapped in thought or a bull or the figure of a calf: these help against incantations and makes the bearer secure in their travels." (Agrippa, TBOP II§47)

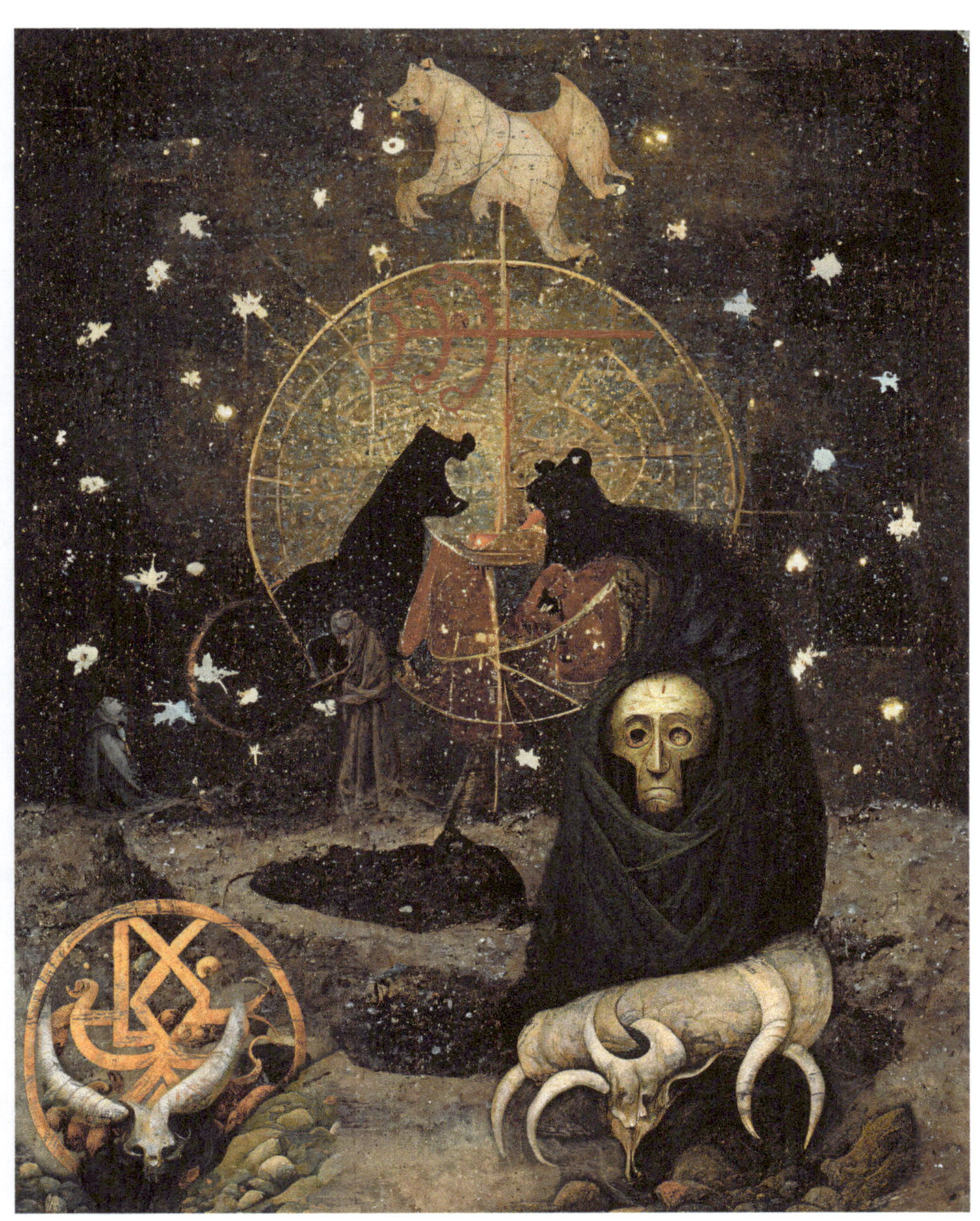

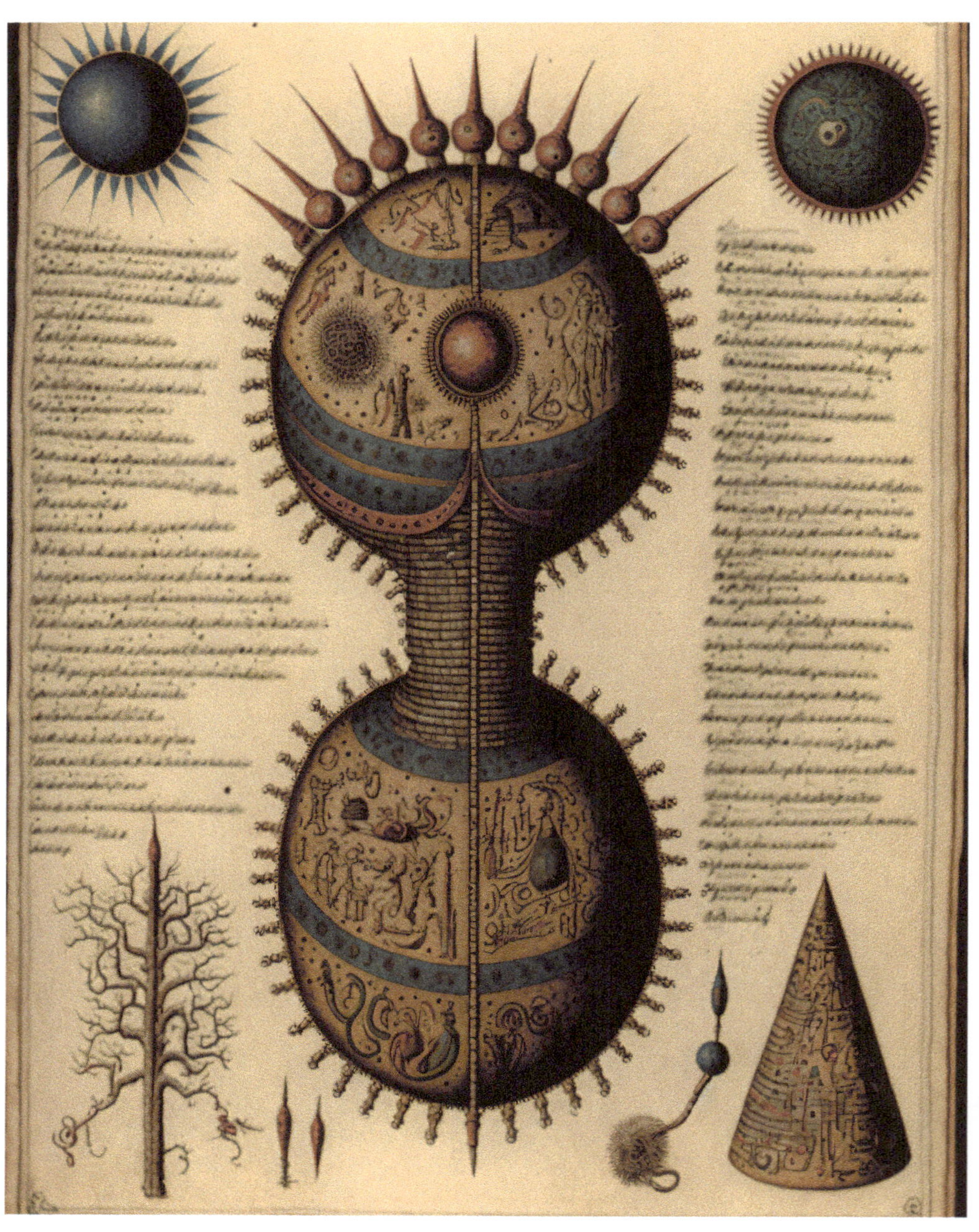

II.12: "Under **Alphecca** they made an image of a hen, or a crowned and raised man: these give benevolence, the love of men, and chastity." (Agrippa, TBOP II§47)

/Oracle of DelphAI

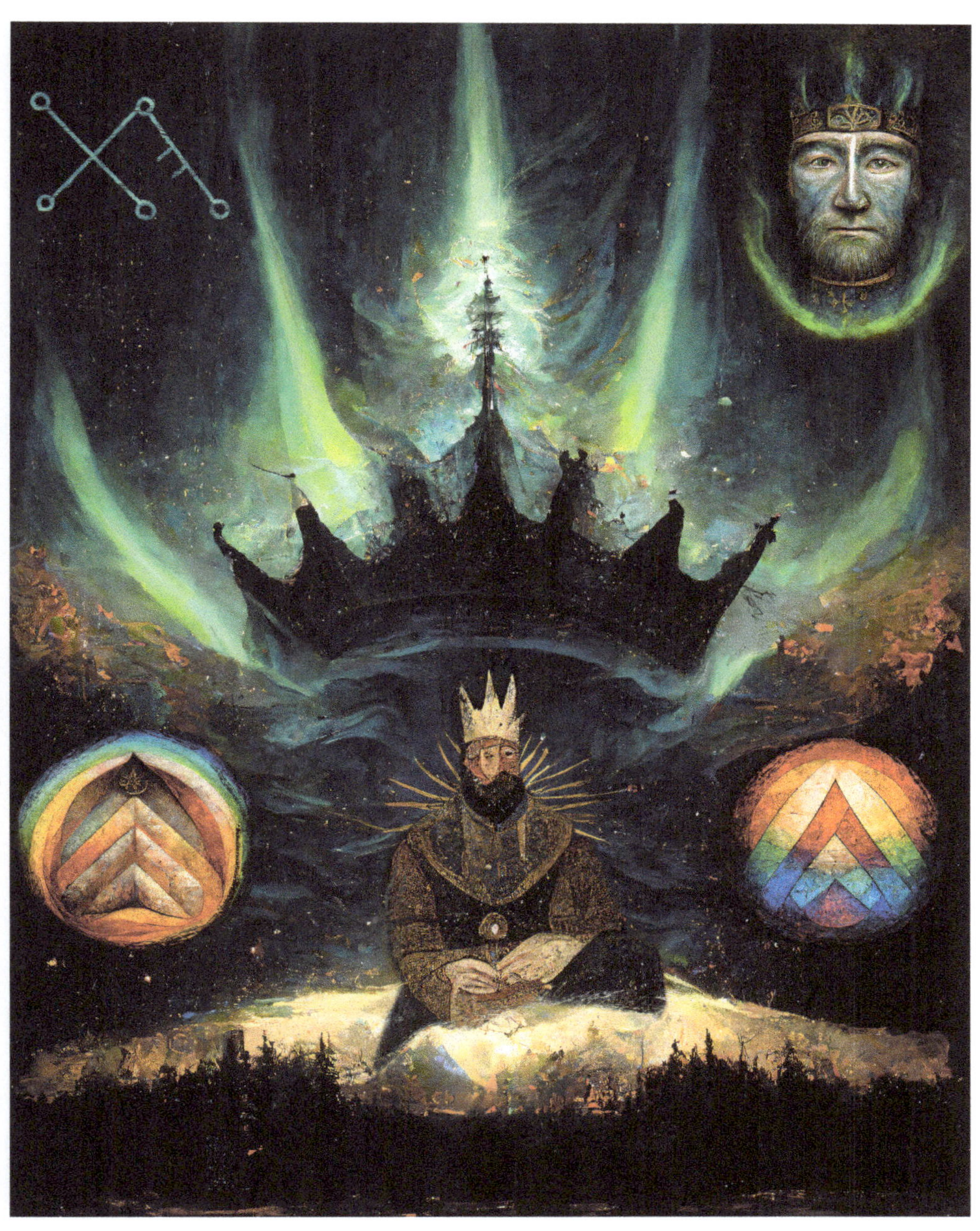

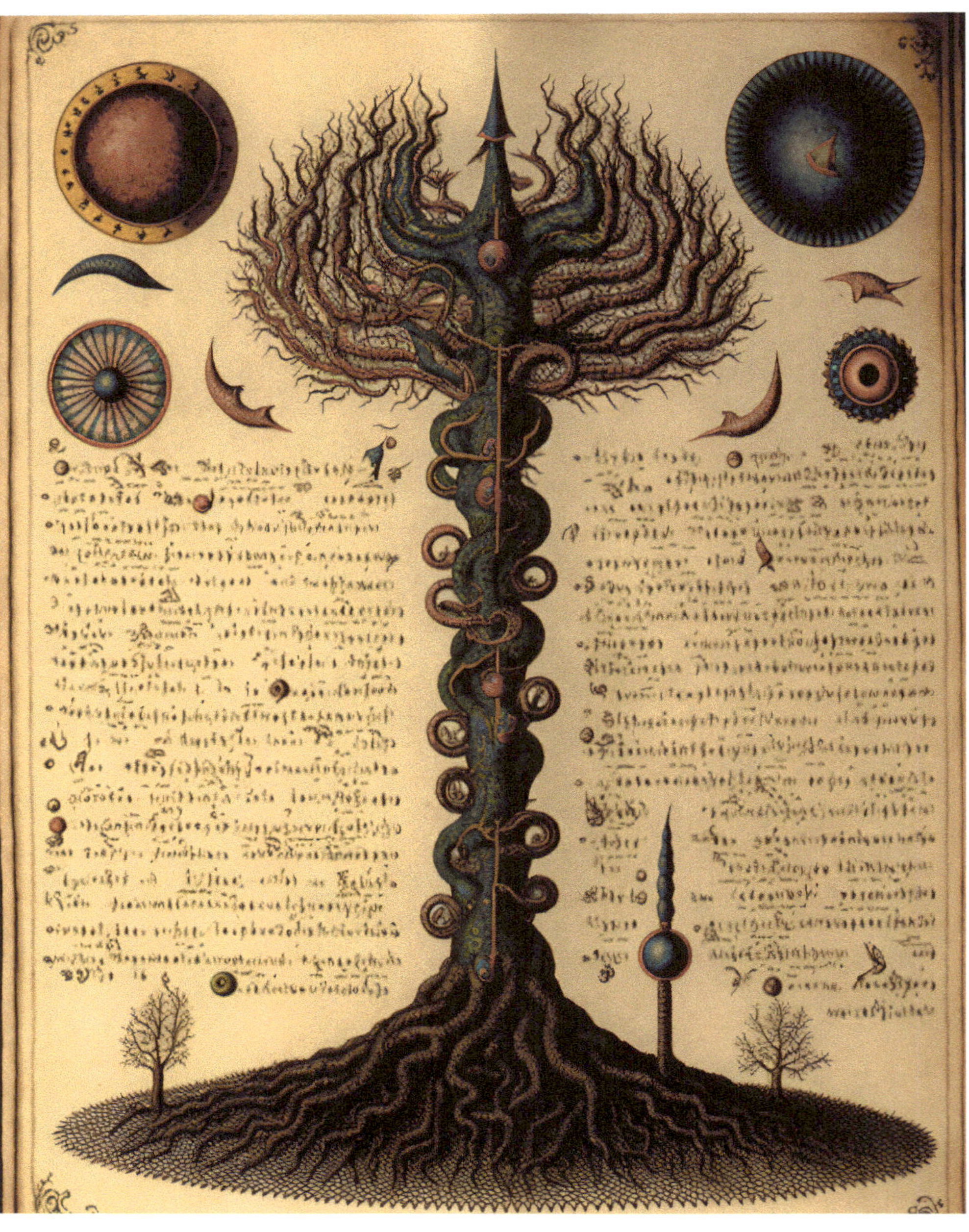

II.13: Antares "Under the Heart of Scorpio, they made an image of an armed man with a breastplate or the figure of a scorpion: these give intellect and memory, as well as causing good color. They help against evil daemons, make them flee, and confine them." (Agrippa, TBOP II§47)

/Oracle of DelphAI

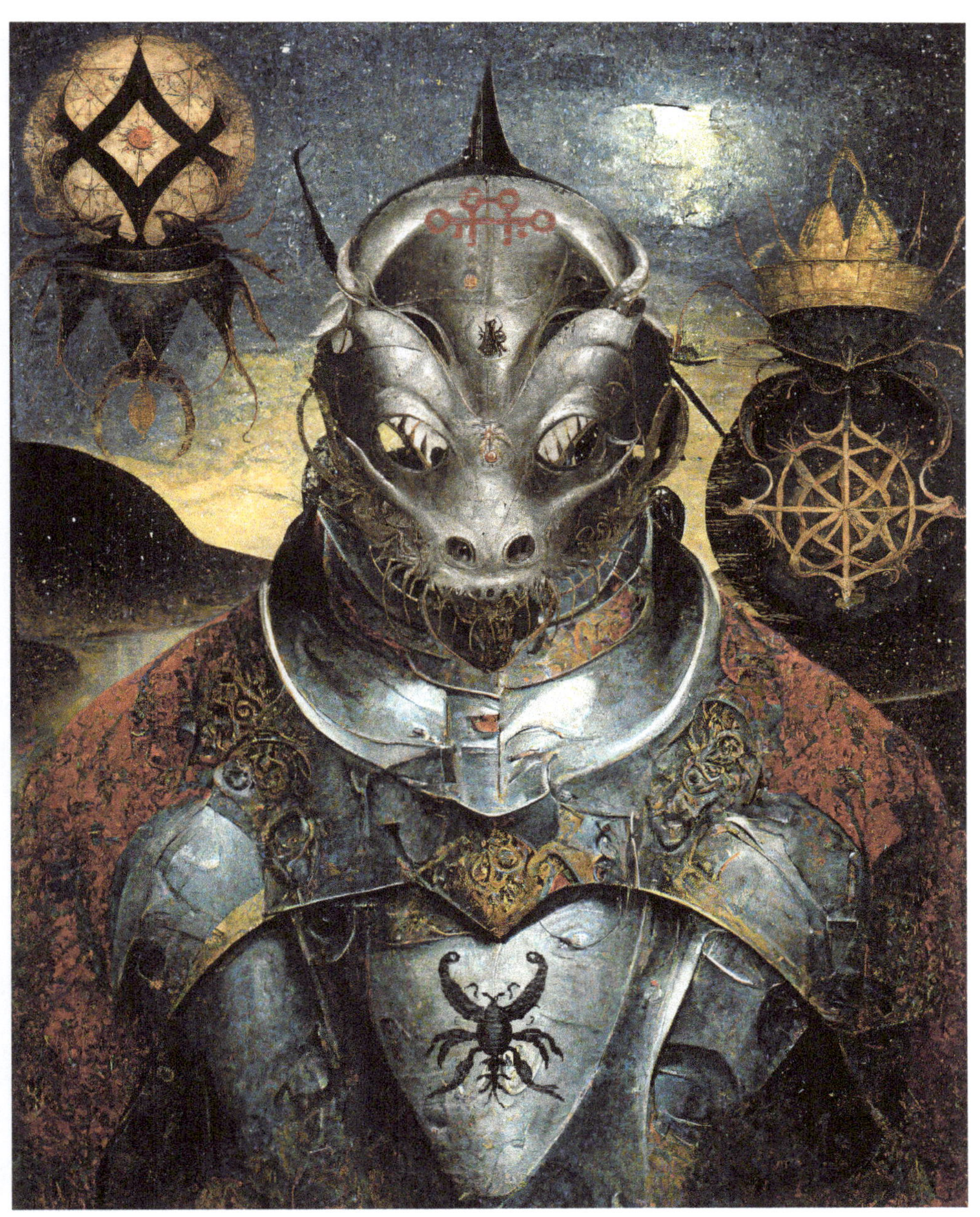

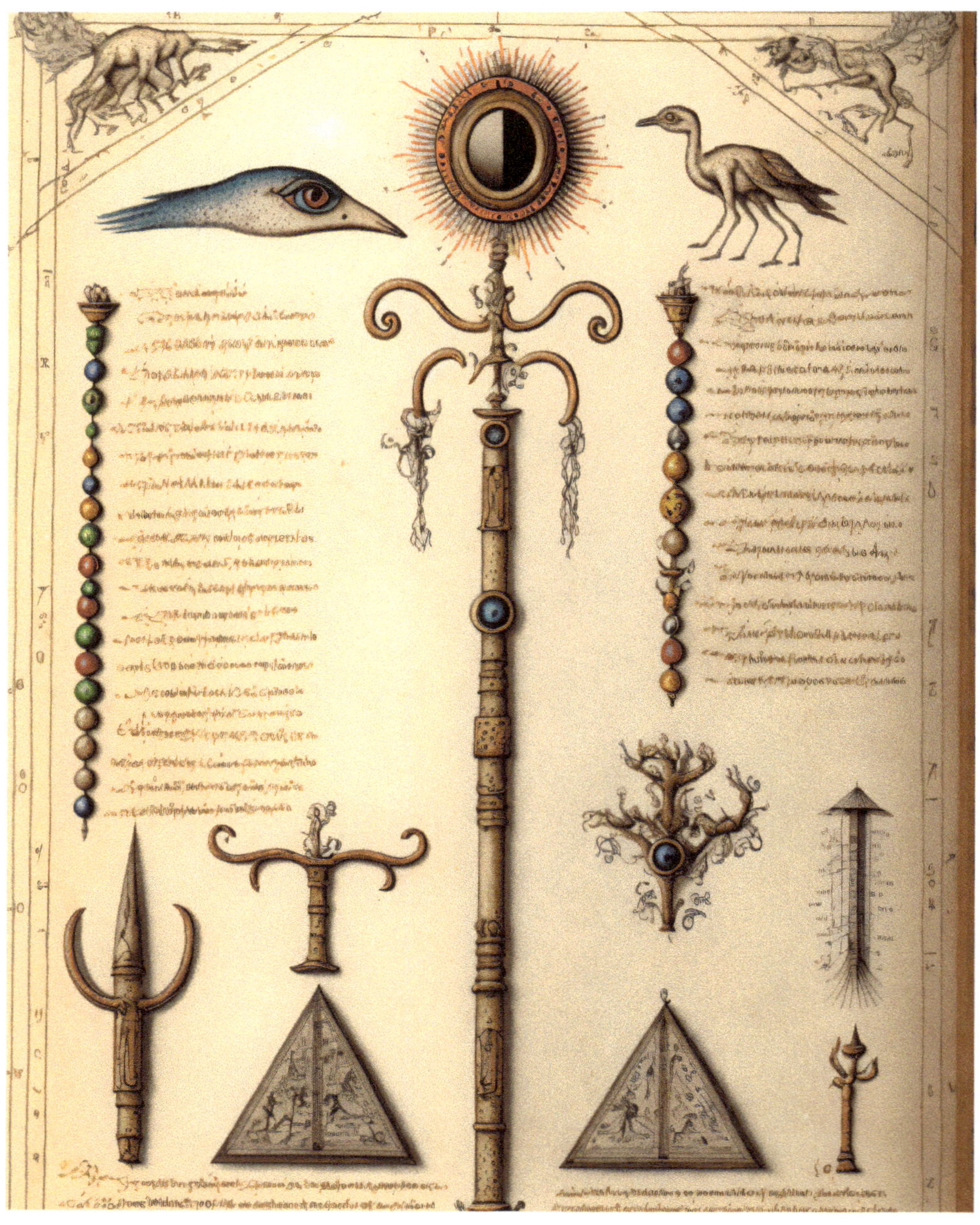

II.14: Vega "Under the Vulture they made an image of a vulture, hen, or traveling man: these make men magnanimous and haughty, and give power over dae-mons and beasts." (Agrippa, TBOP II§47)

/Oracle of DelphAI

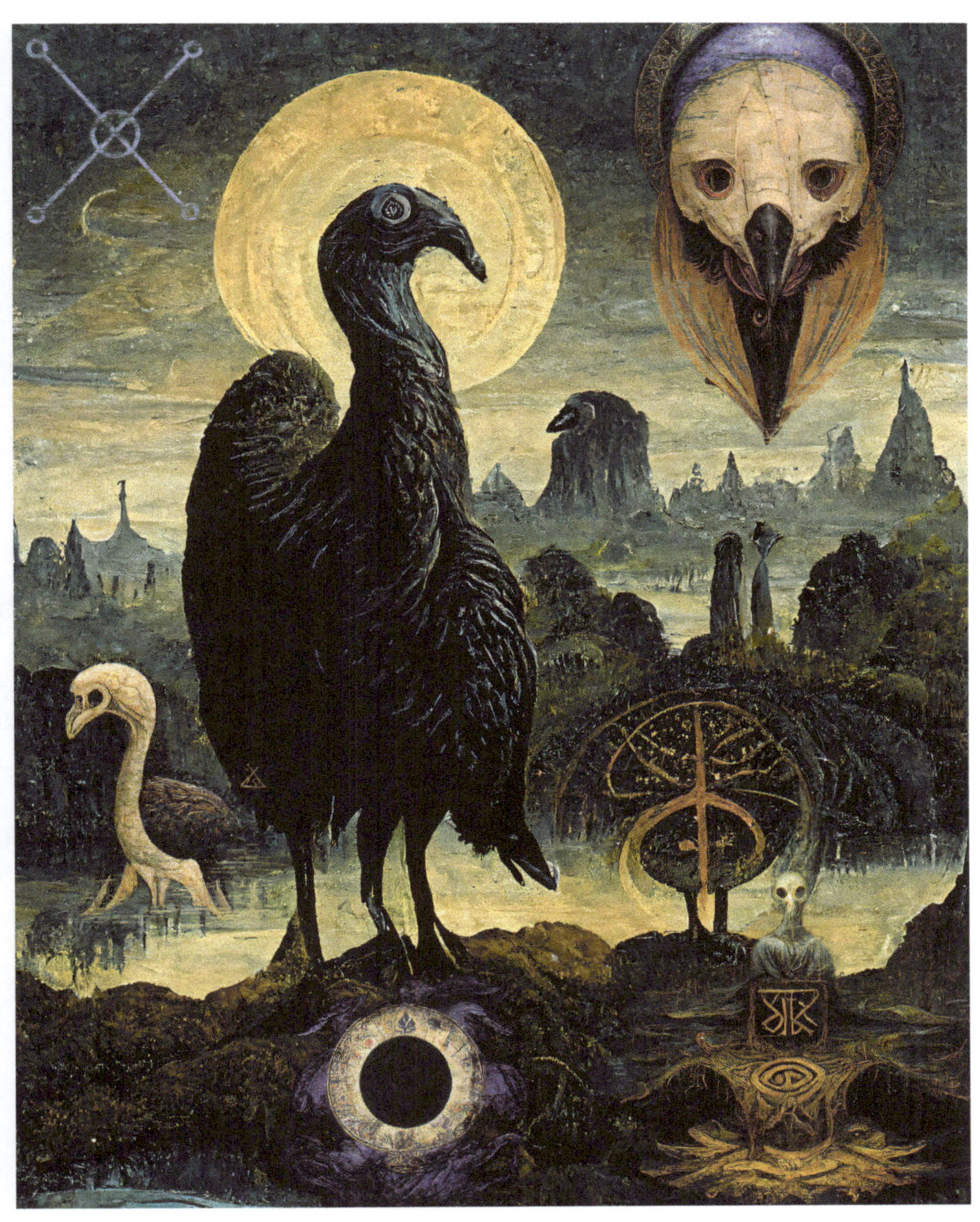

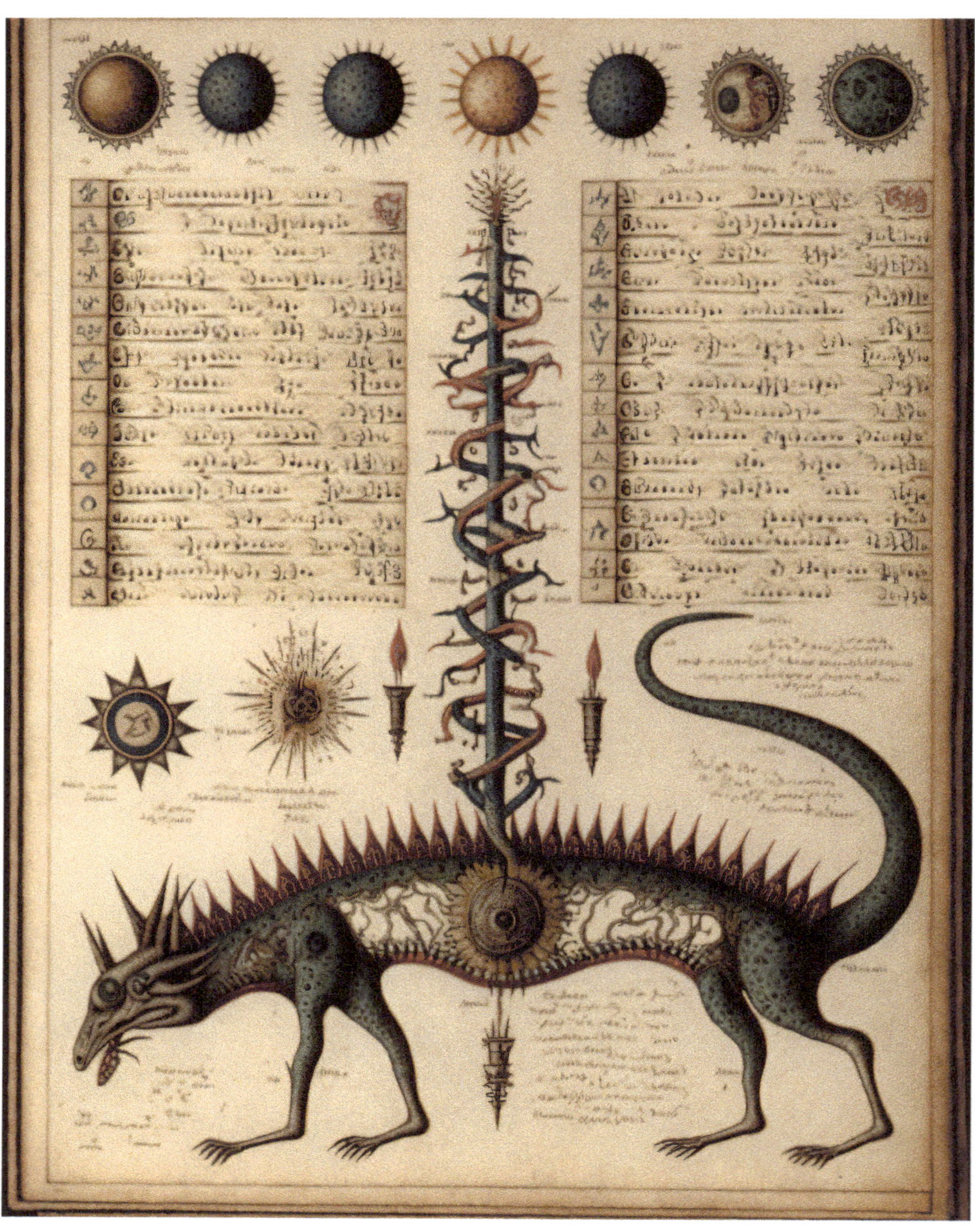

II.15: Deneb Algedi "Under the Tail of Capricorn they made an image of a stag male goat, or an angry man: these give prosperity and increase wealth." (Agrippa, TBOP II§47)

/Oracle of DelphAI

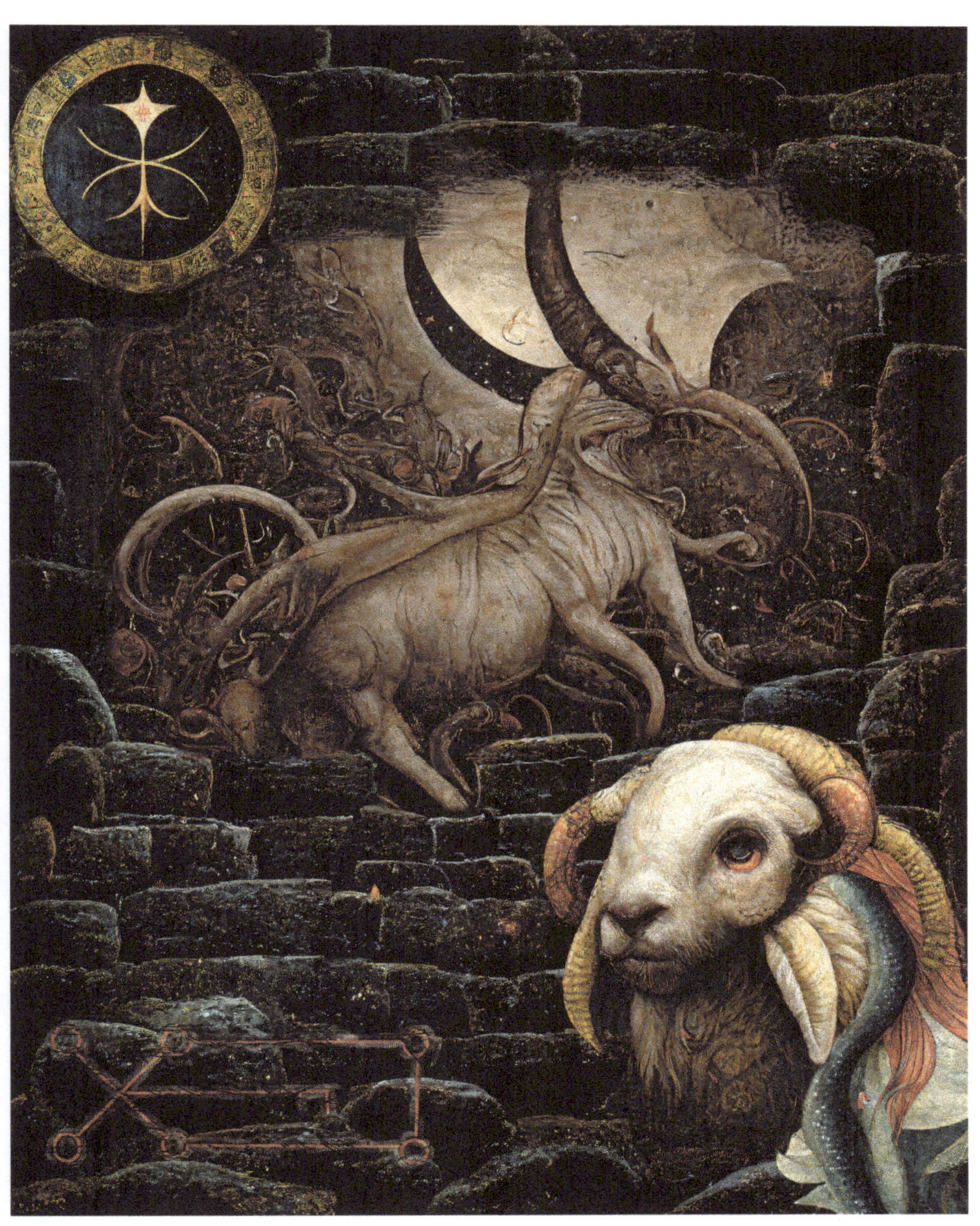

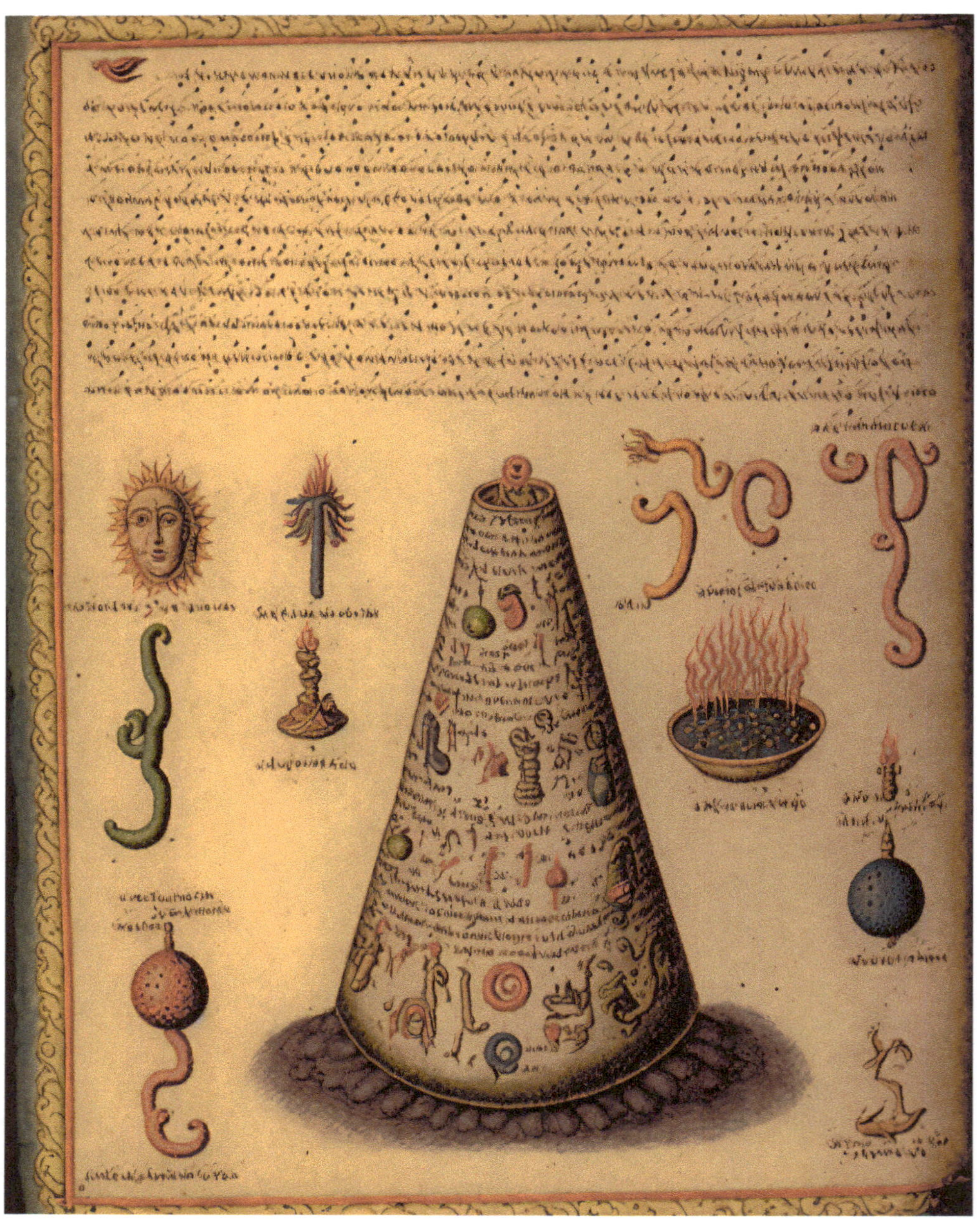

III.I Alnath ... the image of a dark man with his hair wrapped and encircled, standing on his feet, having in his right hand a spear in the manner of a warrior. (Picatrix‡4.IX§29)

/Oracle of Delph∧l

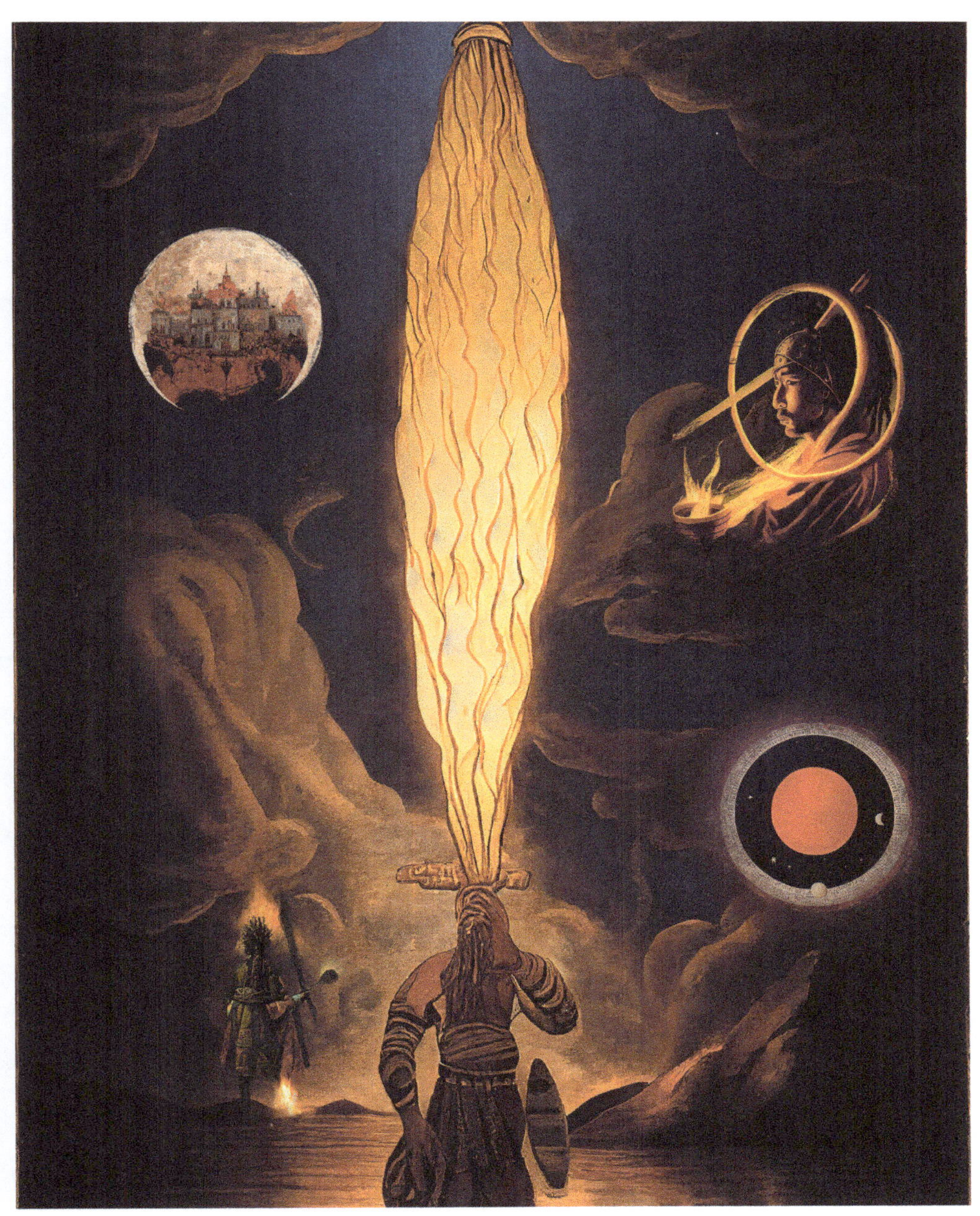

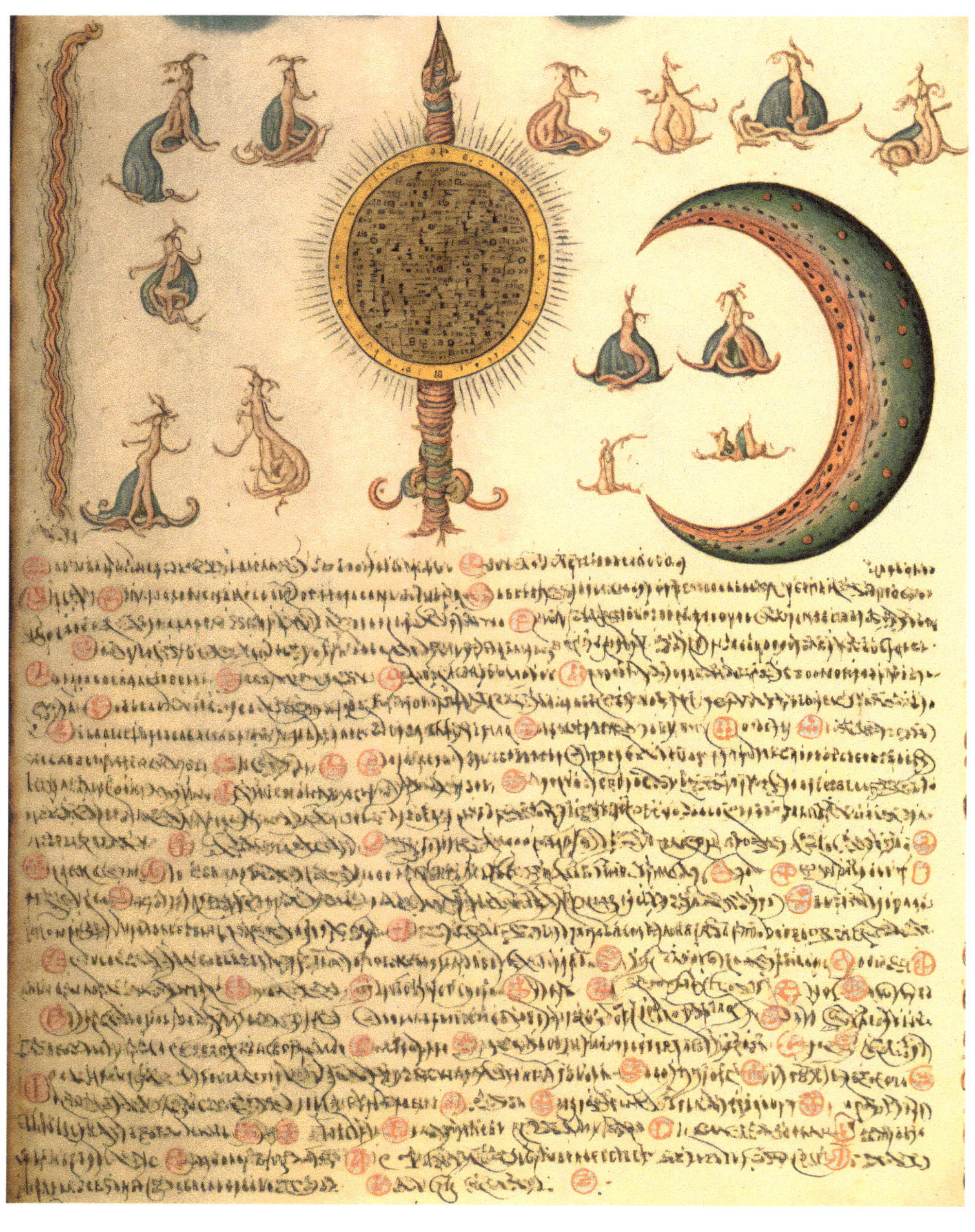

III.2 Albotayn ... the image of a crowned king. (Picatrix‡4.IX§30)

/Oracle of DelphΛI

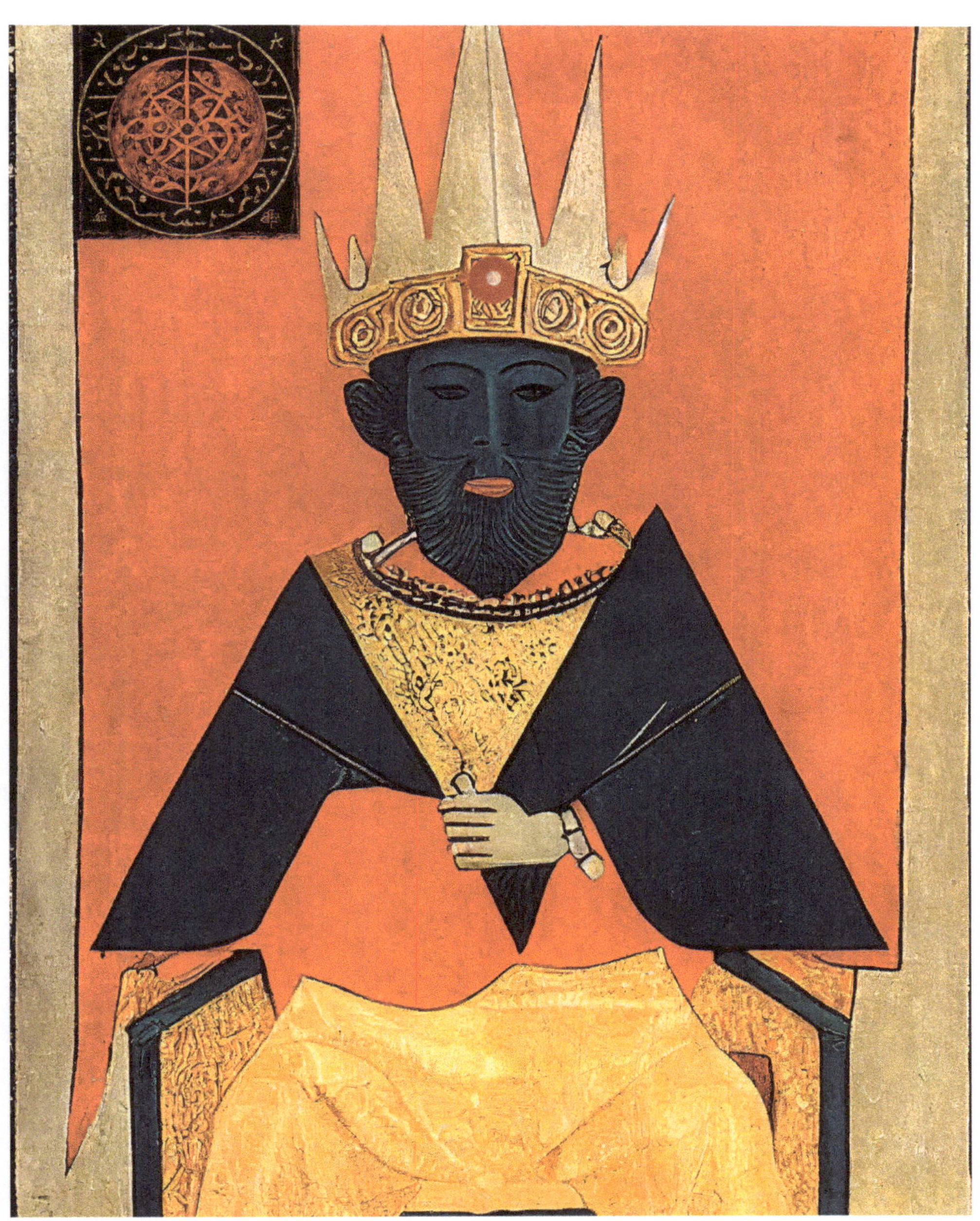

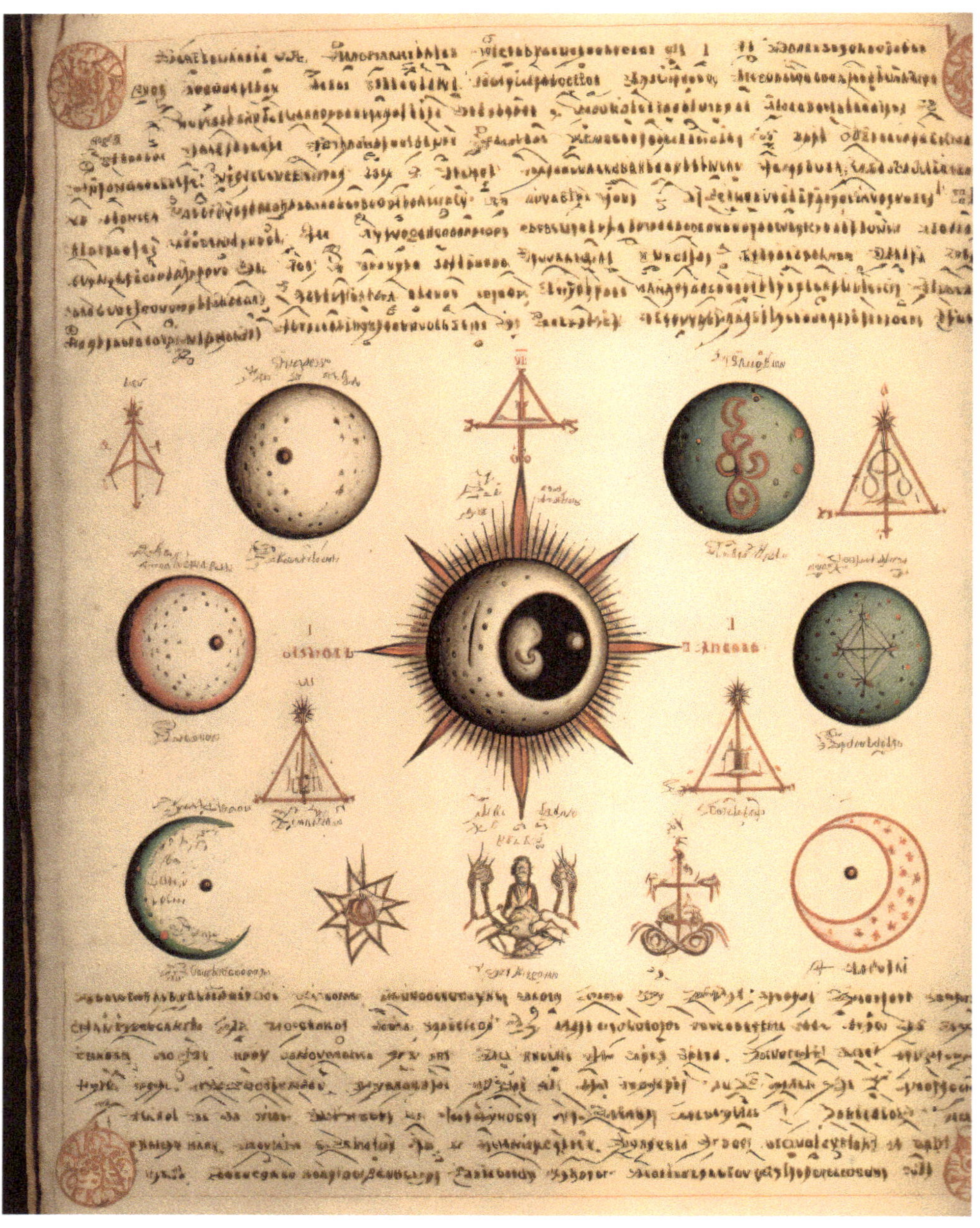

III.3 Azoraye ... a seated woman holding her right hand above her head and dressed in clothes. (Picatrix‡4.IX§31)

/Oracle of DelphAI

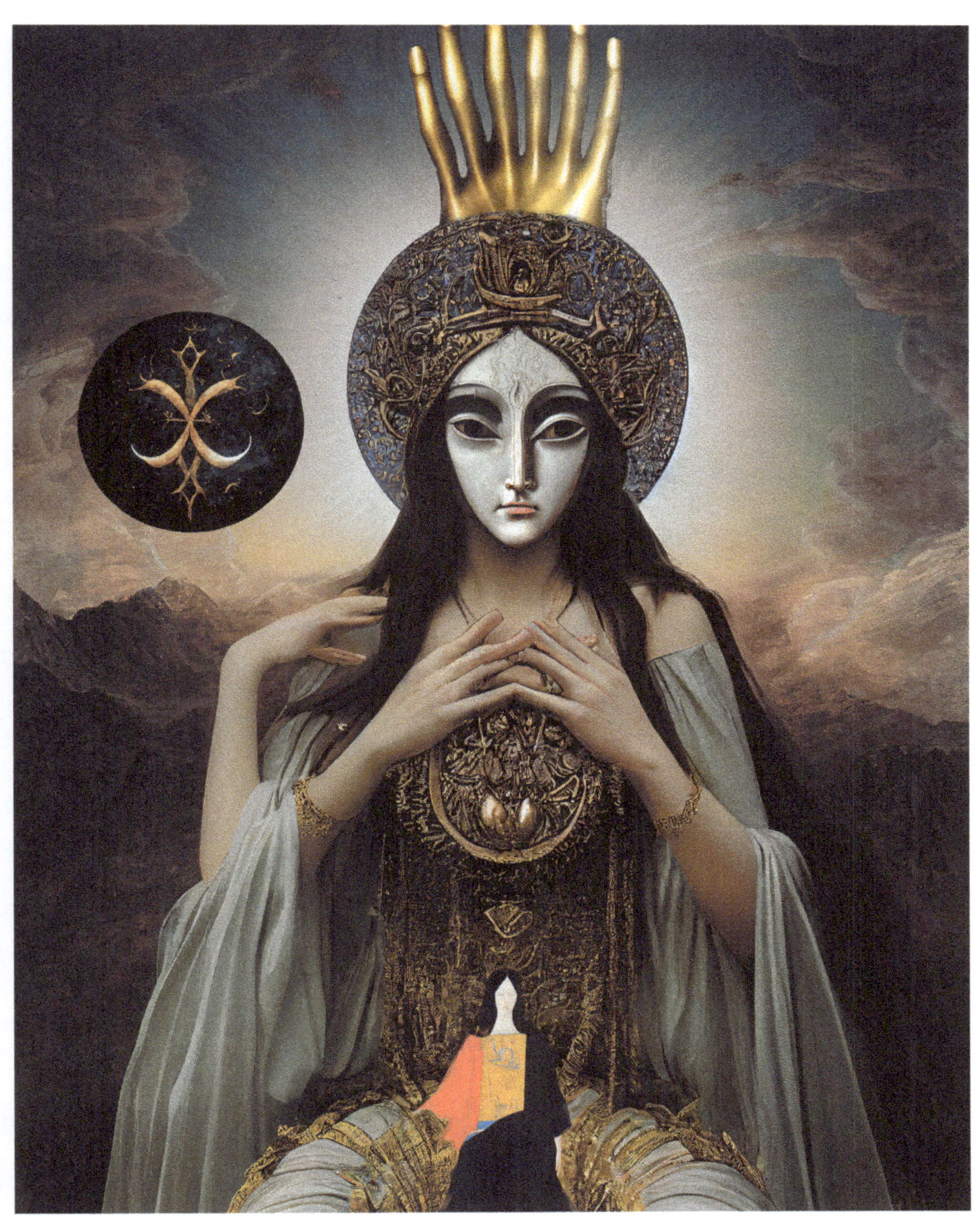

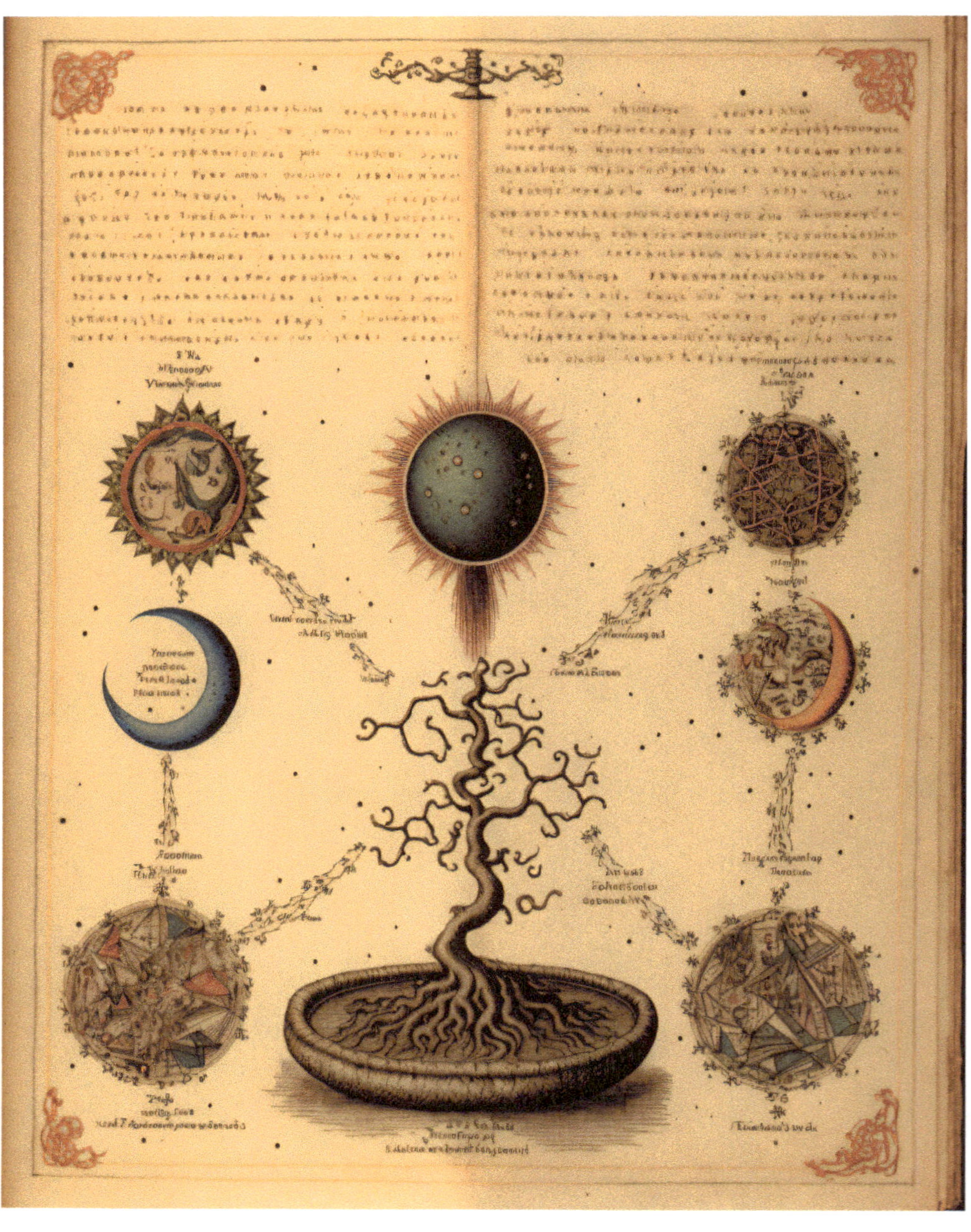

III.4 Aldebaran ... a military man riding upon a horse, holding a snake in his right hand. (Picatrix‡4.IX§32)

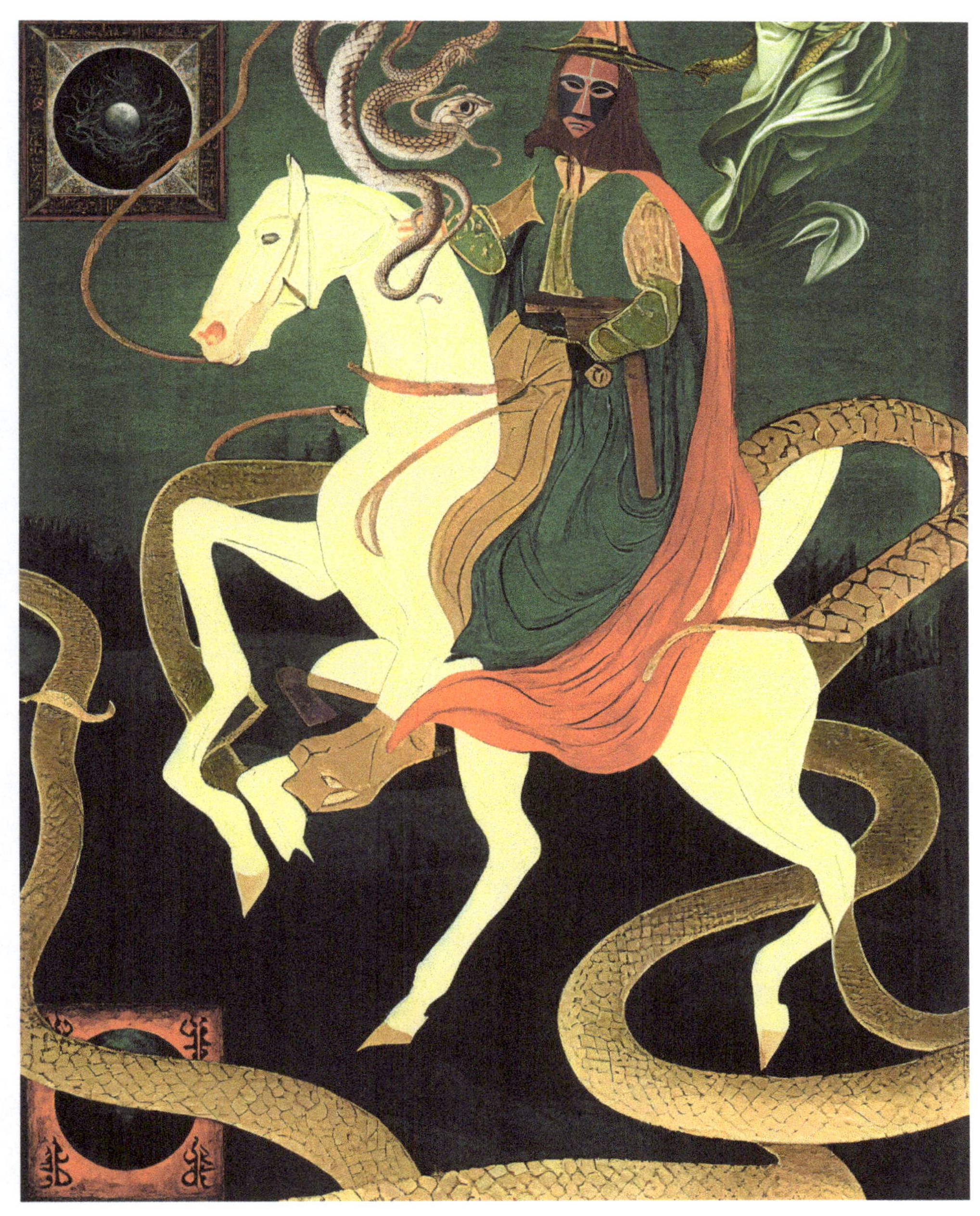

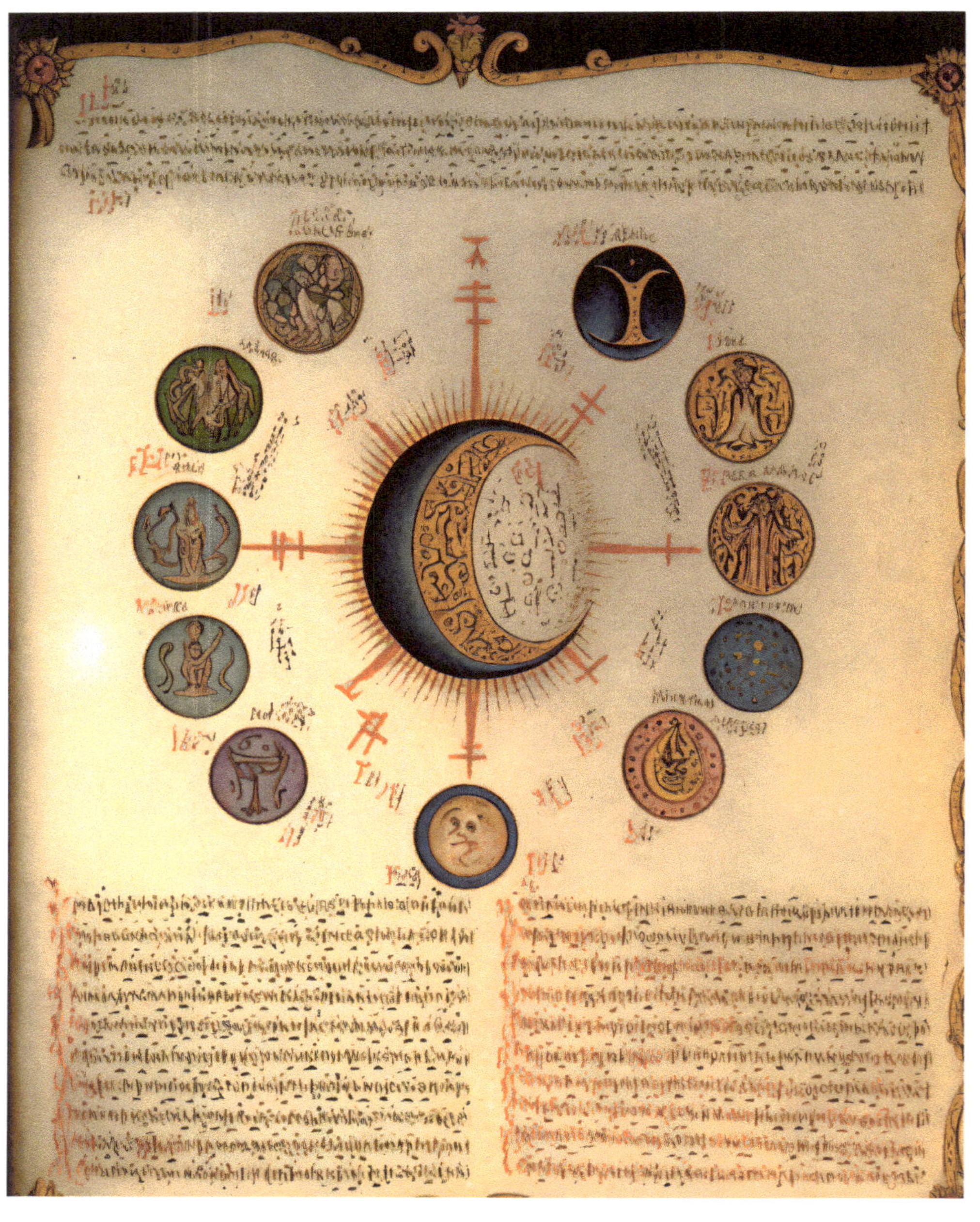

III.5 Almizen ... the head of a man without a body. (Picatrix‡4.IX§33)

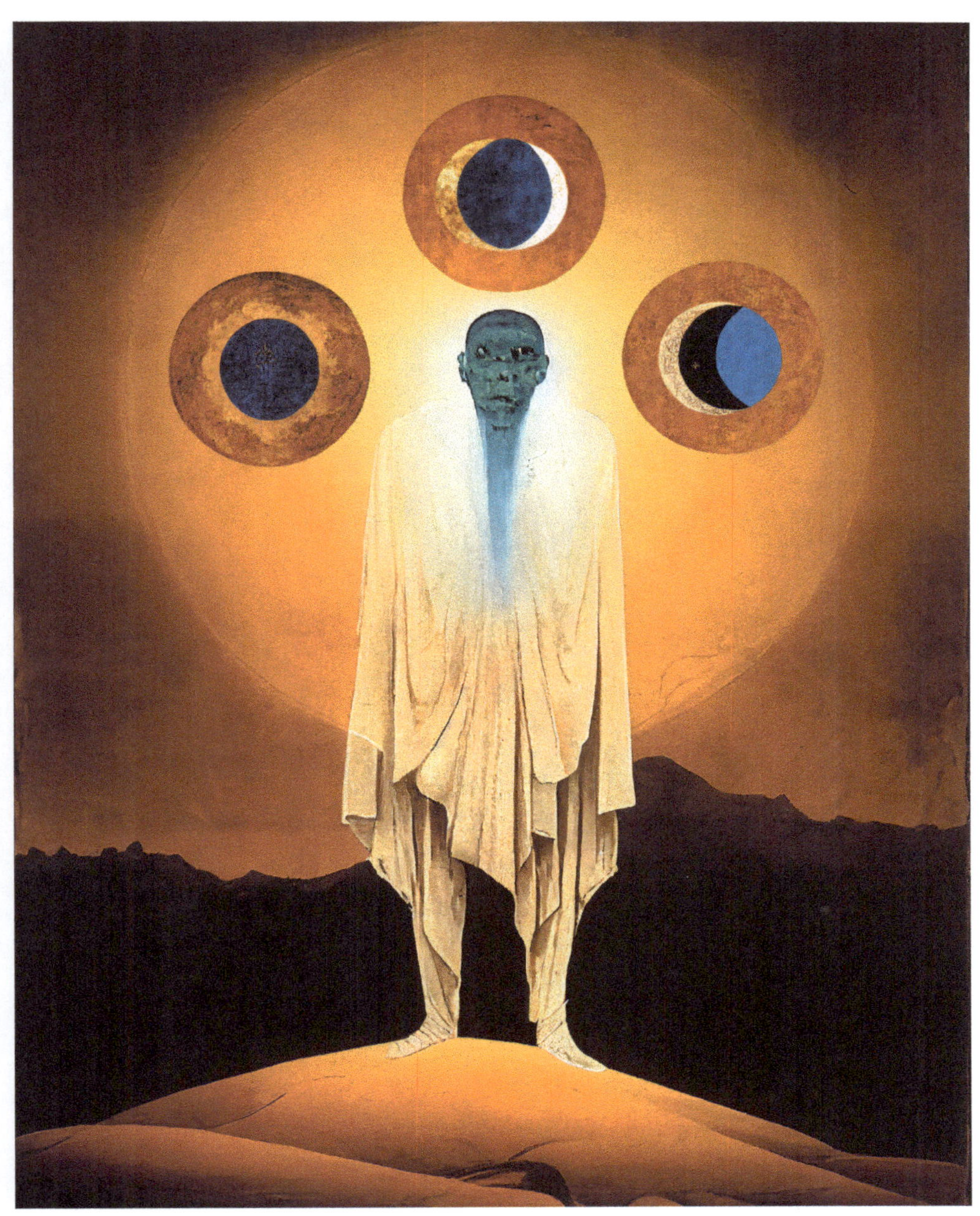

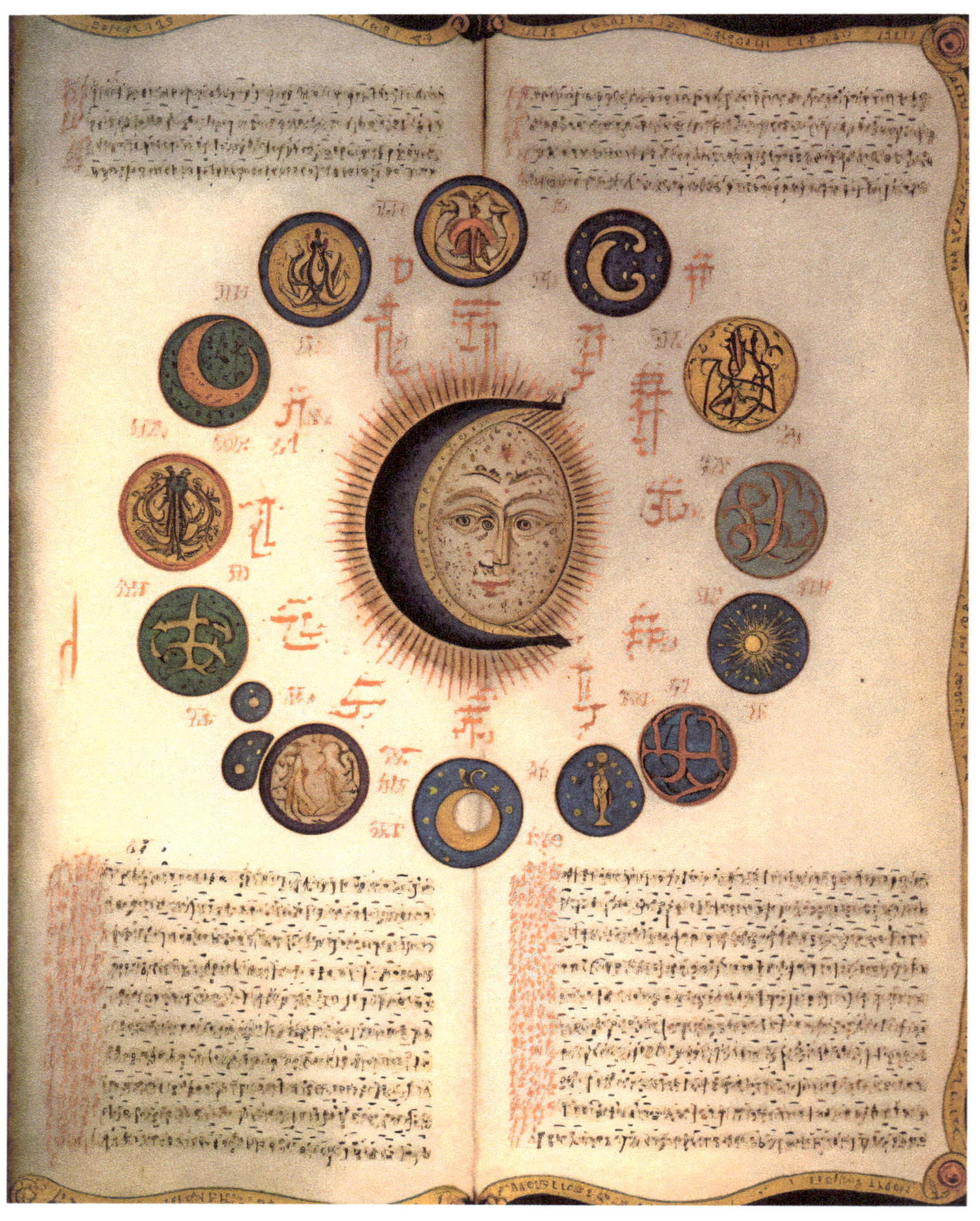

III.6 Achaya ... Make two images from white wax and make them embrace each other... (Picatrix[†]4.IX§34)

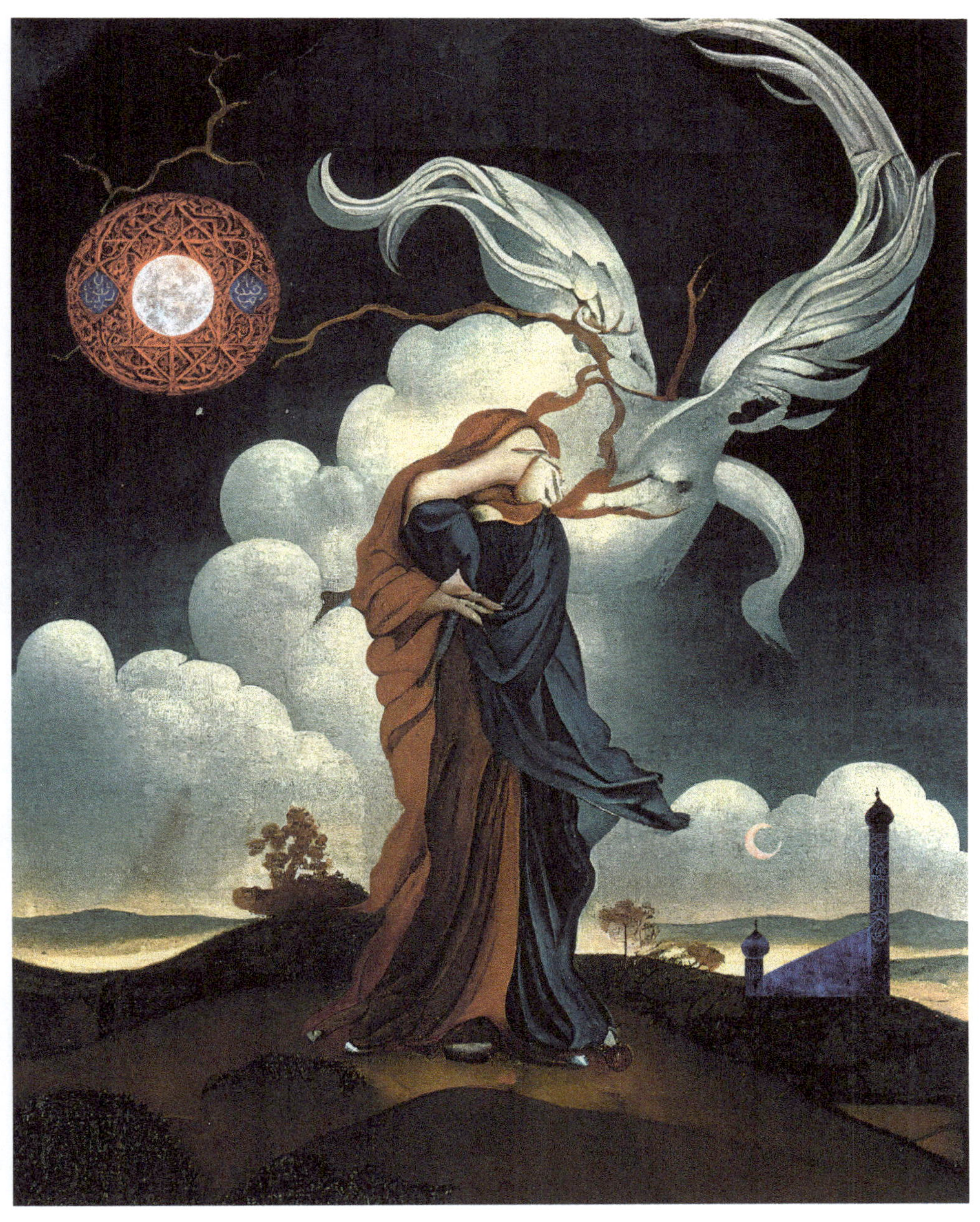

/63

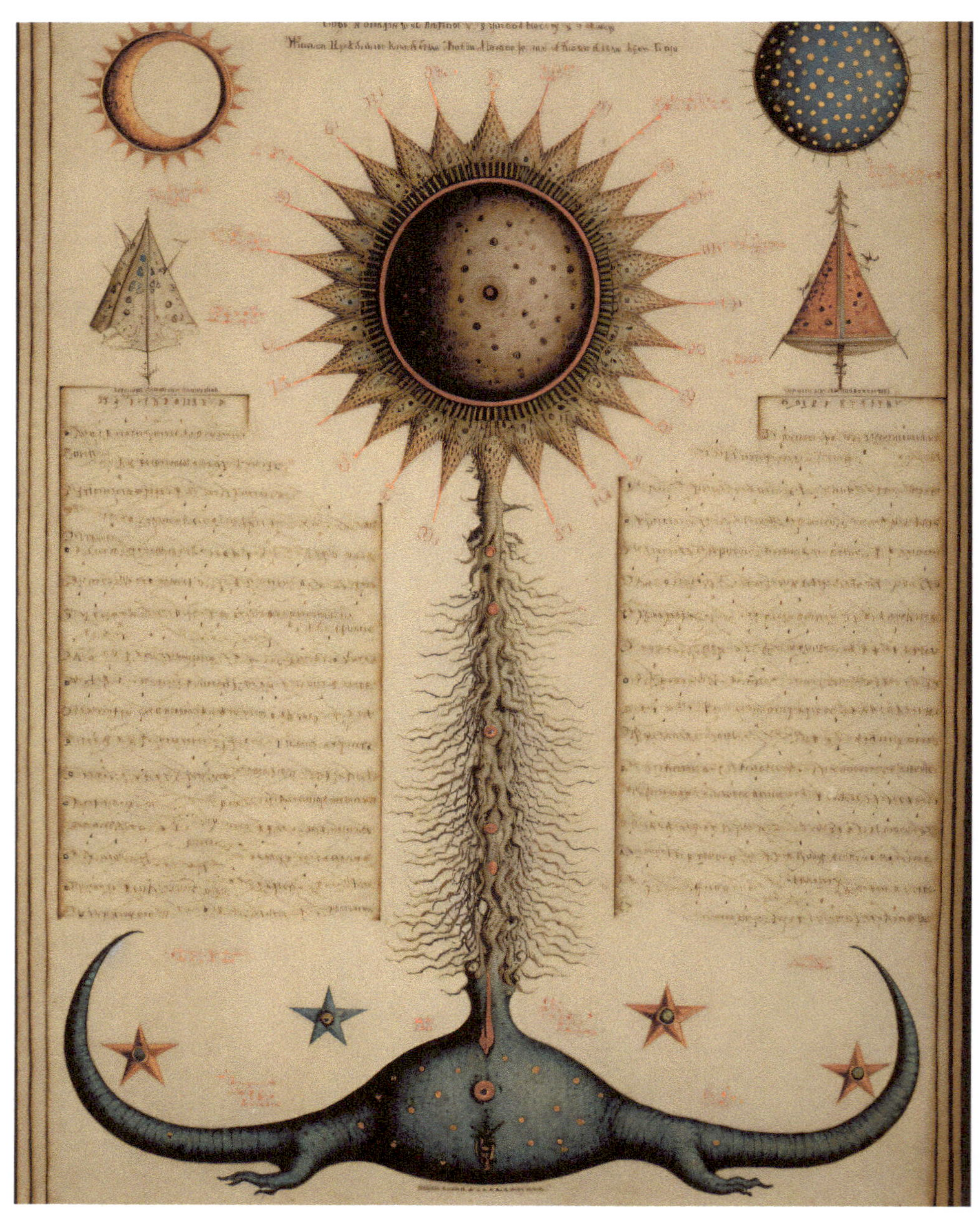

III.7 Aldira ... a man clothed in robes and with his hands extended to heaven in the manner of a man who is praying and supplicating. (Picatrix[†]4.IX§35)

/Oracle of DelphAI

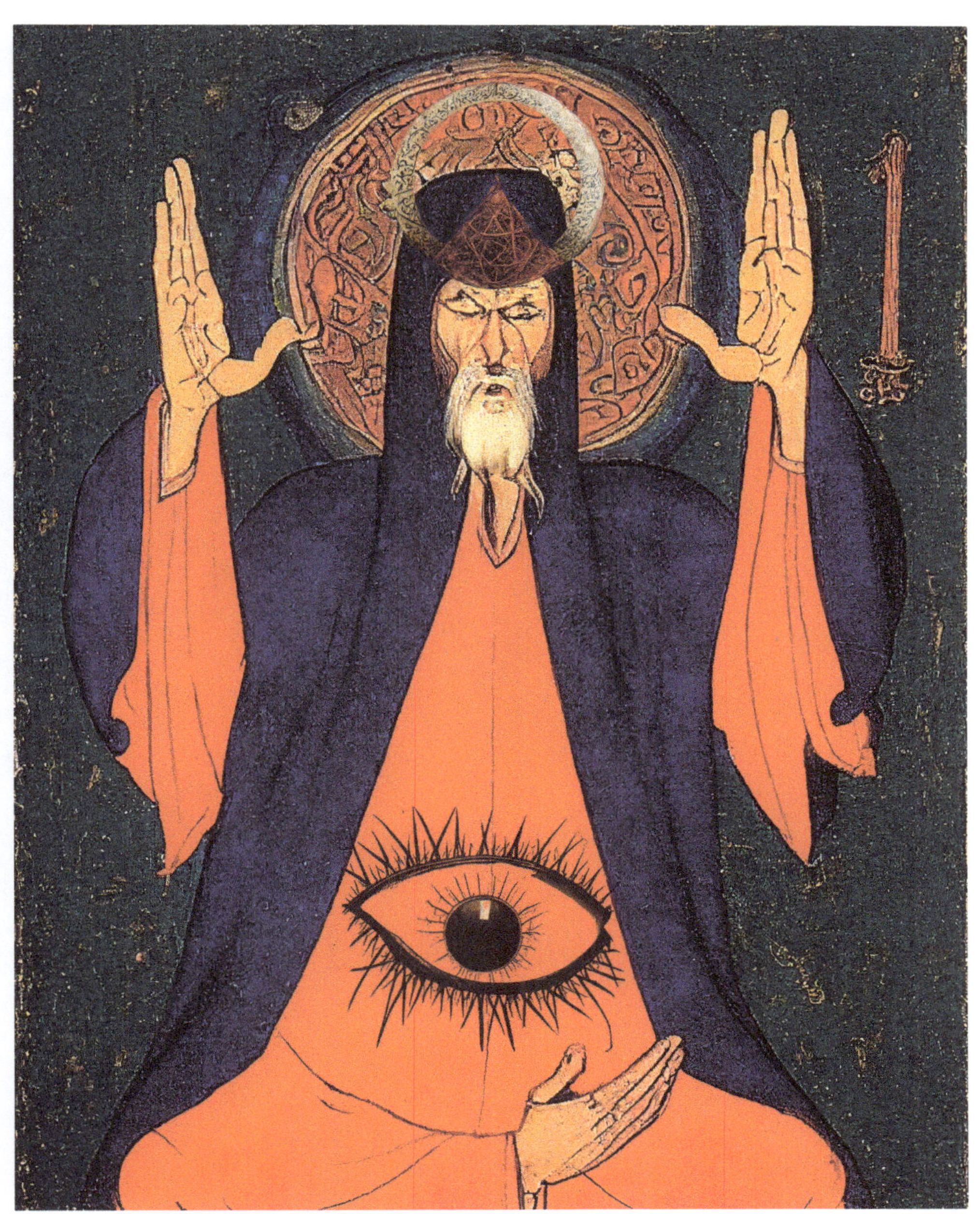

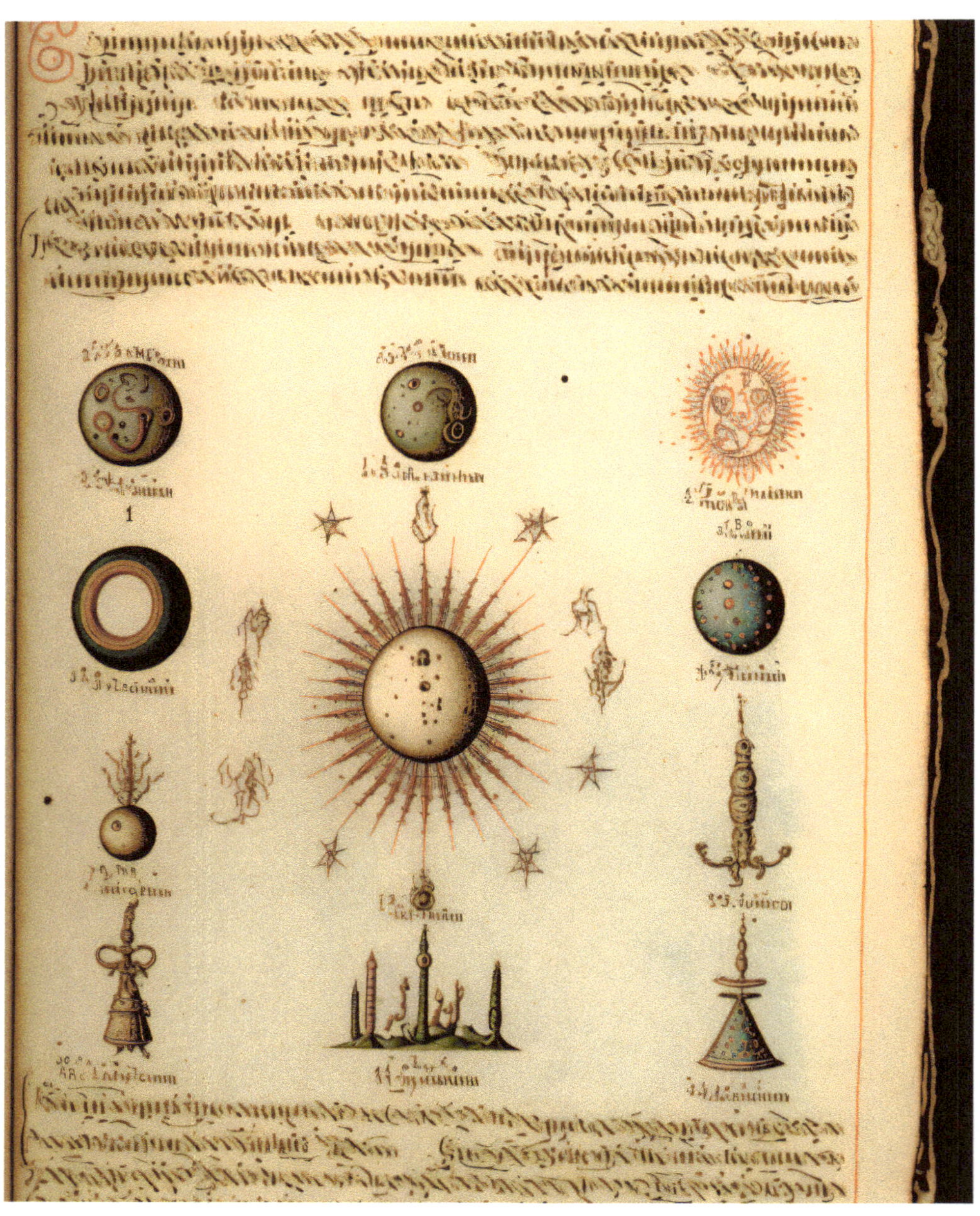

III.8 Annathra ... the image of an eagle with the face of a man. (Picatrix[†]4.IX§36)

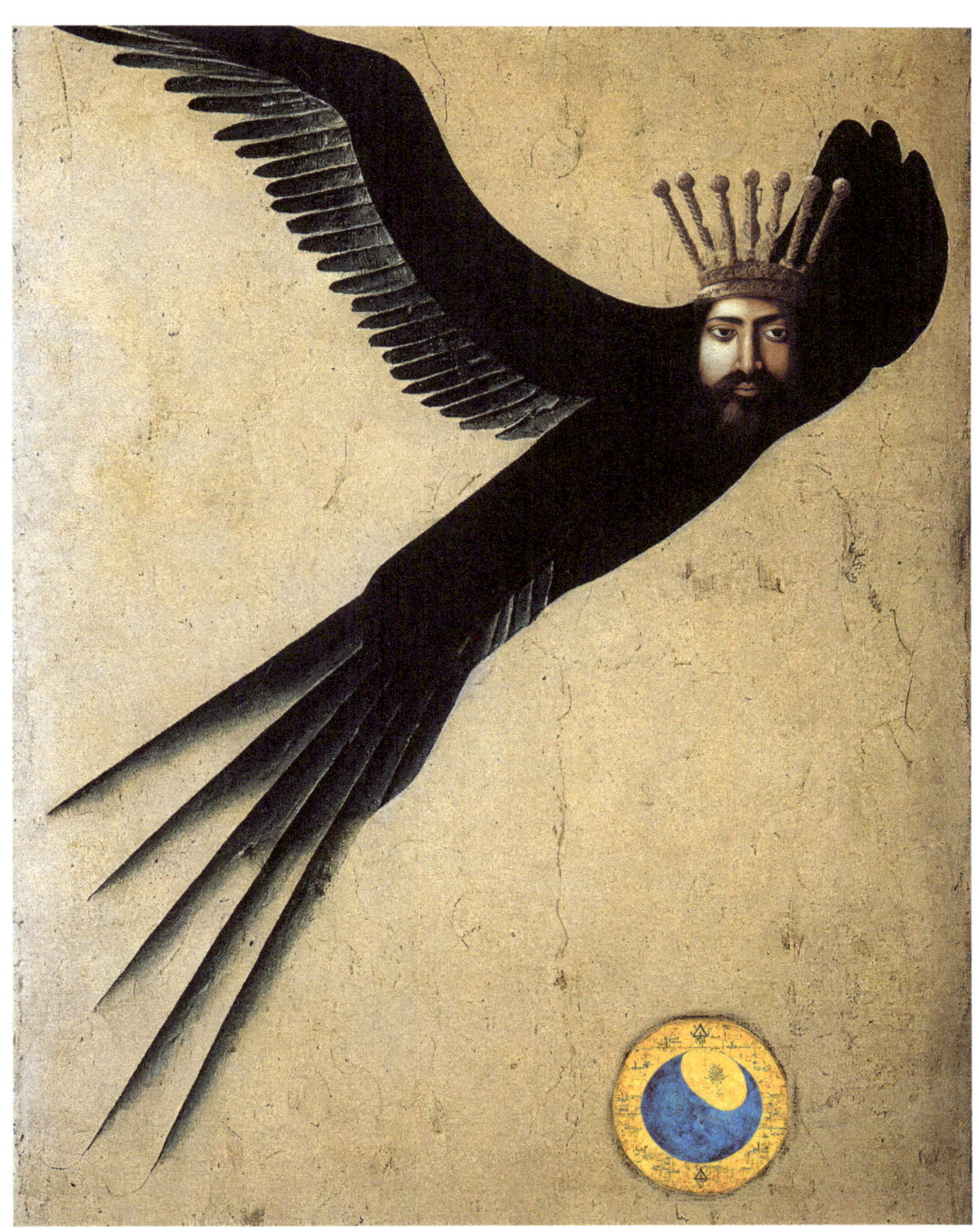

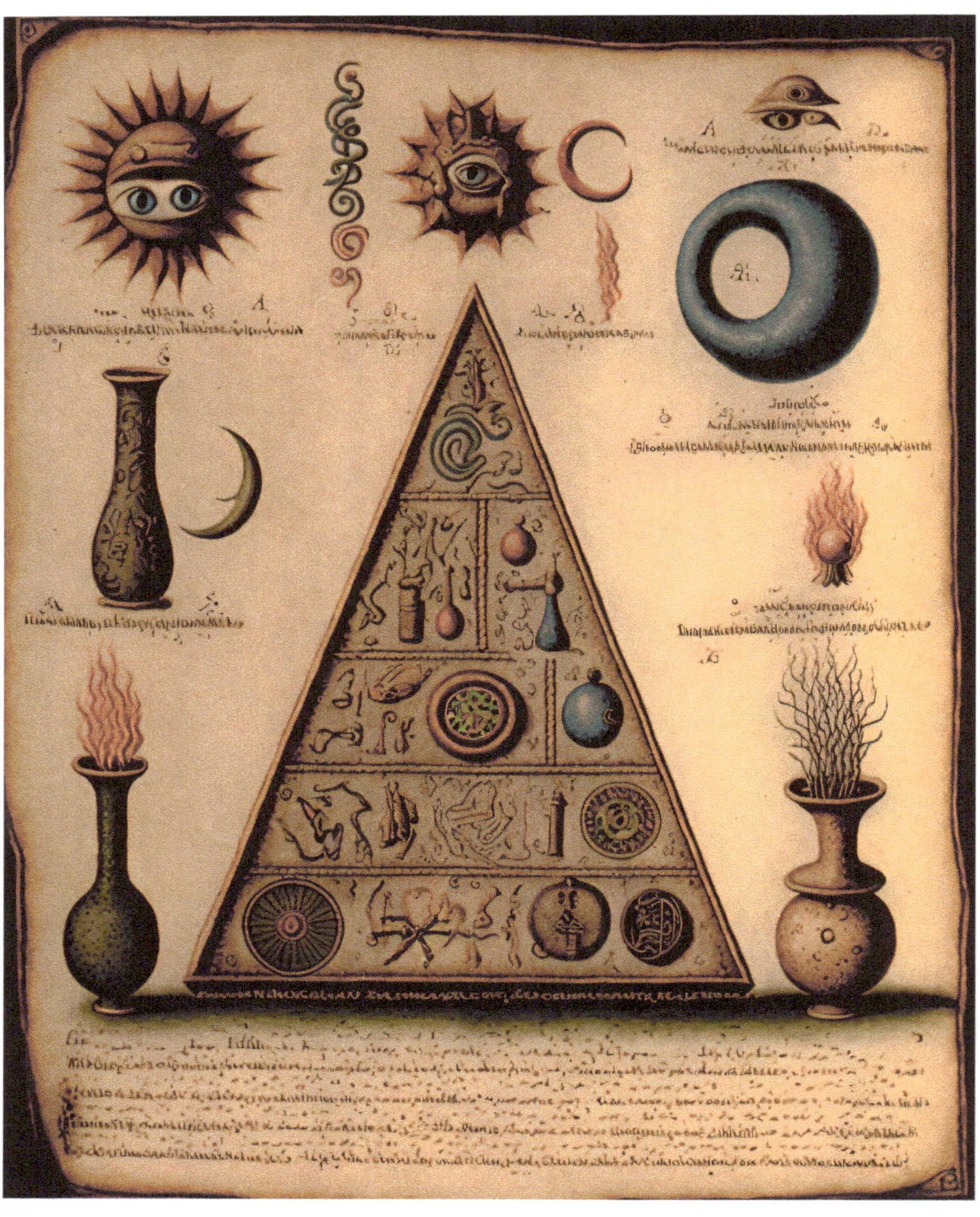

III.9 Atarfa ... a eunuch holding his hands over his eyes. (Picatrix[†]4.IX§37)

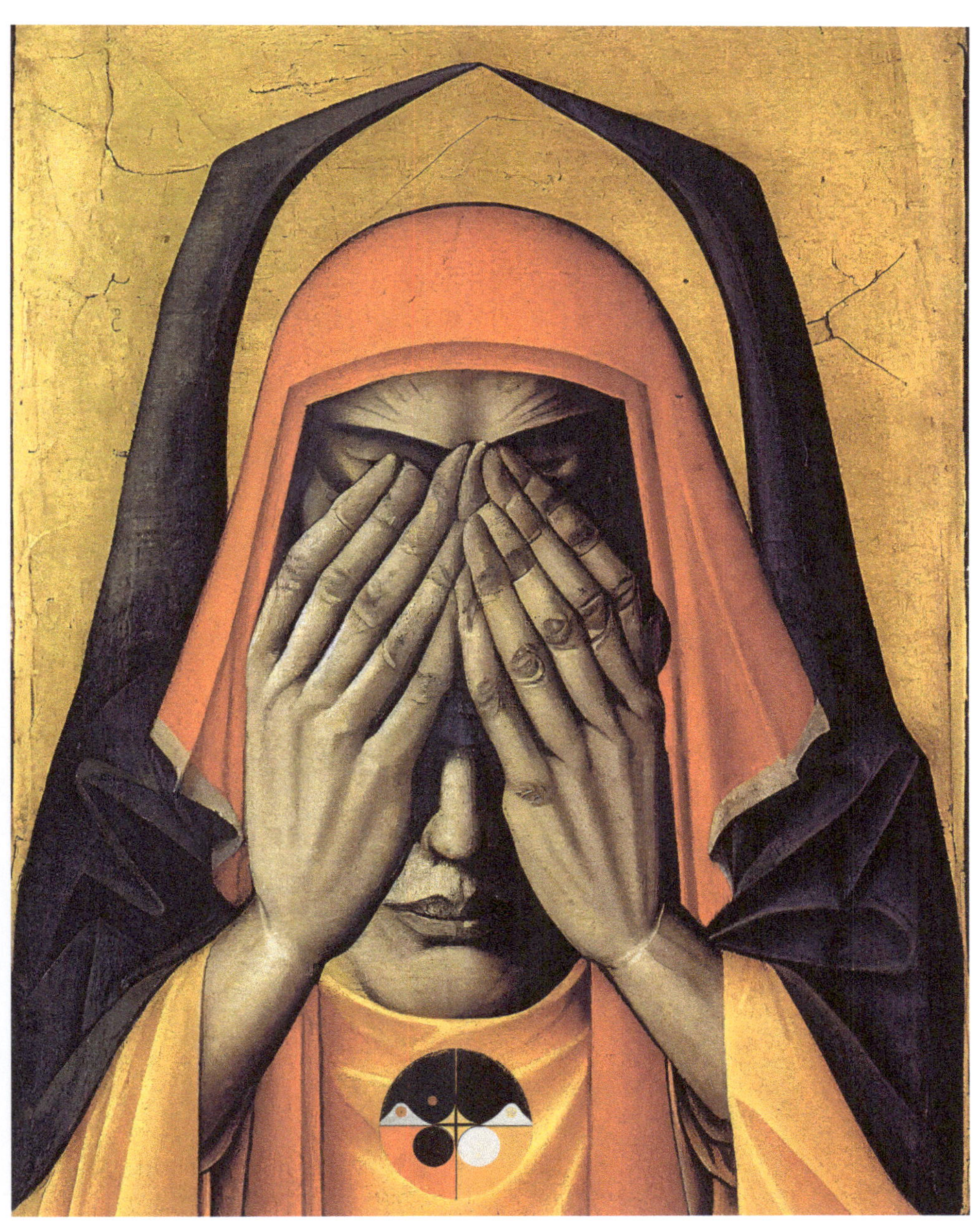

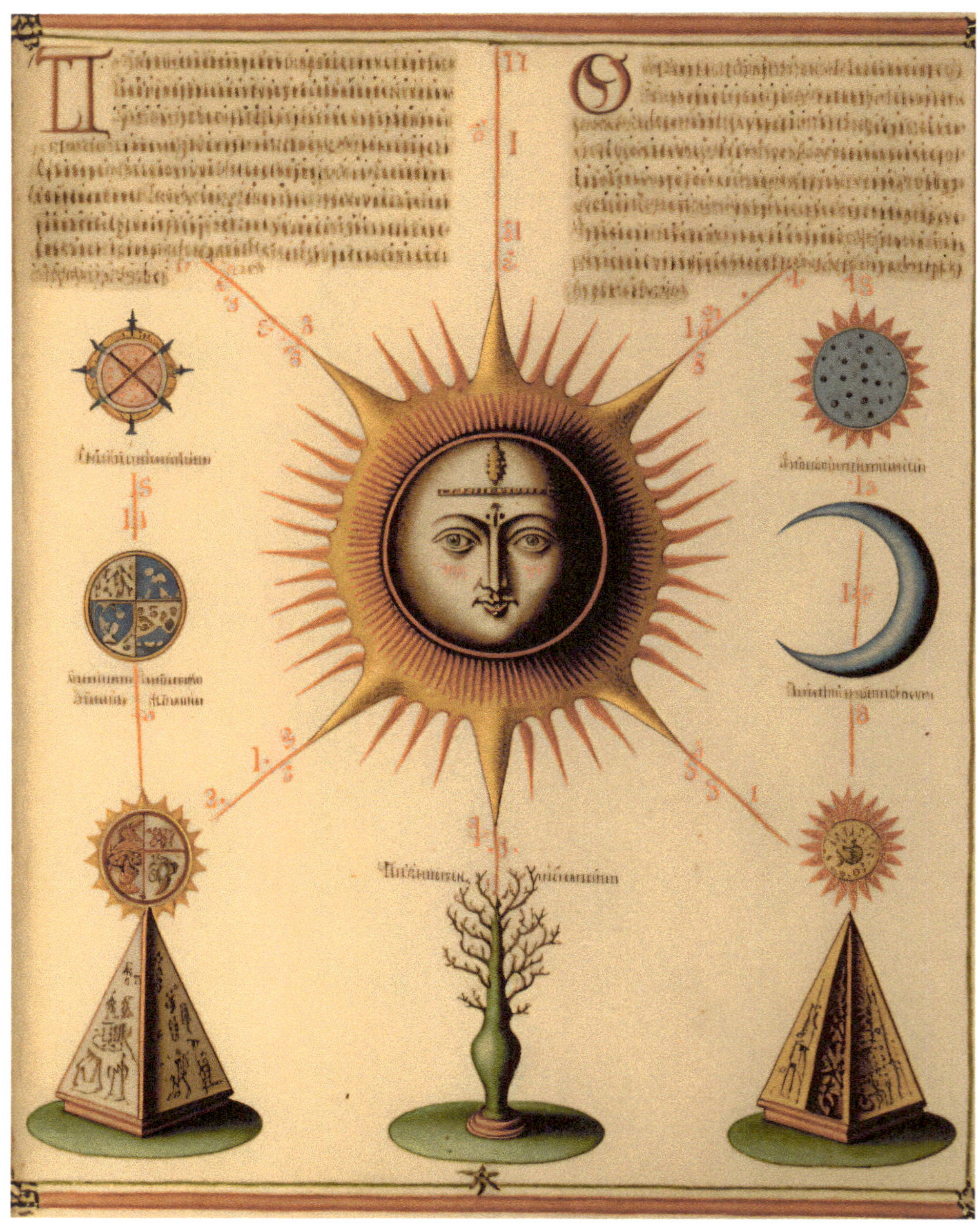

III.10 Algebha ... image of a lion head. (Picatrix‡4.IX§38)

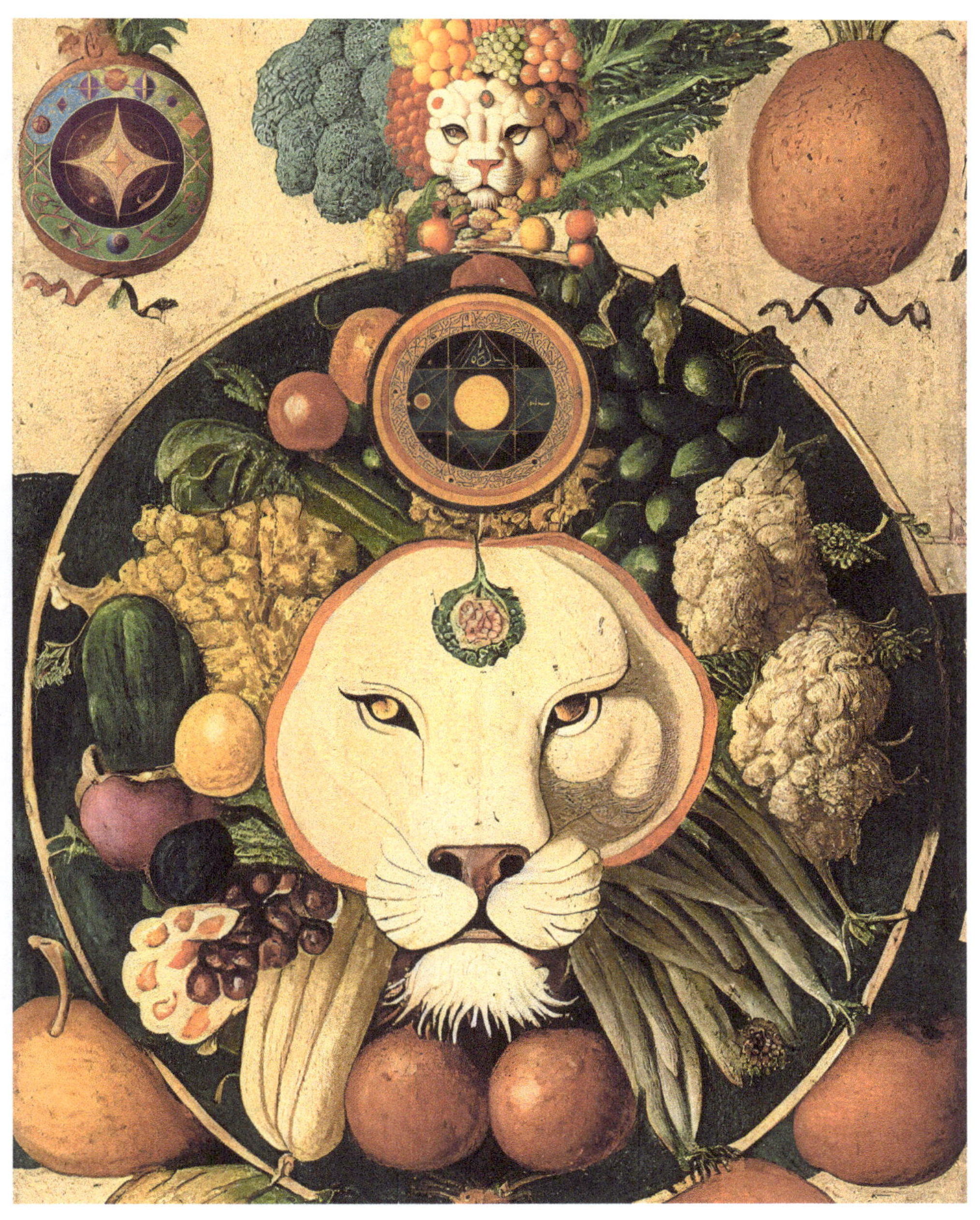

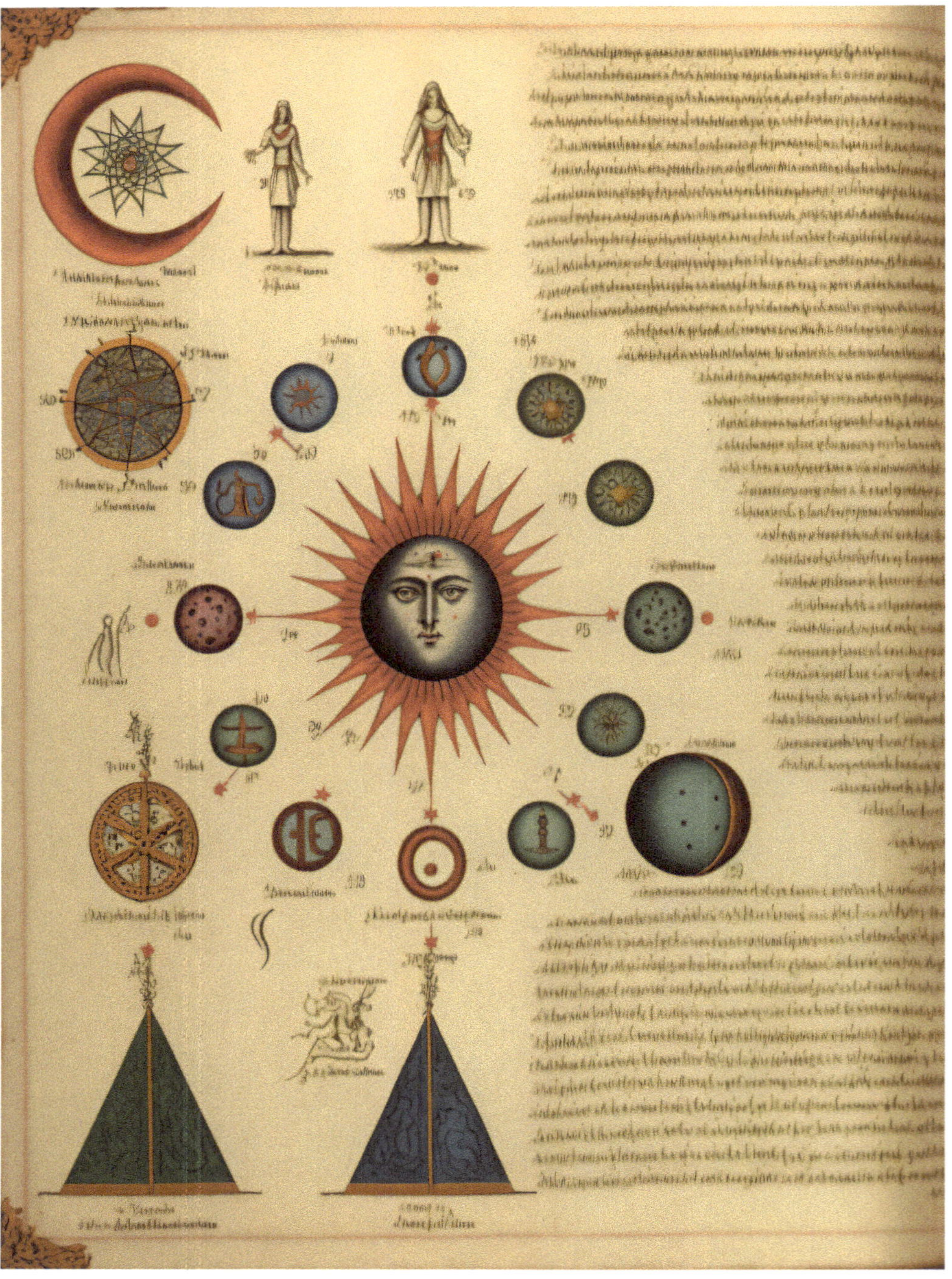

III.11 Azobra … a man riding a lion, holding a lance in his right hand and holding the ear of the lion with his left hand. (Picatrix[†]4.IX§39)

/Oracle of DelphΛI

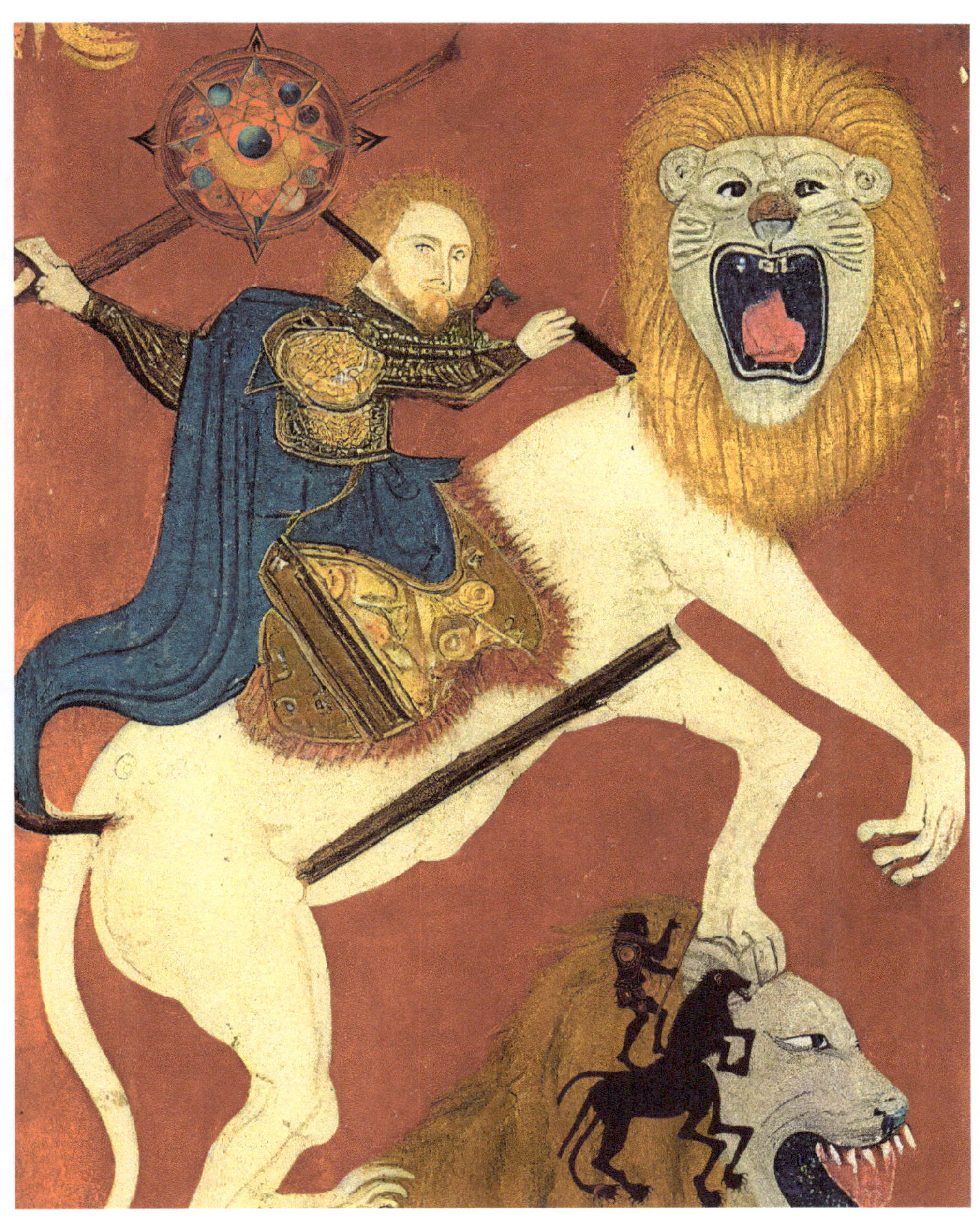

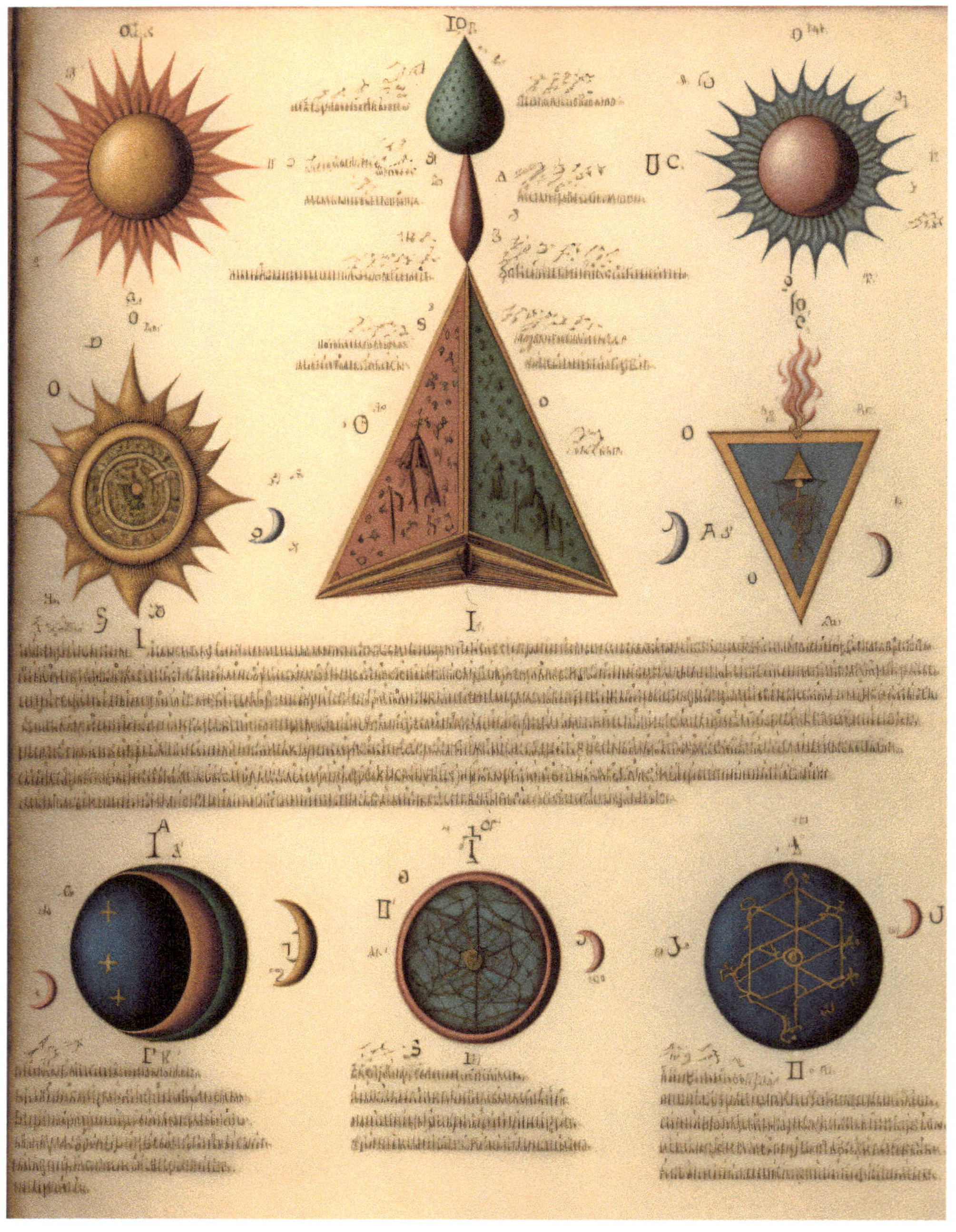

III.12 Azarfa ... a dragon fighting with a man. (Picatrix[1] 4.IX§40)

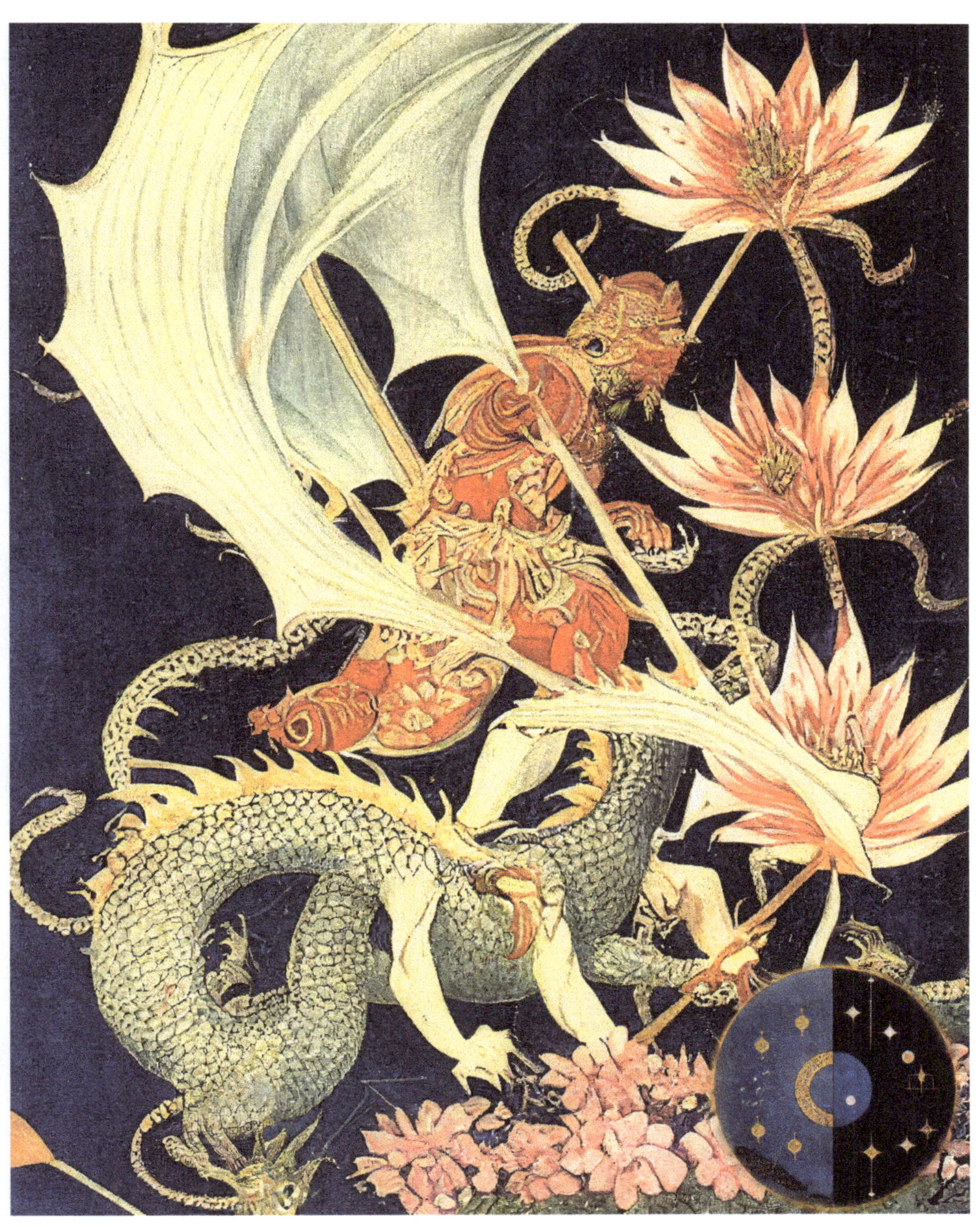

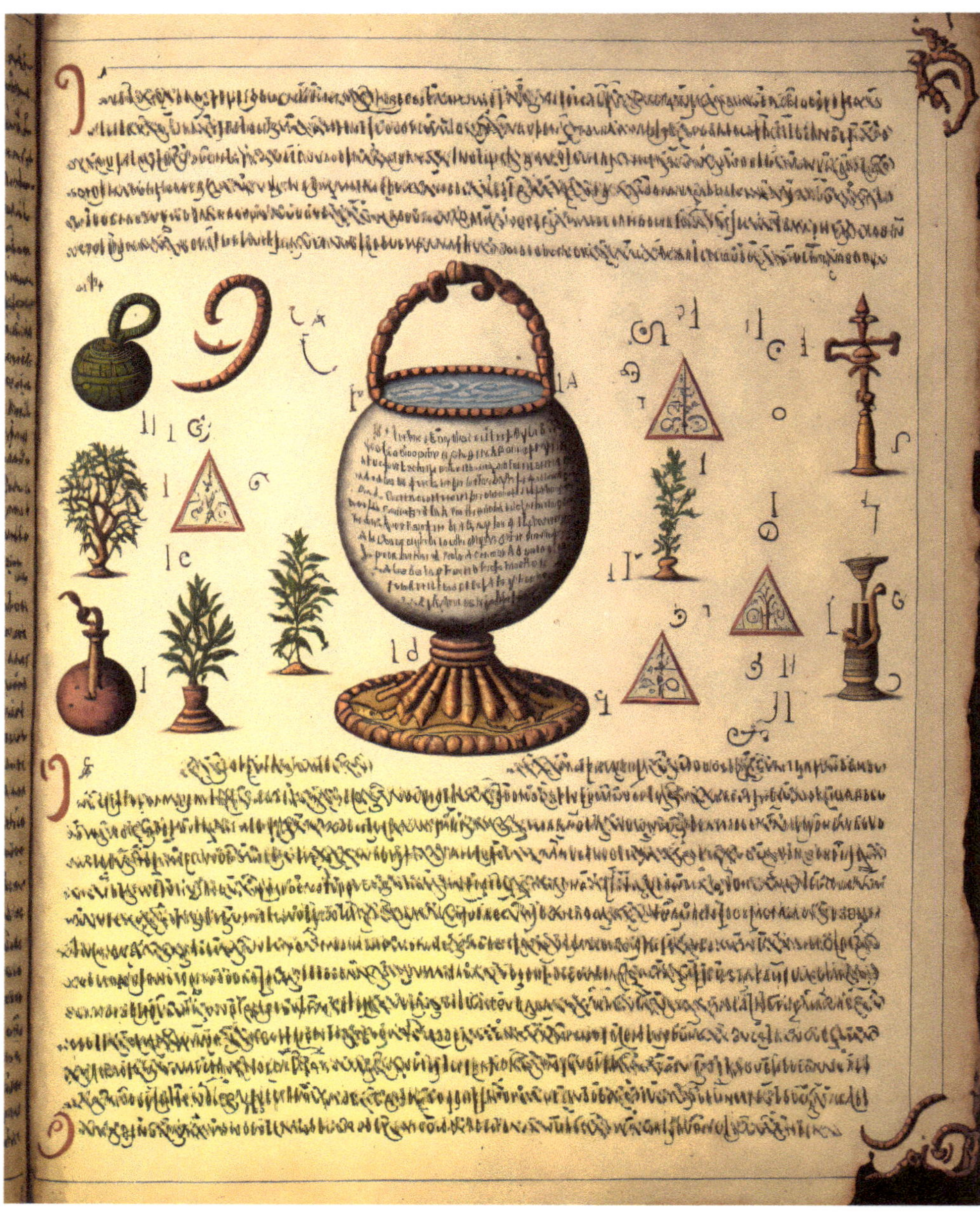

III.13 Alahue ... an erect man (that is, with an erect penis); and let it be in all ways the image of a man desiring to couple with a woman. (Picatrix[1] 4. IX§41)

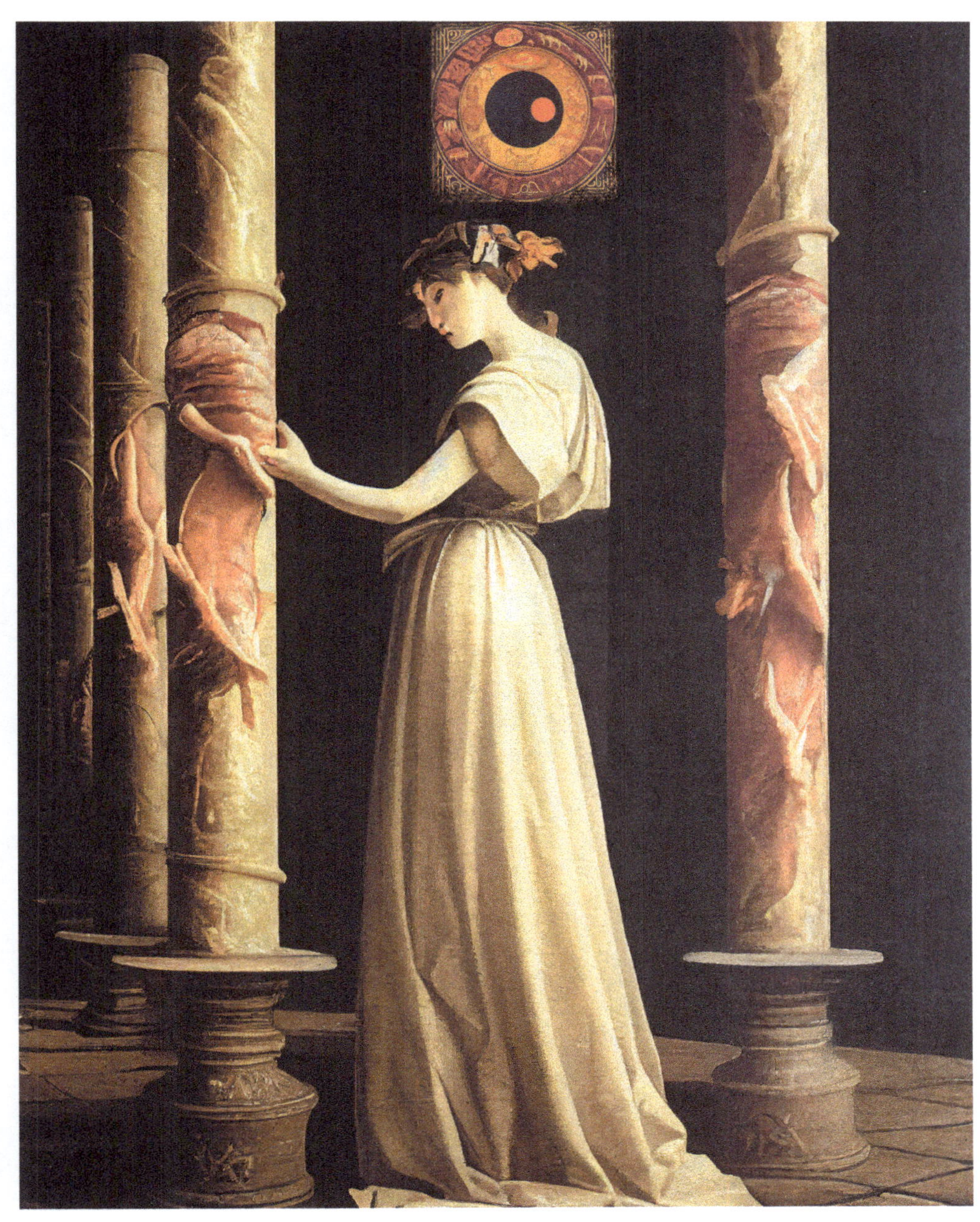

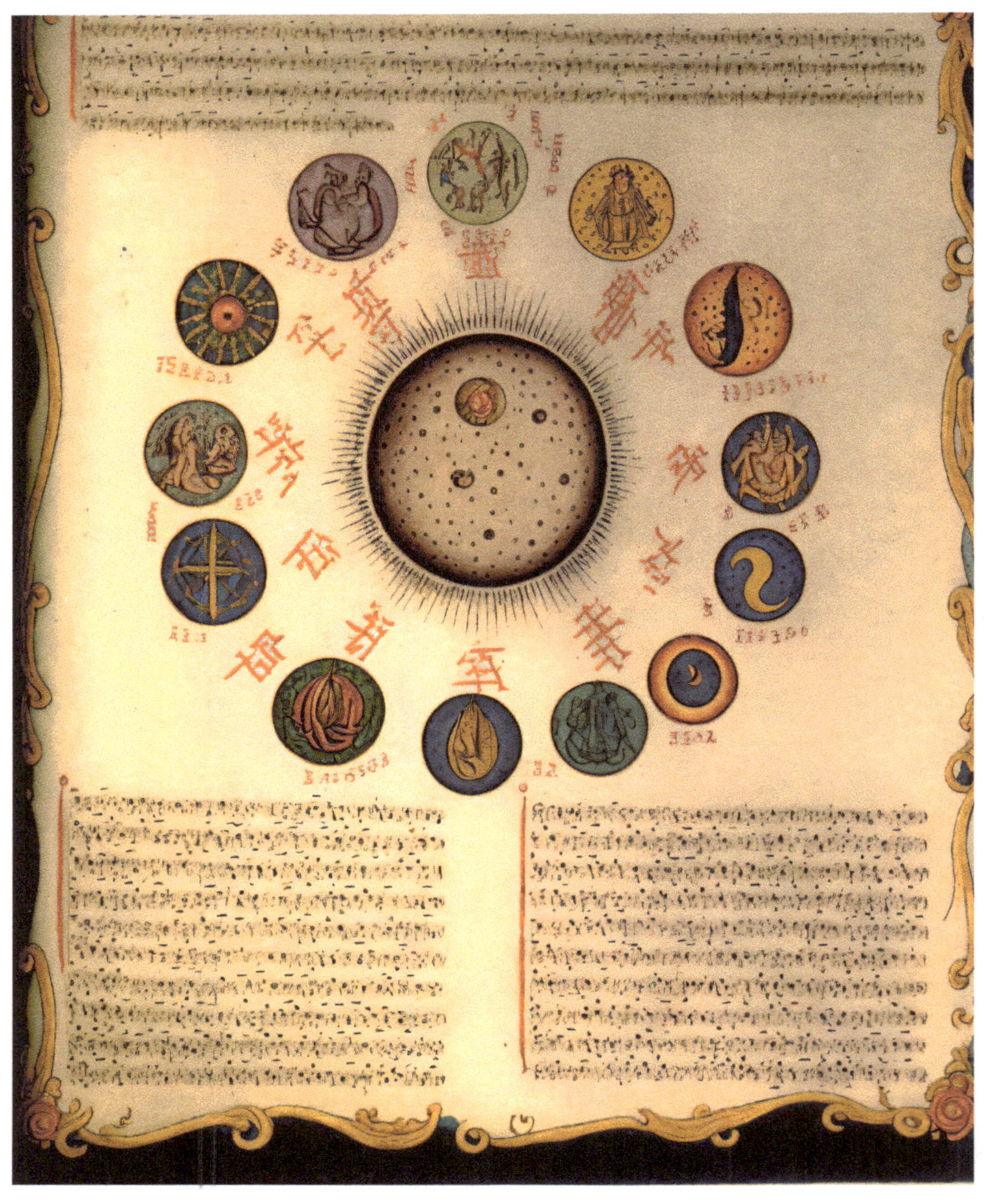

III.14 Azimech … a dog with his own tail held in his mouth. (Picatrix[†]4.IX§42)

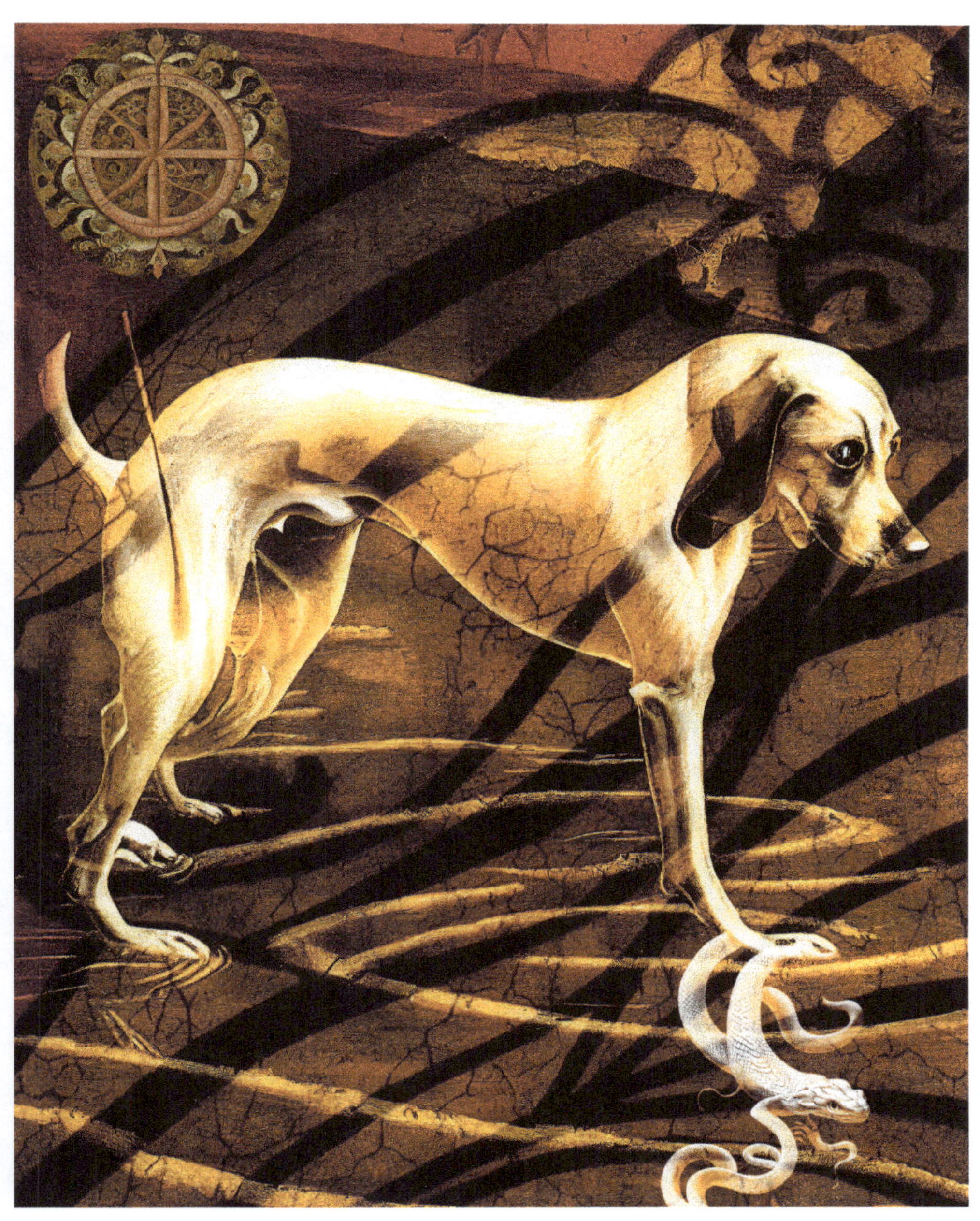

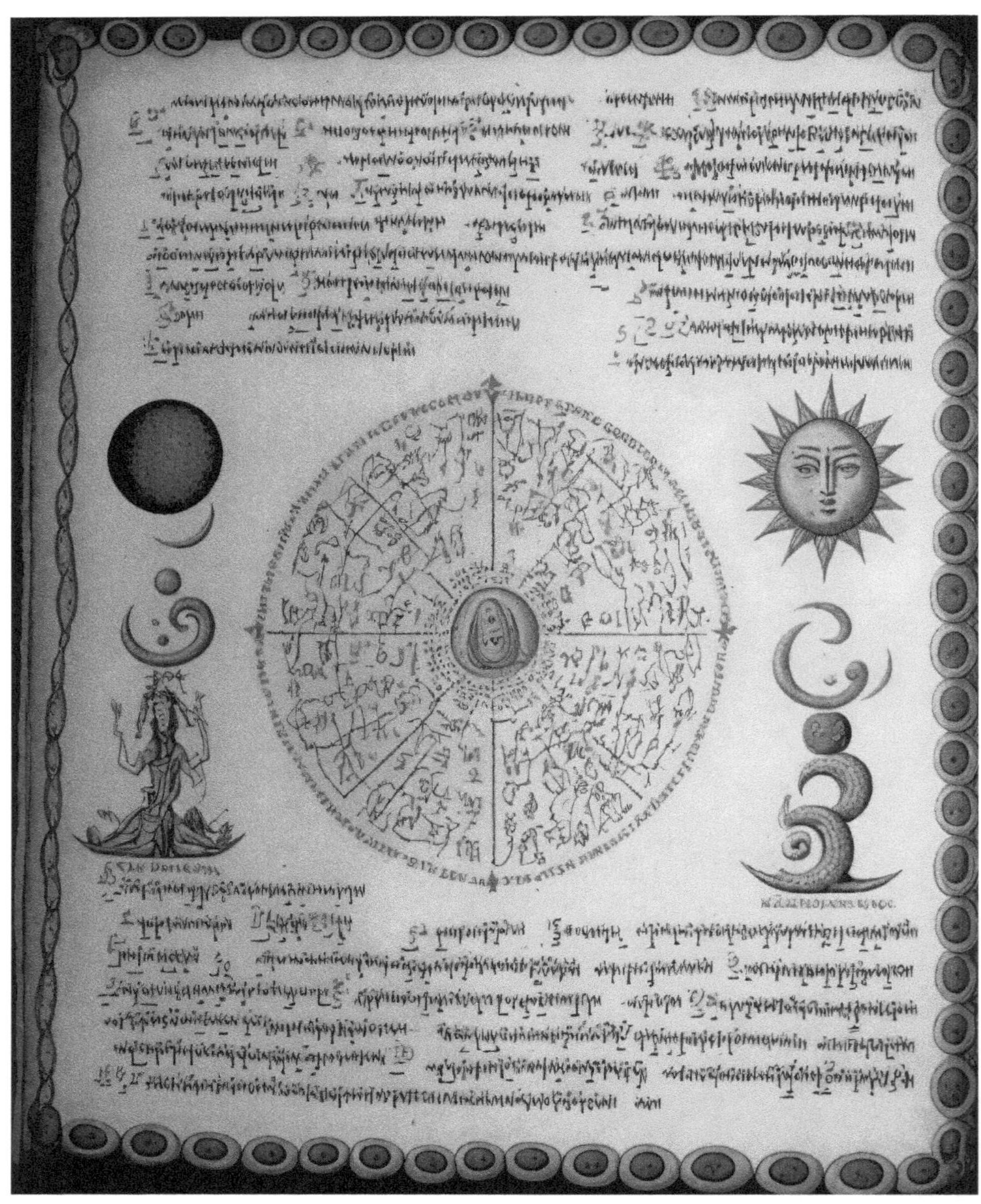

III.15 Algafra ... the figure of a seated man, holding scrolls in his hand as if reading them. (Picatrix[†]4.IX§43)

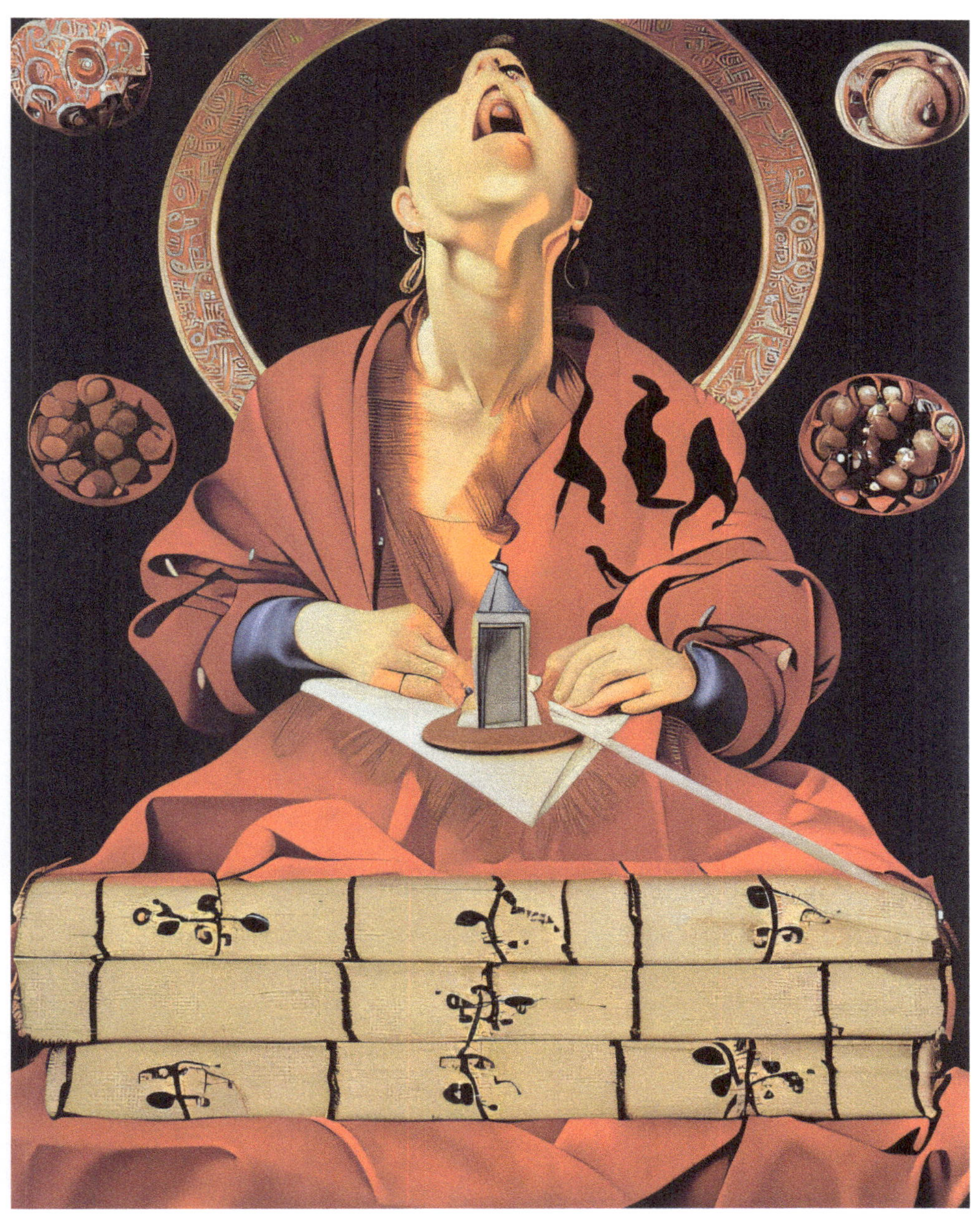

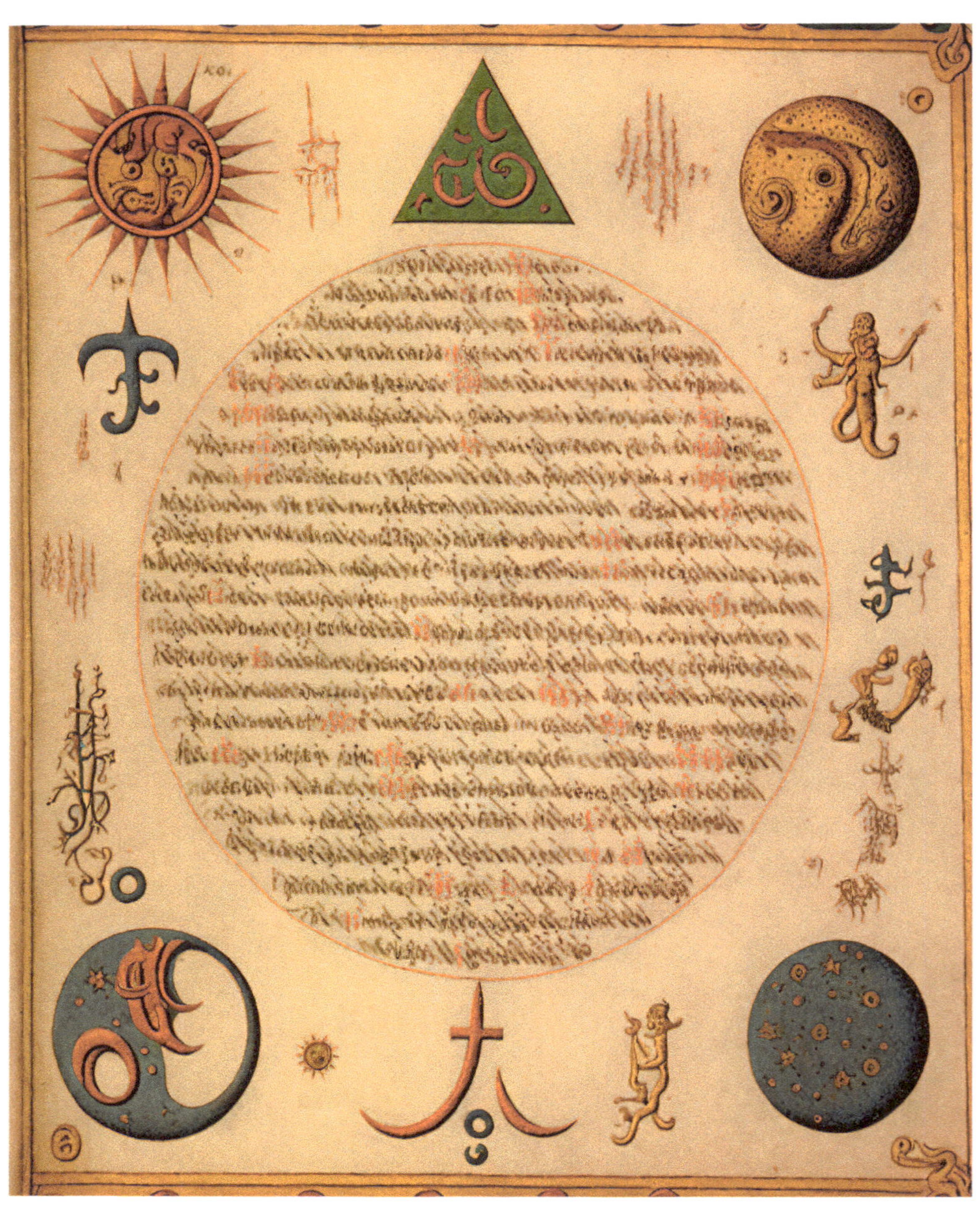

III.16 Azebene ... a man seated in a throne and carrying a scale in his hands.
(Picatrix‡4.IX§44)

/Oracle of DelphΛl

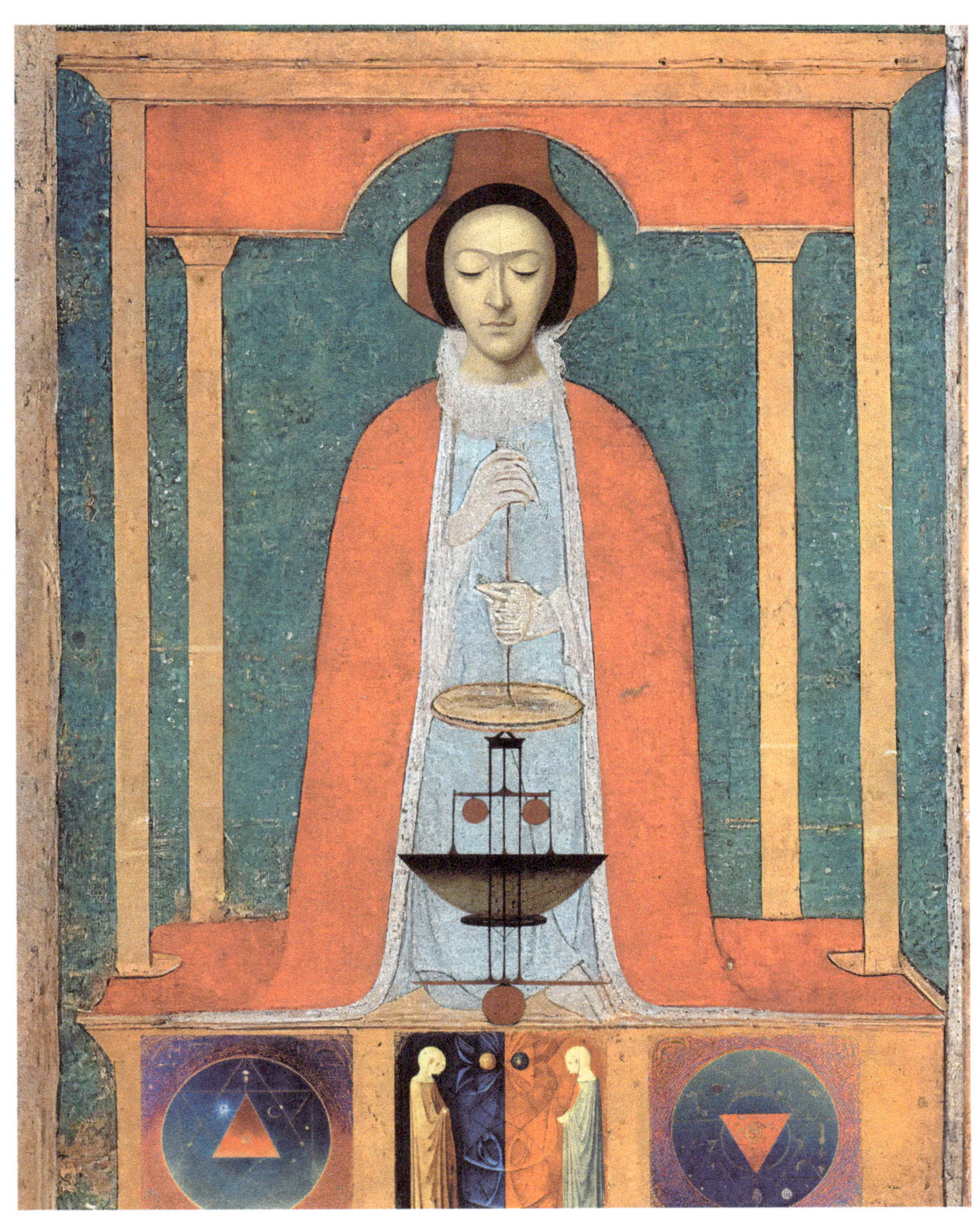

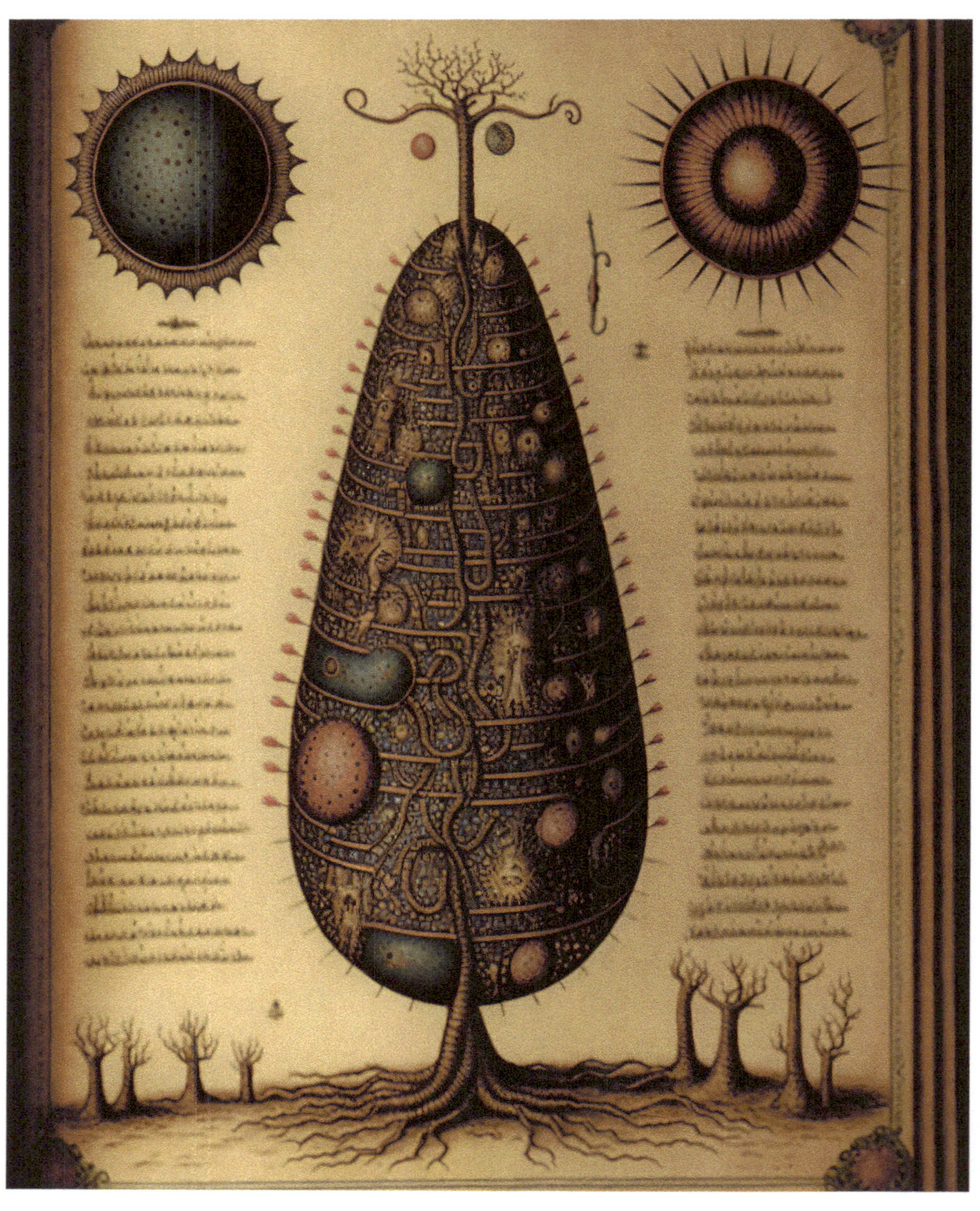

III.17 **Alichil** … the figure of a monkey in an iron seal, holding his hands above his shoulders. (Picatrix[†]4.IX§45)

/Oracle of DelphAI

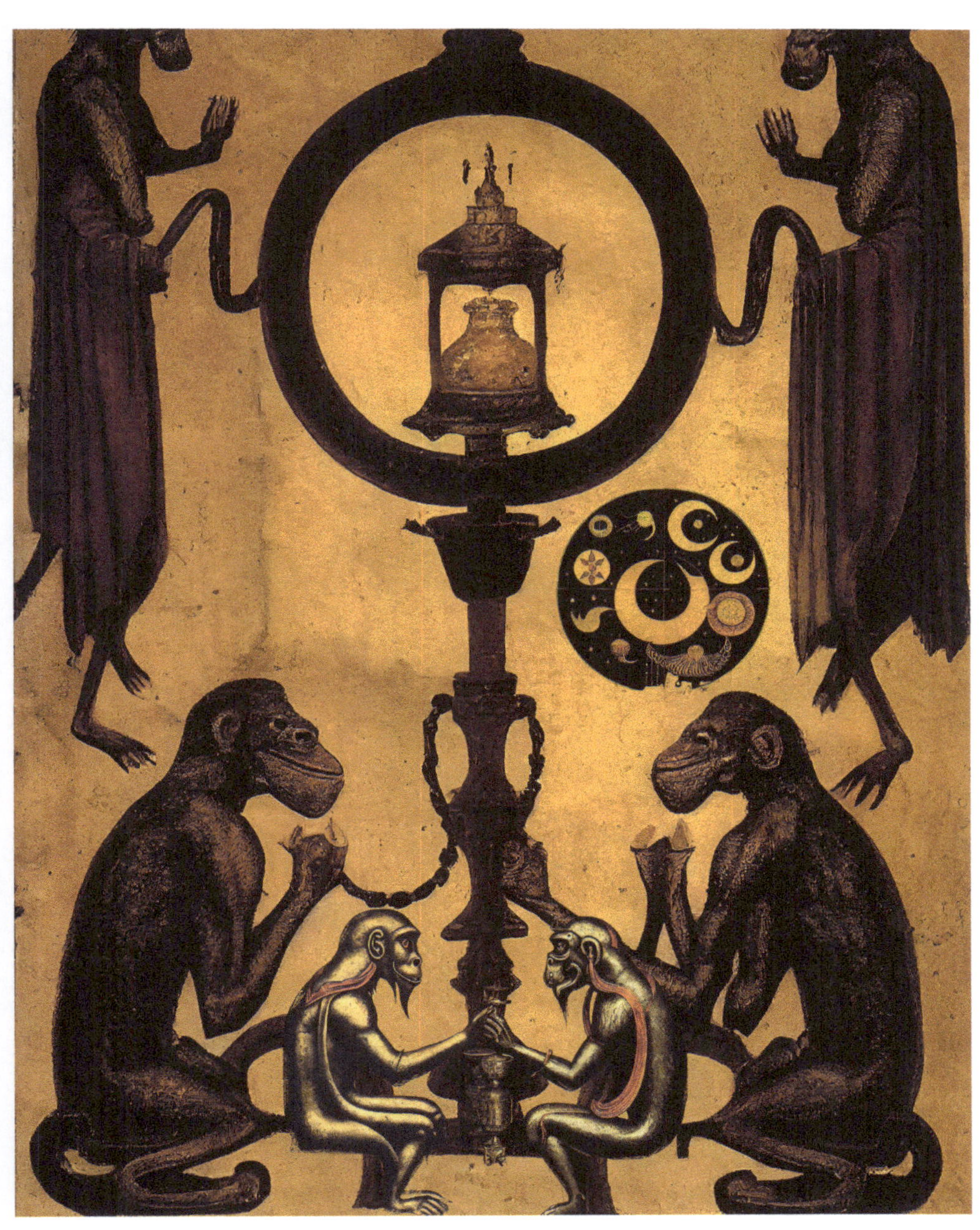

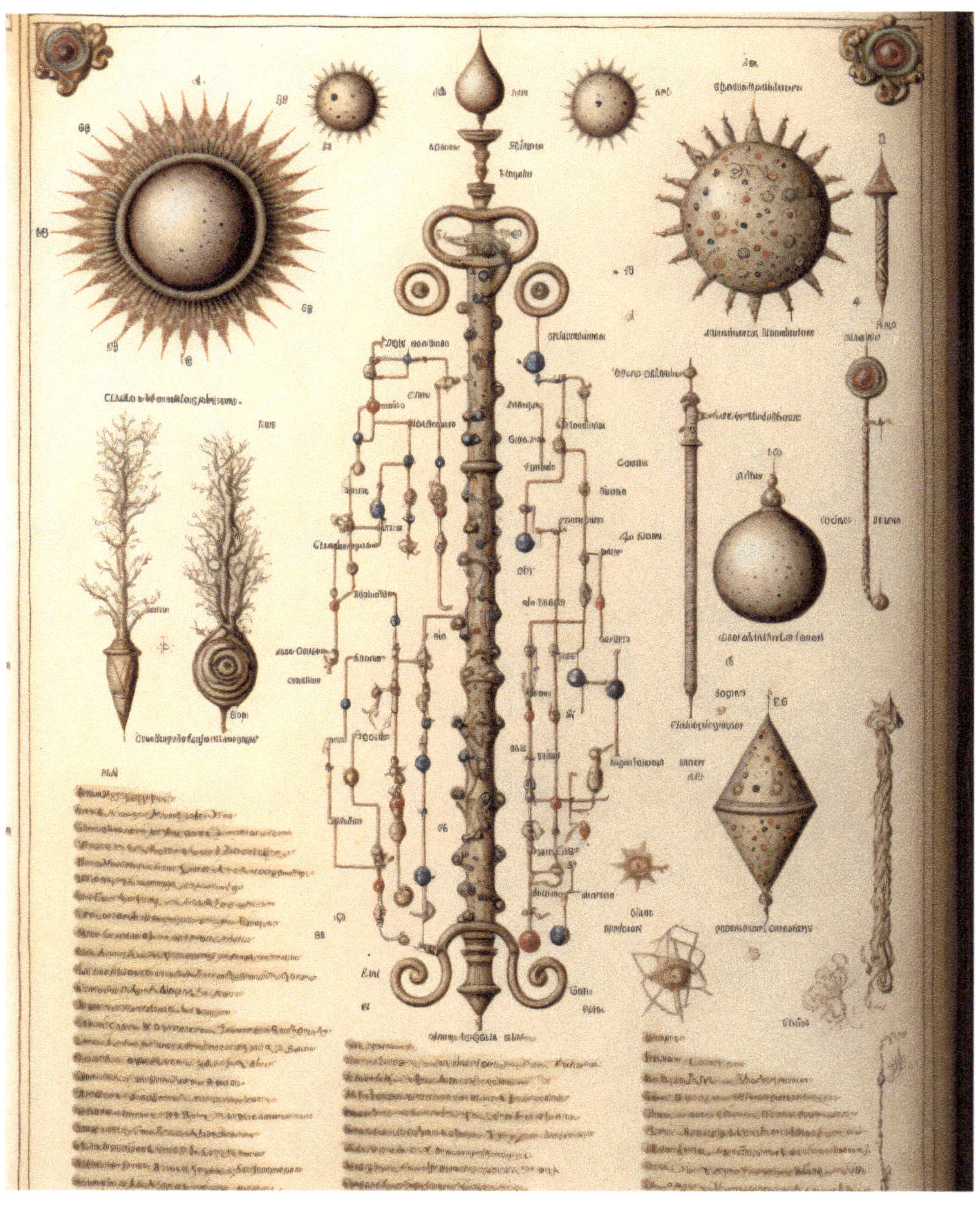

III.18 Alcab … the image of an adder holding its tail above its head. (Picatrix‡4.IX§46)

/Oracle of DelphΛI

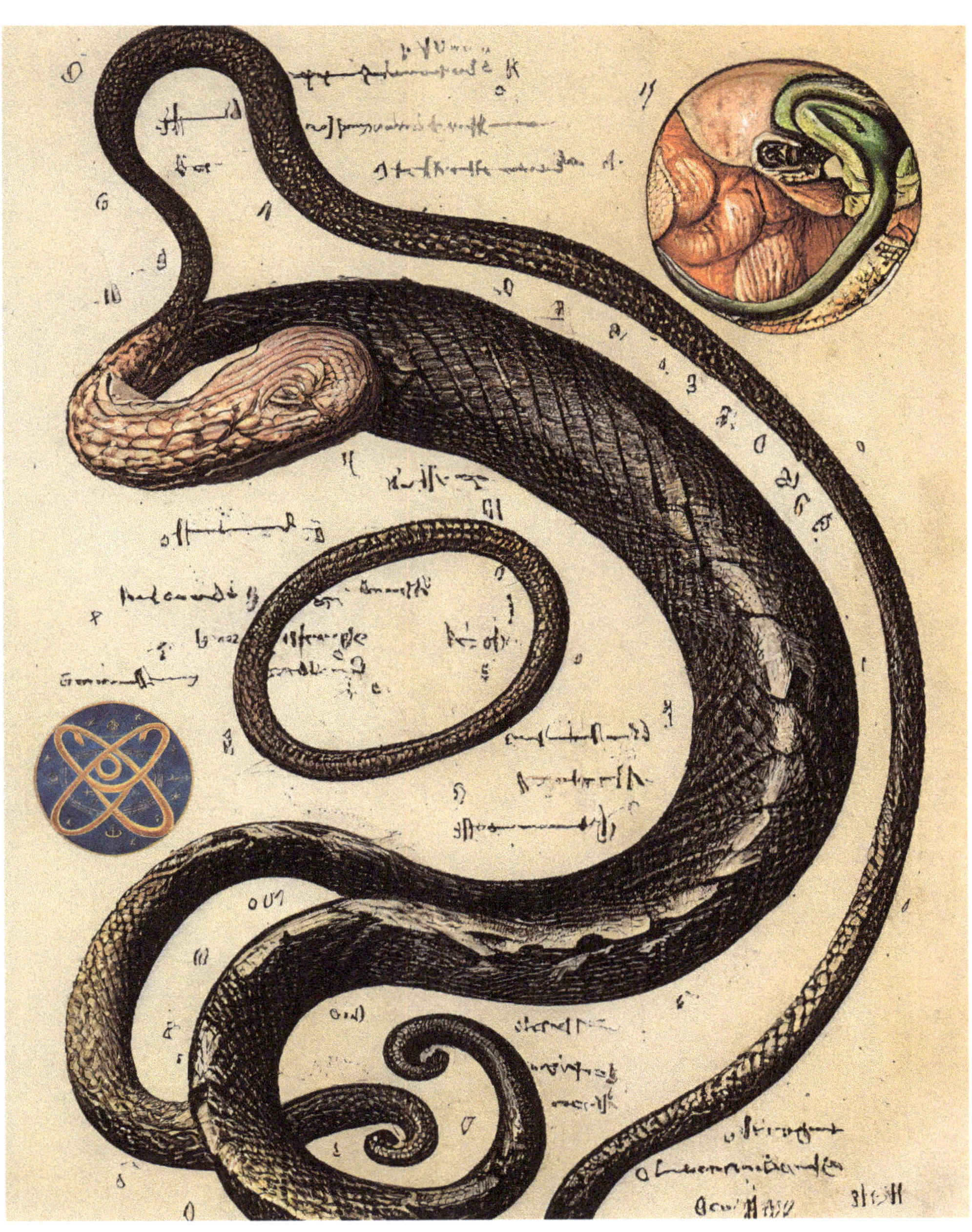

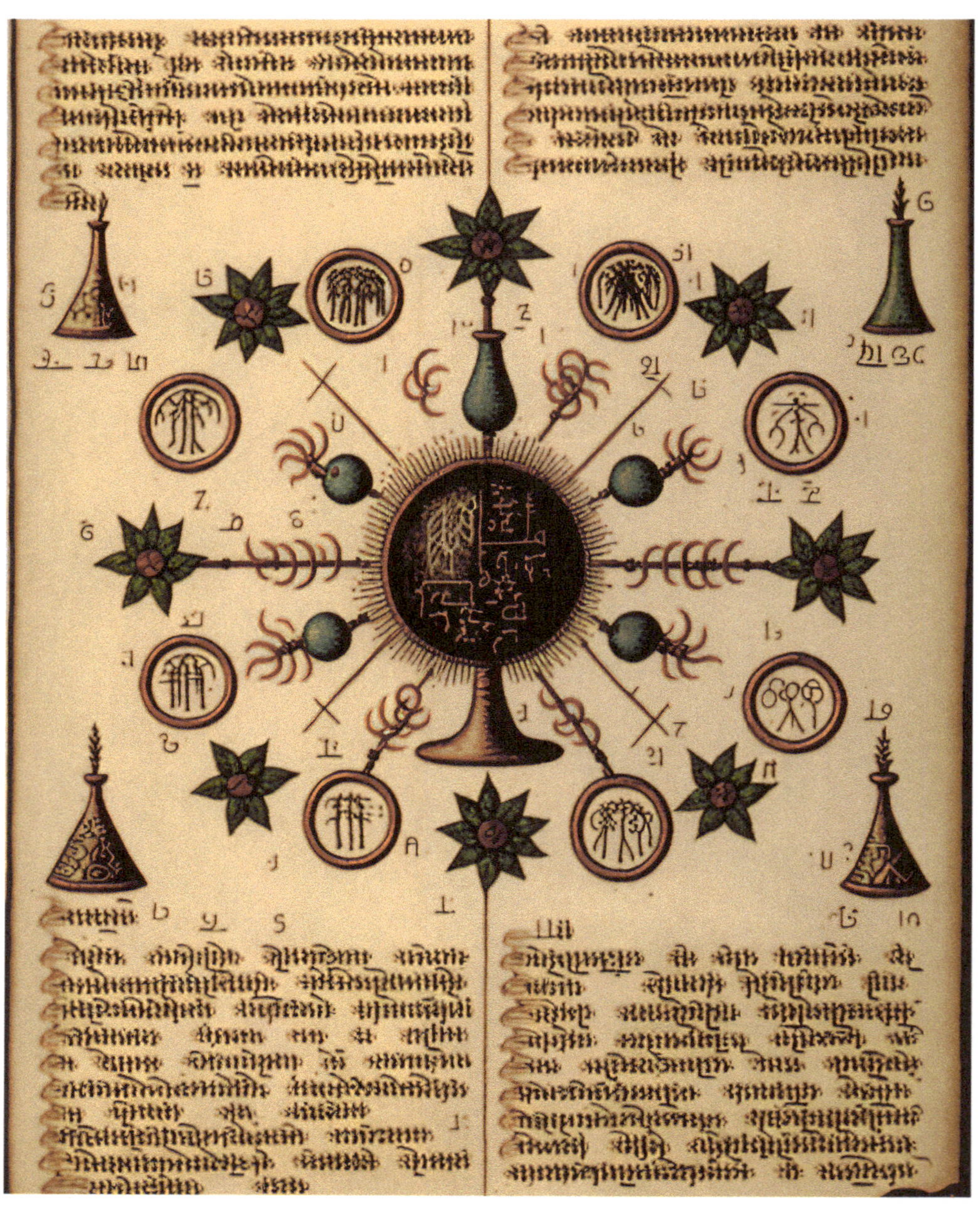

III.19 Axaula ... the image of a woman holding her hands before her face. (Picatrix[†]4. IX§47)

/Oracle of DelphAl

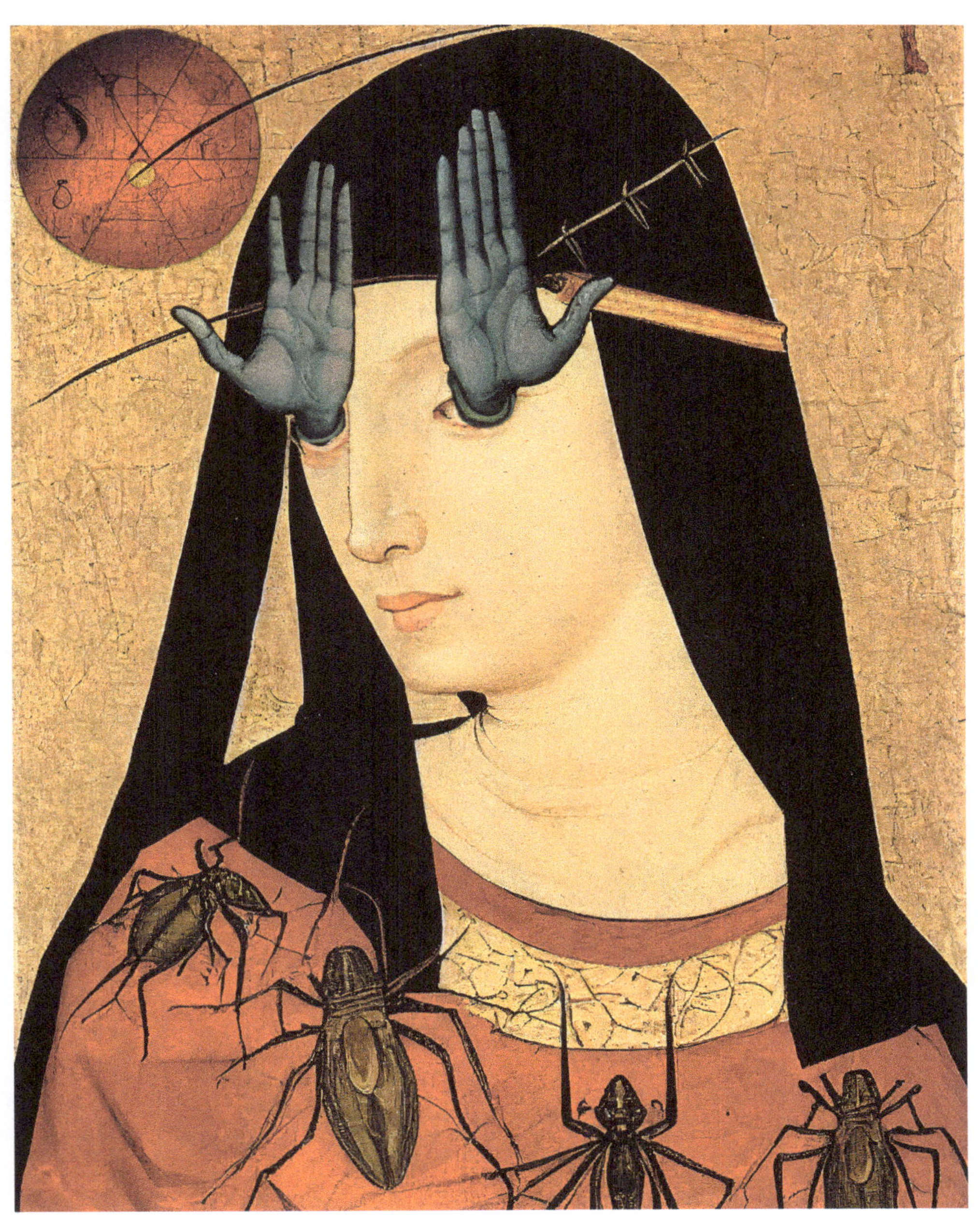

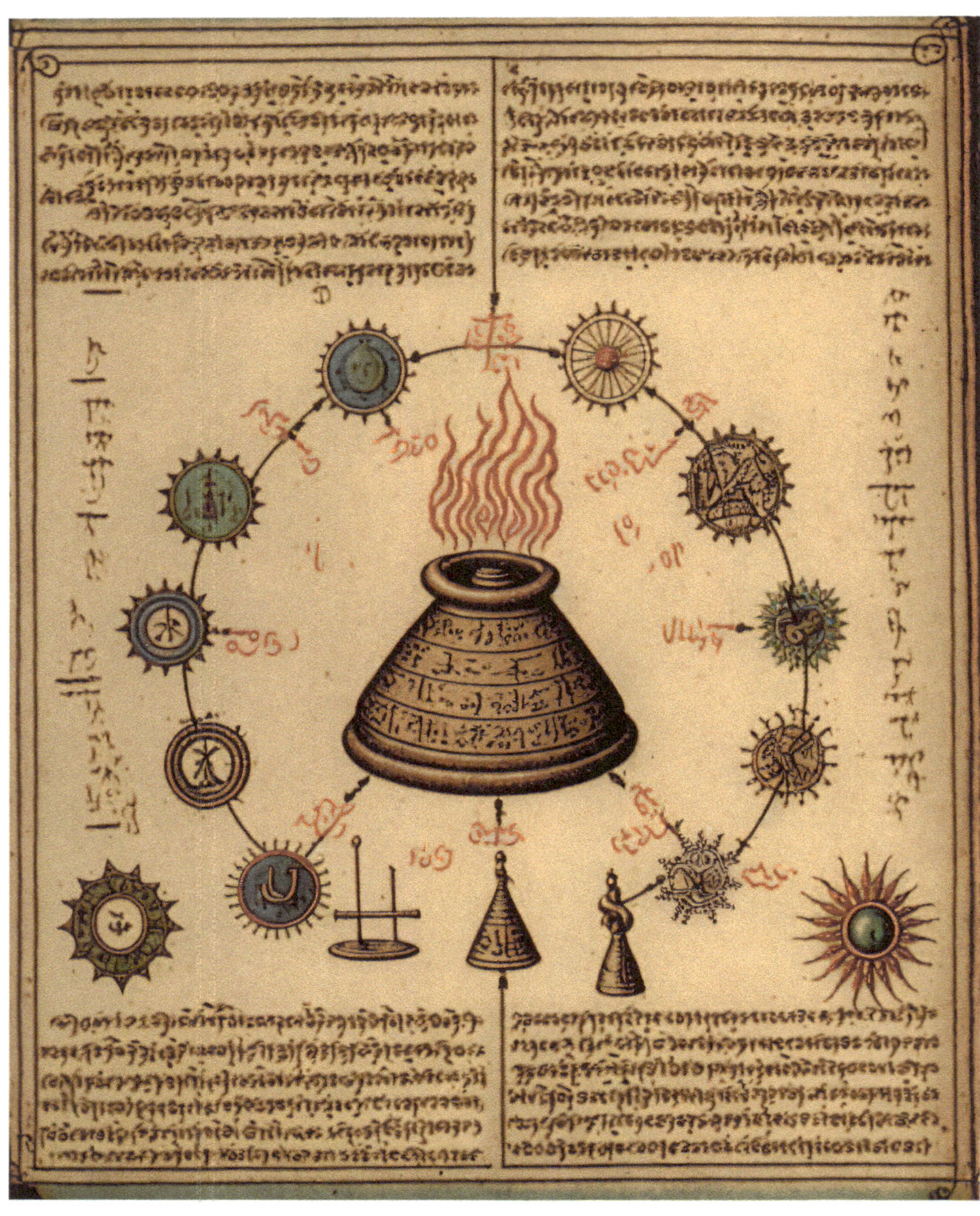

III.20 Alnaym … a figure having the head and arms of a man, the body of a horse with four feet and having a tail, holding a bow in its hands. (Picatrix[†]4. IX§48)

/Oracle of DelphAI

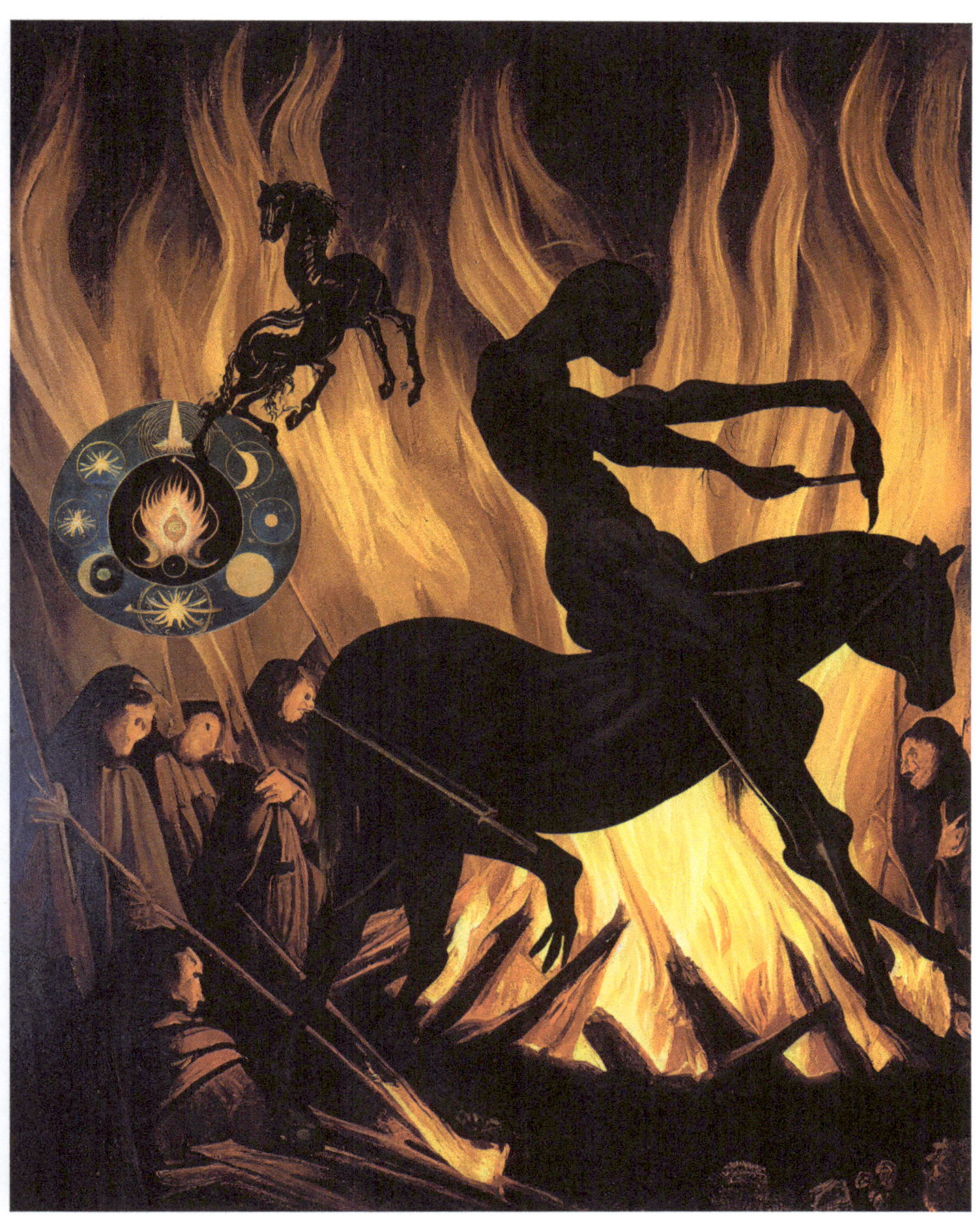

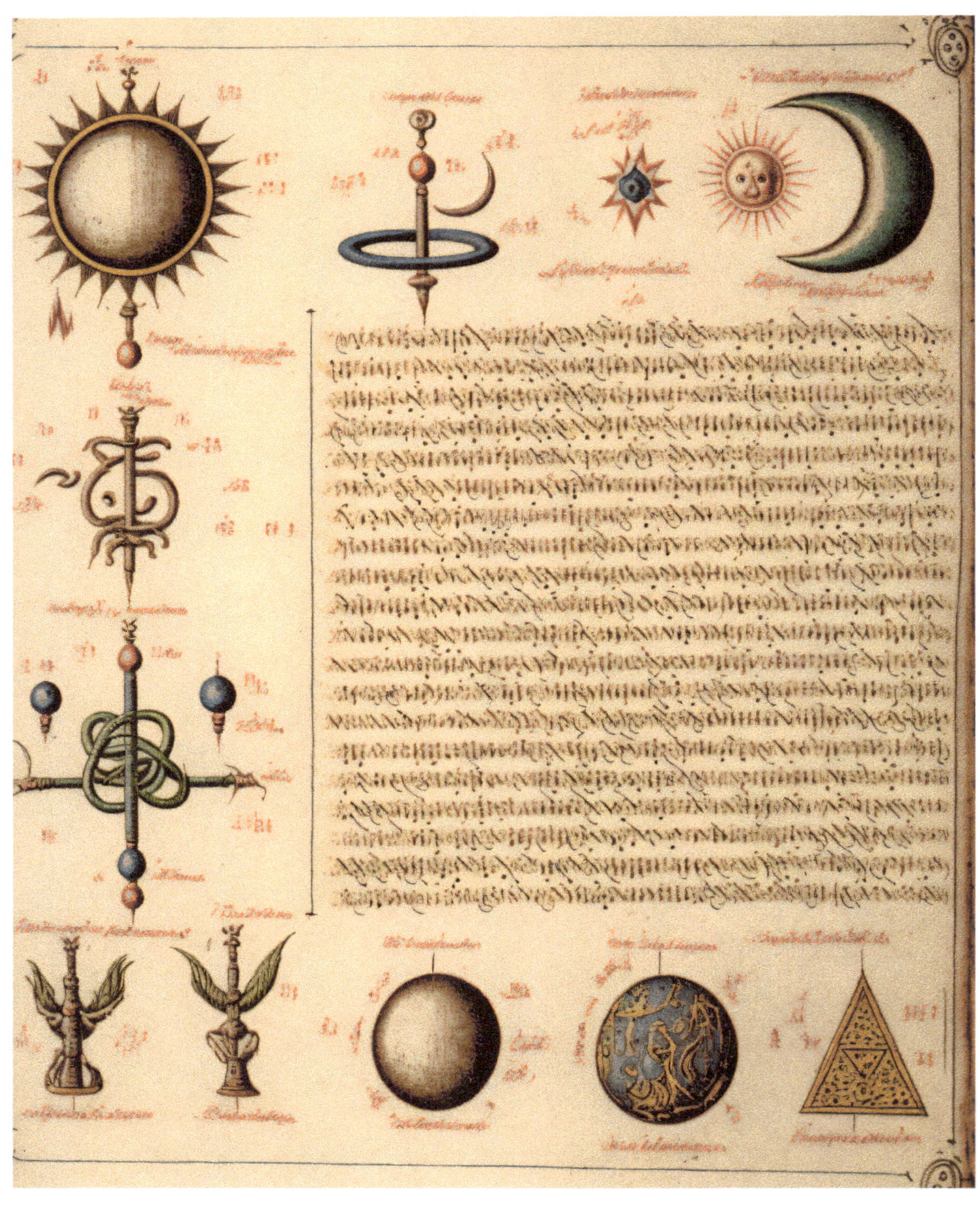

III.21 Albelda ... the image of a man having two faces, with one facing forward and one facing behind. (Picatrix[†]4.IX§49)

/Oracle of DelphAI

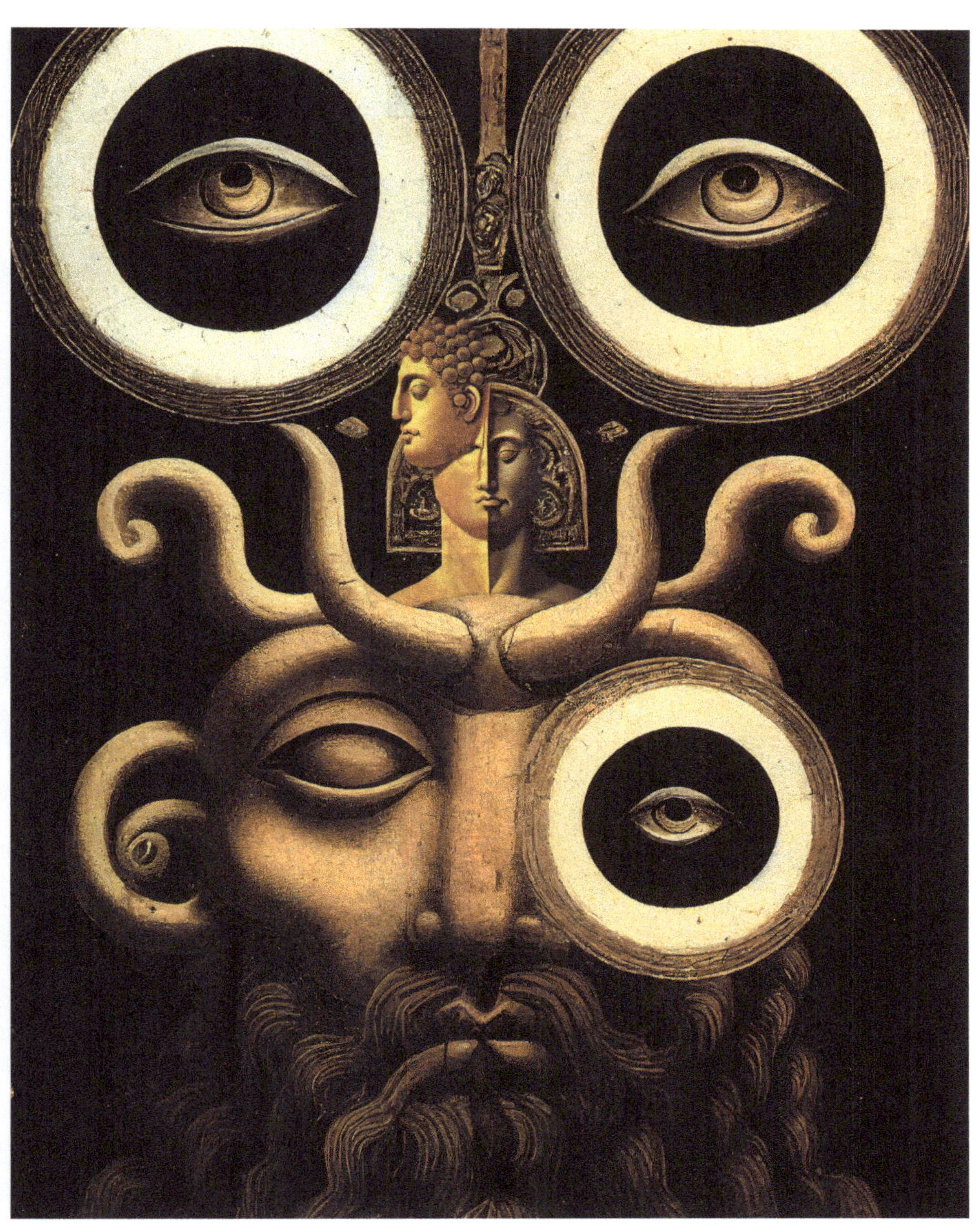

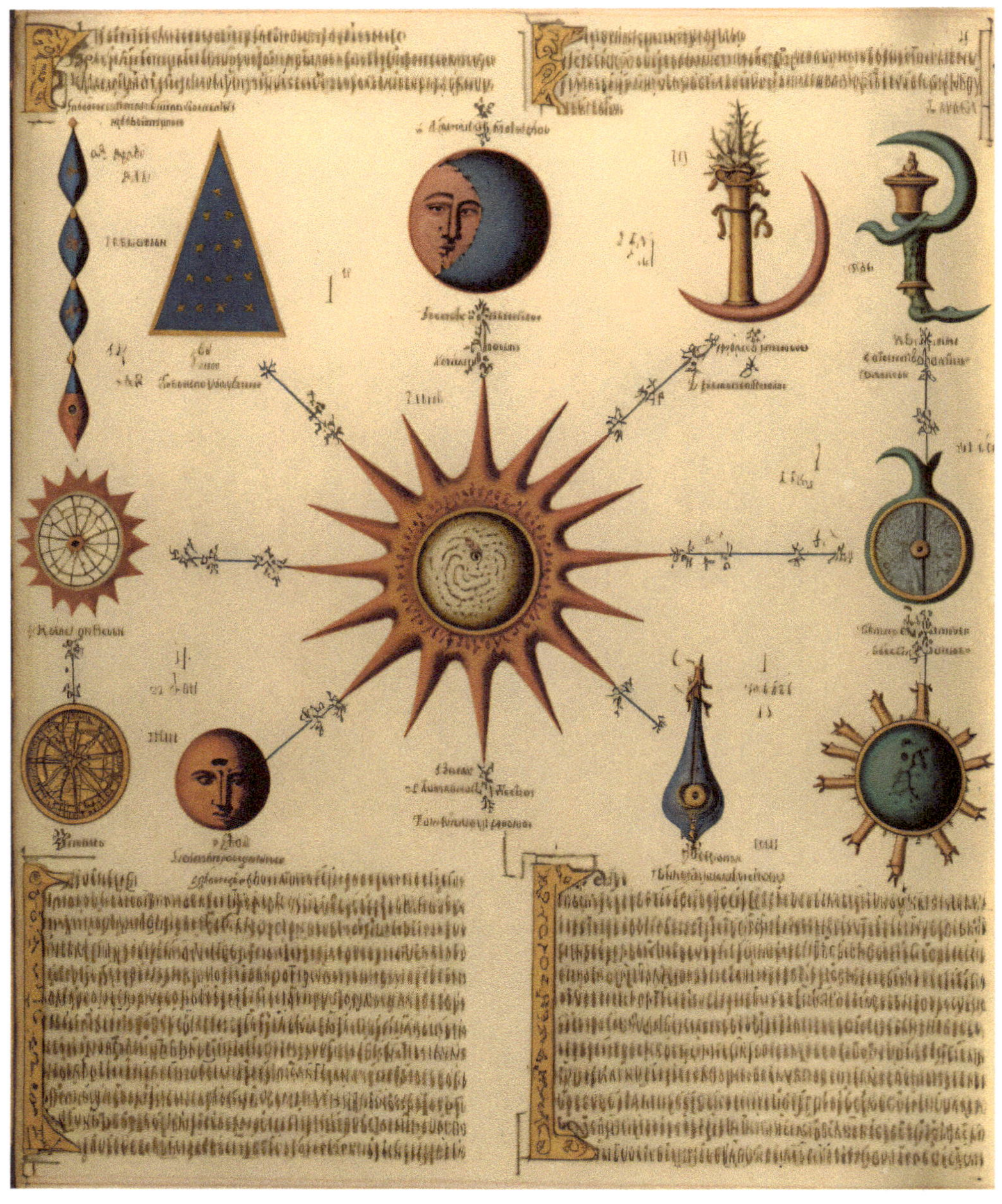

III.22 Sadahaca … the figure of a man with winged feet wearing a helmet. (Picatrix[†]4. IX§50

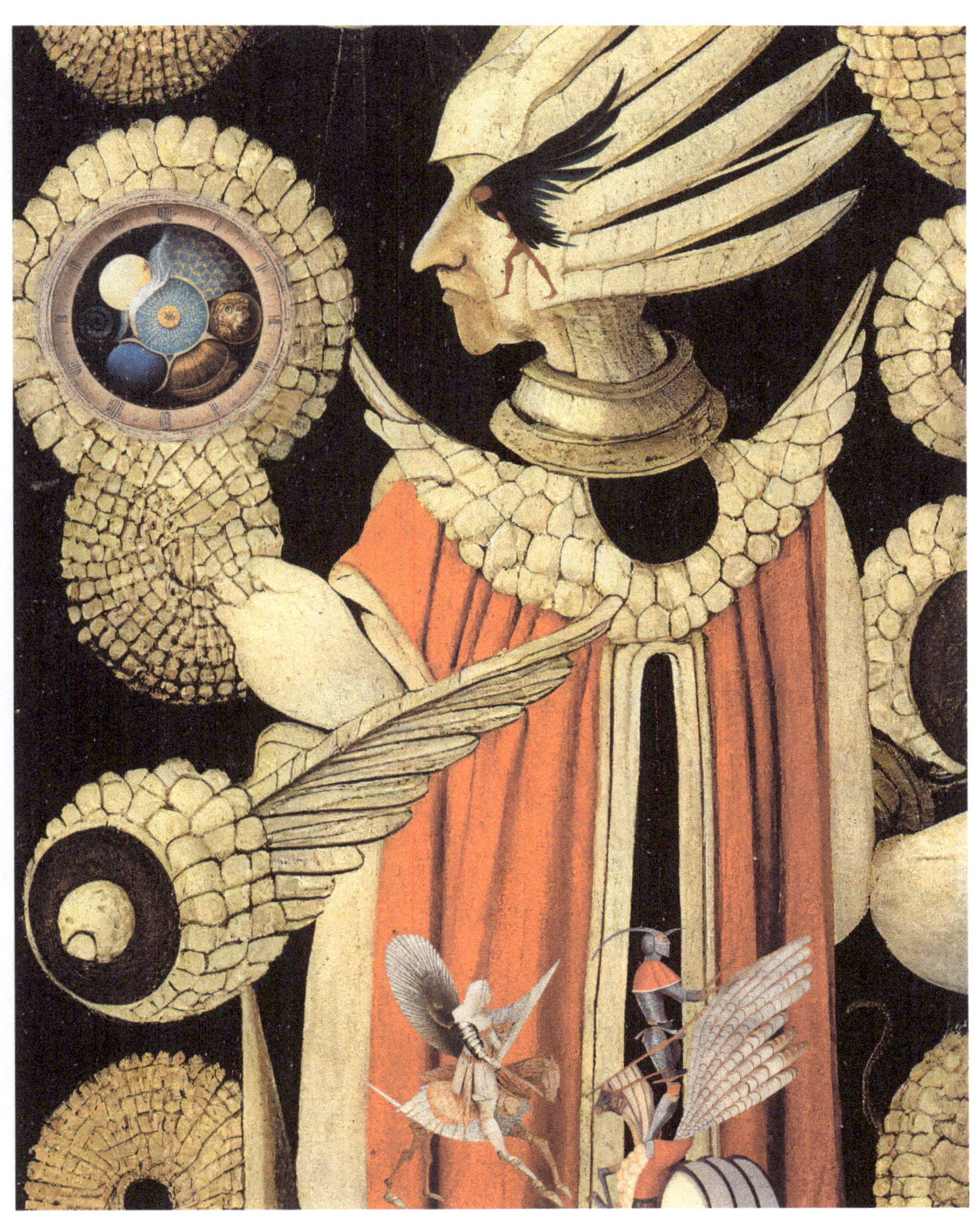

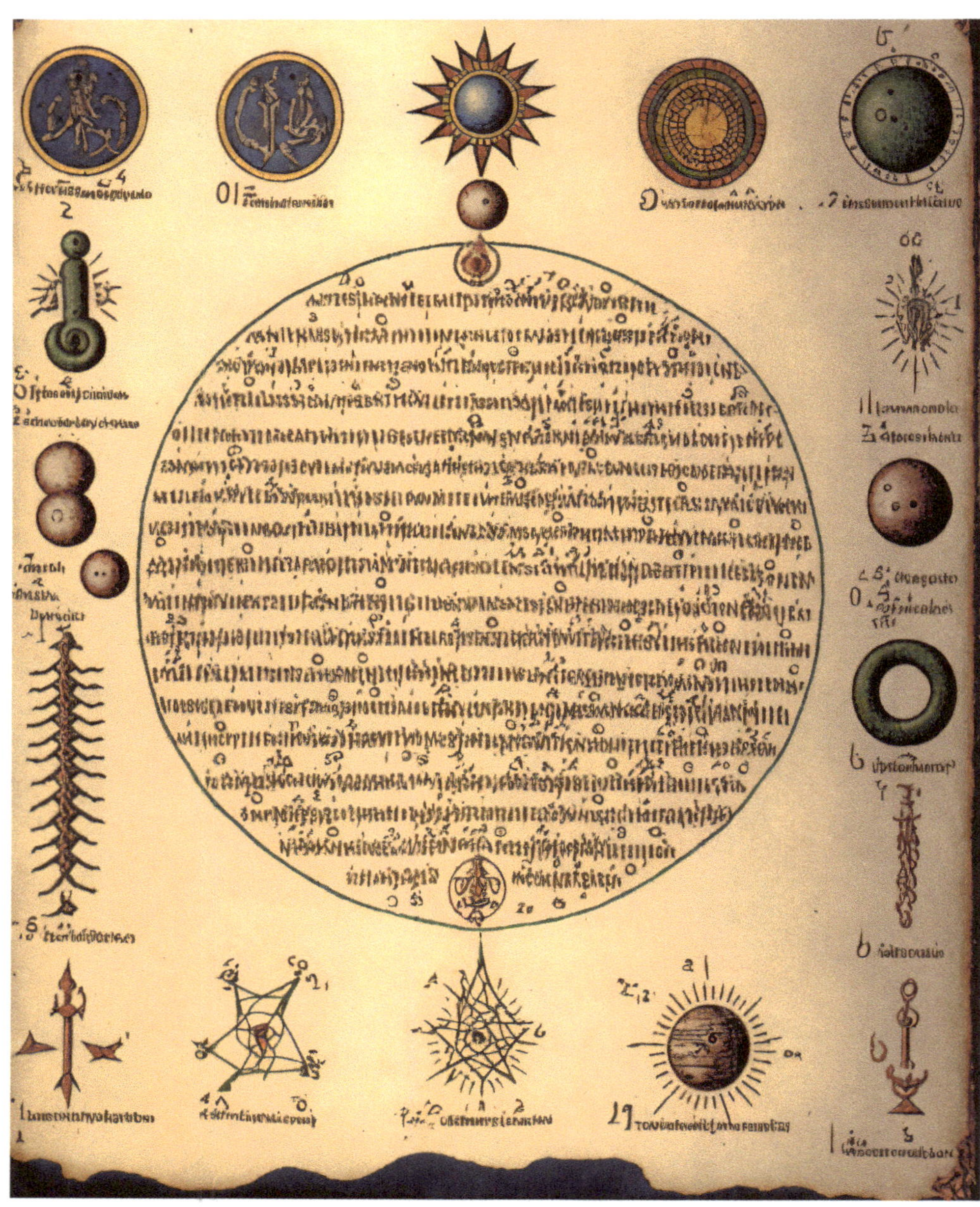

III.23 Zaadebola … the image of a cat with a dog's head. (Picatrix‡4.IX§51)

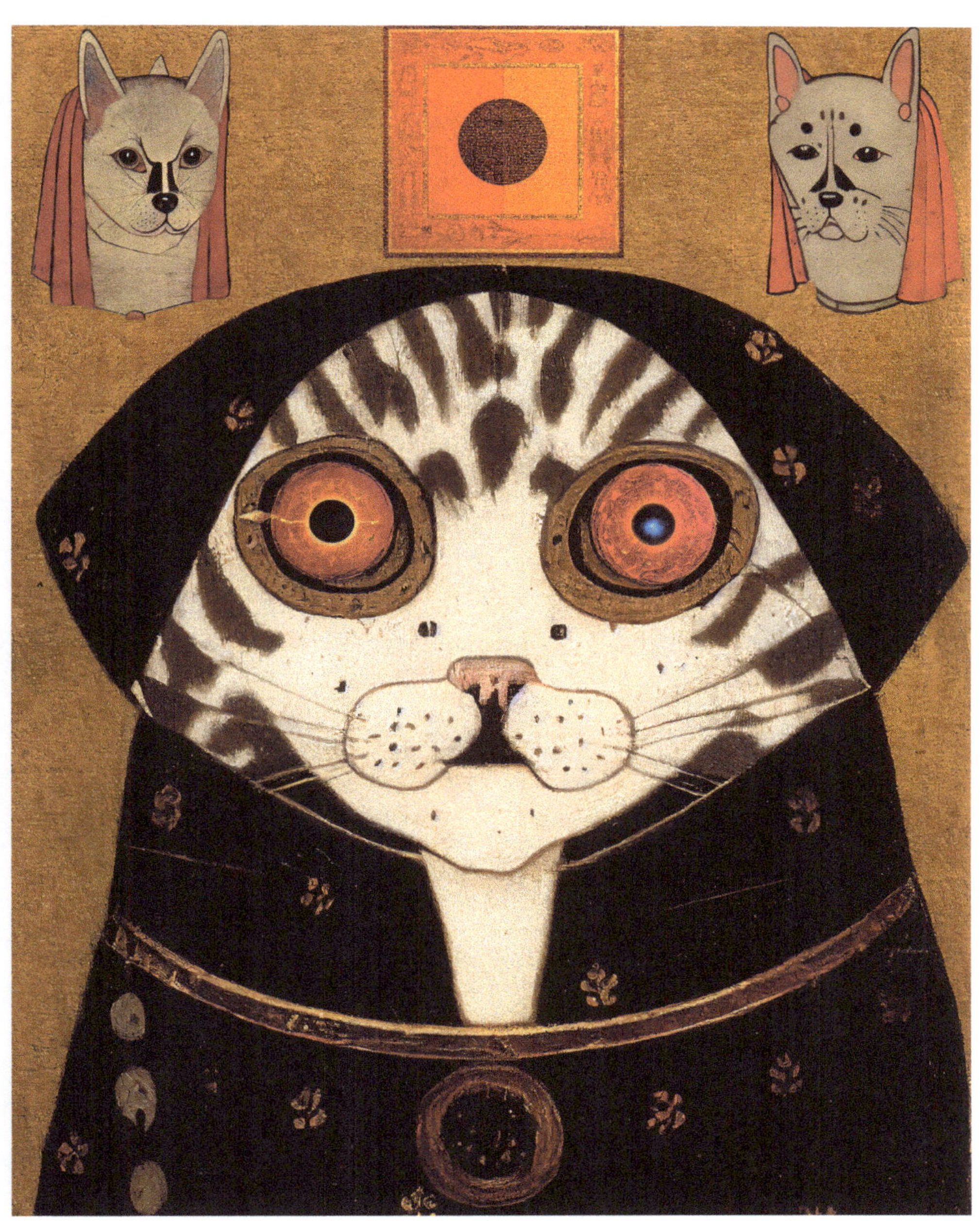

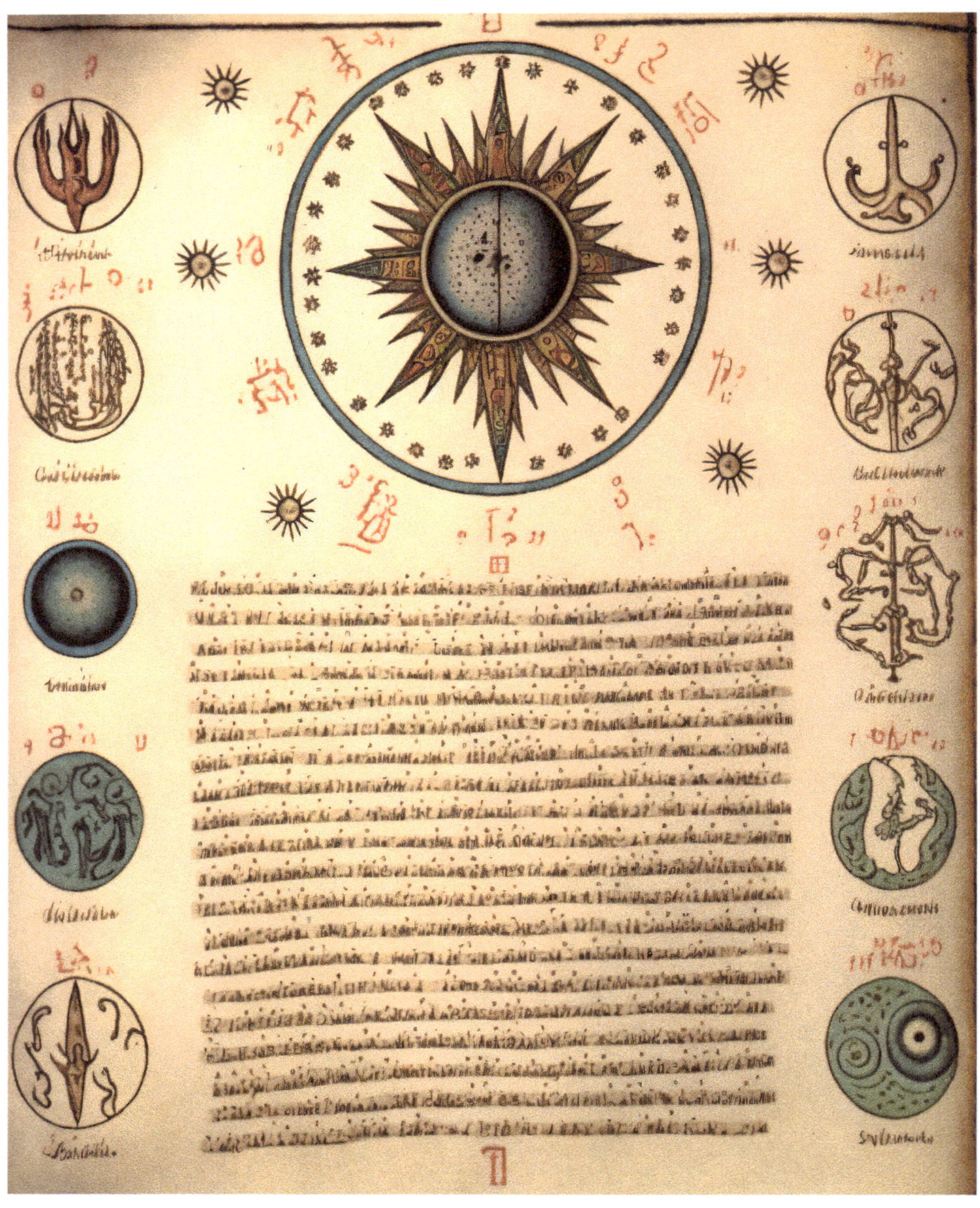

III.24 Caadazod ... a woman holding and nursing her son in her arms. (Picatrix‡4.IX§52)

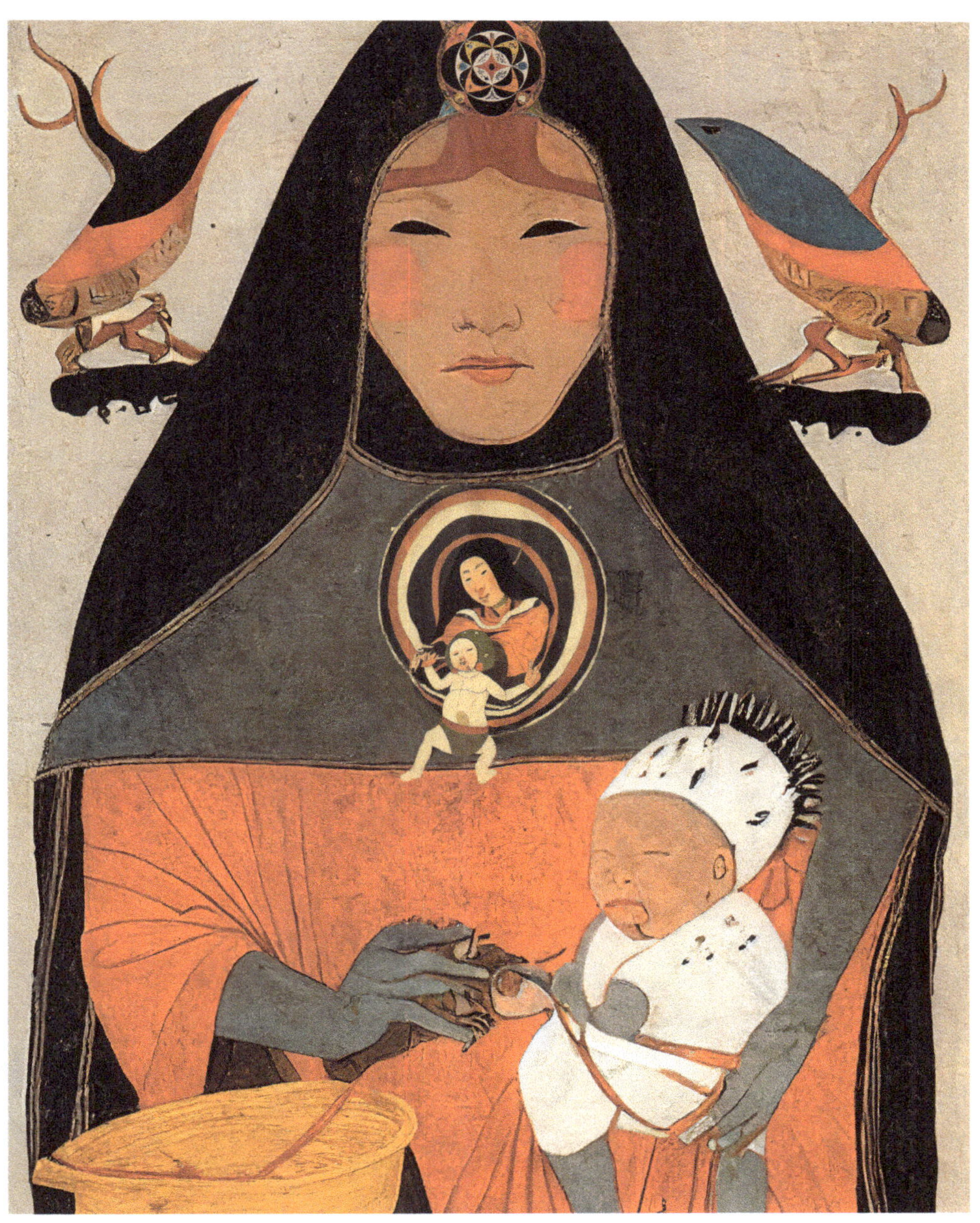

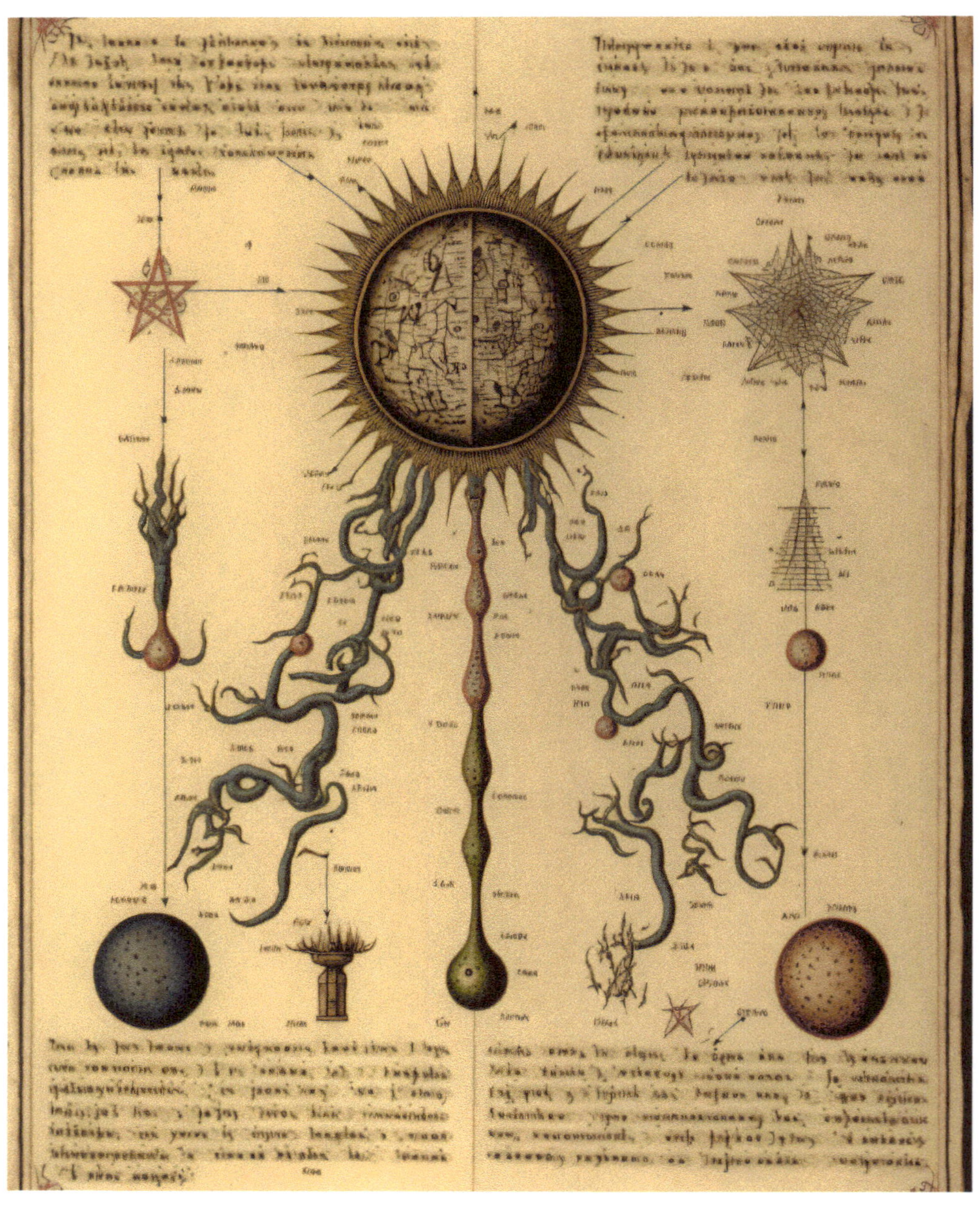

III.25 Zaadalahbia ... the figure of a man in the likeness of one who is planting trees.
(Picatrix‡4.IX§53)

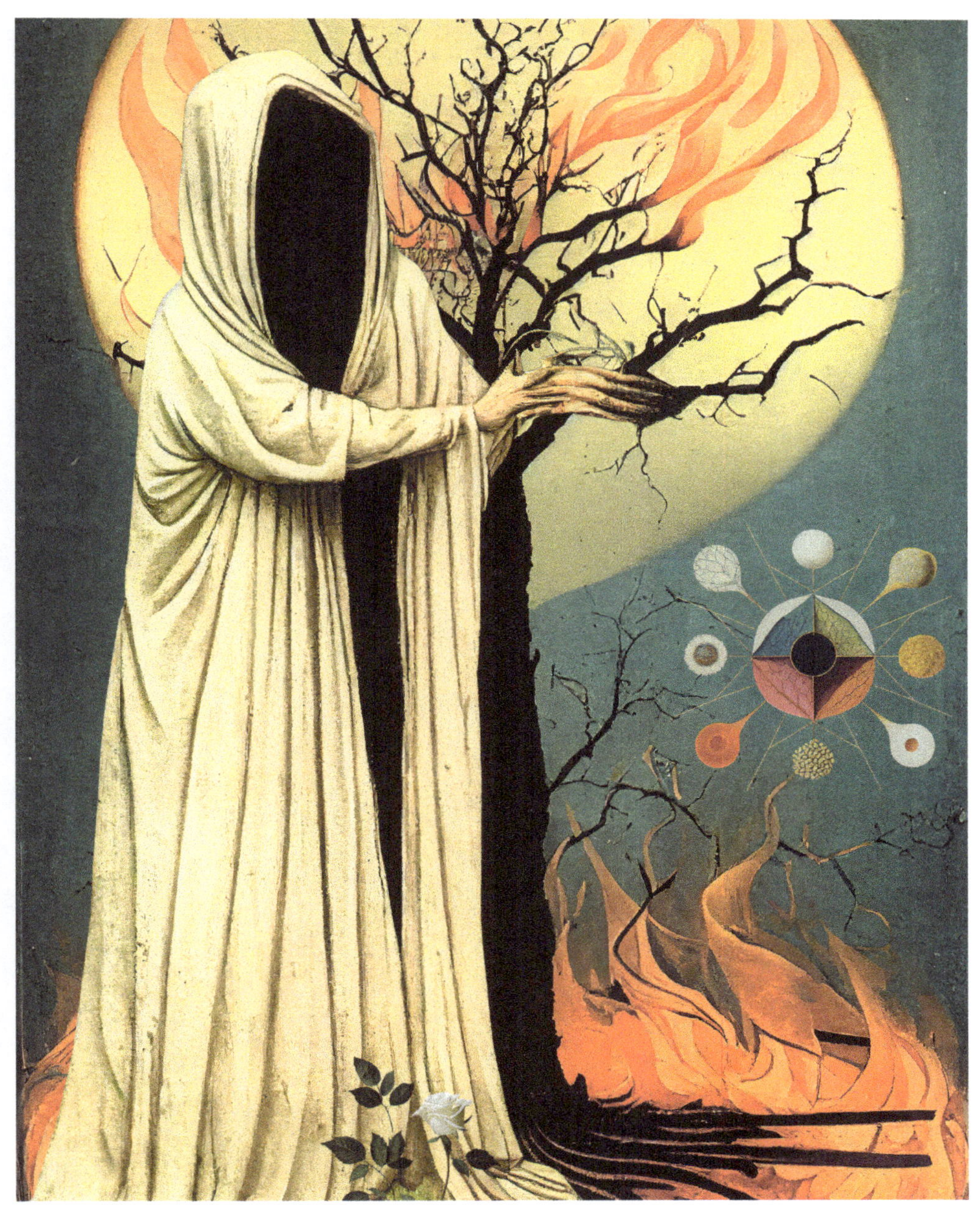

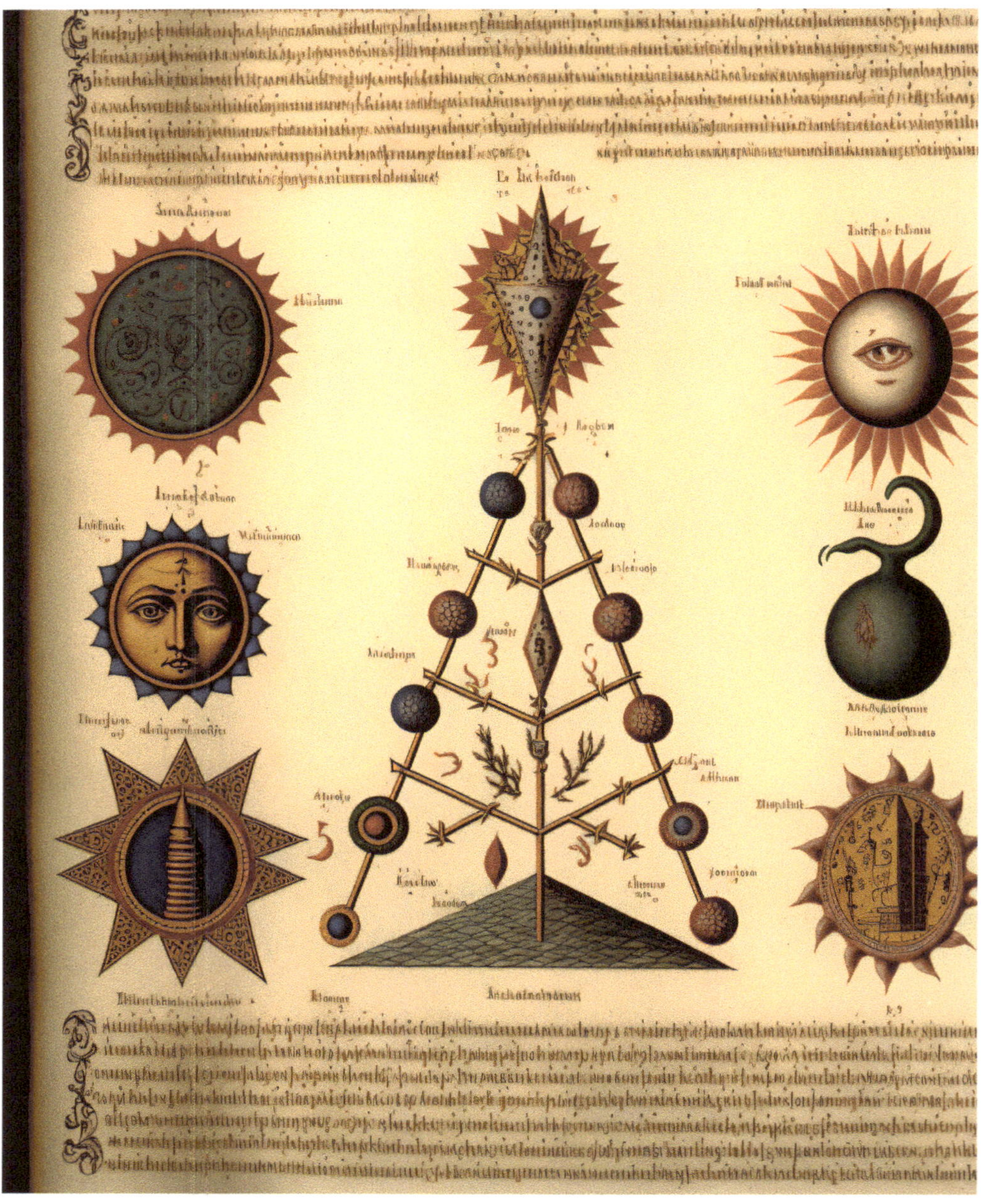

III.26 **Alfarg, the former** ... the image of a woman with her hair unbound and before her a vessel placed as if to receive her hair figure of a man in the likeness of one who is planting trees. (Picatrix[†]4.IX§54)

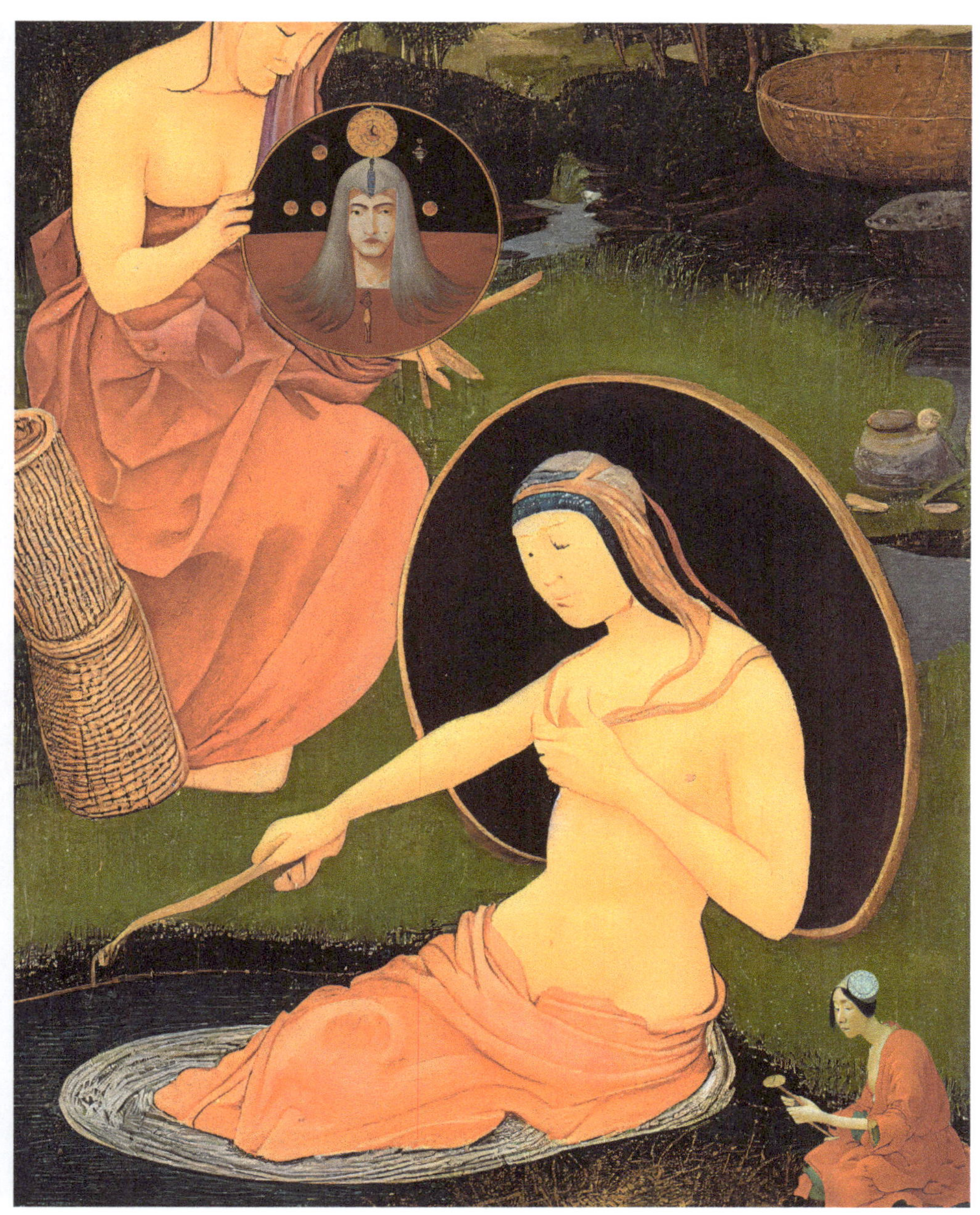

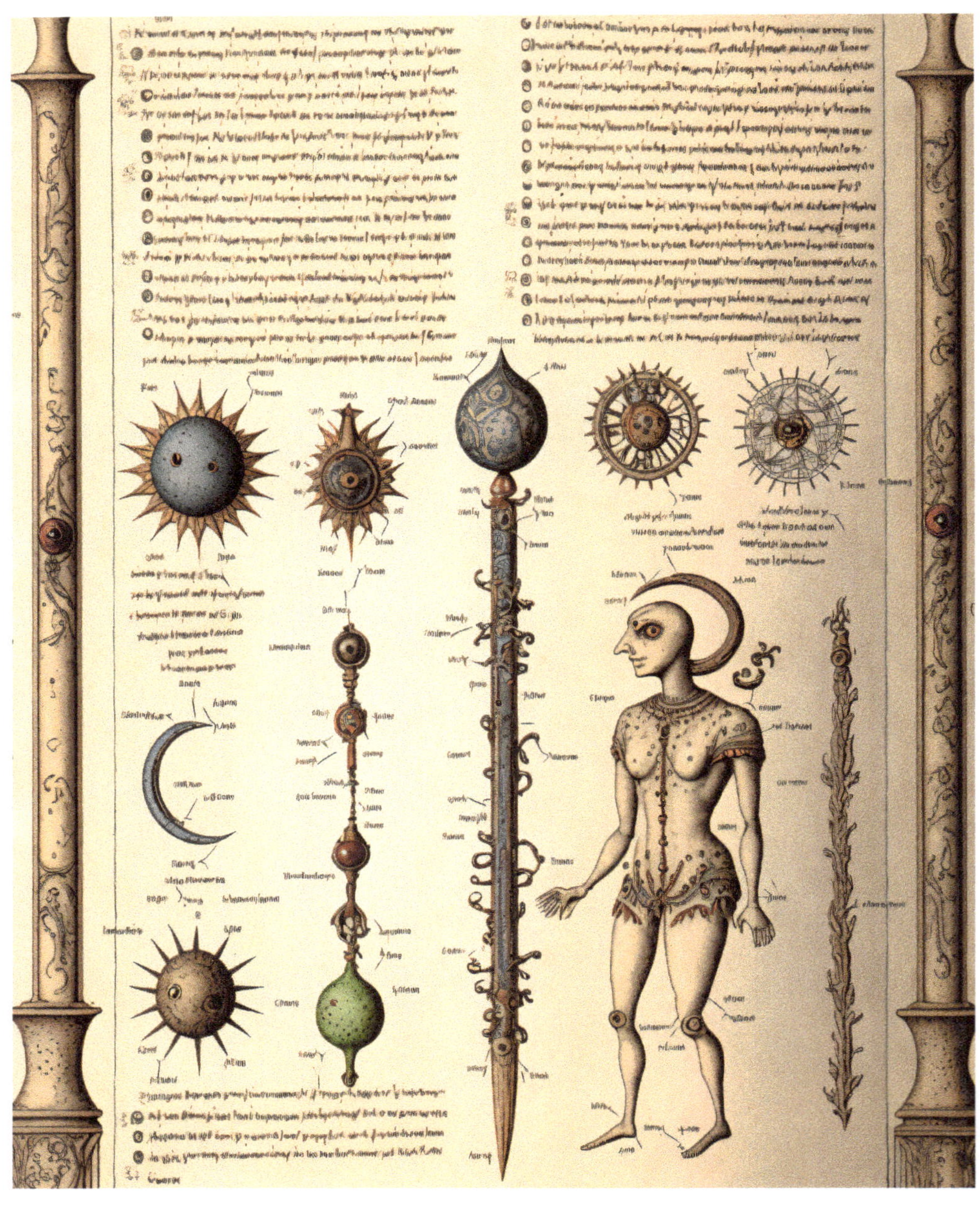

III.27 Alfarg, the latter ... the image of a winged man, holding a perforated dish in his hands, and raising it to his mouth. (Picatrix[‡]4.IX§55)

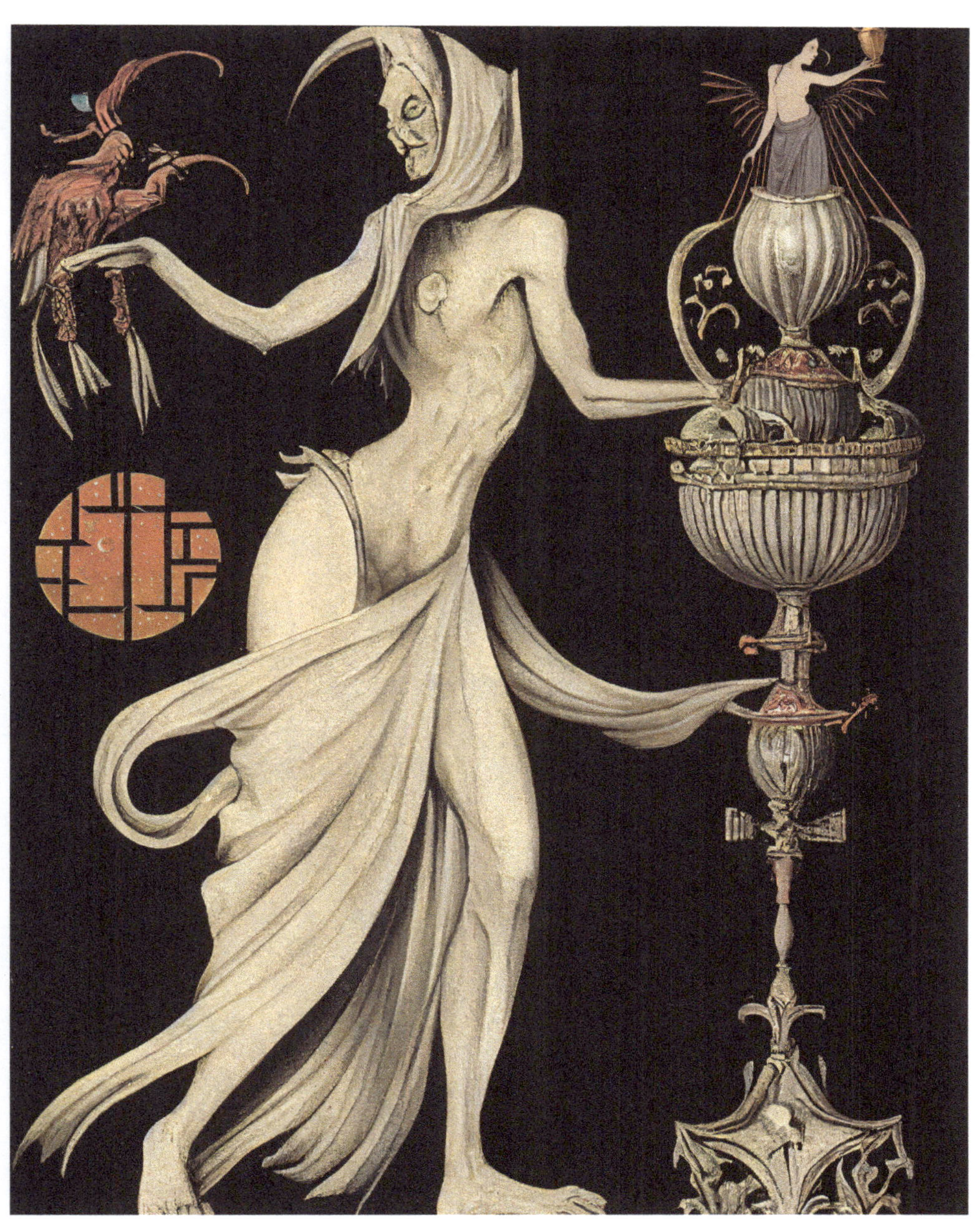

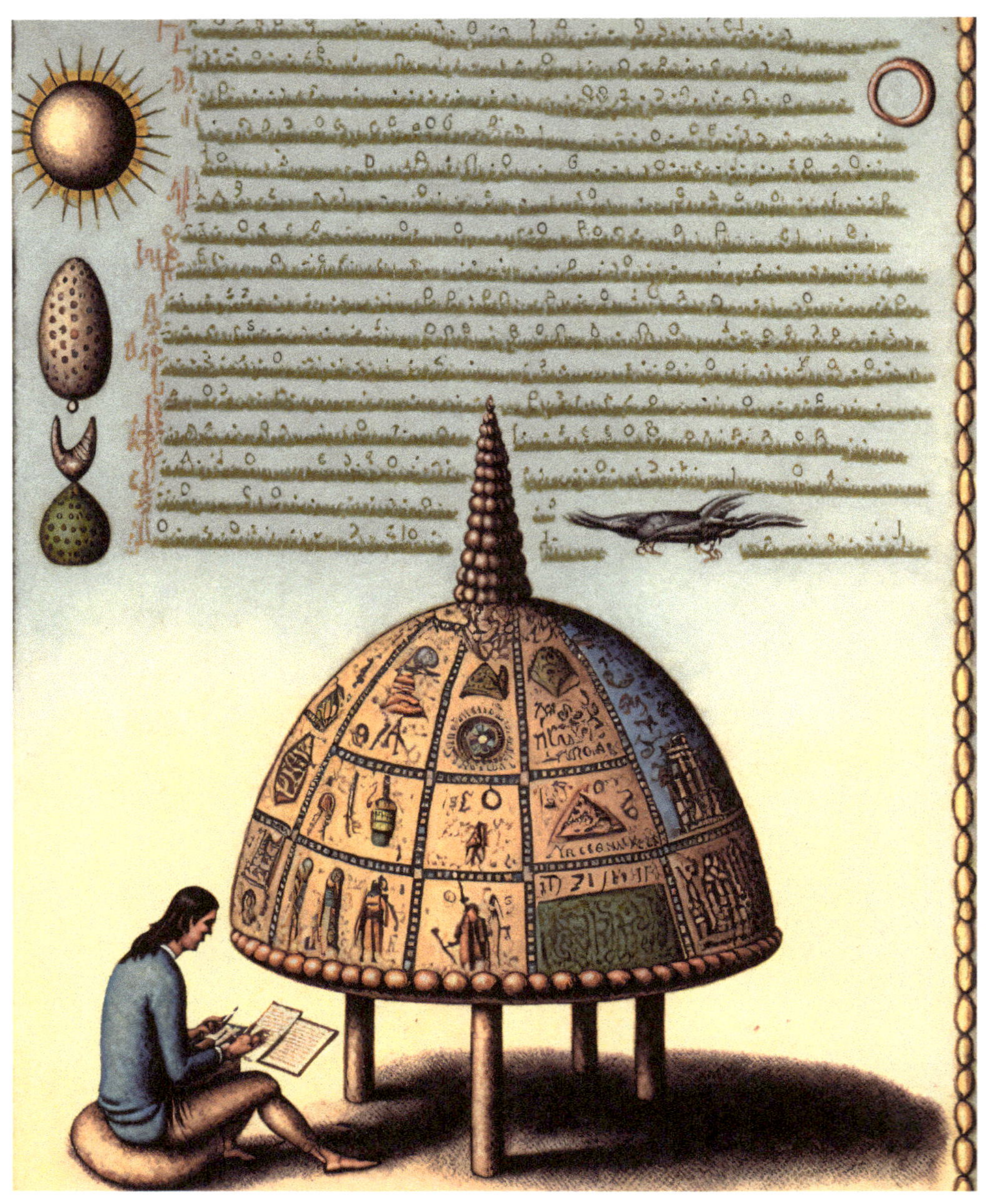

III.28 Arrexe ... the image of a fish with a colored spine. (Picatrix‡4.IX§56)

/Oracle of DelphΛI

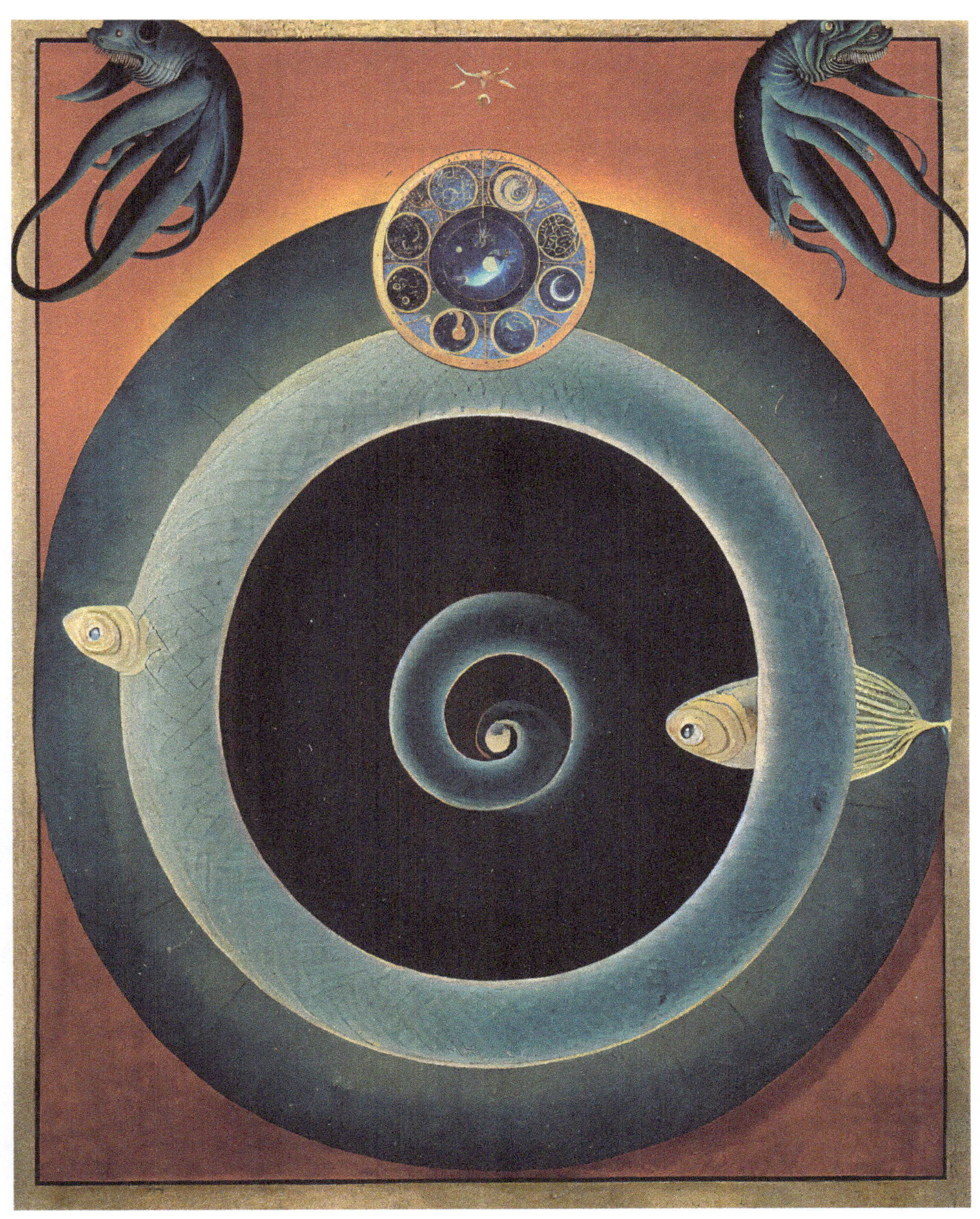

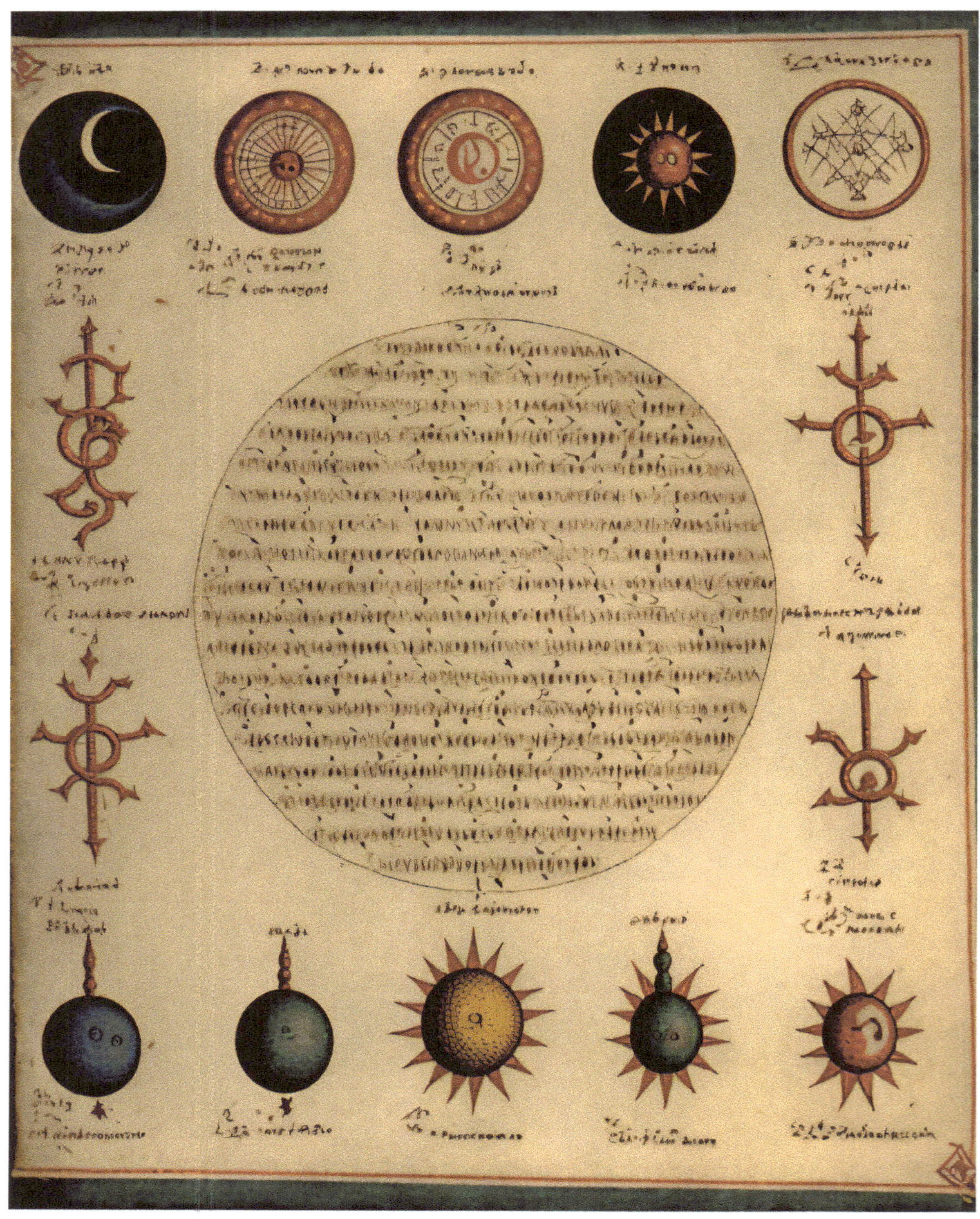

IV.1 Aries I ... A black man, anxious, with a large body, red eyes, holding a chopping axe in his hand, and girded in a white cloth. (Picatrix‡2.XI§3)

/Oracle of DelphAI

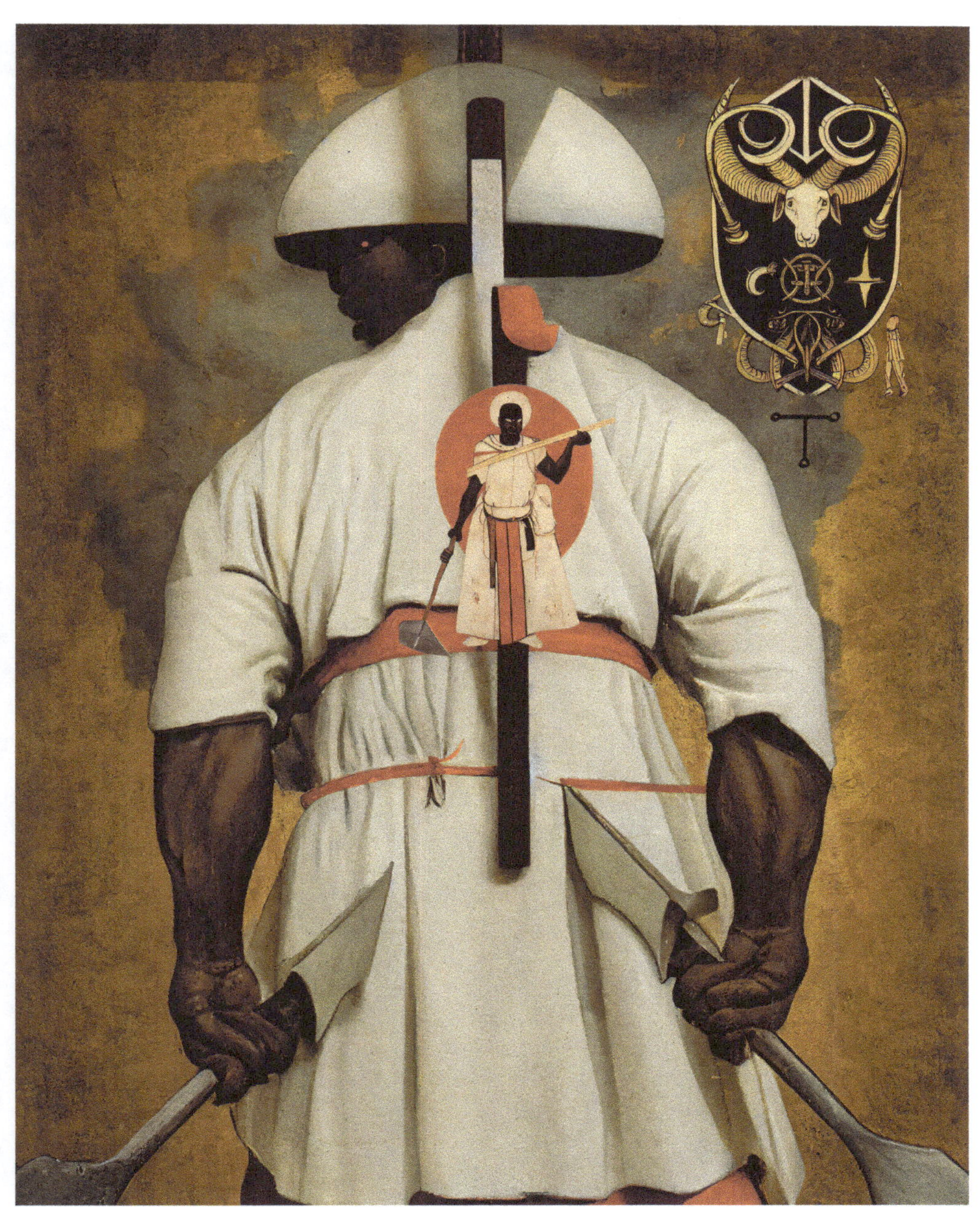

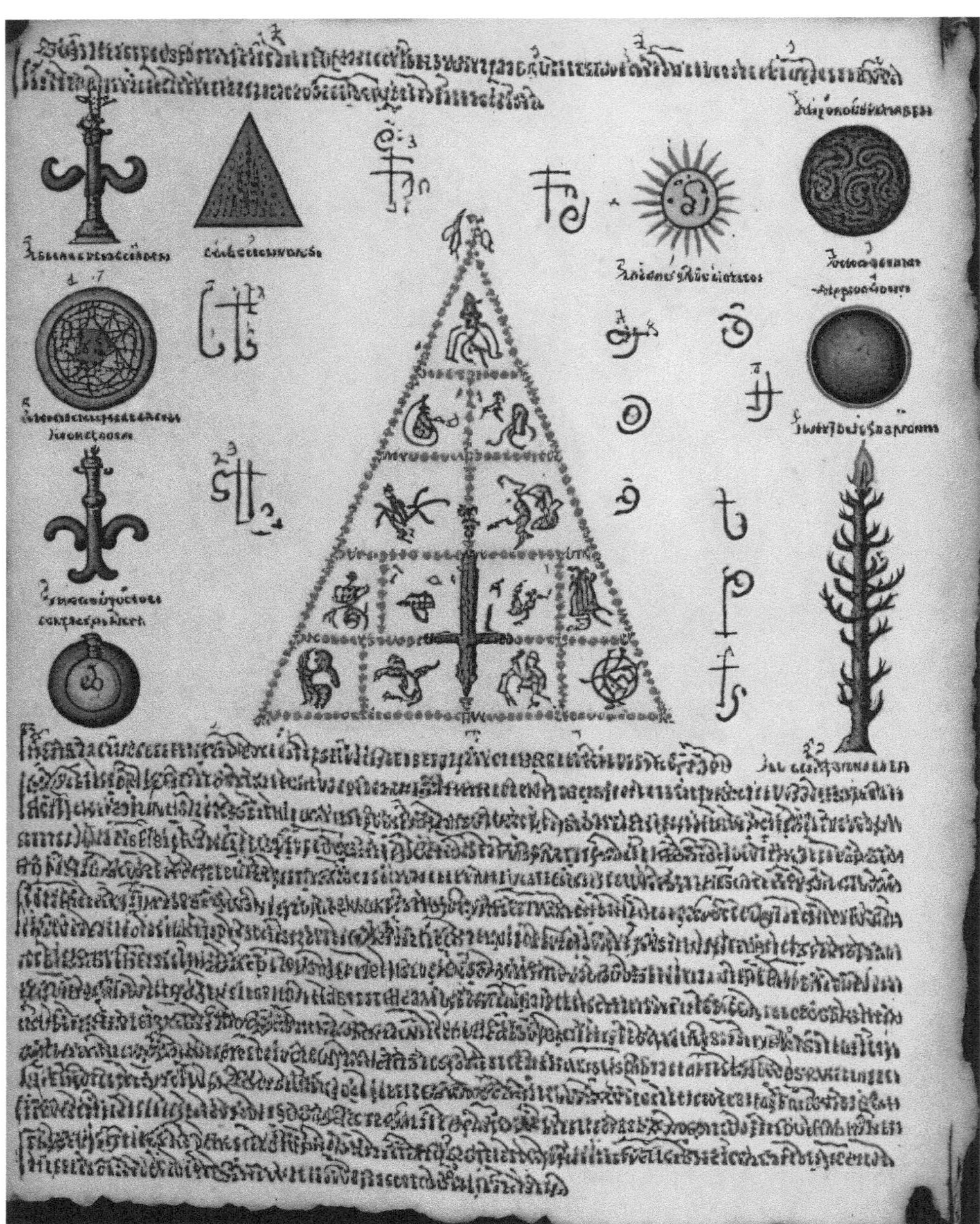

IV.2 Aries II … A woman dressed in green clothes and missing a leg. (Picatrix‡2.XI§4)

/Oracle of DelphΛI

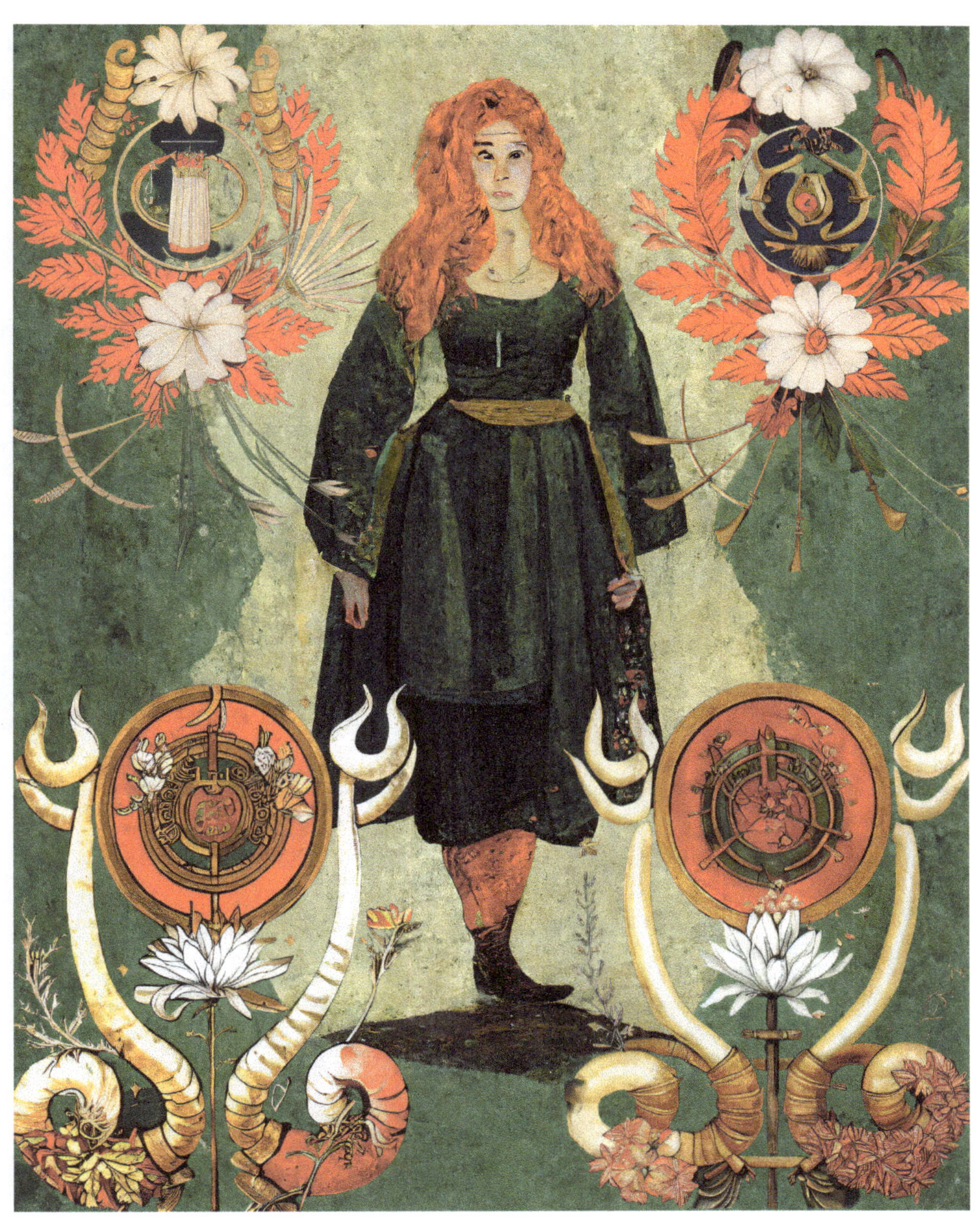

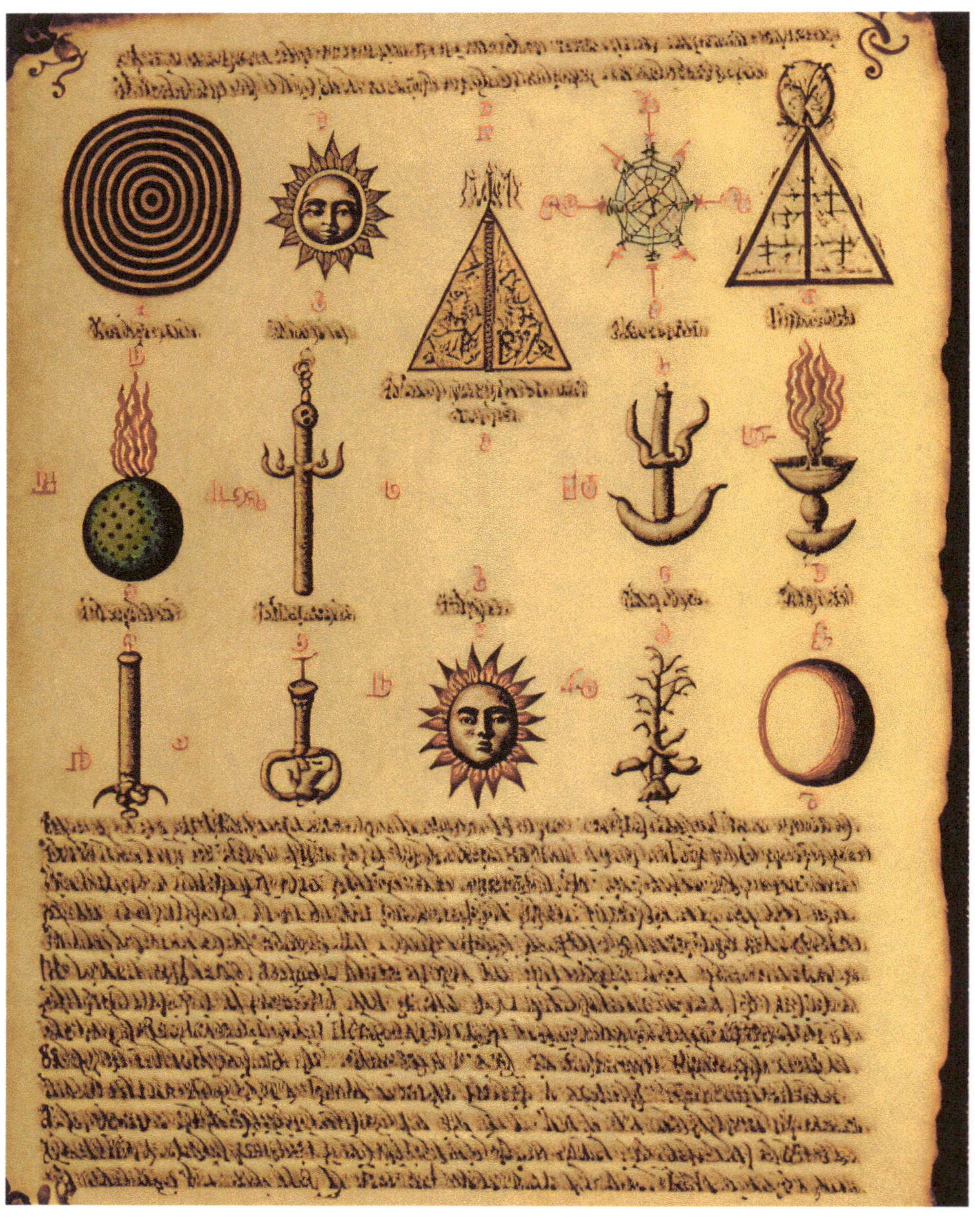

IV.3 Aries III ... An unsettled man, holding a golden bracelet in his hands and dressed in red clothes, desiring to do good yet incapable. (Picatrix‡2. XI§5)

/Oracle of DelphΛI

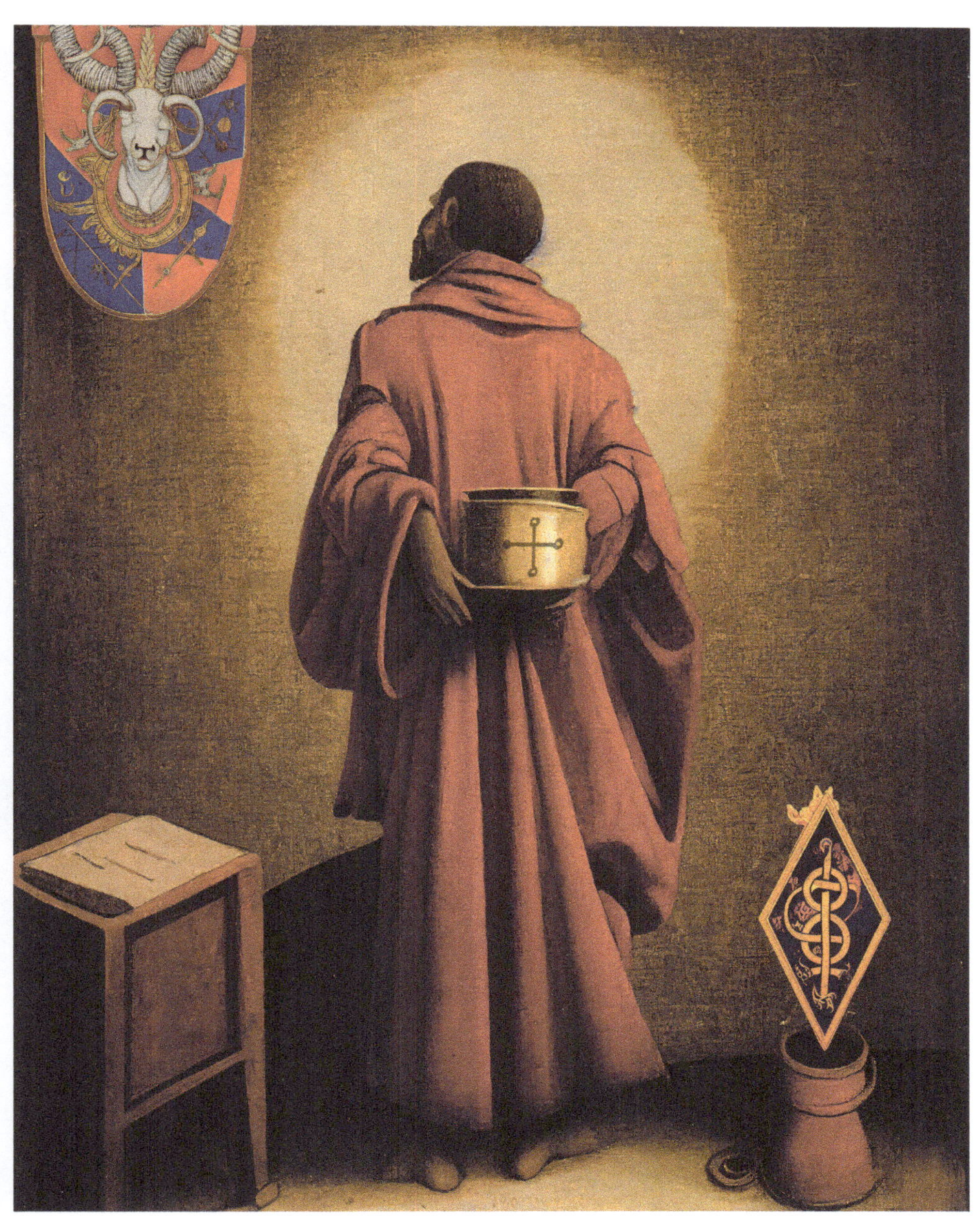

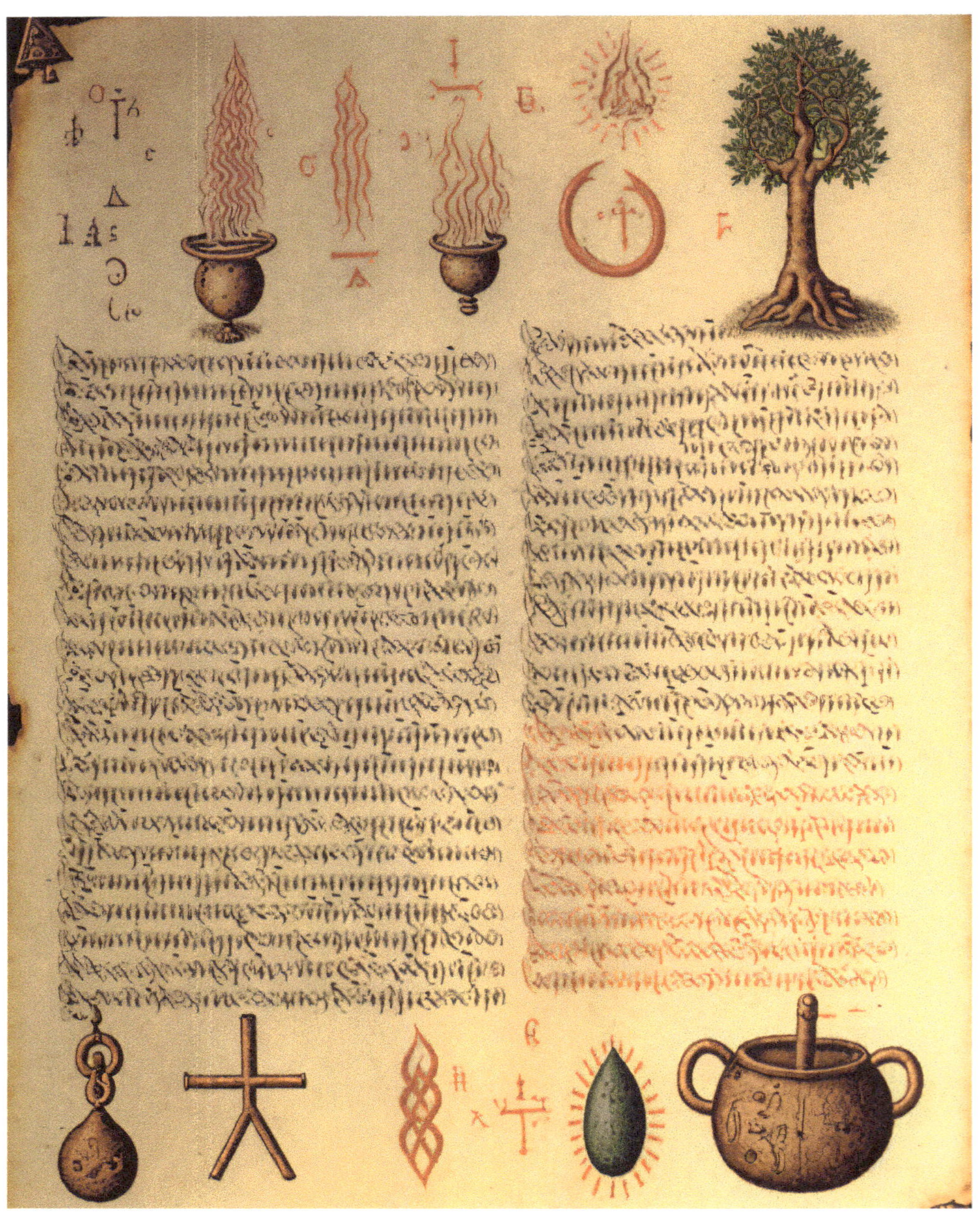

IV.4 Taurus I ... A woman with curly hair, with a single son wearing clothes similar to fire, and she also is dressed in similar clothes. (Picatrix‡2.XI§6)

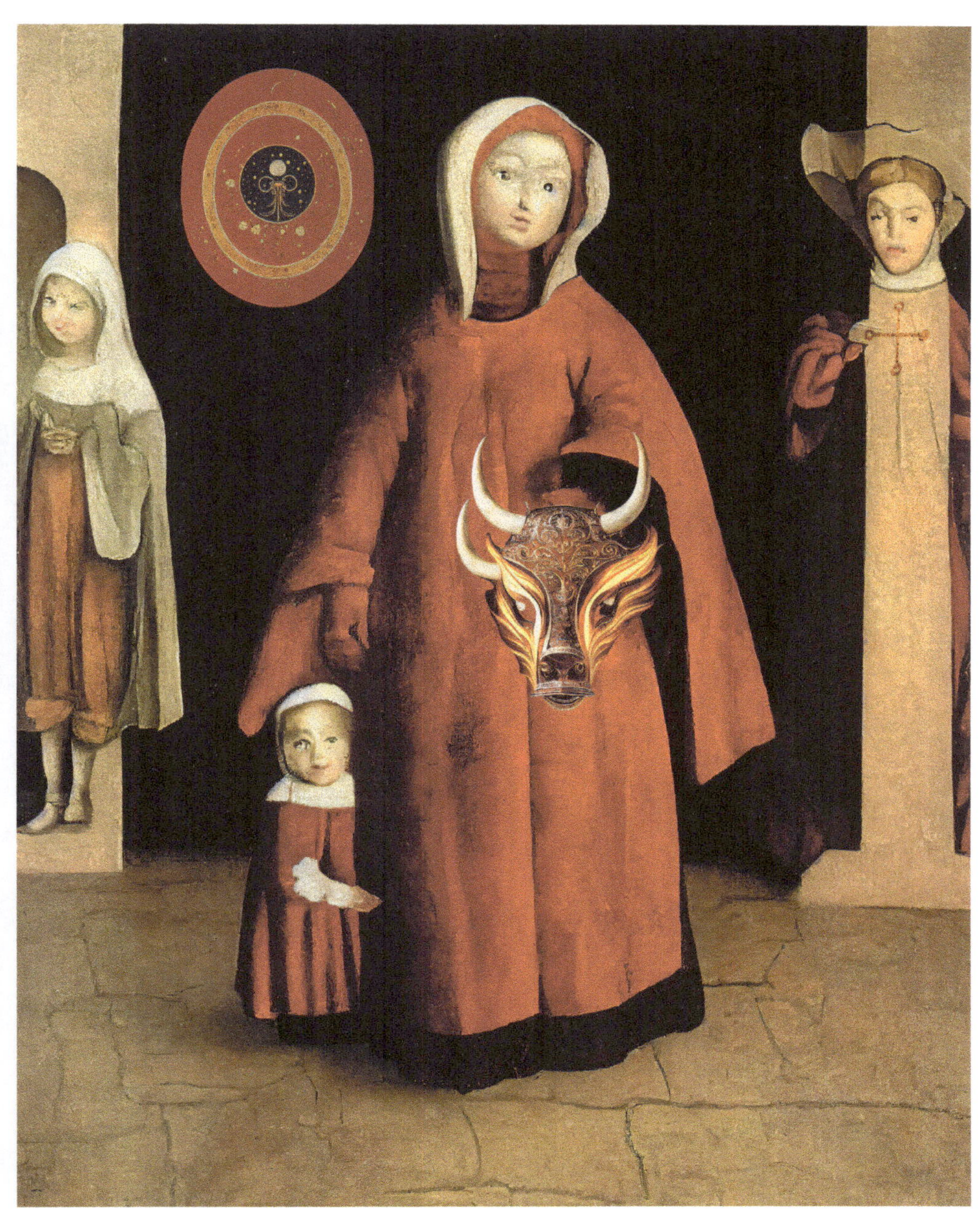

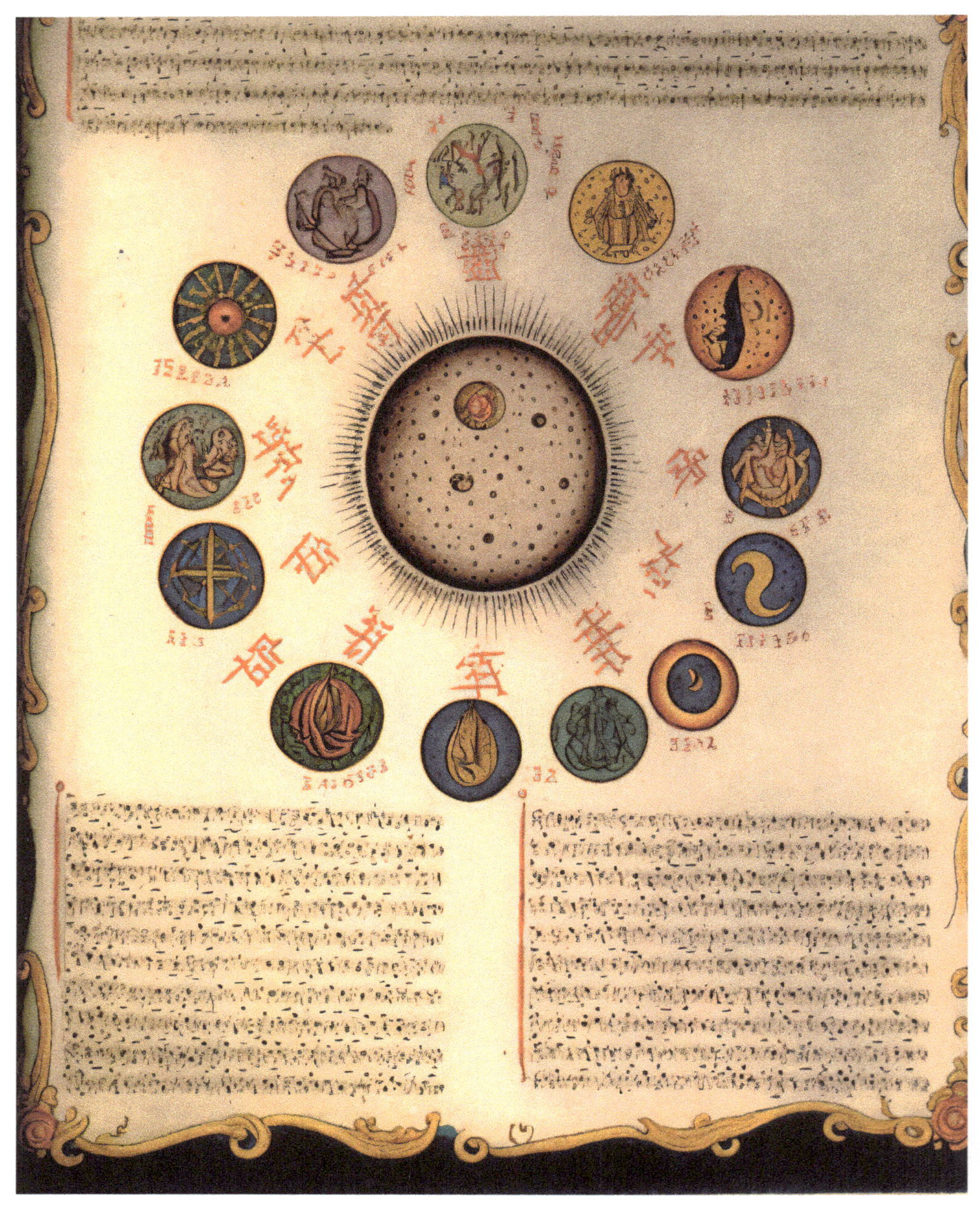

IV.5 Taurus II ... ∧ man looking like a camel, with hooves in place of his fingers like cattle. He himself is wholly covered with a torn linen cloth. (Picatrix‡2. XI§7)

/Oracle of Delph∧l

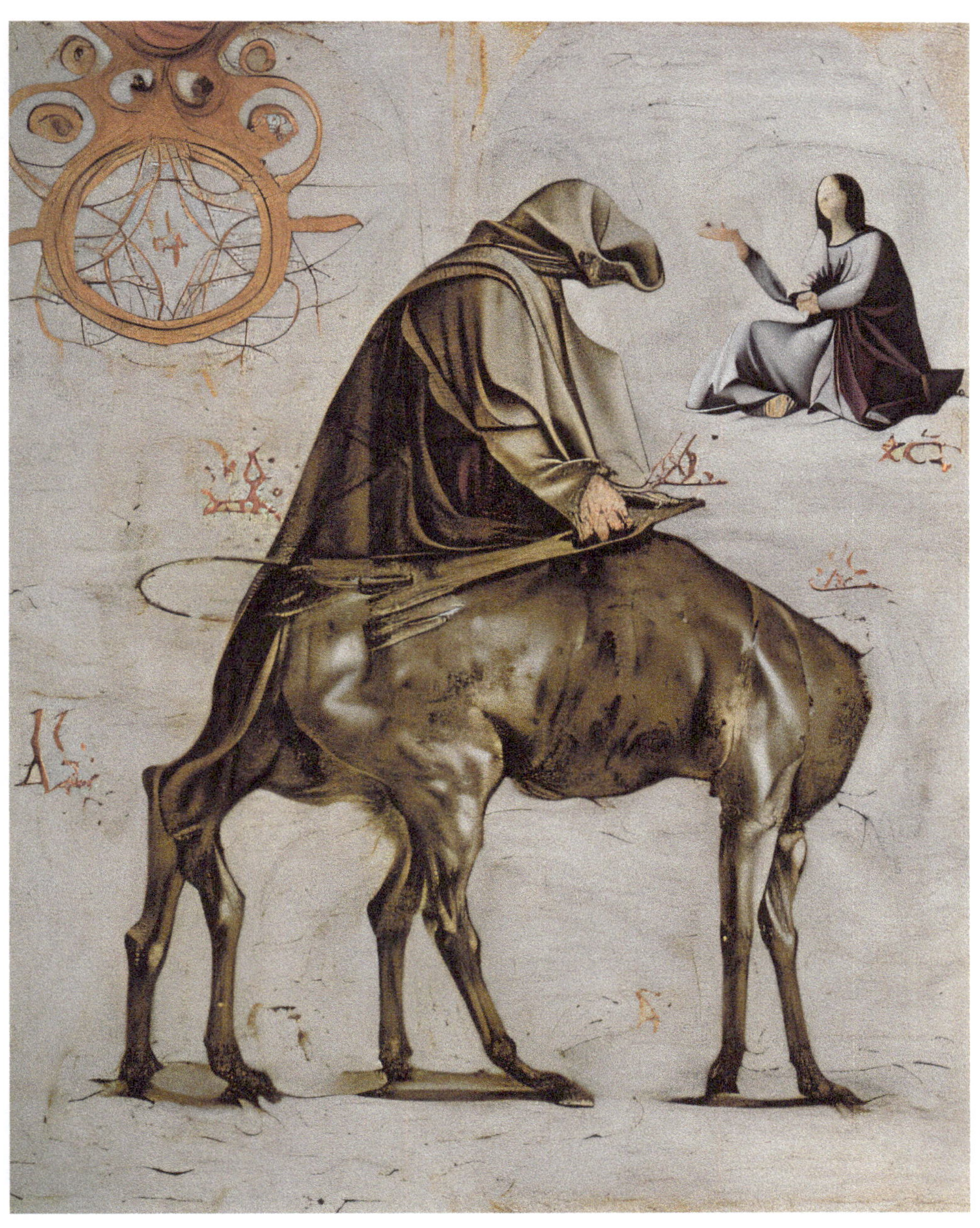

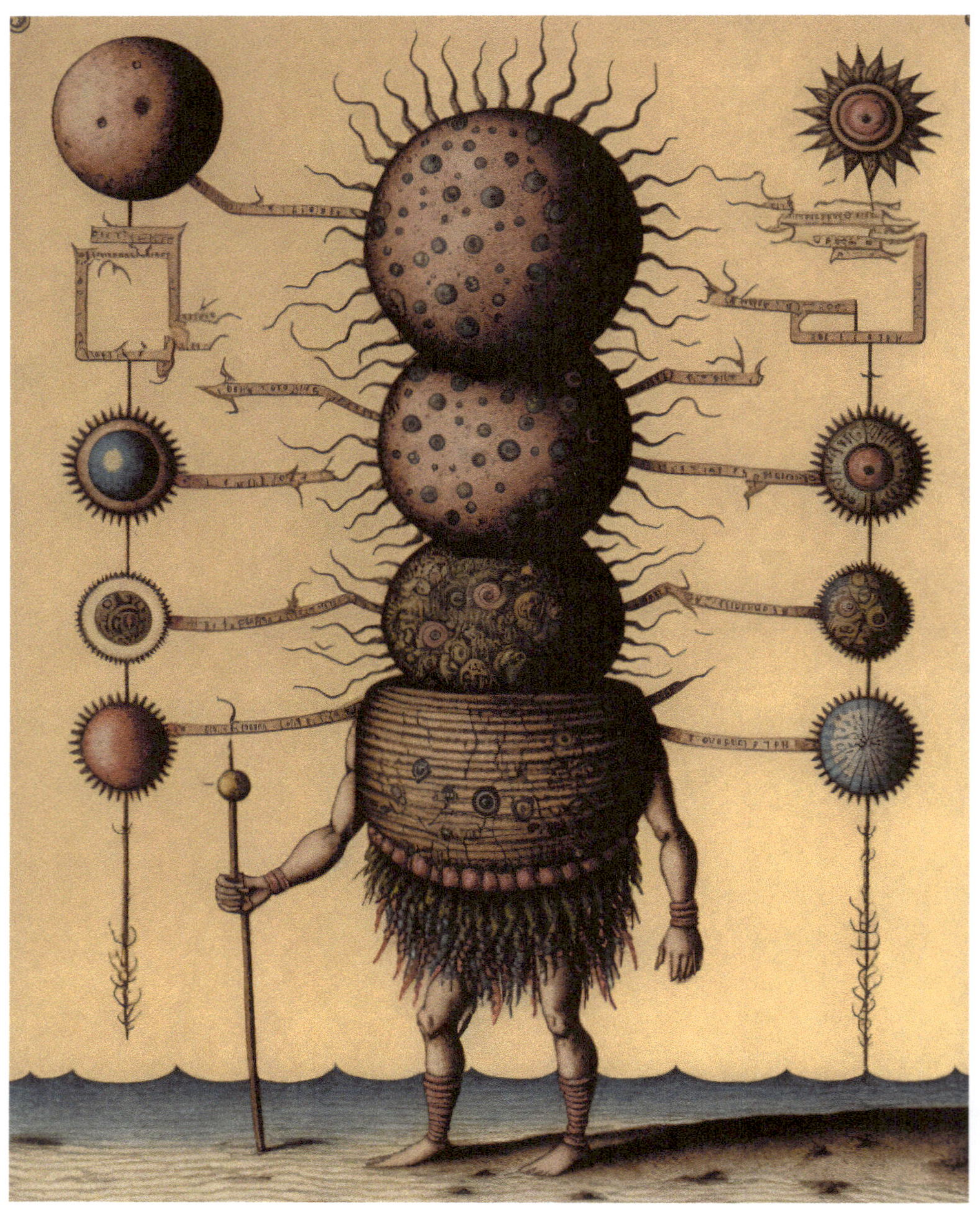

IV.6 Taurus III ... Λ red-colored man with very large, white teeth visible outside his mouth and with a body similar to an elephant with long legs. (Picatrix‡2.XI§8)

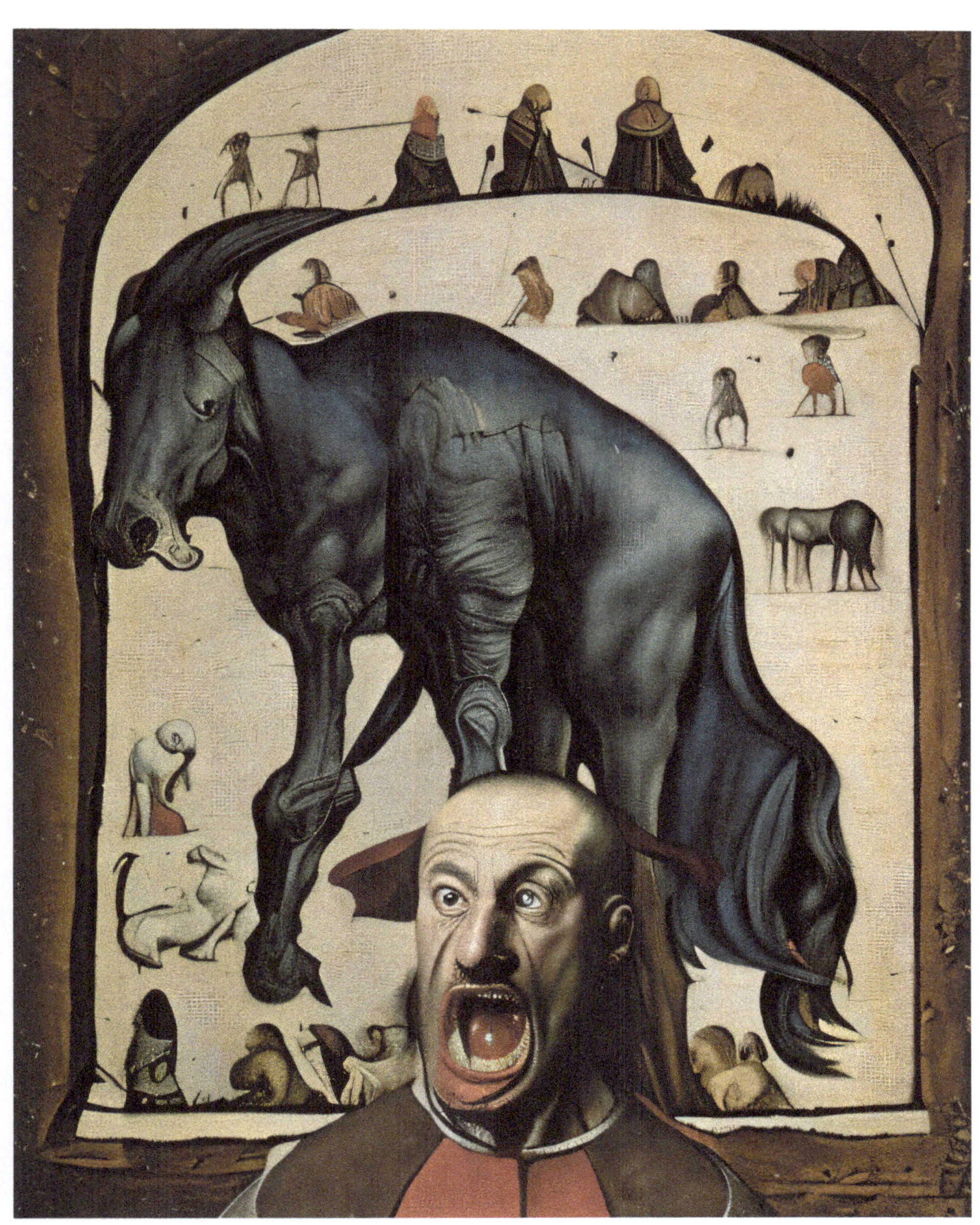

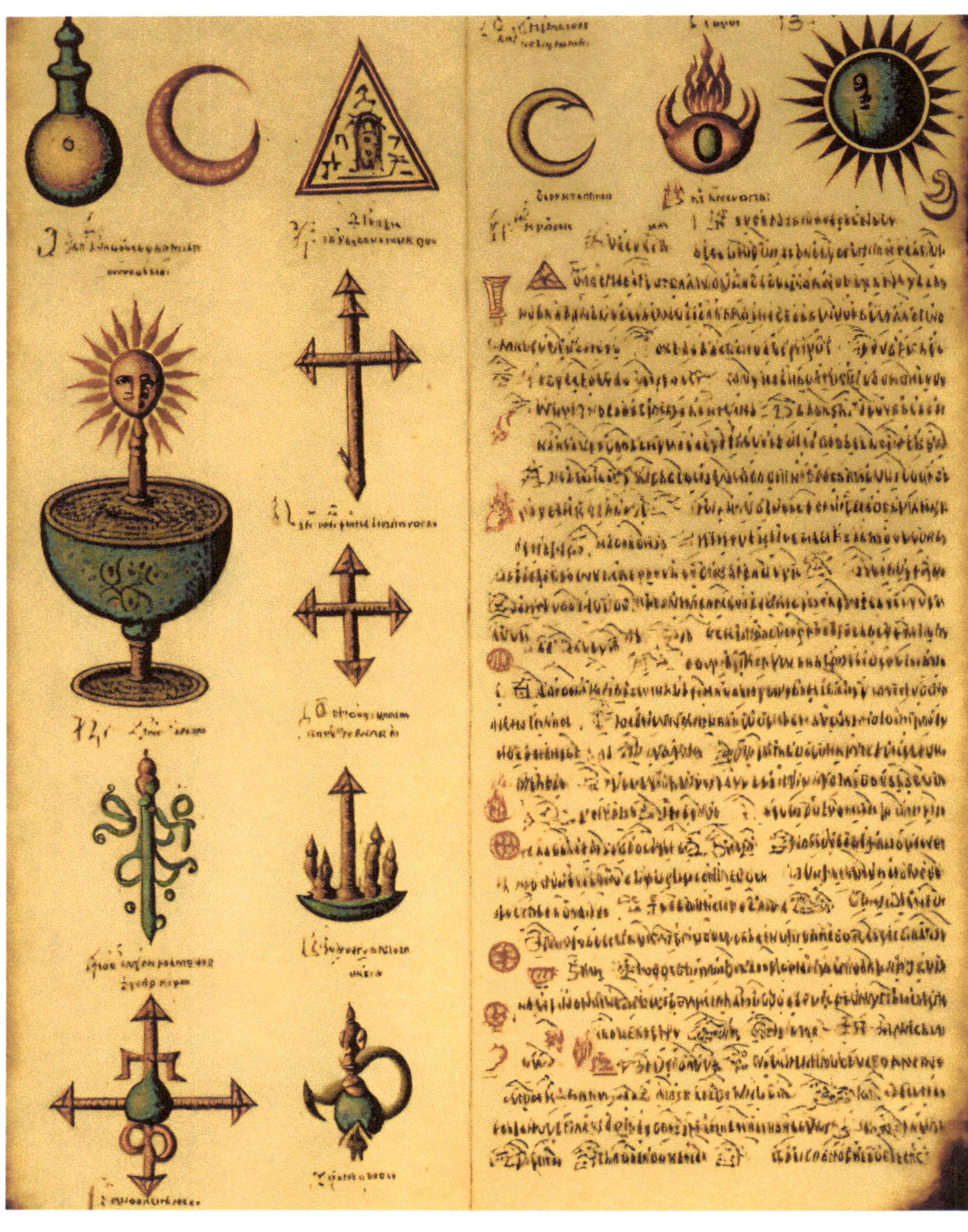

IV.7 **Gemini I** ... Λ beautiful woman, the mistress of stitching, and with her ascend two calves and two horses. (Picatrix‡2.XI§9)

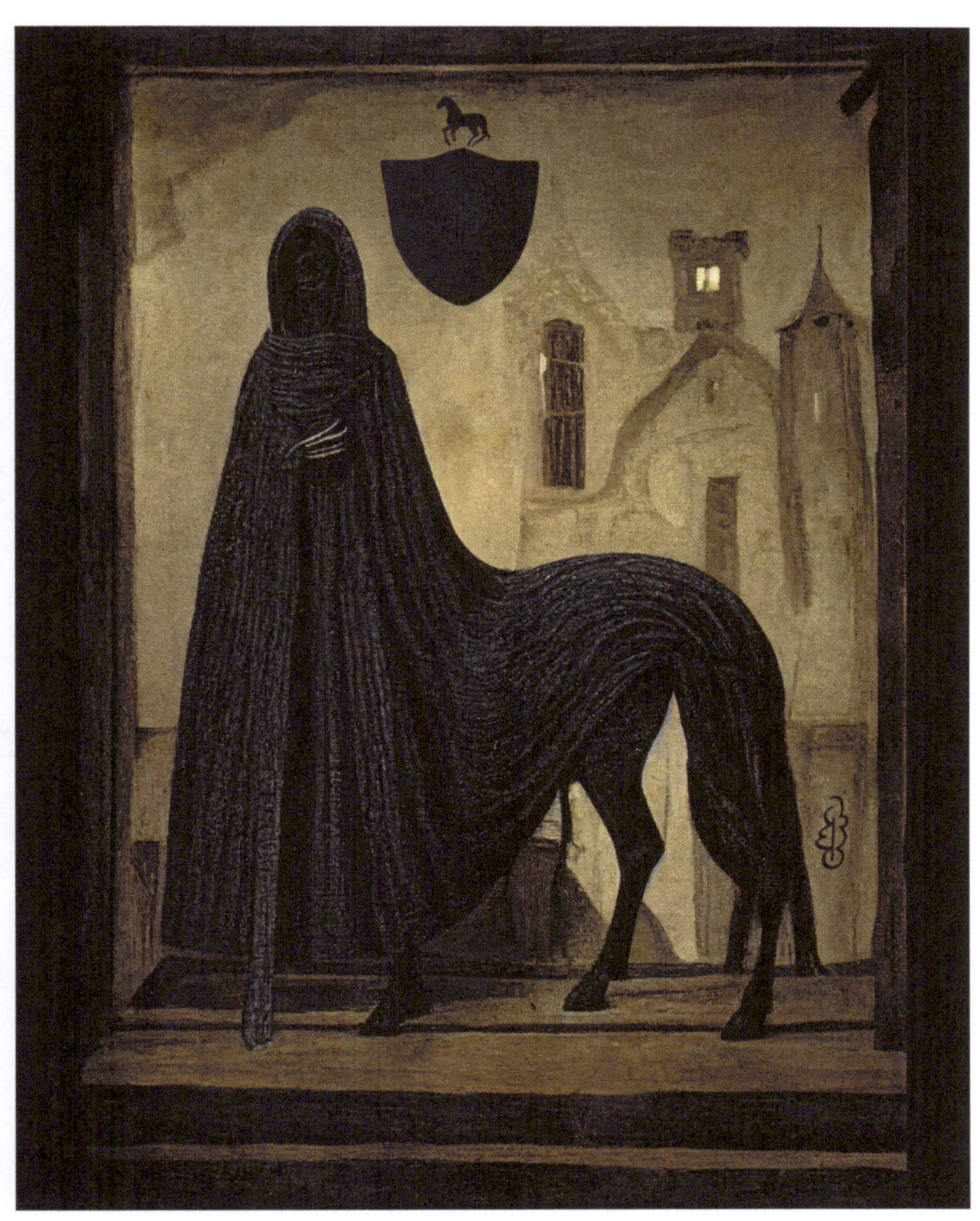

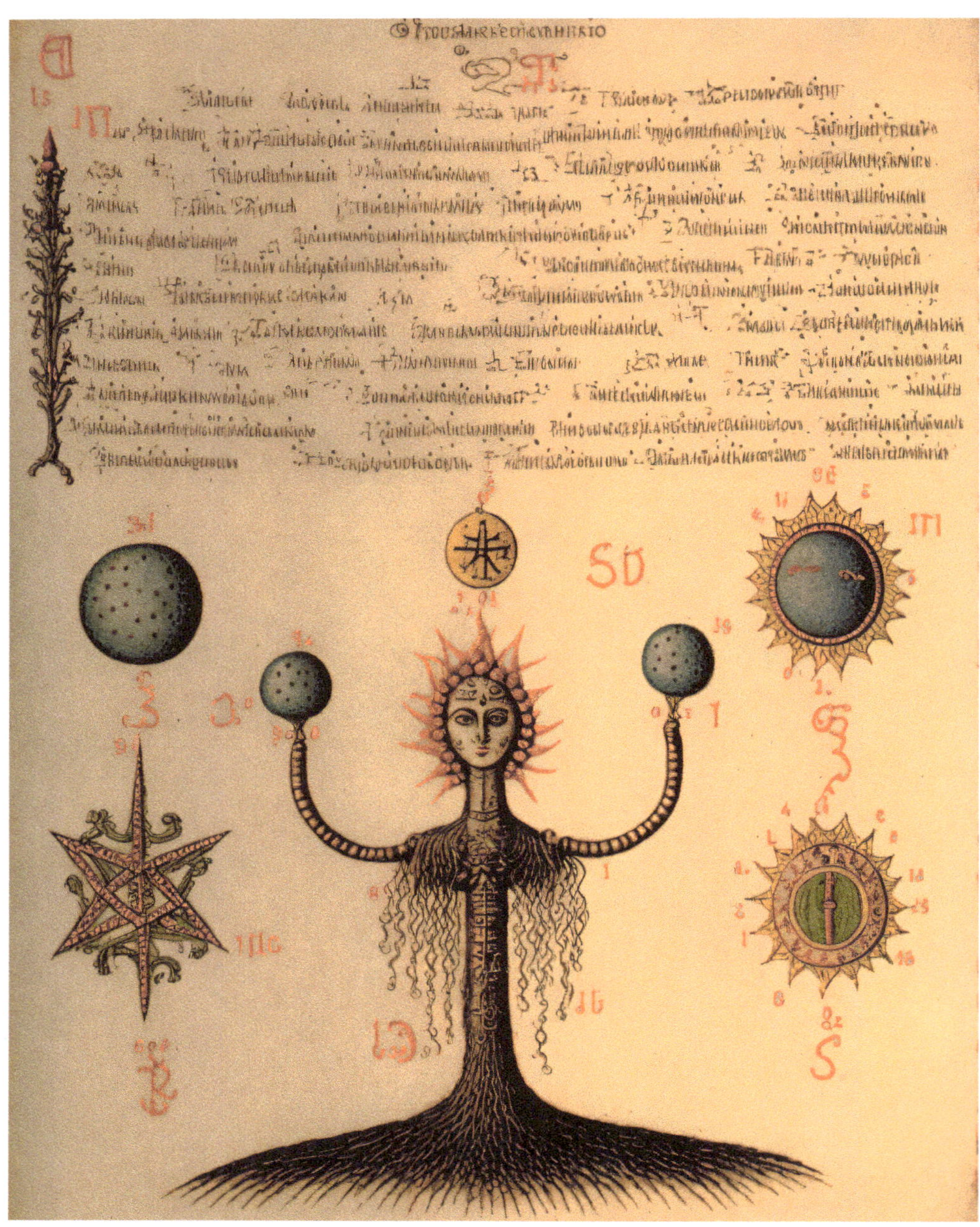

IV.8 Gemini II ... A man whose face is like an eagle and his head is covered with a linen cloth; he is garbed and protected in a leaden cuirass, and on his head an iron helmet upon which is a silken wreath; and he is holding in his hand a bow and arrows. (Picatrix†2.XI§10)

/Oracle of DelphAI

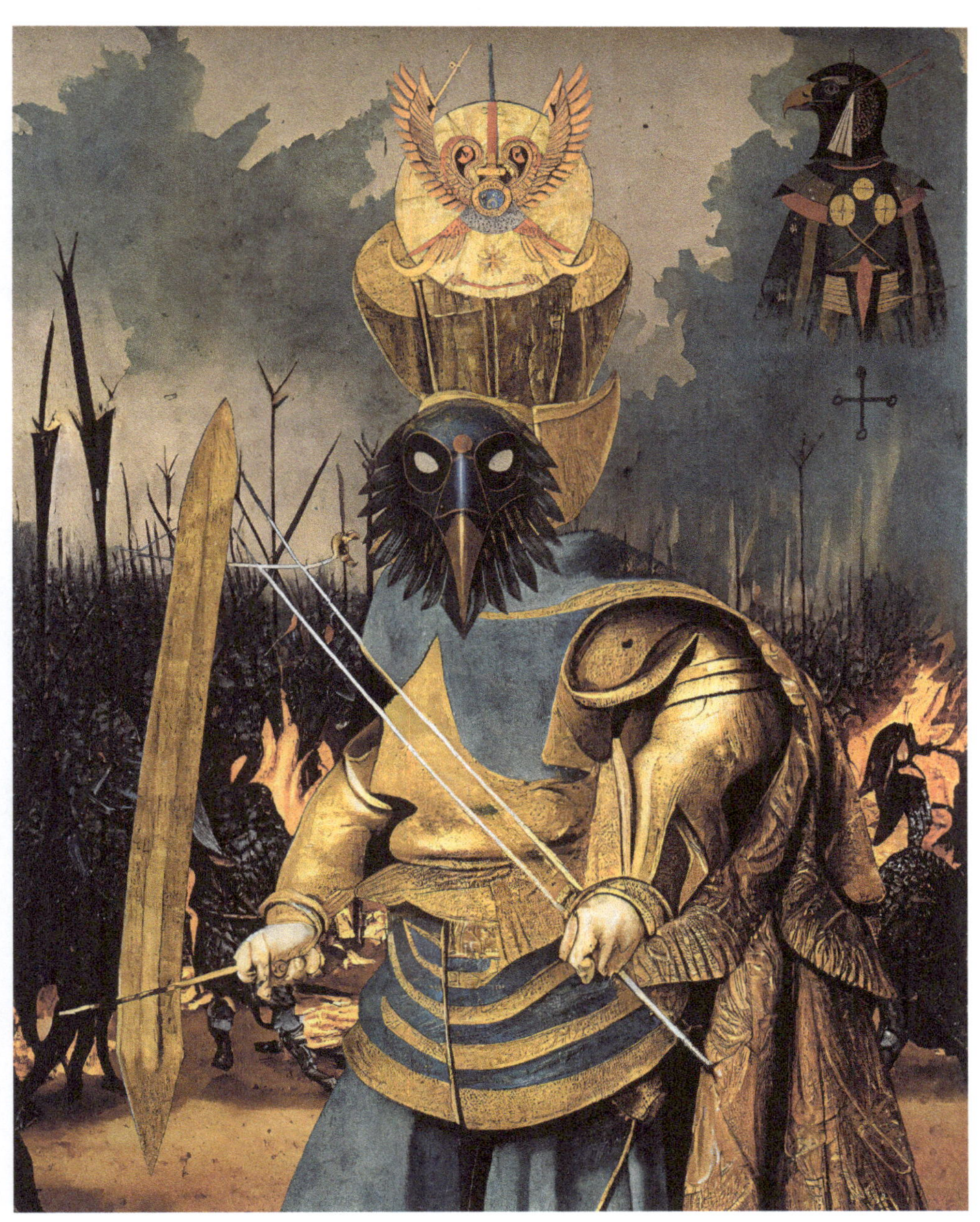

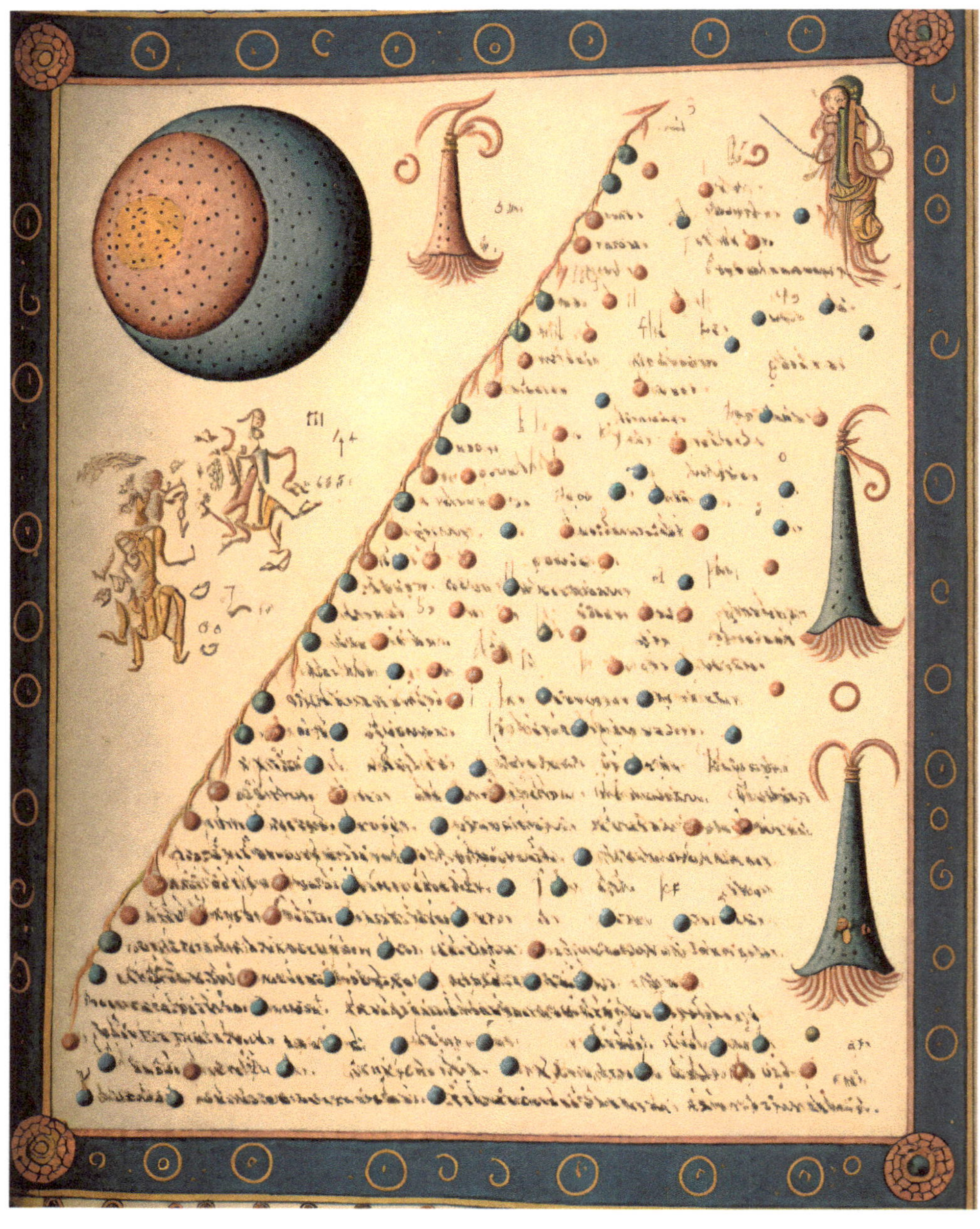

IV.9 Gemini III ... ∧ man garbed with a cuirass holding a bow and arrows, and a quiver.
(Picatrix‡2.XI§11)

/Oracle of Delph∧l

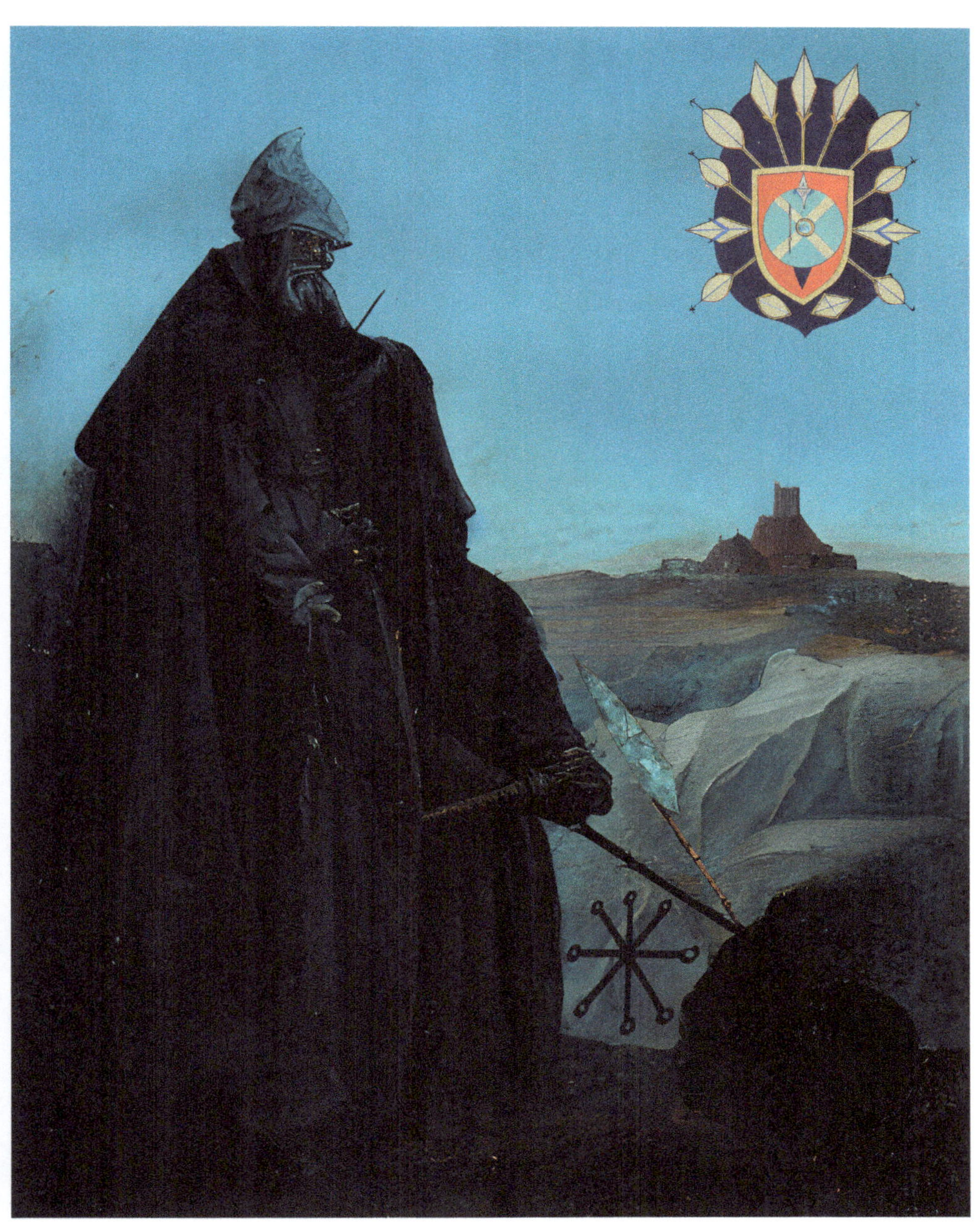

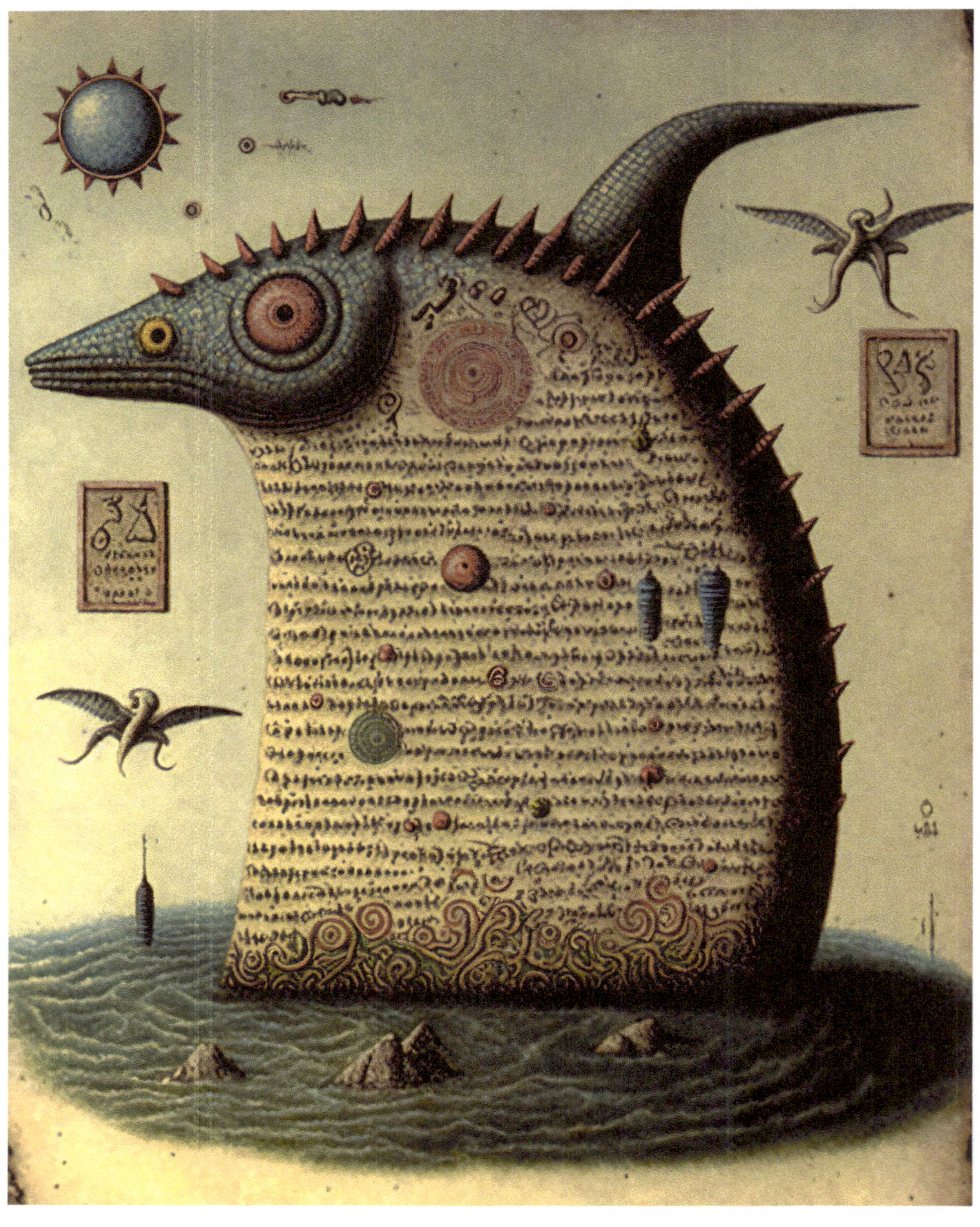

IV.10 Cancer I ... Λ man with crooked fingers and a bent over head. His body is like a horse. He has white feet, and fig leaves cover his body. (Picatrix‡2. XI§12)

/Oracle of DelphΛI

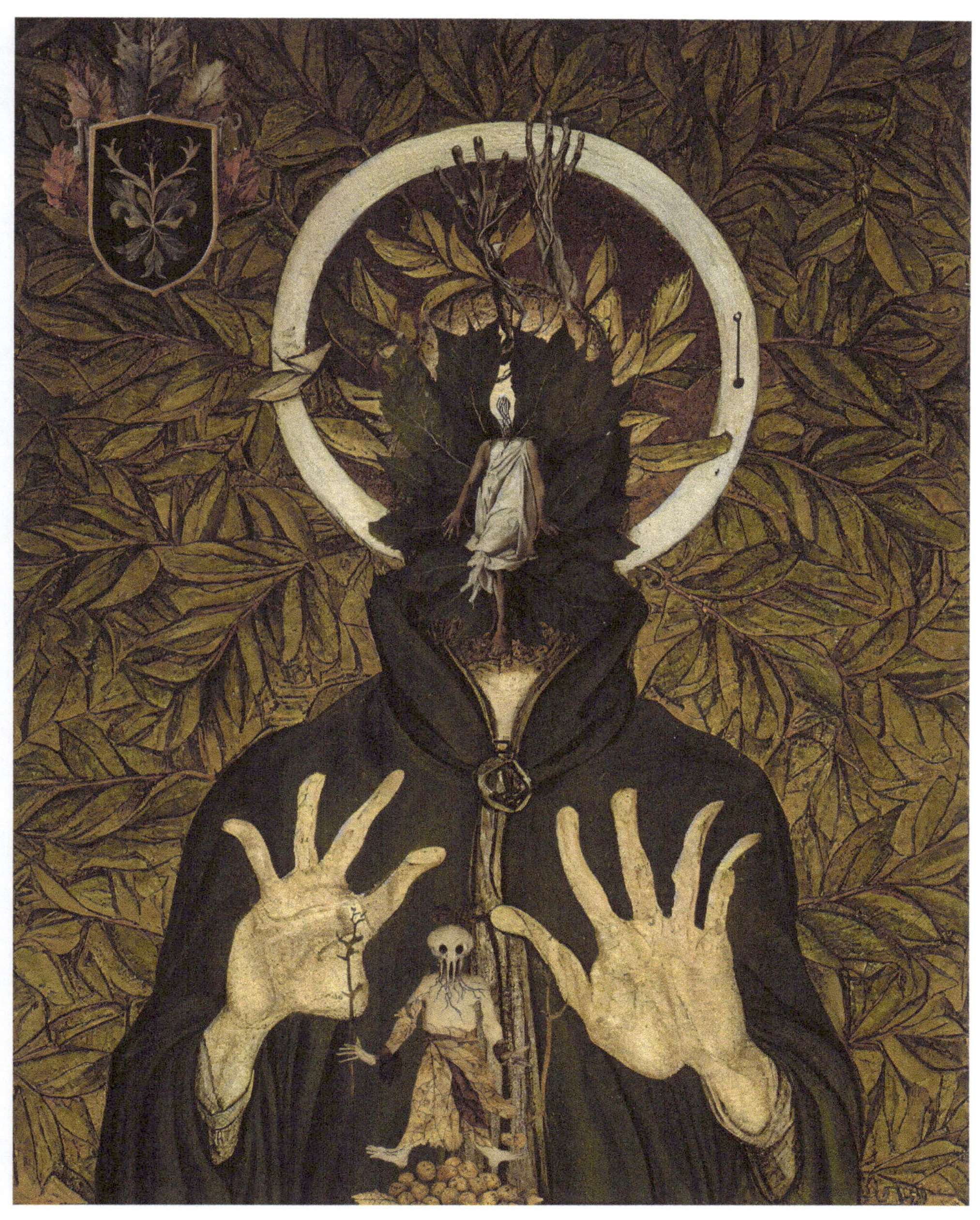

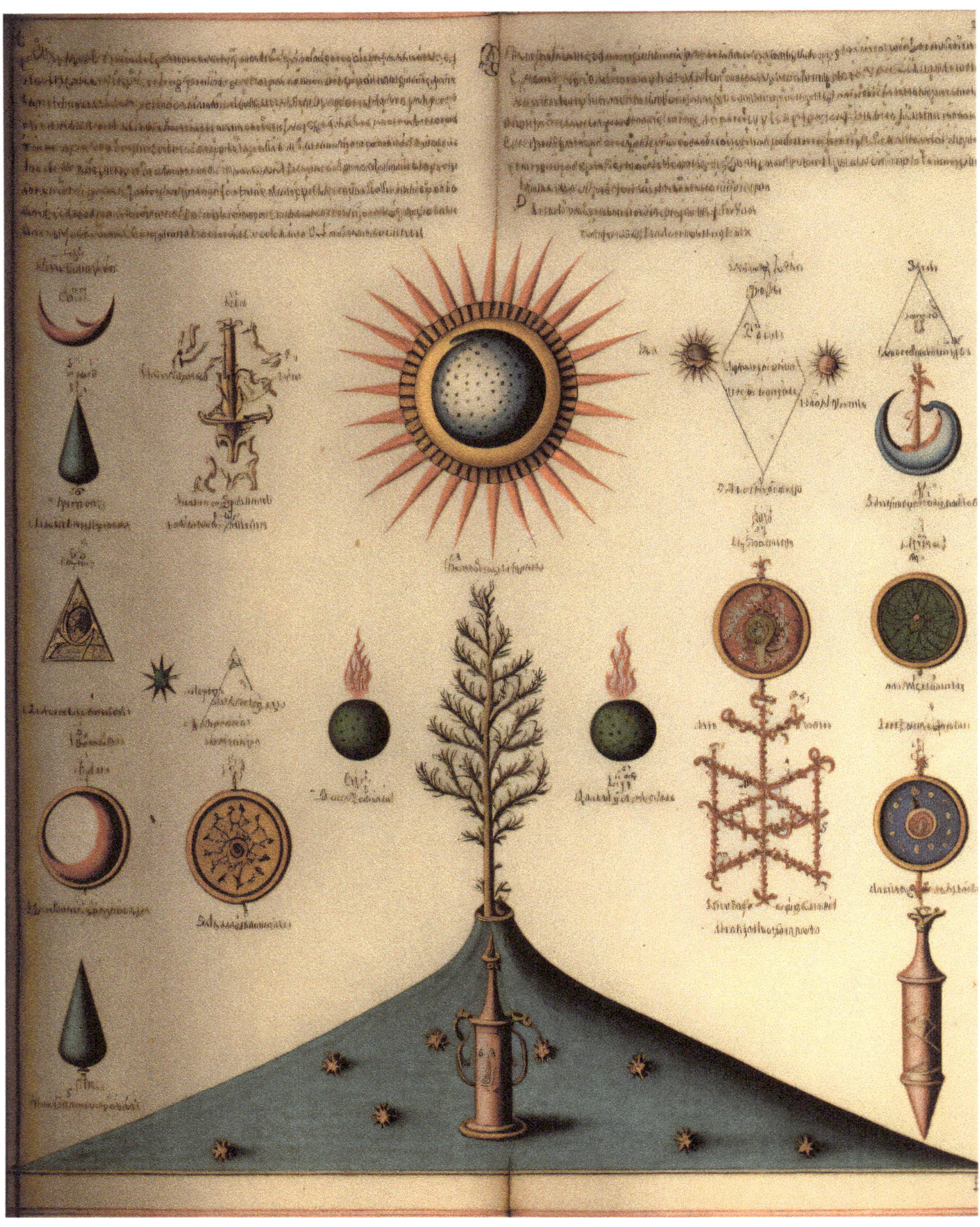

IV.11 Cancer II ... Λ woman with a beautiful face with a crown of green myrtle on her head and the stem of a plant that is called the water lily in her hand, singing songs of love and joy. (Picatrix‡2.XI§13)

/Oracle of DelphΛI

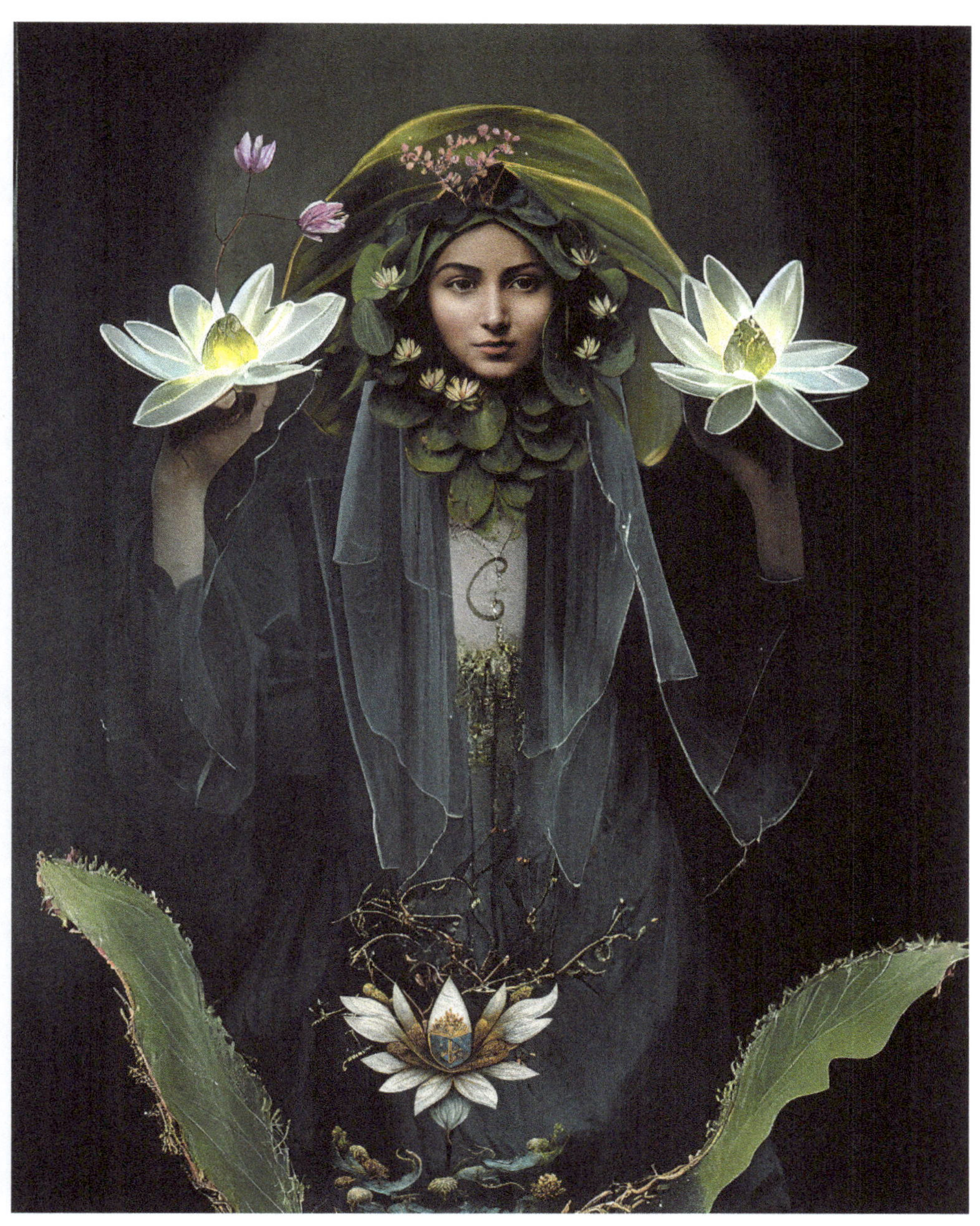

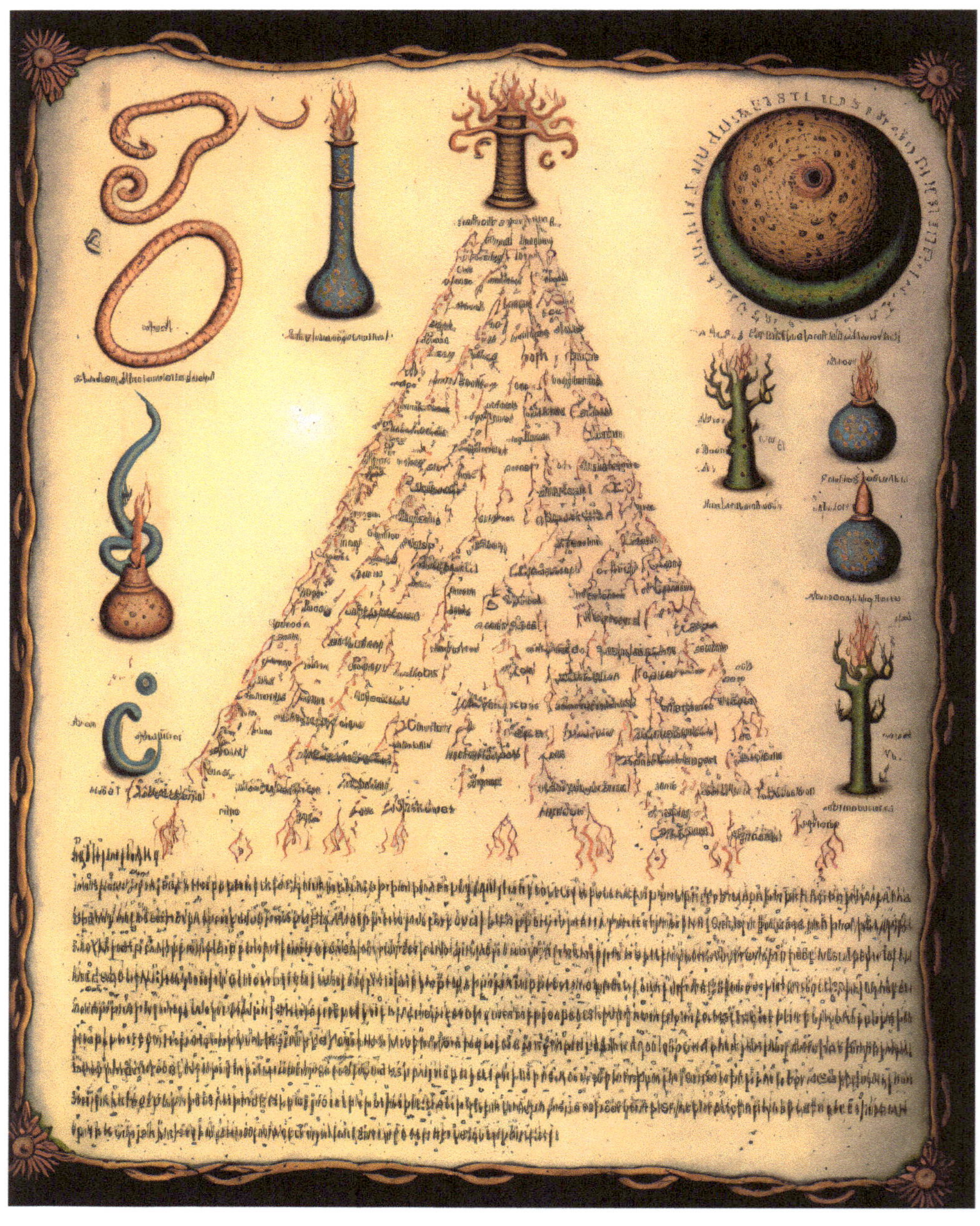

IV.12 Cancer III ... Λ man with a turtle under his feet and he holds a serpent in his hand holding before him golden chains. (Picatrix†2.XI§14)

/Oracle of DelphΛl

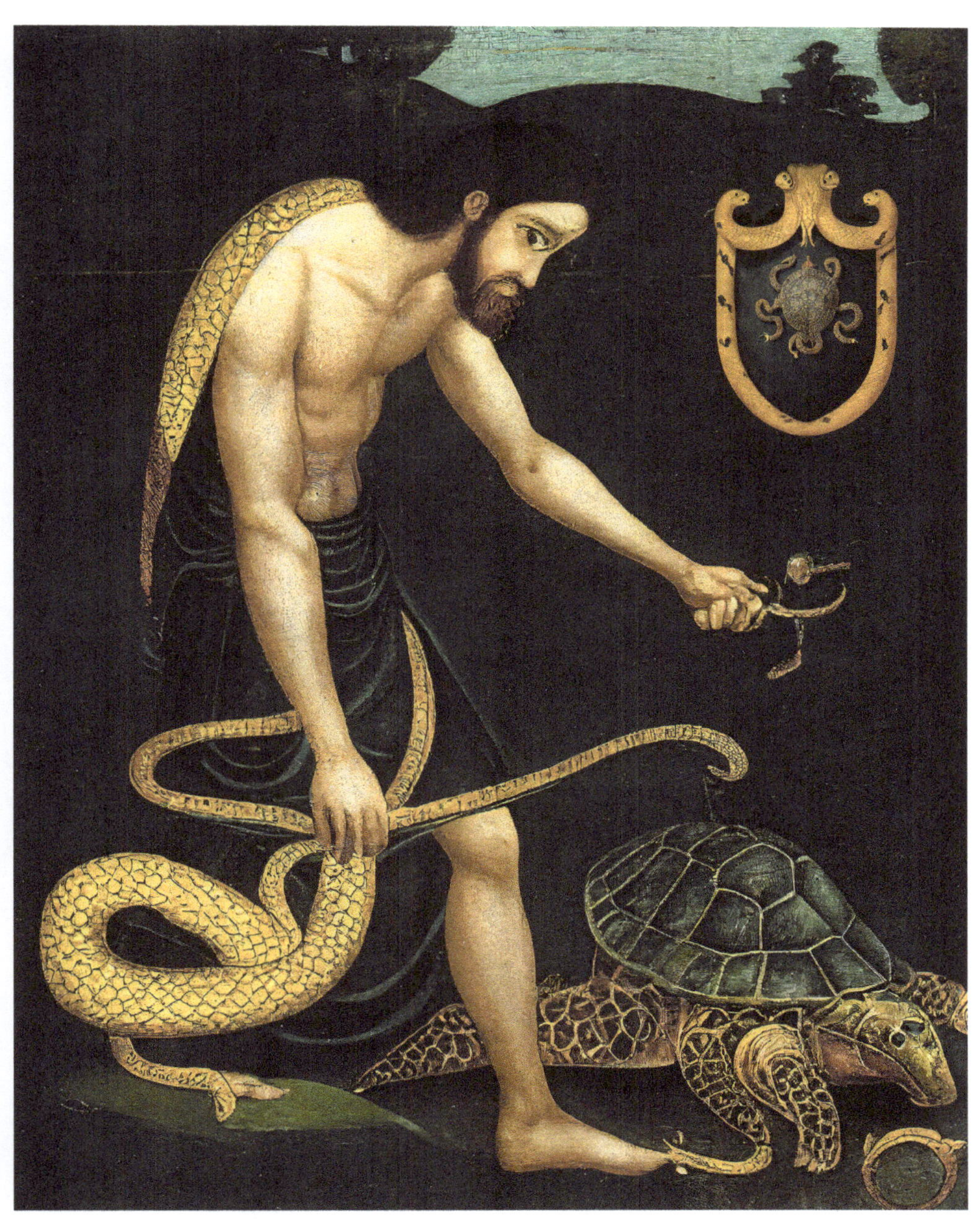

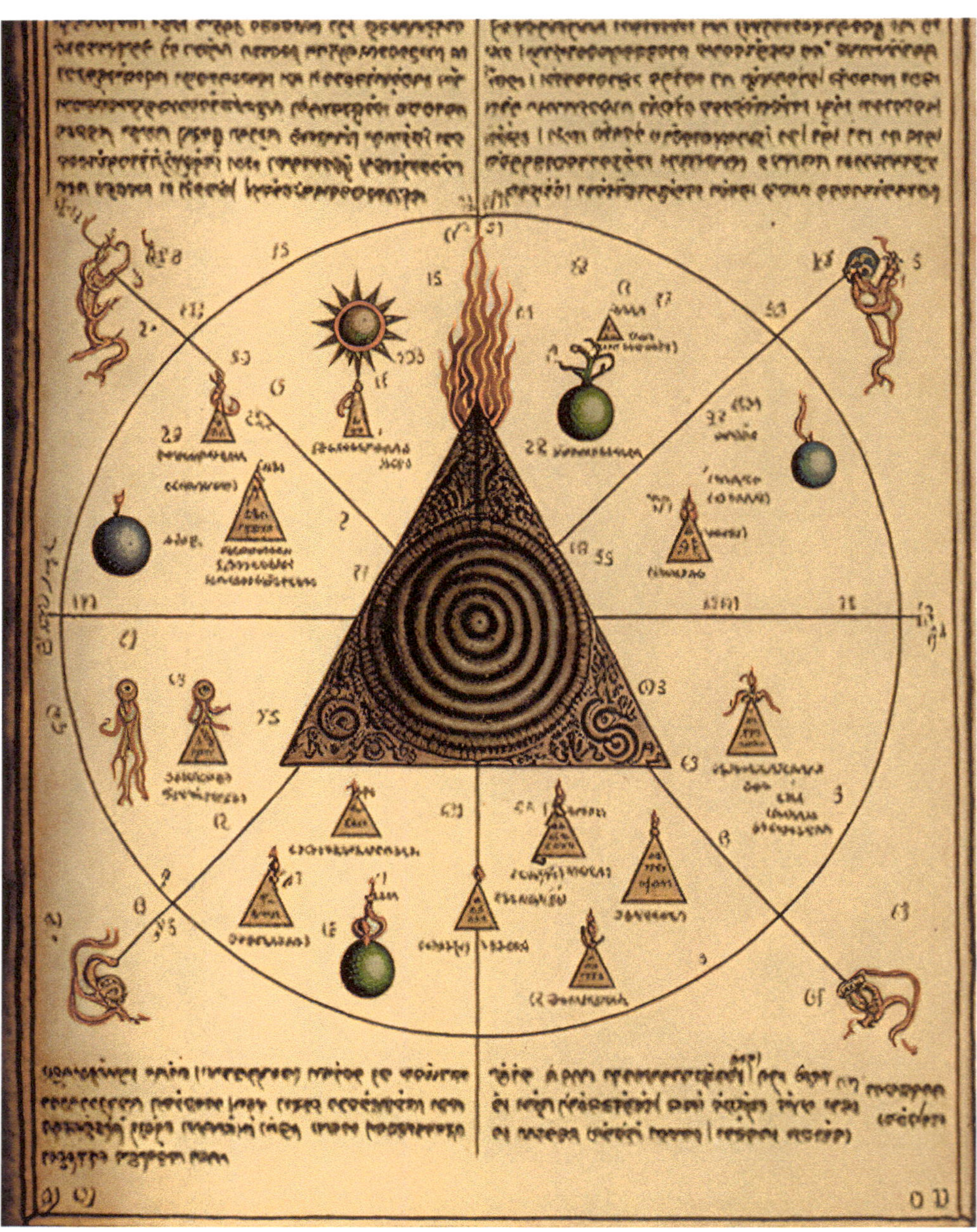

IV.13 Leo I ... A man dressed in dirty clothes. With him ascends the figure of a master of the horse looking northward. His figure is that of a bear and a dog. (Picatrix‡2.XI§15)

/Oracle of DelphΛI

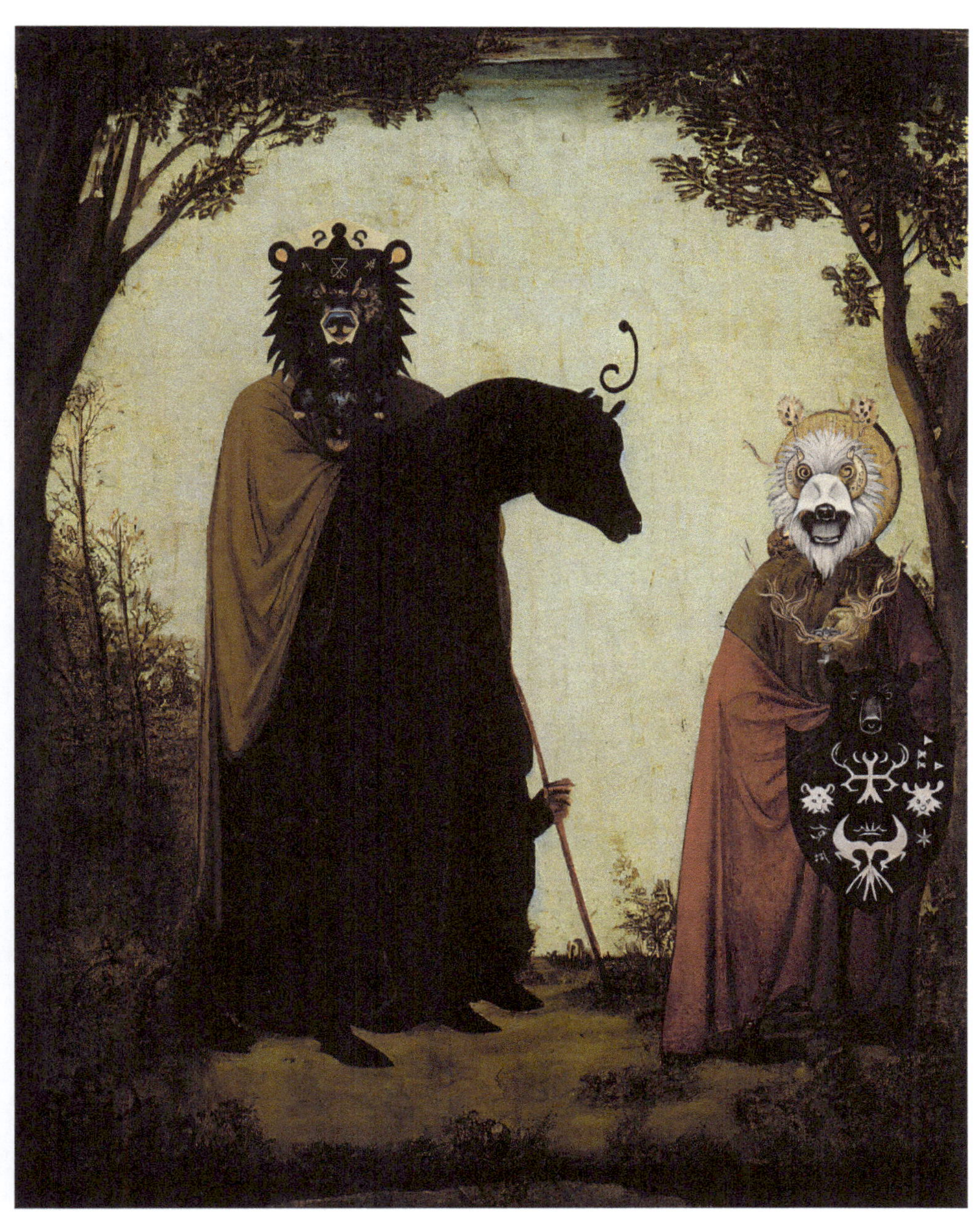

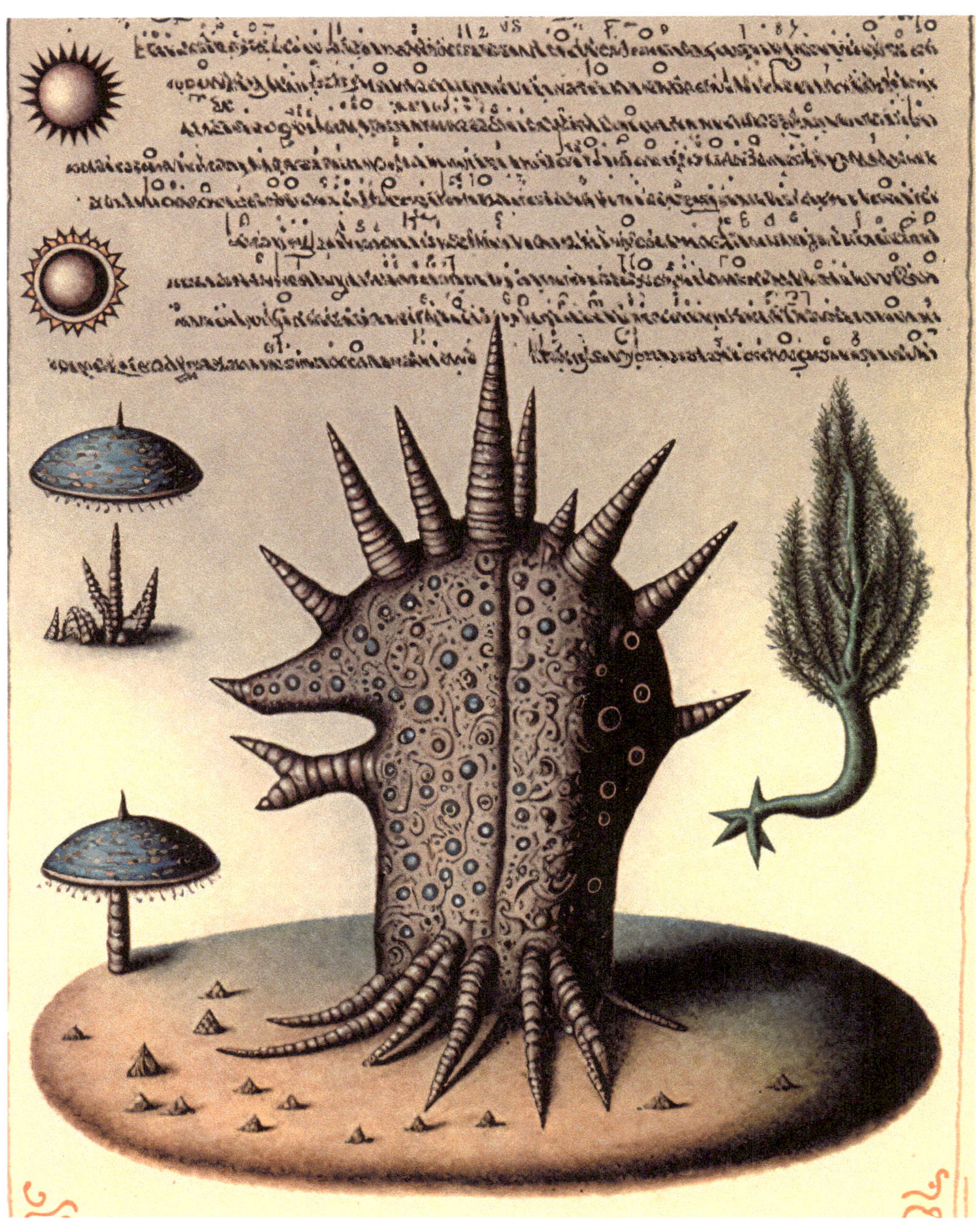

IV.14 Leo II ... Λ man with a crown of white myrtle on his head and a bow in his hand.
(Picatrix‡ 2.XI§16)

/Oracle of DelphΛl

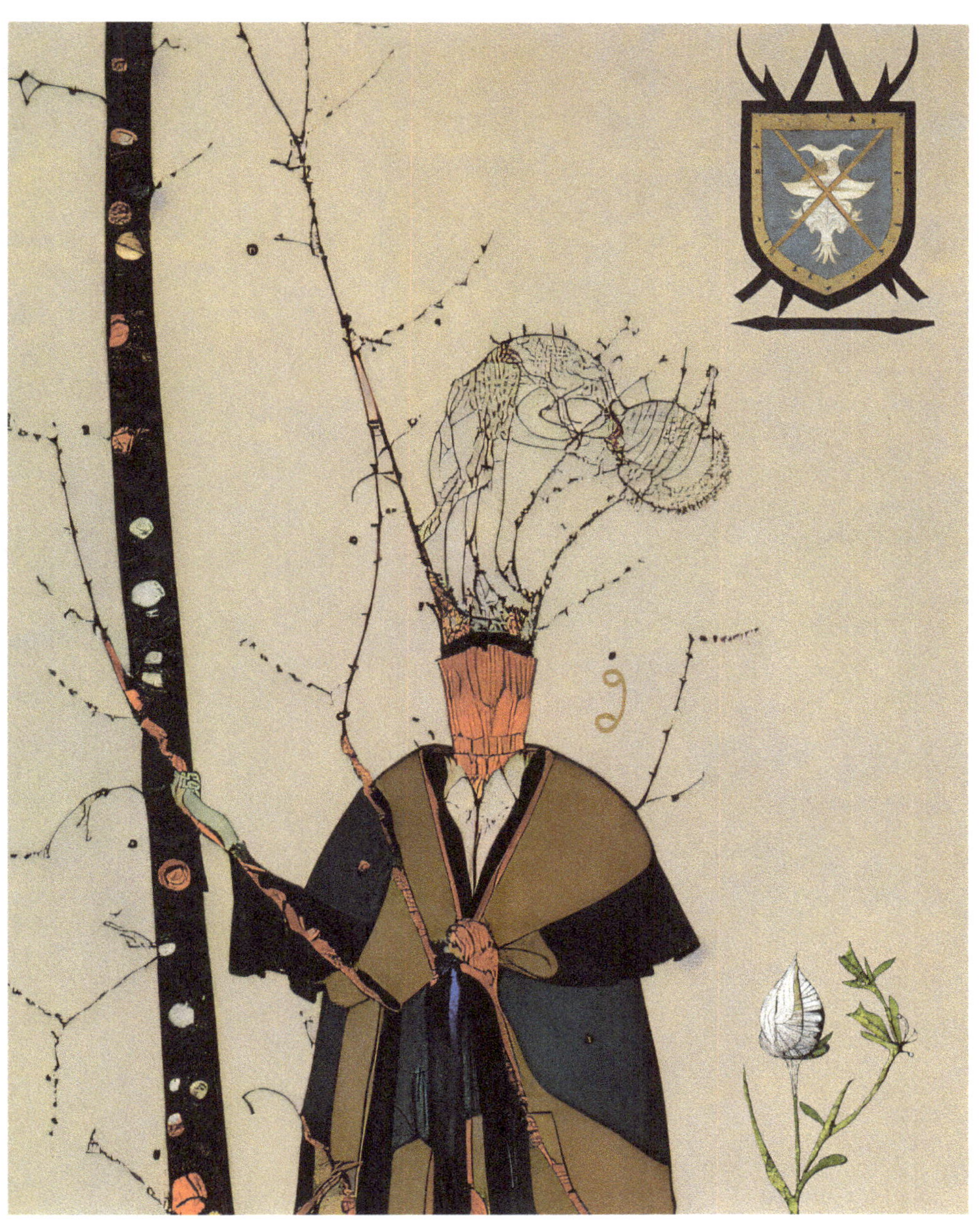

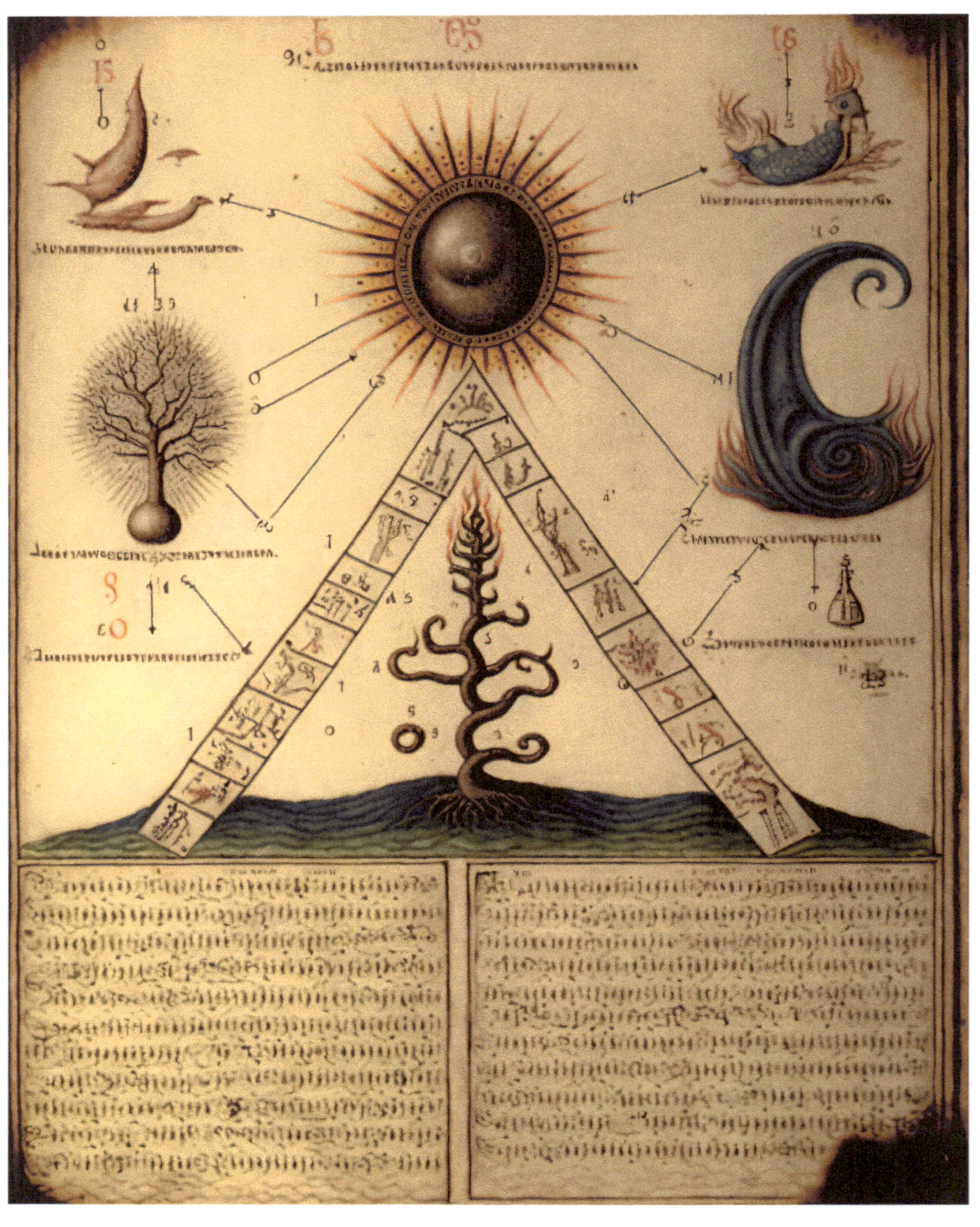

IV.15 Leo III ... an old man dark and foul, holding fruit and meat in his mouth and a jug covered with copper in his hand. (Picatrix†2.XI§17)

/Oracle of DelphΛI

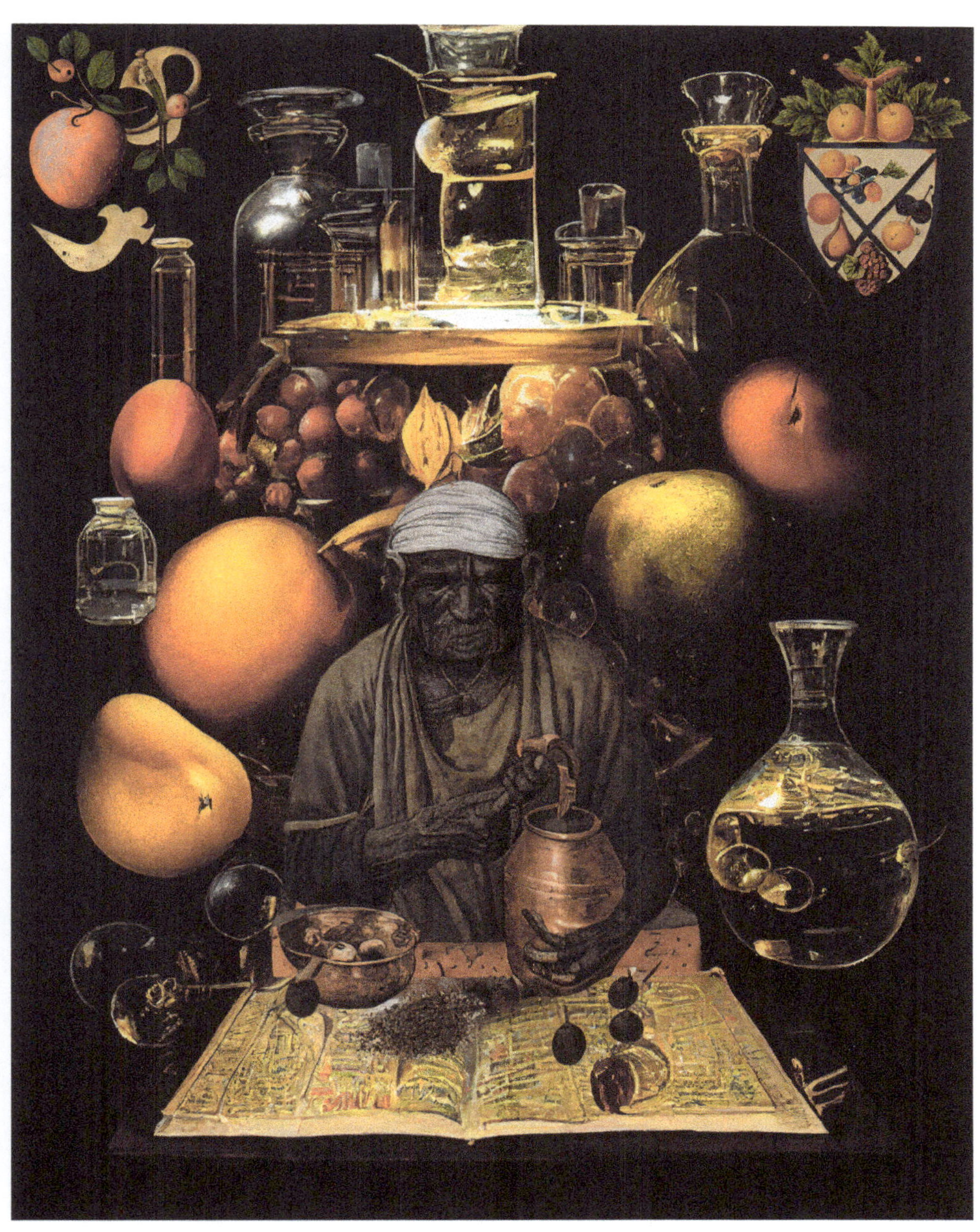

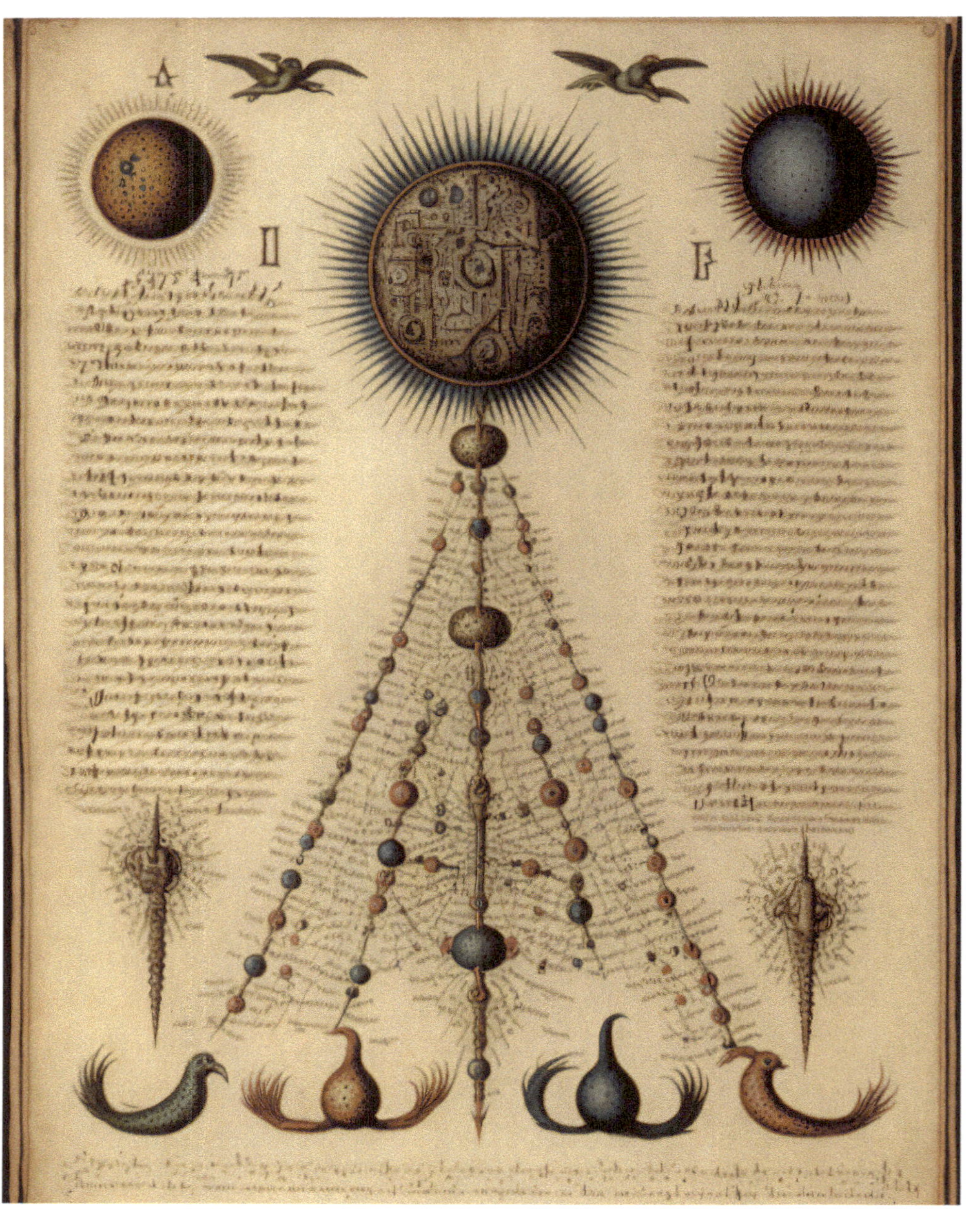

IV.16 Virgo I ... a beautiful girl covered over with a woolen sheet and holding in her hand a pomegranate. (Picatrix[†]2.XI§18)

/Oracle of DelphAI

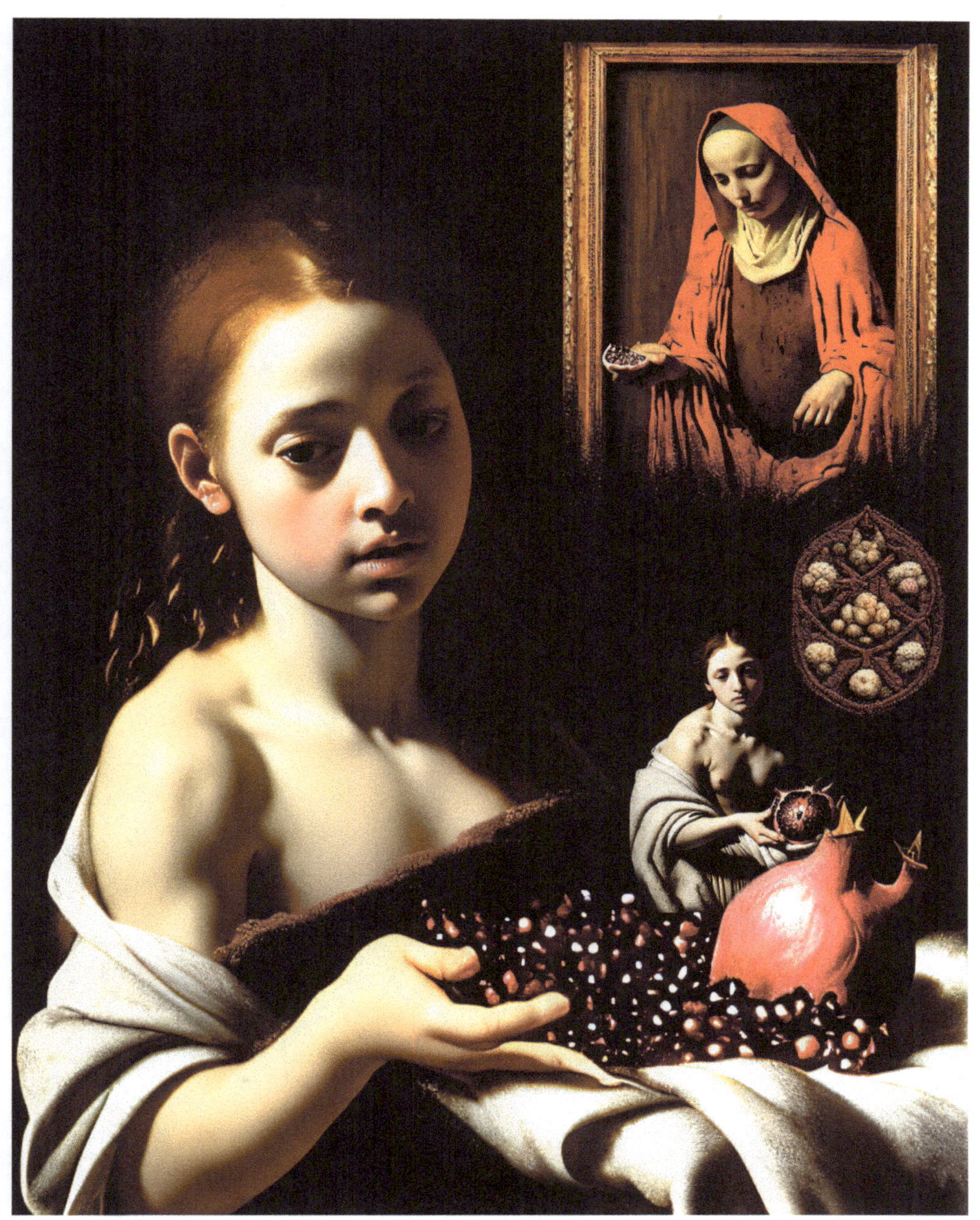

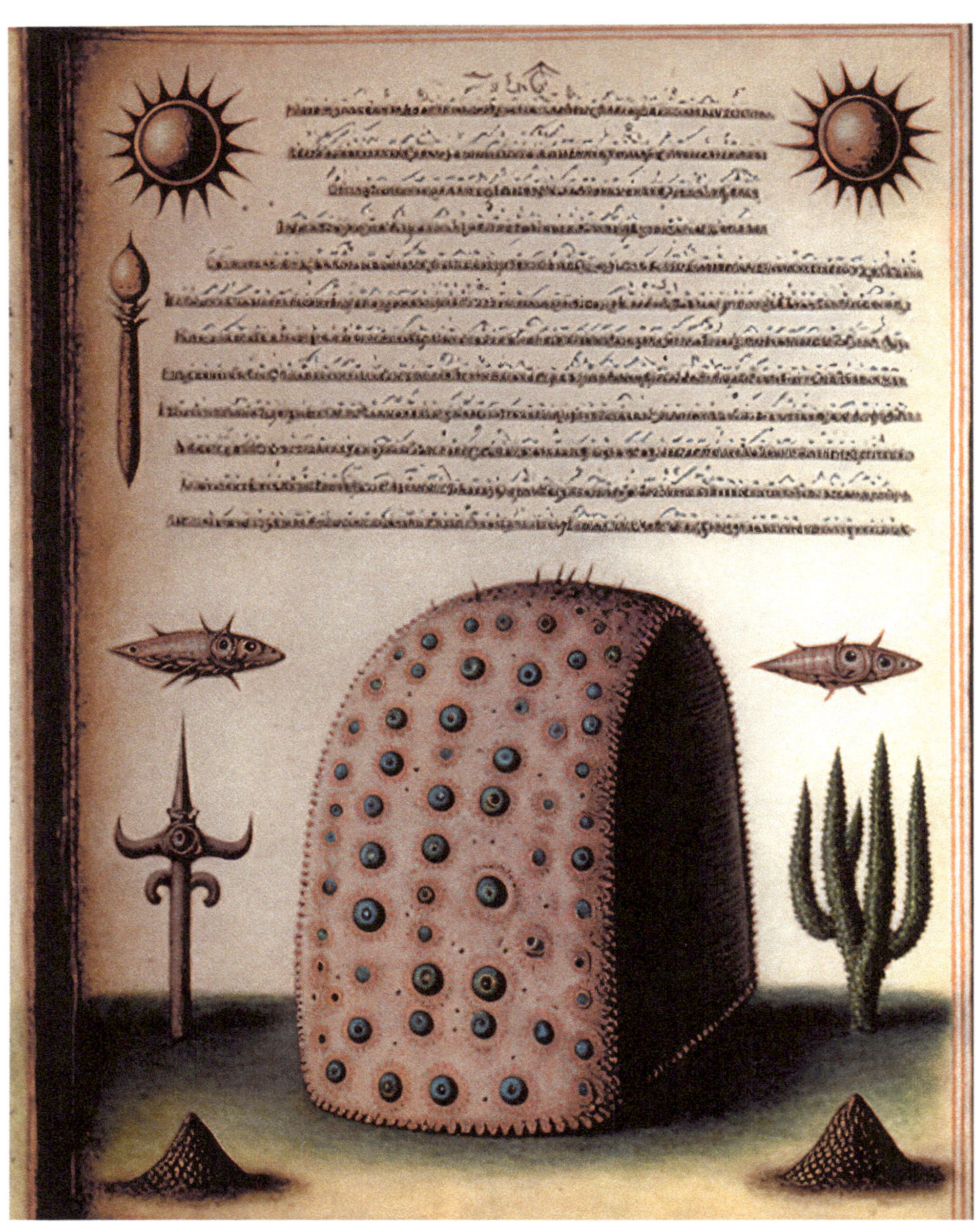

IV.17 Virgo II ... a man of beautiful color, dressed in leather and upon the vestment of leather another vestment of iron. (Picatrix[†]2.XI§19)

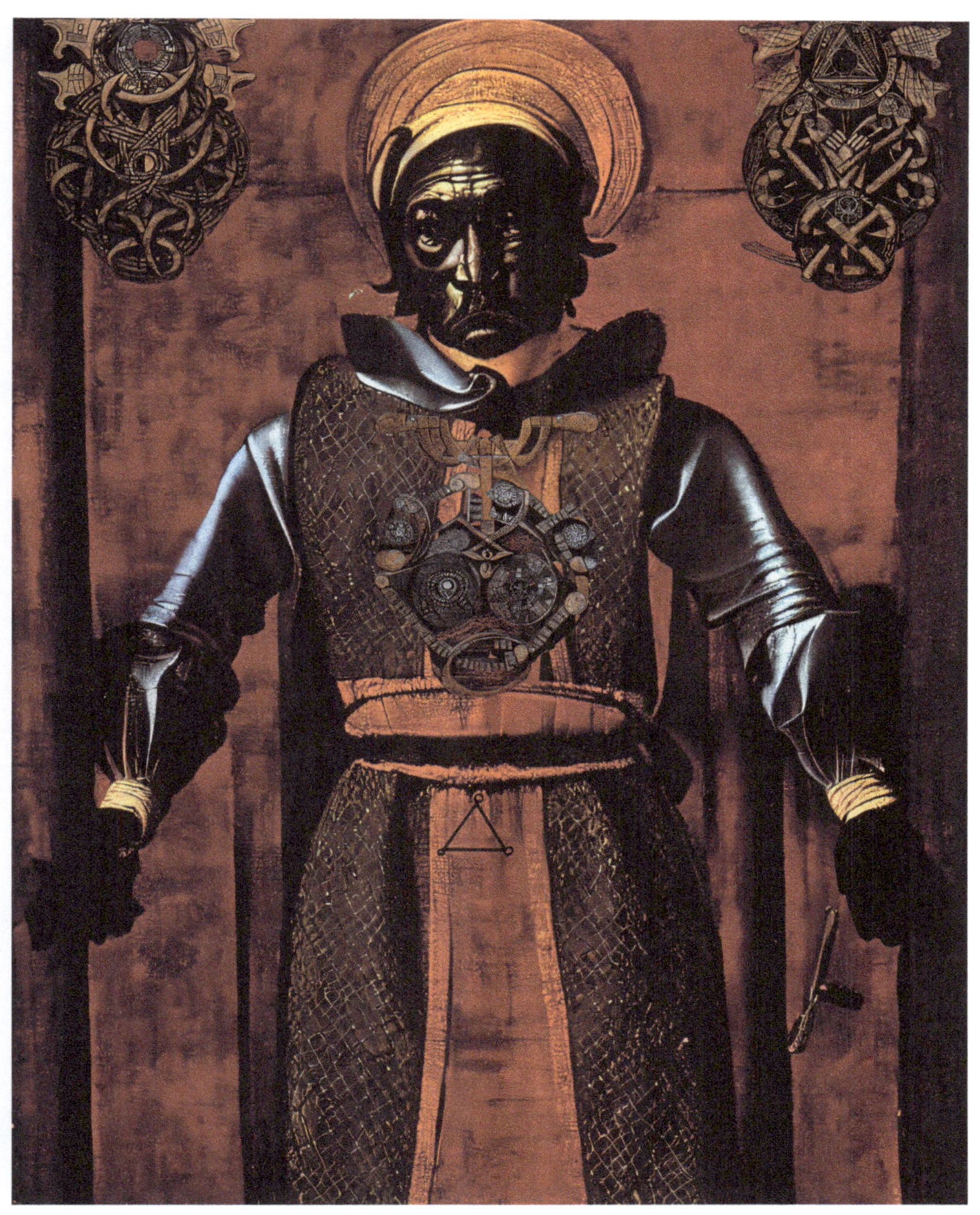

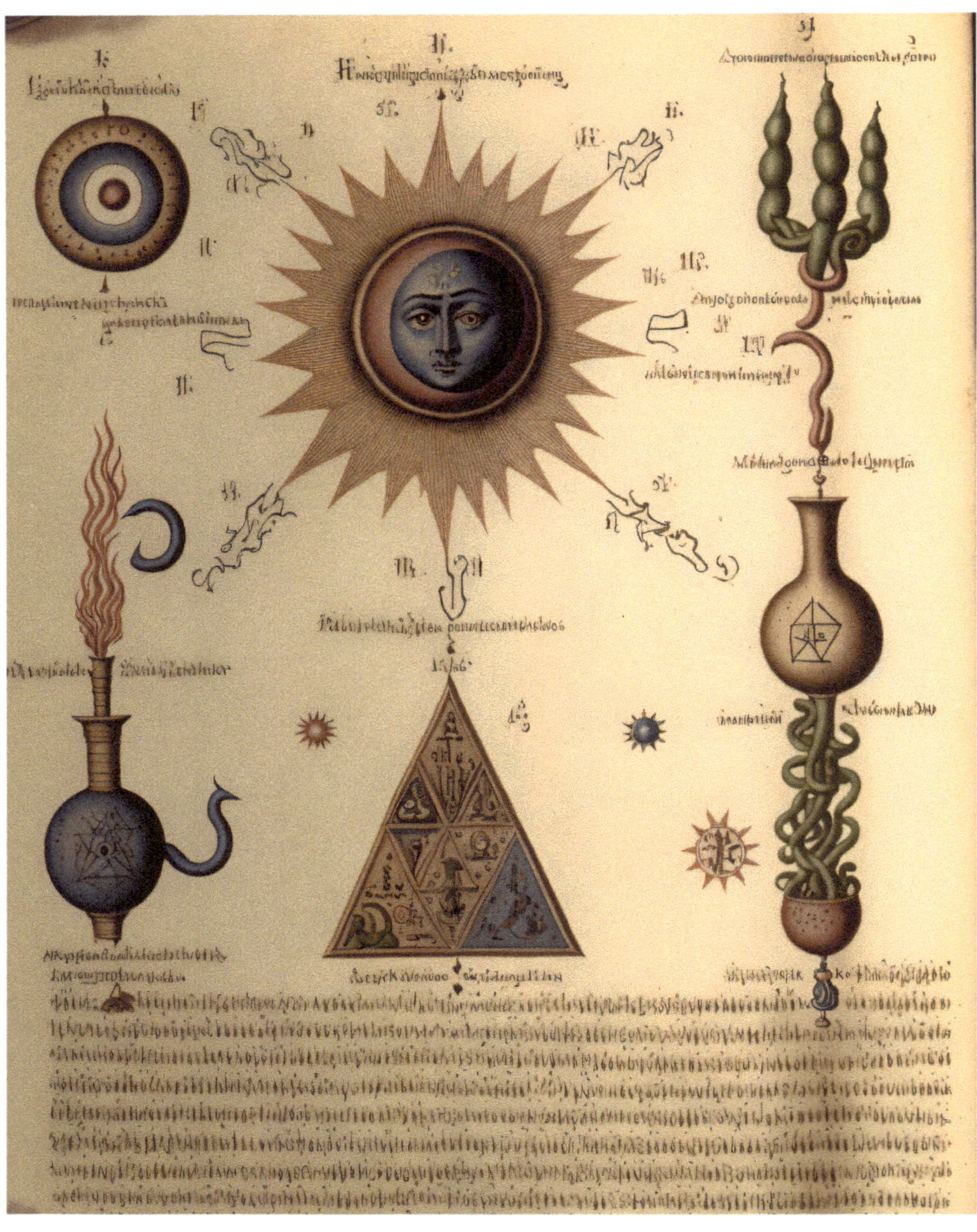

IV.18 Virgo III ... a pale man of large body wrapped in a white linen cloth, and with him a woman holding in her hand black olive oil. (Picatrix[†]2.XI§20)

/Oracle of DelphΛI

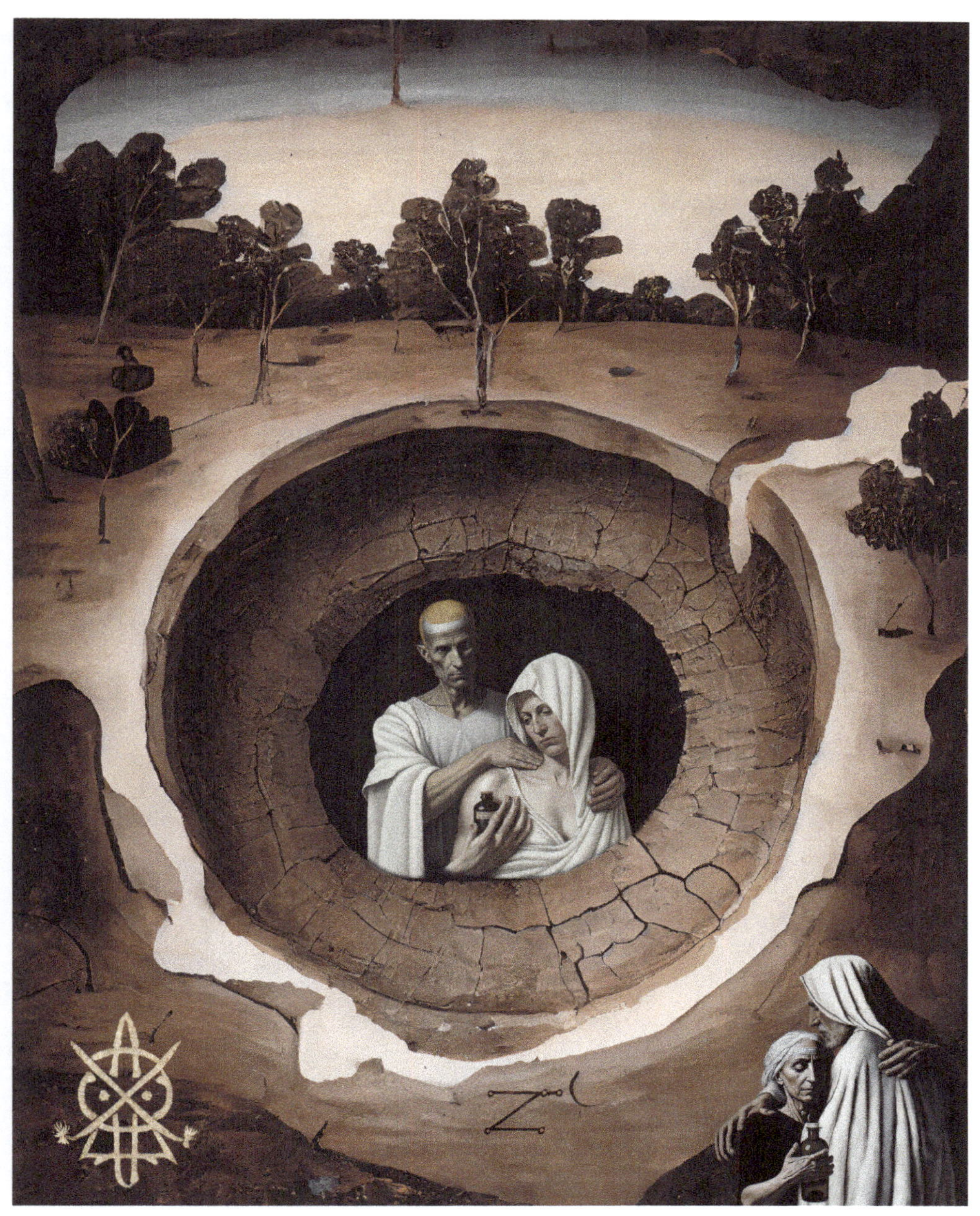

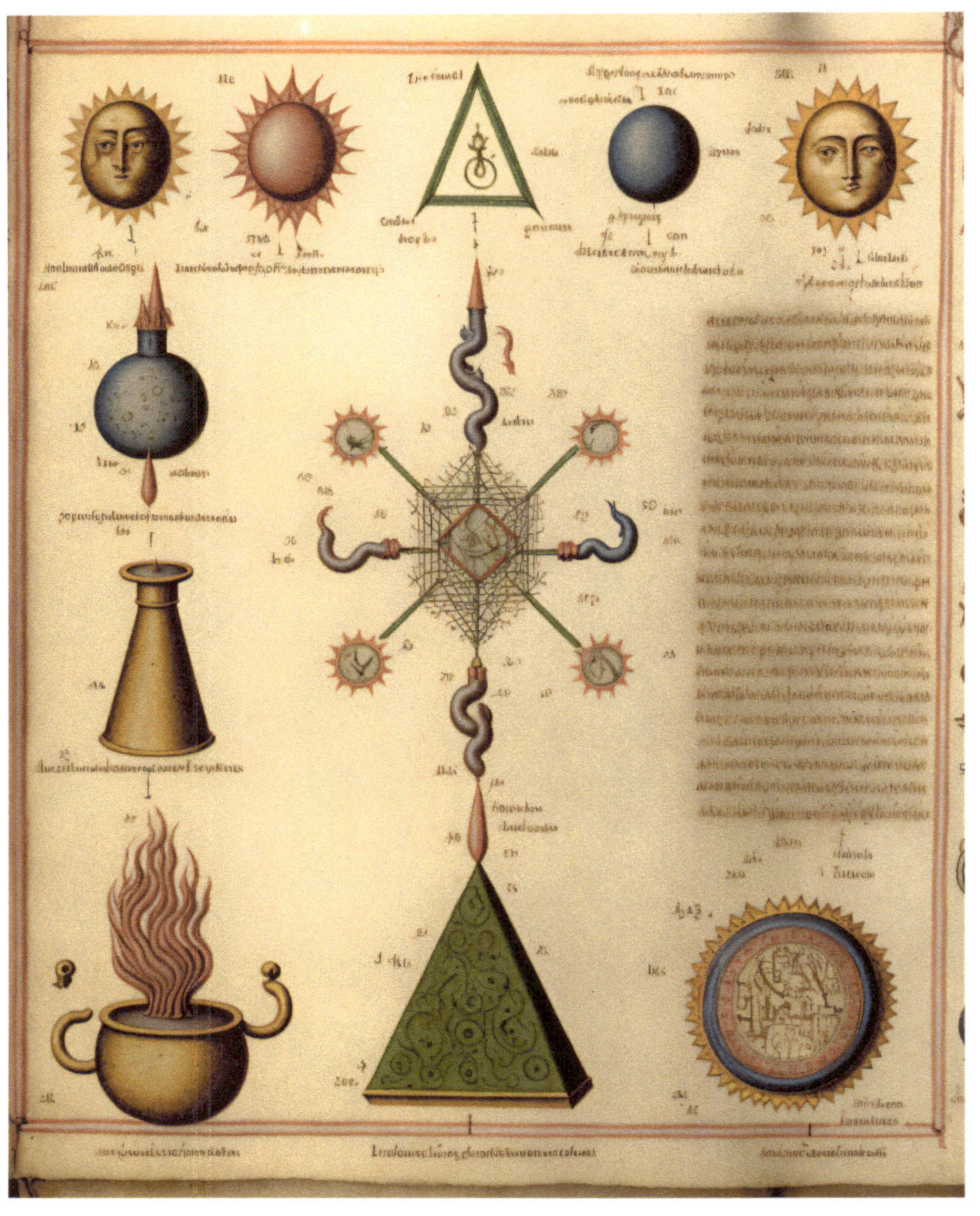

IV.19 Libra I ... a man holding a lance in his right hand but in the left a bird hanging by its feet. (Picatrix†2.XI§21)

/Oracle of DelphΛI

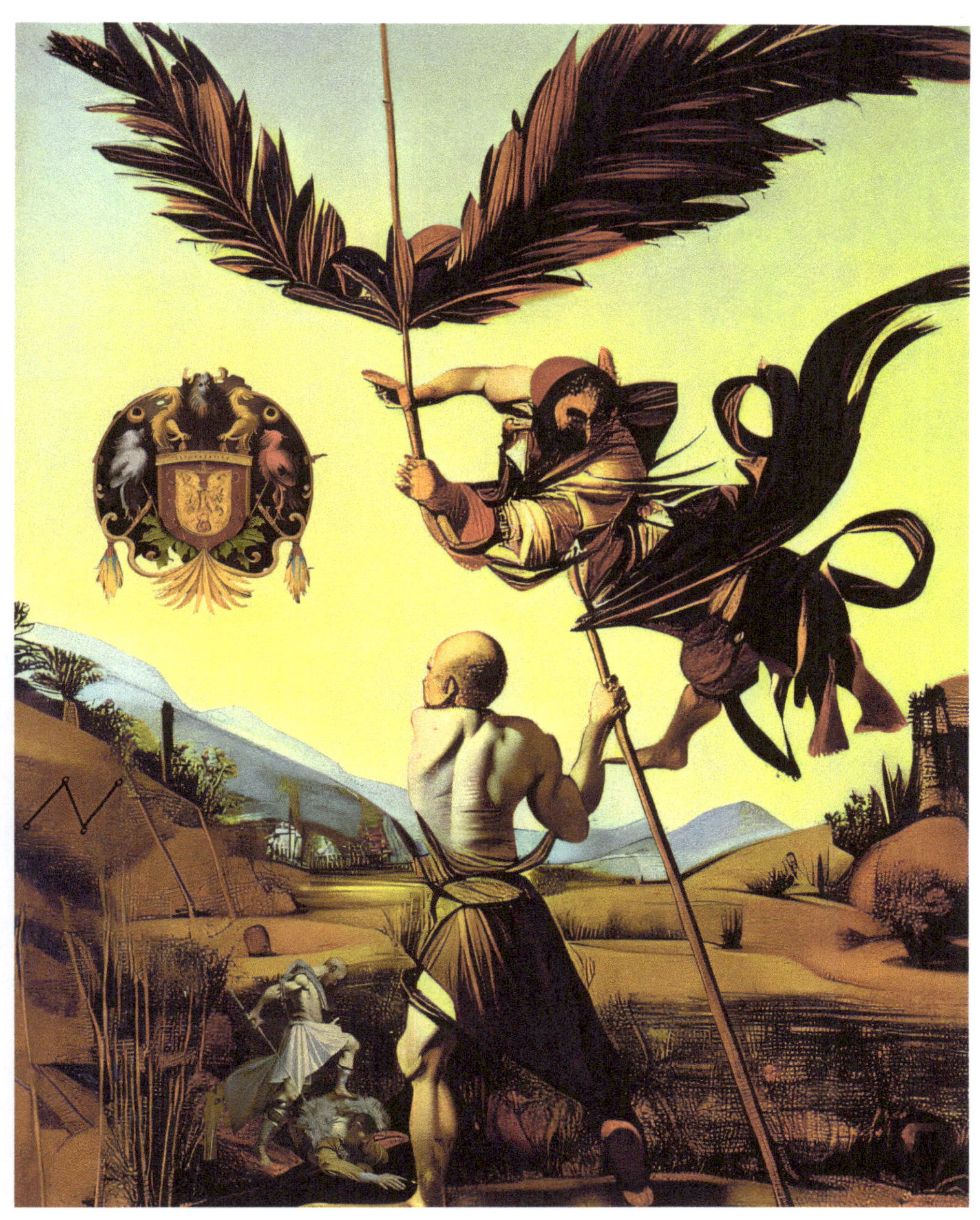

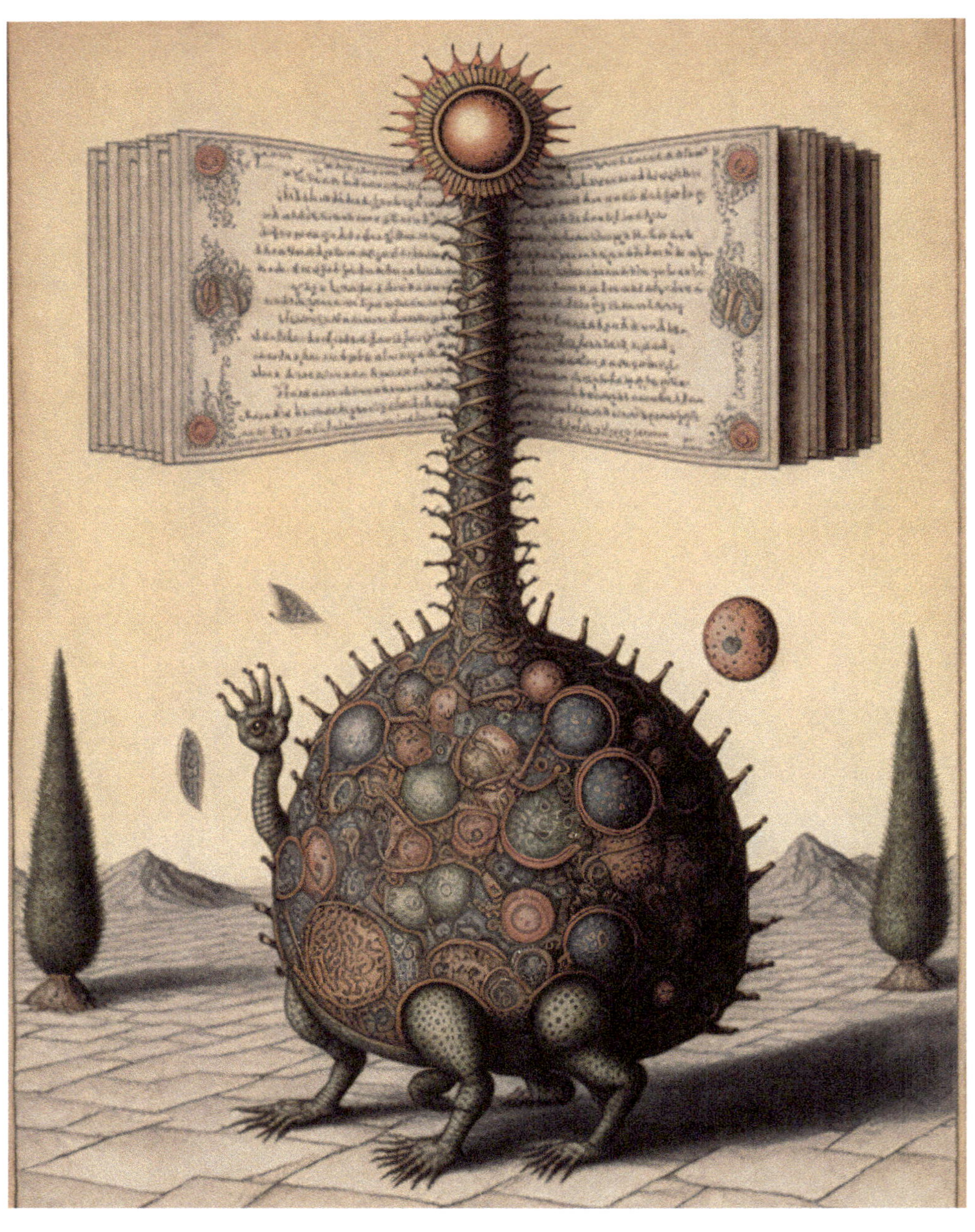

IV.20 Libra II ... a black man having a journey of marriage and joy. (Picatrix†2.XI§22)

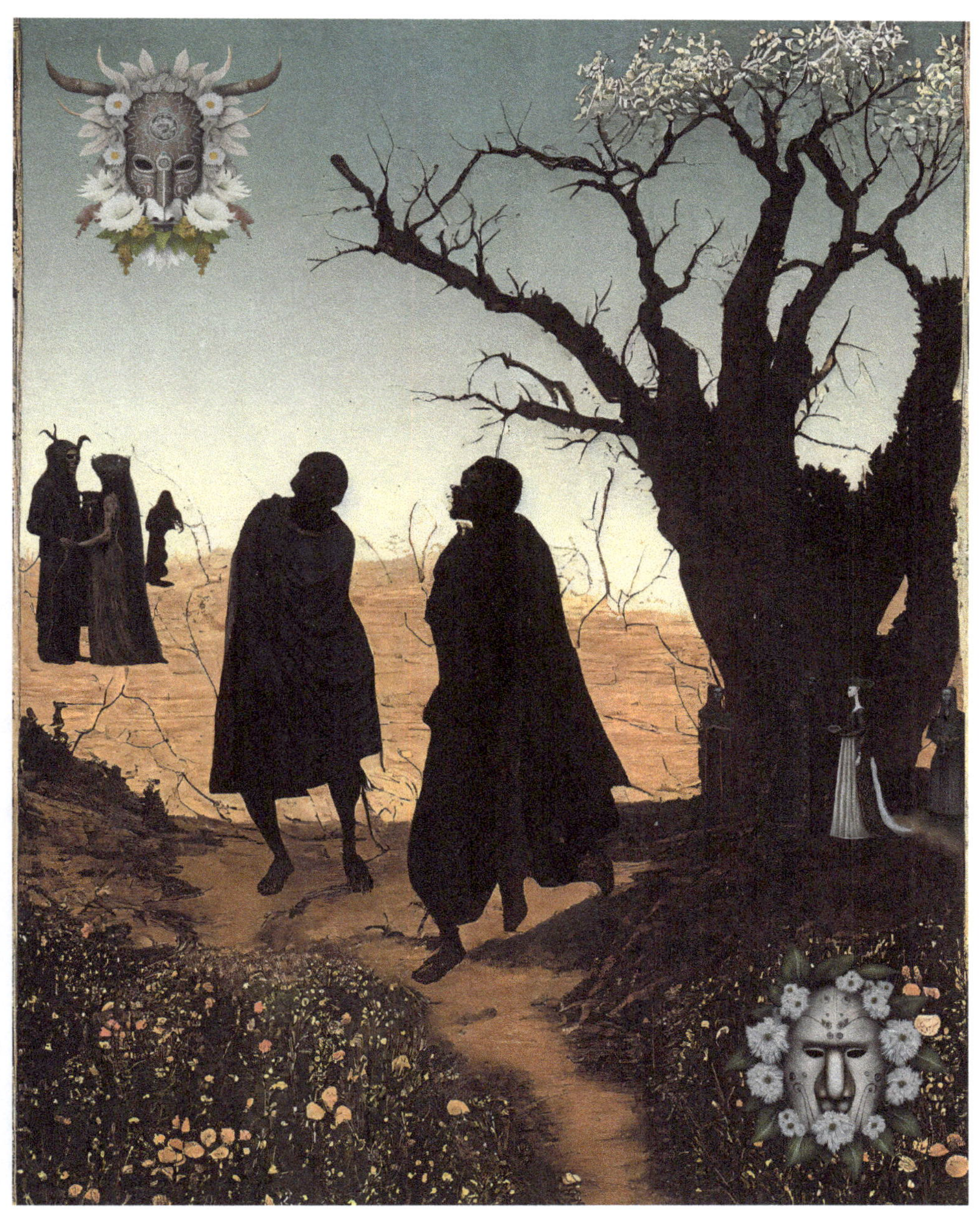

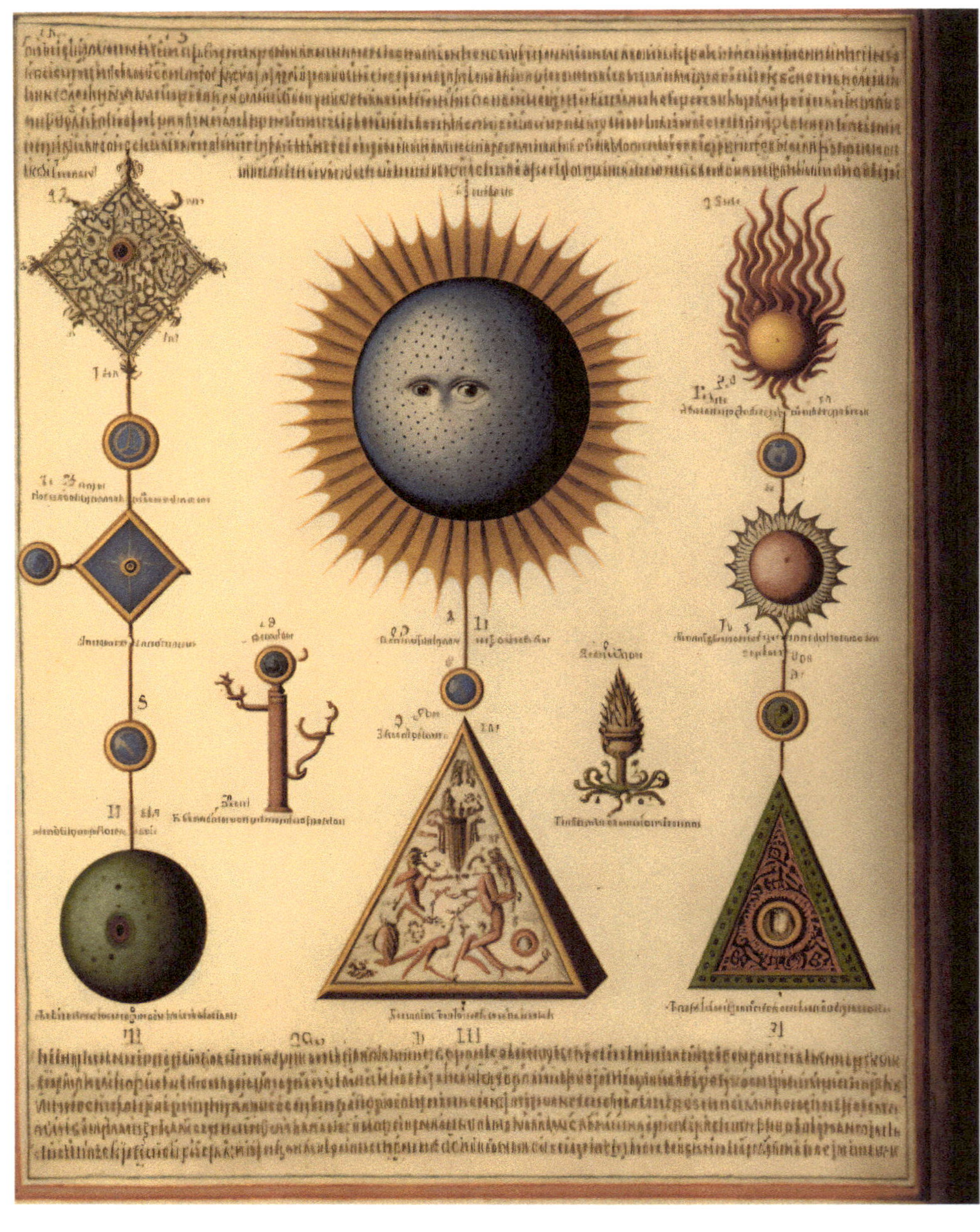

IV.21 Libra III ... a man upon a donkey, and before him a wolf. (Picatrix[†]2.XI§23)

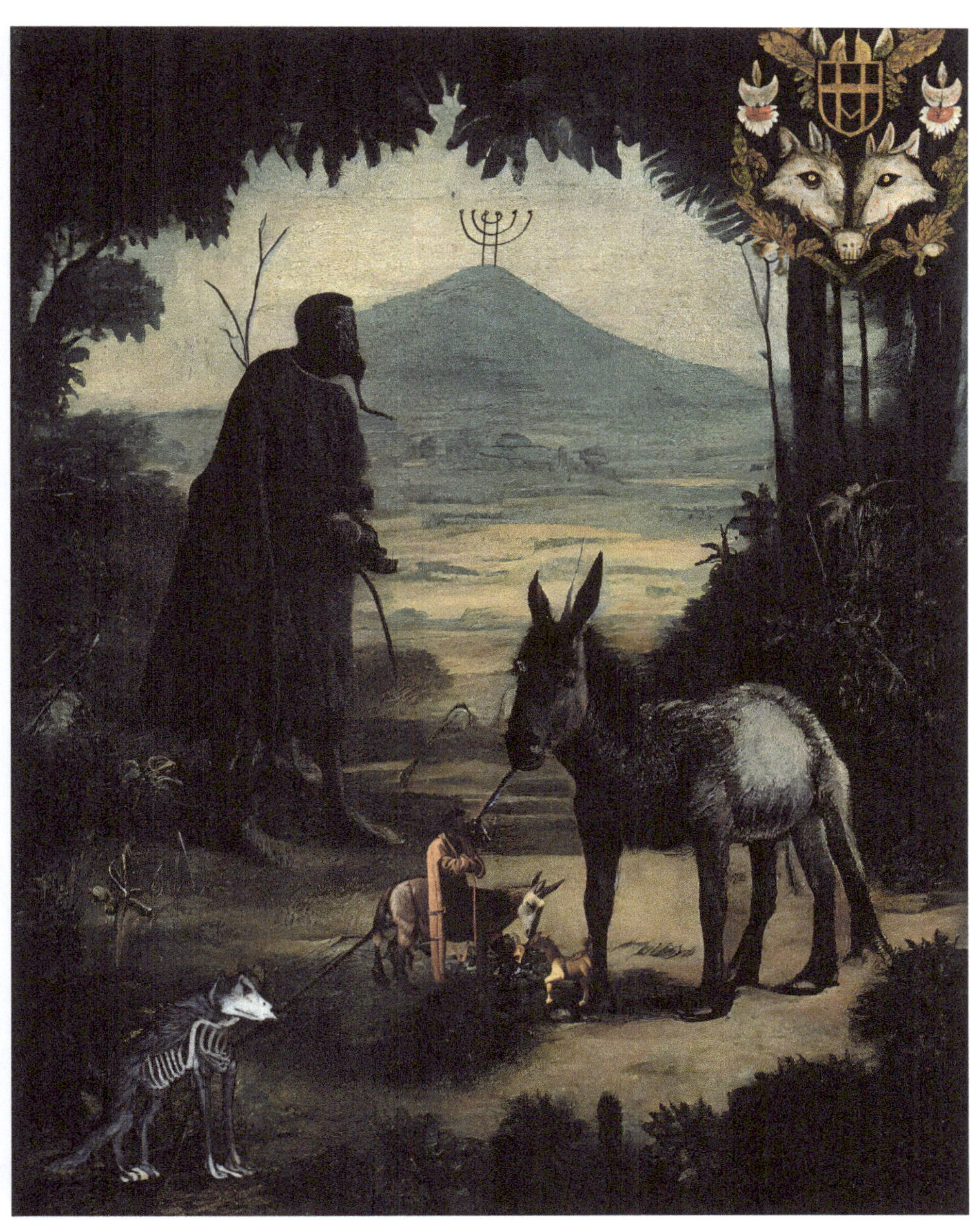

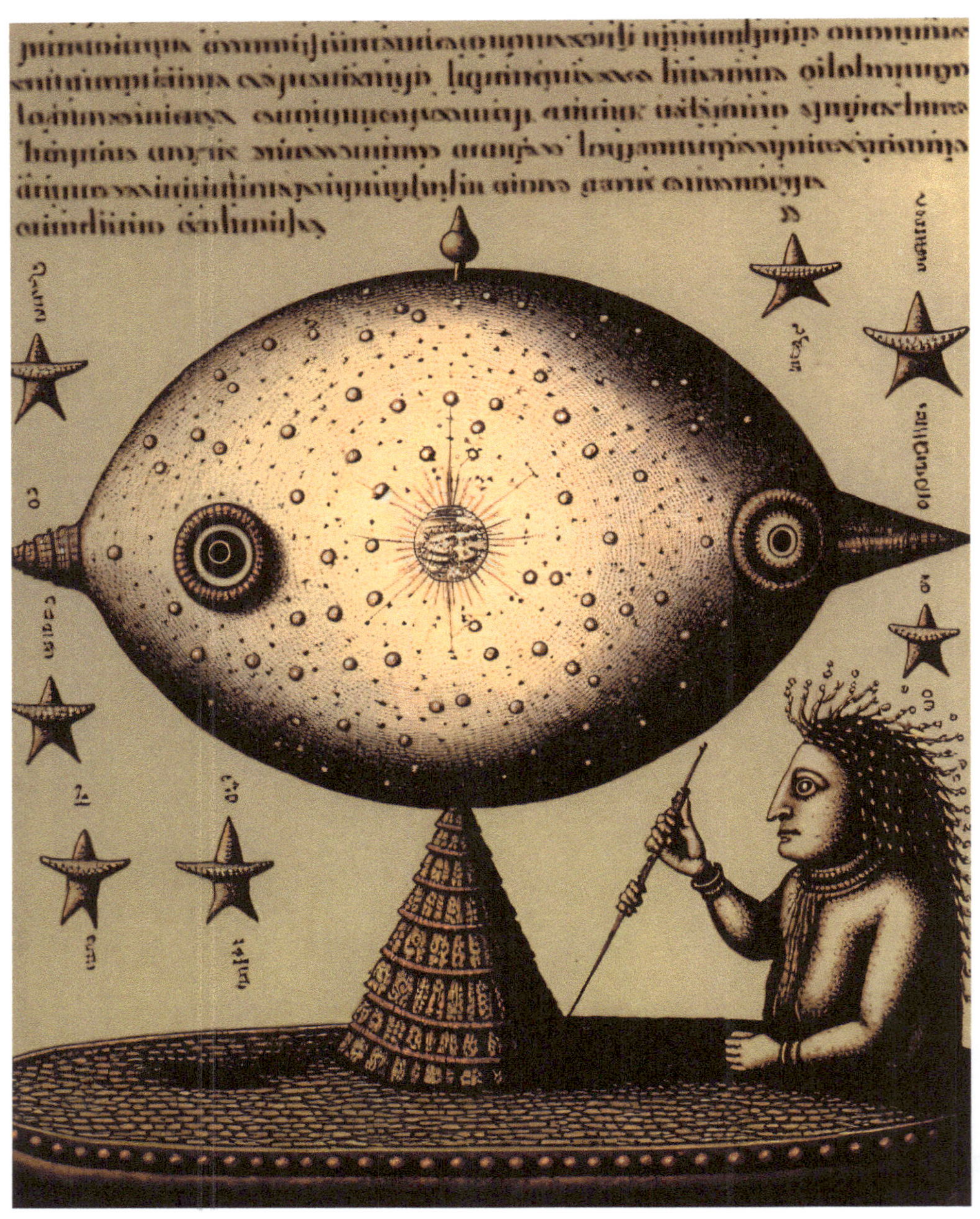

IV.22 Scorpio I … a man holding a lance in his right hand, but a human head in his left. (Picatrix[†]2.XI§24)

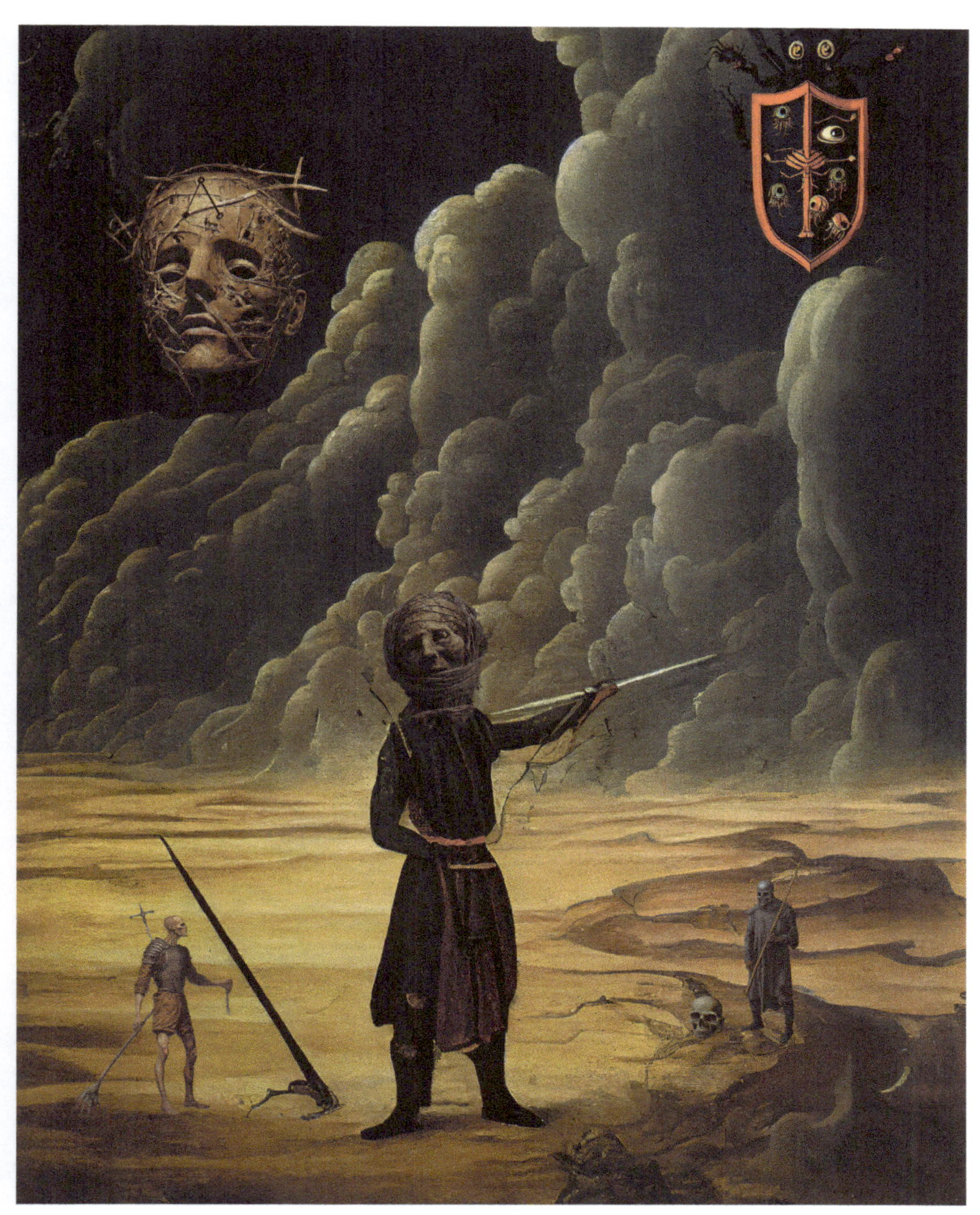

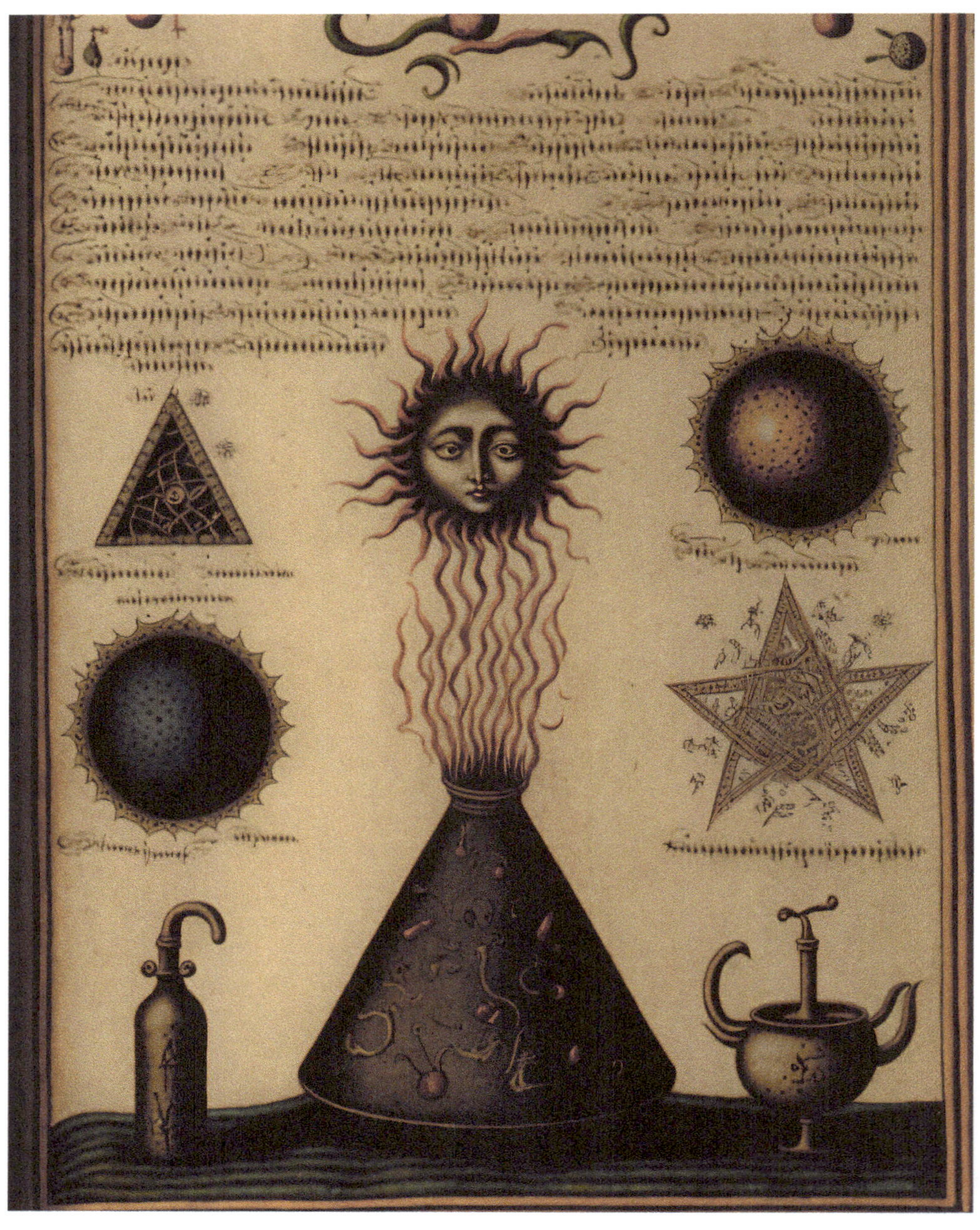

IV.23 Scorpio II ... a man riding upon a camel holding a scorpion in his hand. (Picatrix[†]2.XI§25)

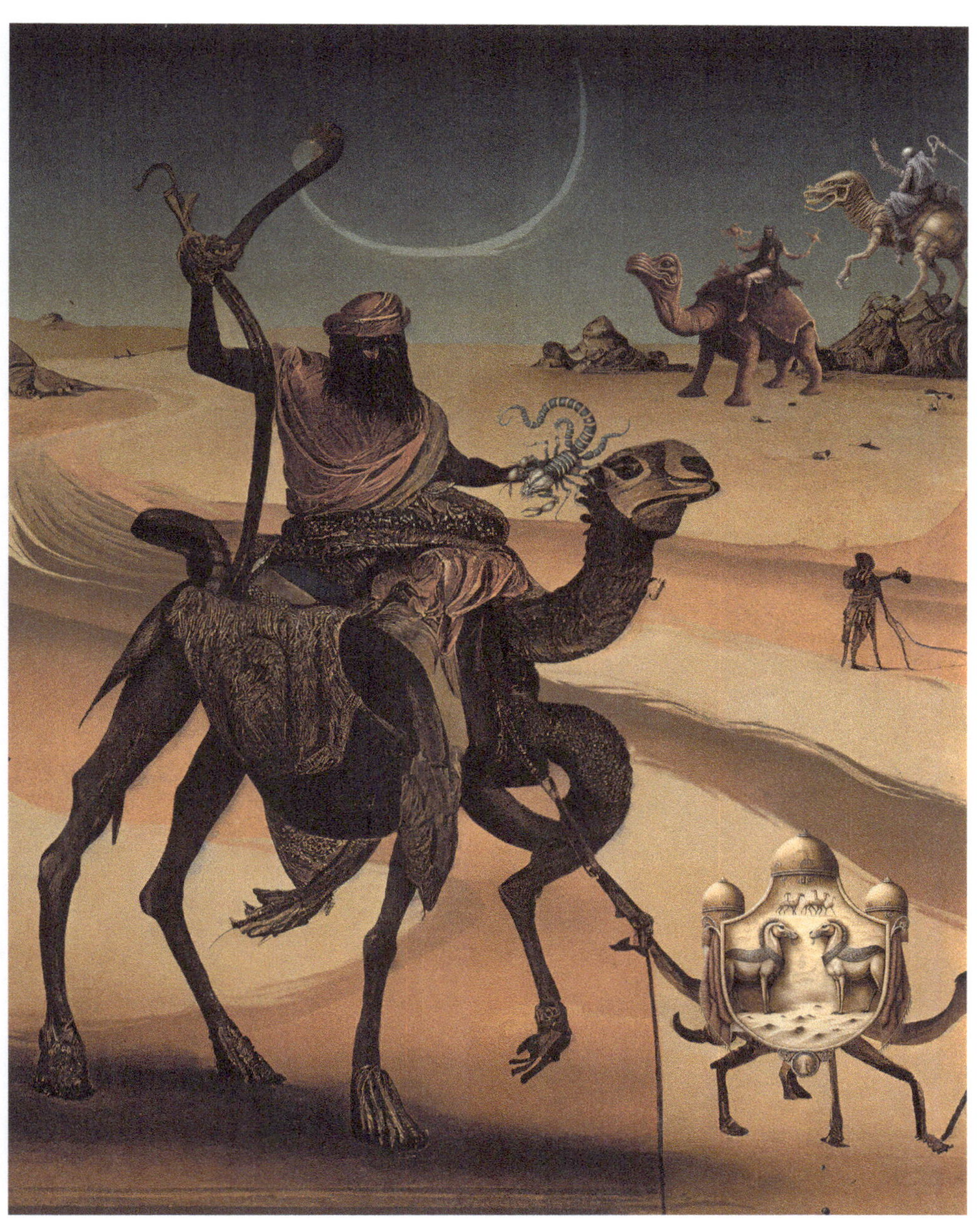

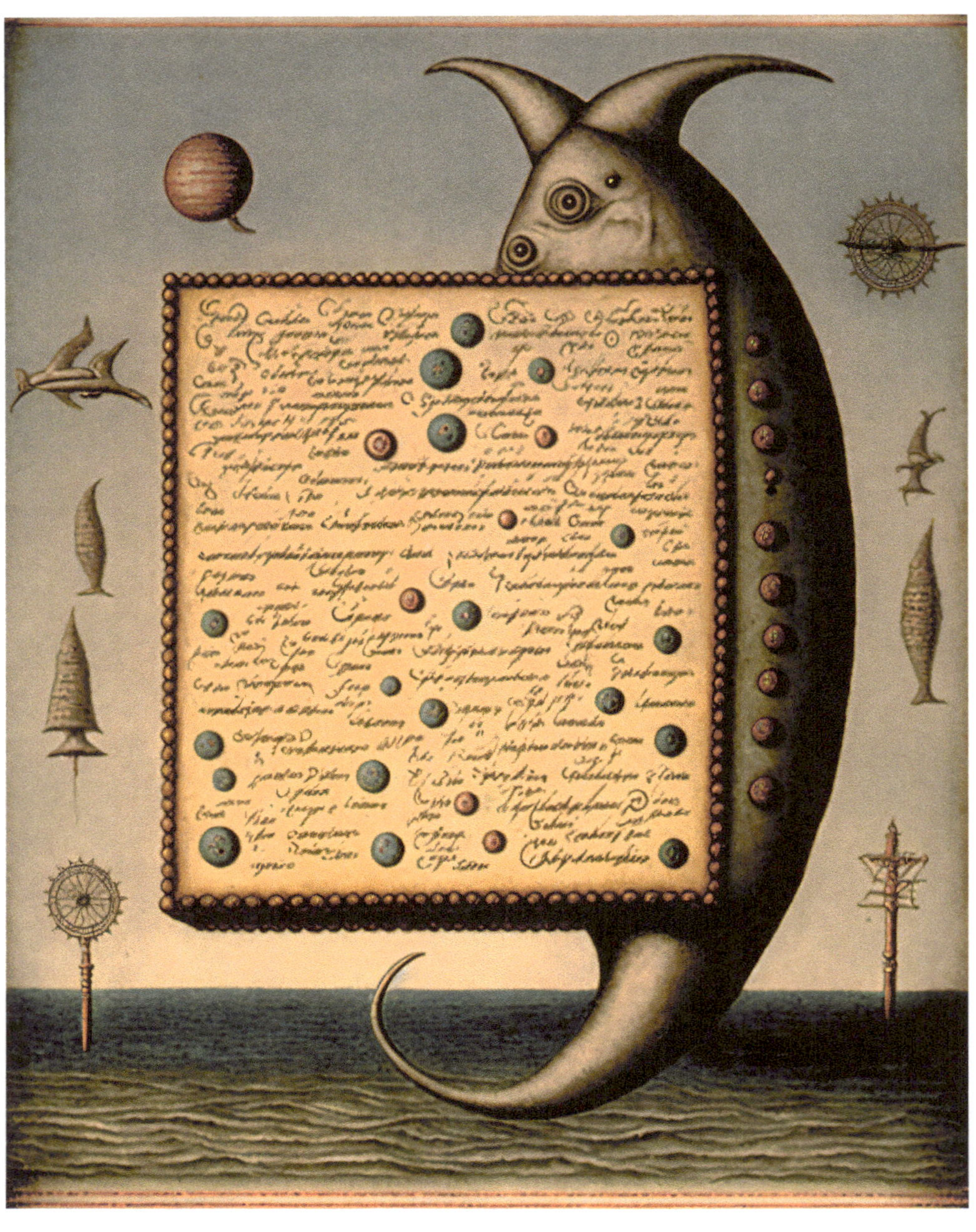

IV.24 Scorpio III … a horse and a rabbit with it. (Picatrix†2.XI§26)

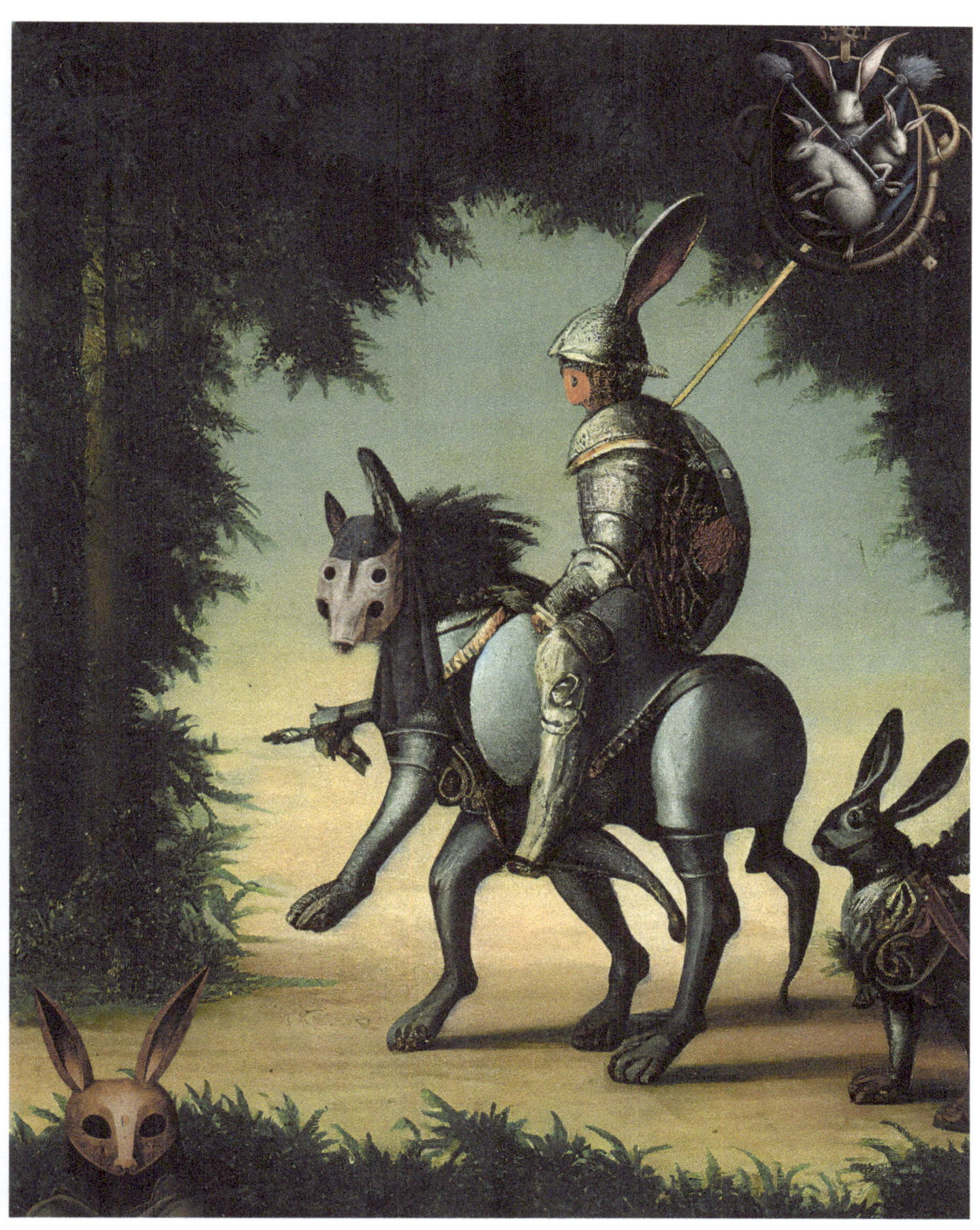

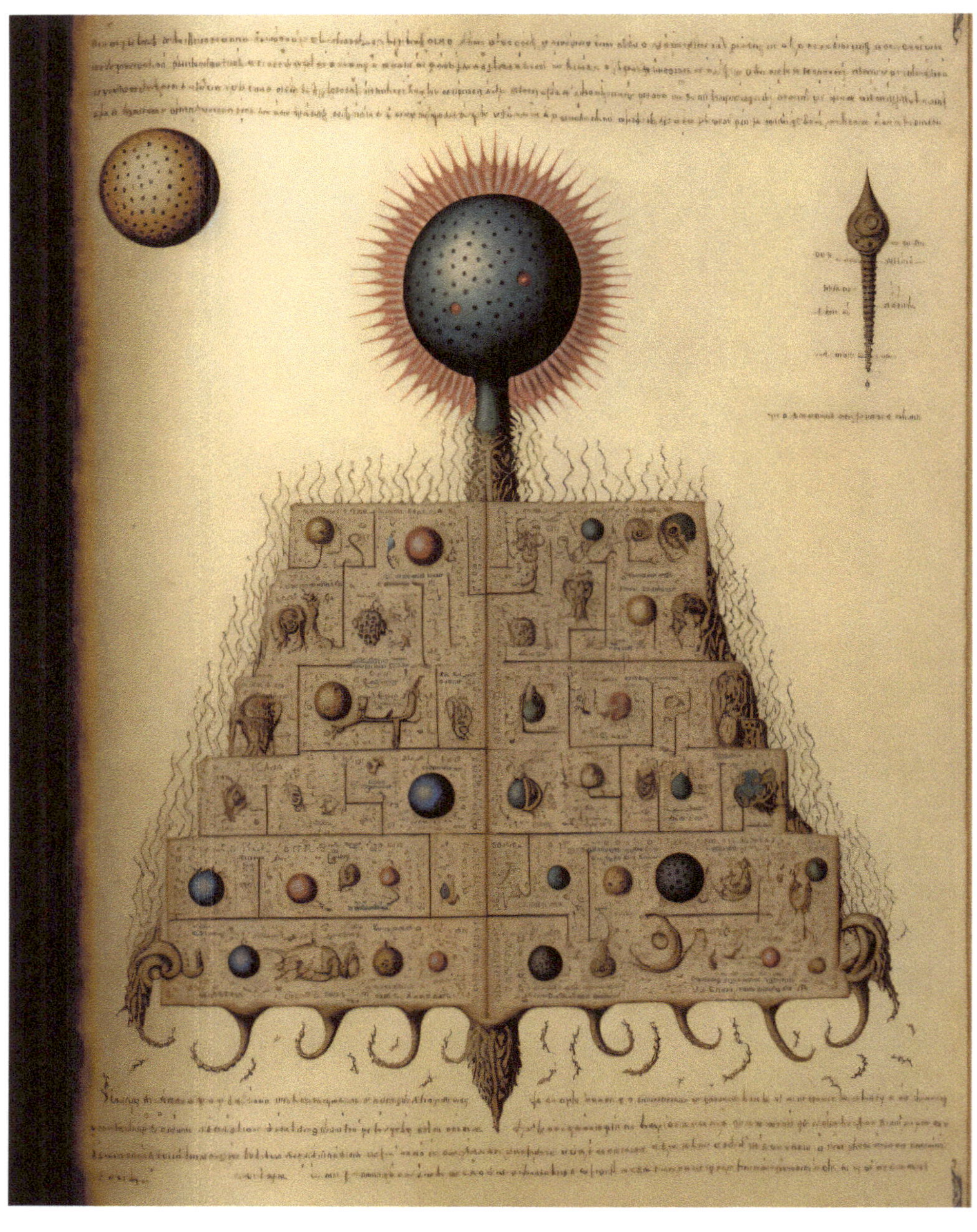

IV.25 Sagittarius I ... three bodies of men of which one is yellow, another white, but the third red. (Picatrix[†]2.XI§27)

/Oracle of DelphΛI

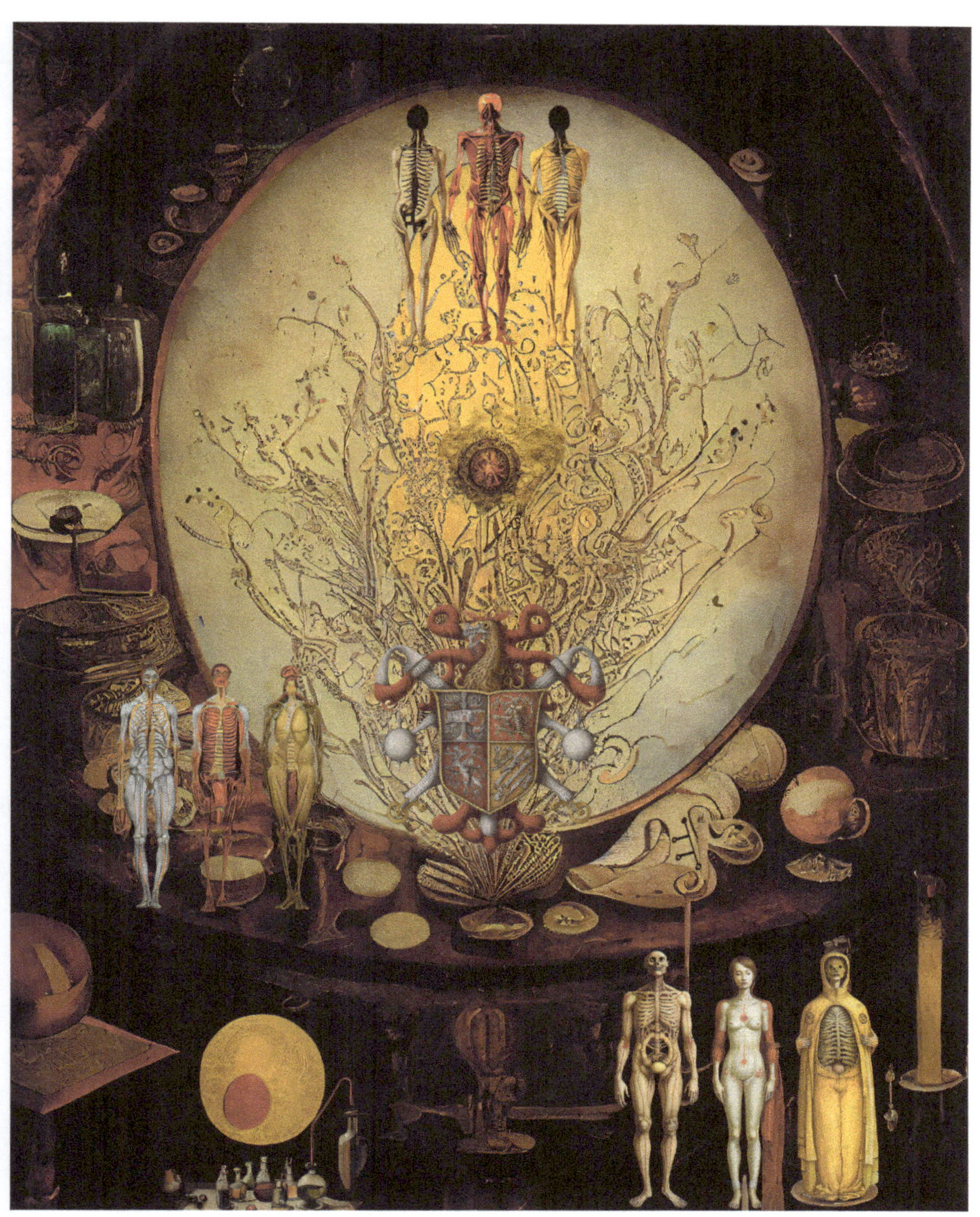

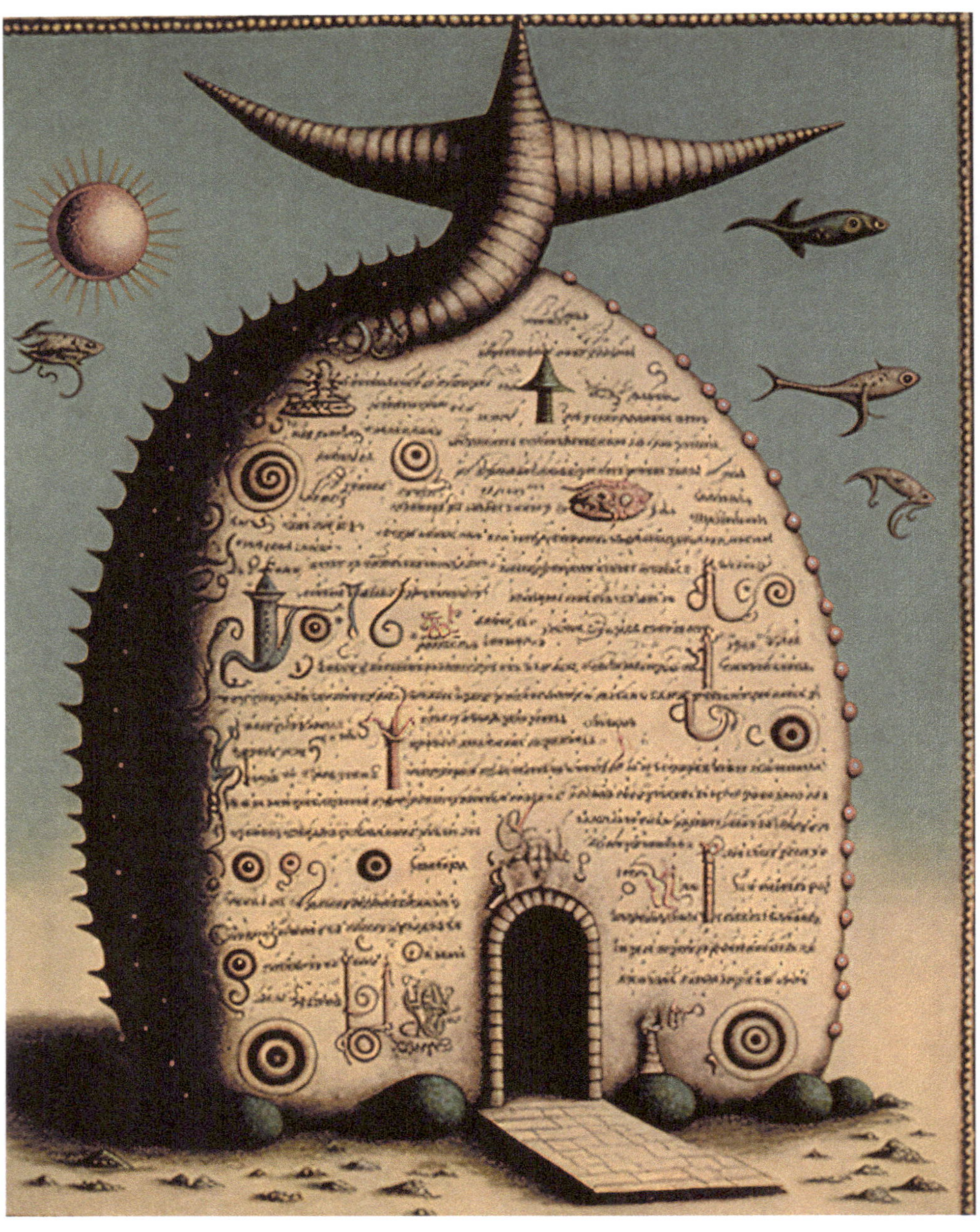

IV.26 Sagittarius II … a man leading two cows with a monkey and a bear before him.
(Picatrix‡2.XI§28)

/Oracle of DelphΛI

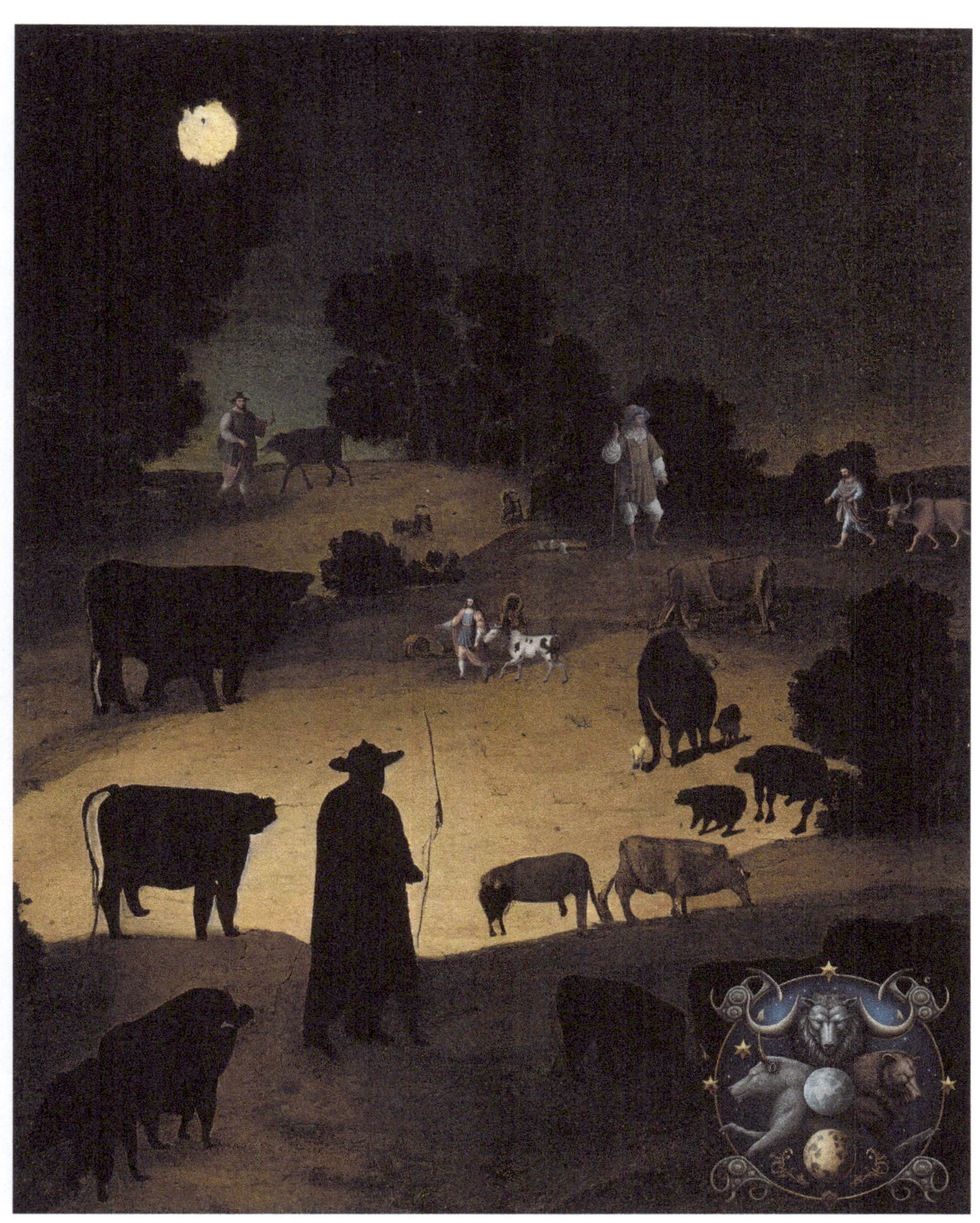

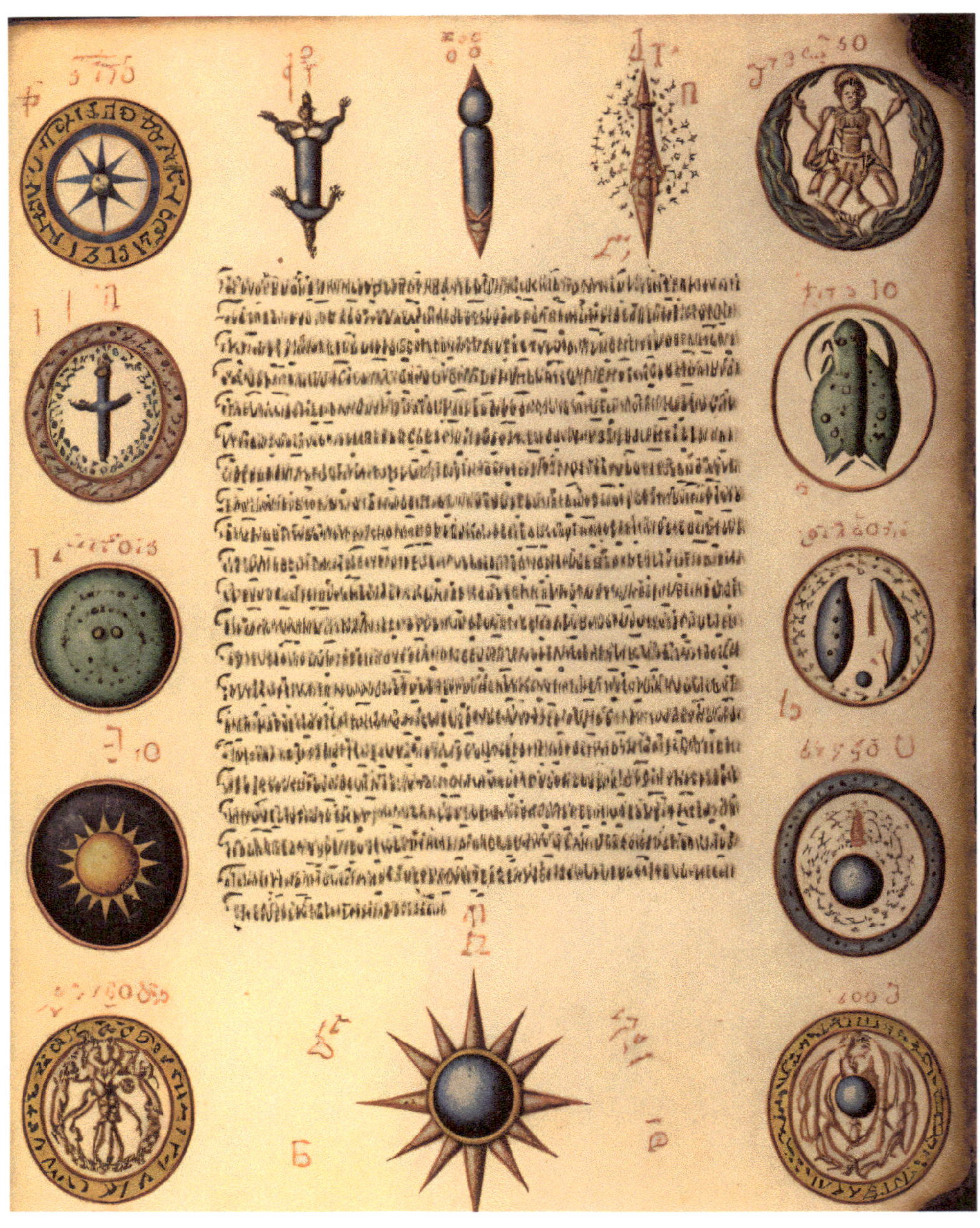

IV.27 Sagittarius III ... a man with a hat on his head killing another man. (Picatrix‡ 2.XI§29)

/Oracle of DelphΛI

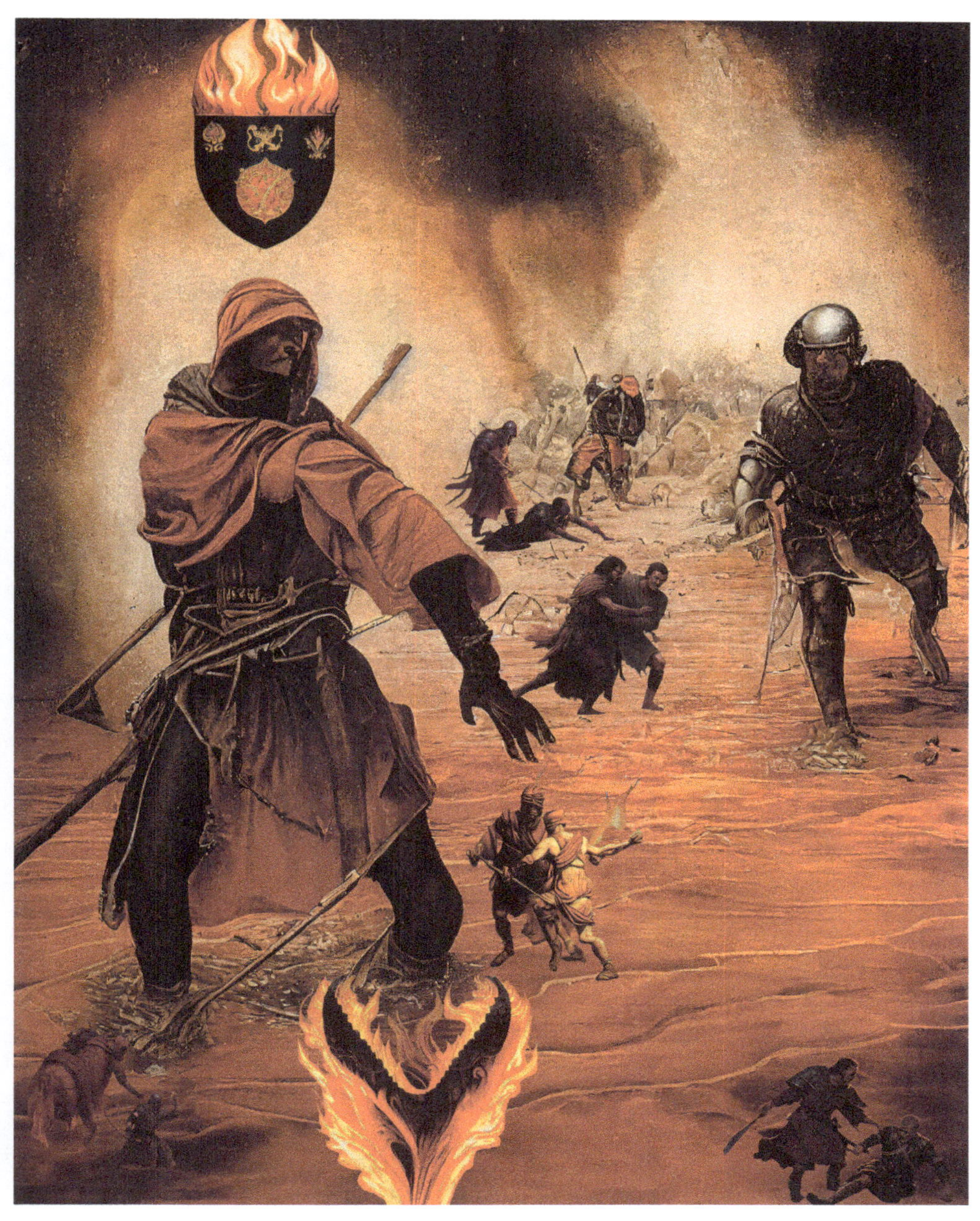

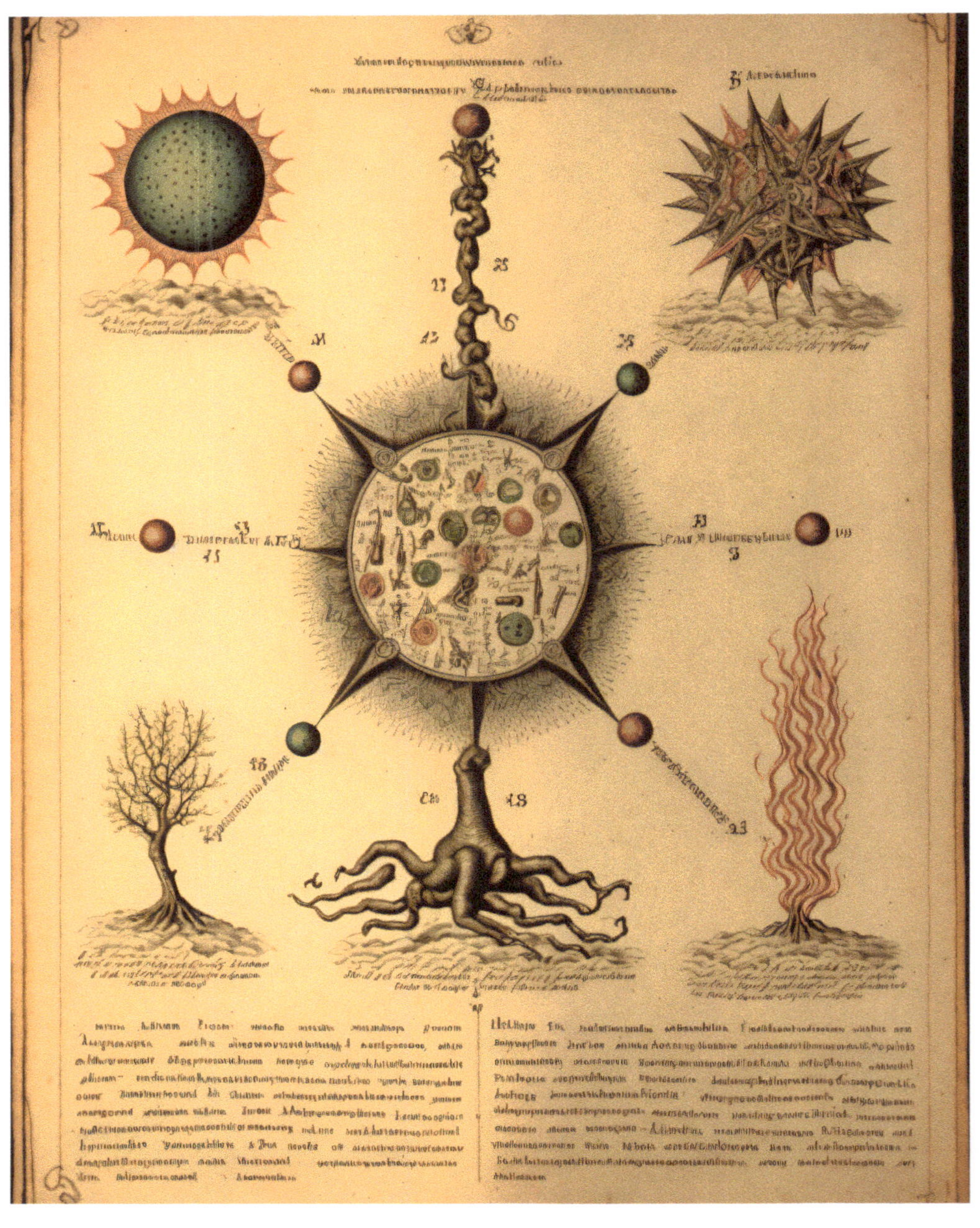

IV.28 Capricorn I ... a man holding a pipe in his right hand but a hoe in his left hand.
(Picatrix†2.XI§30)

/Oracle of DelphAI

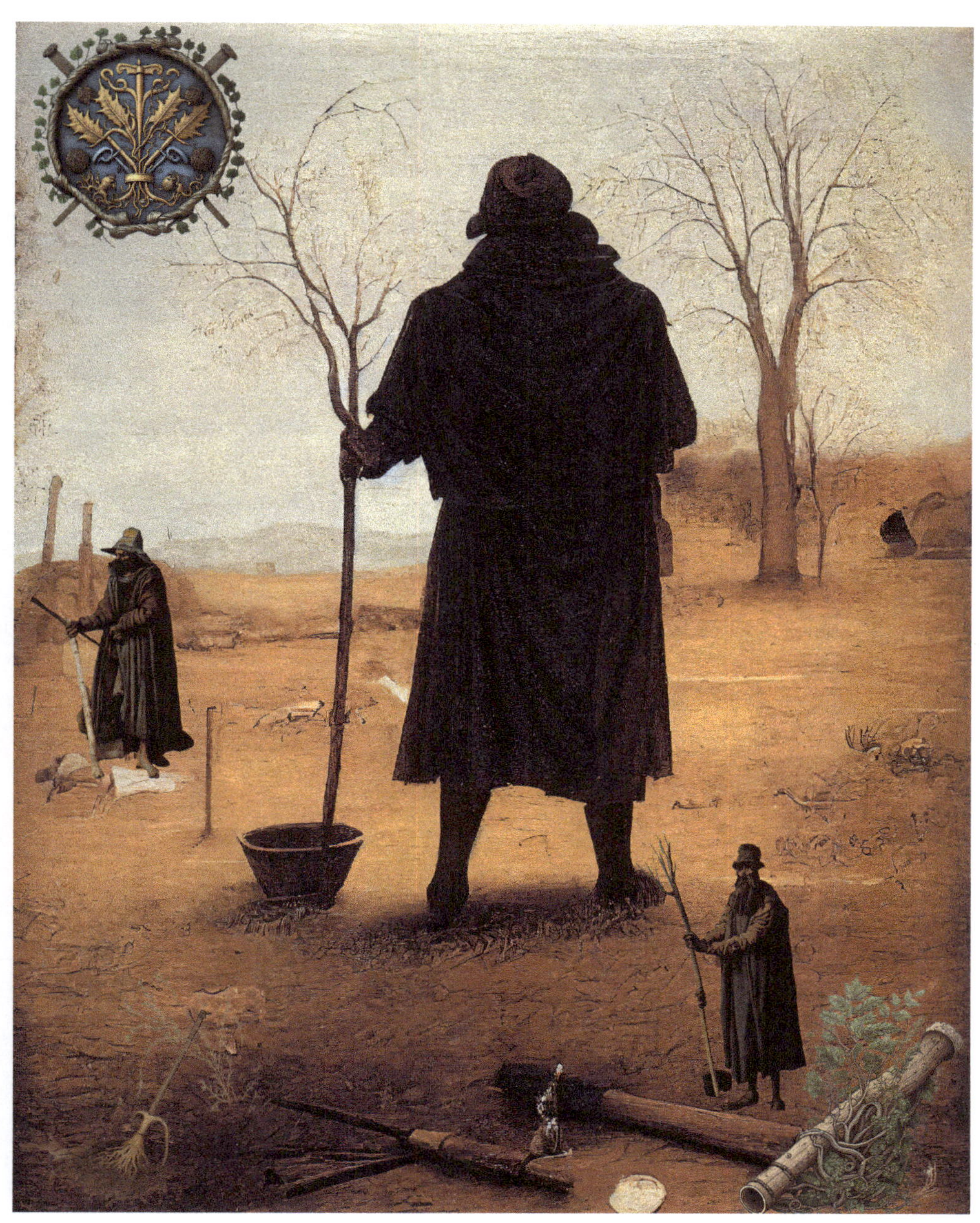

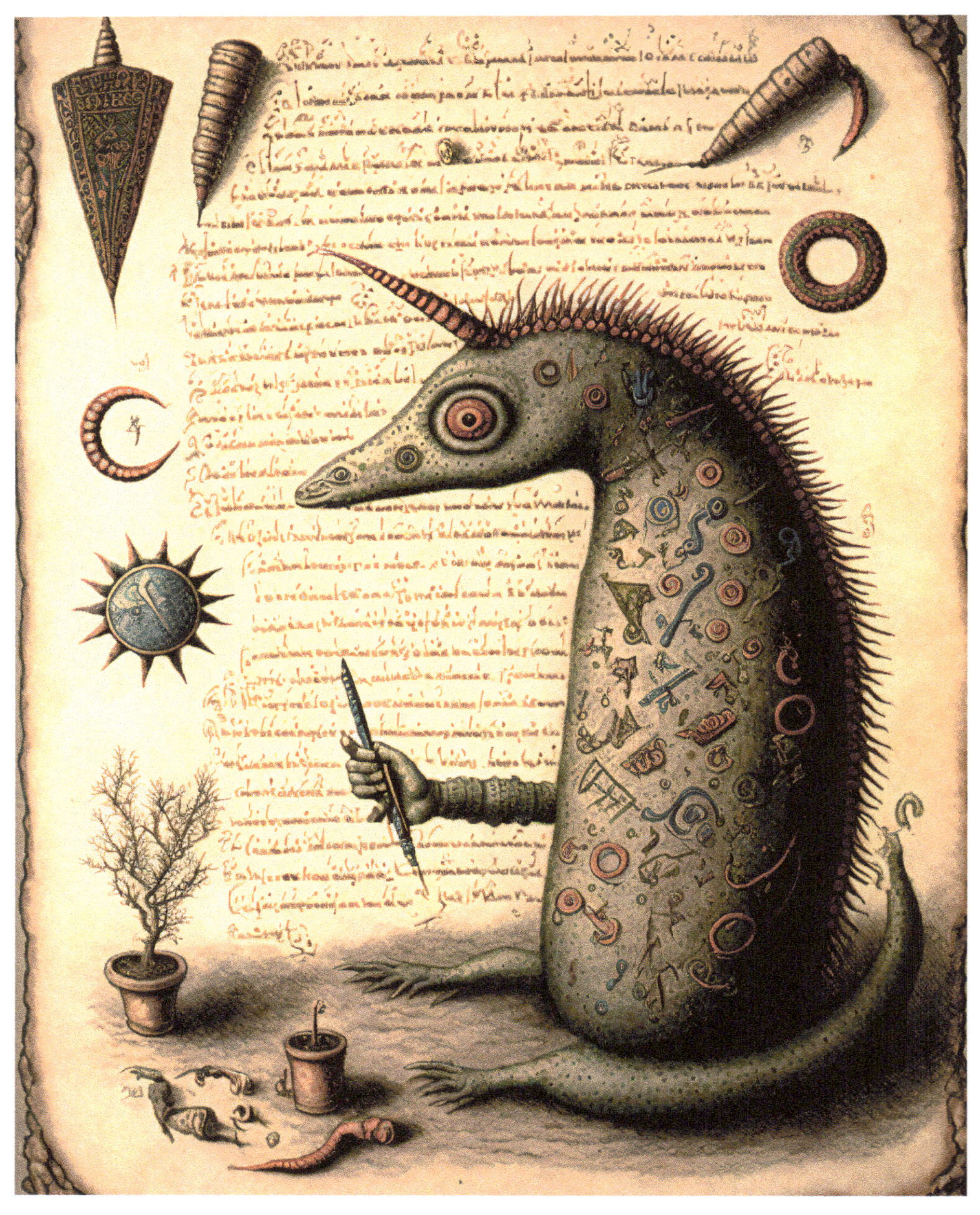

IV.29 Capricorn II … a man having before him half of a monkey. (Picatrix[†]2.XI§31)

/Oracle of DelphAI

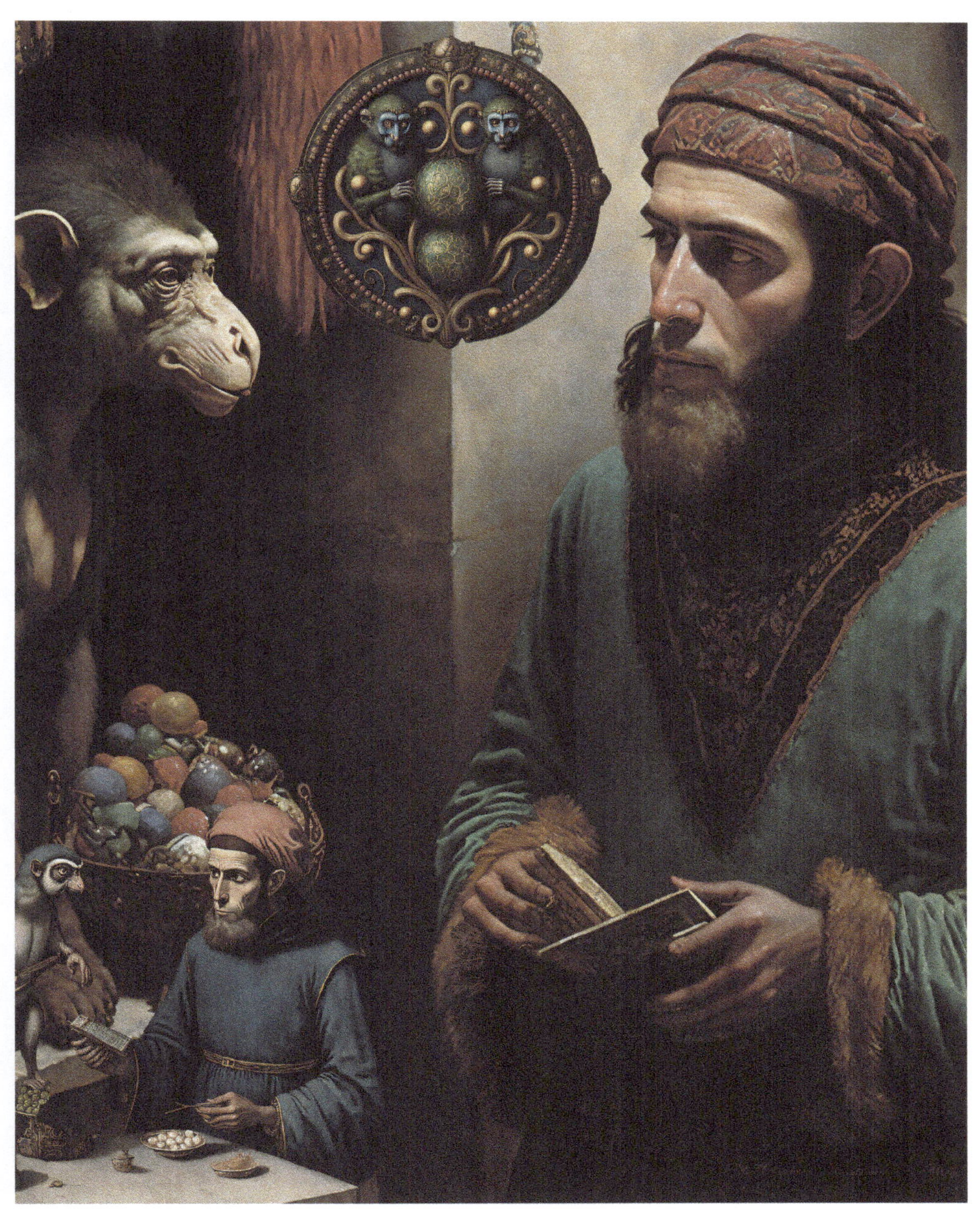

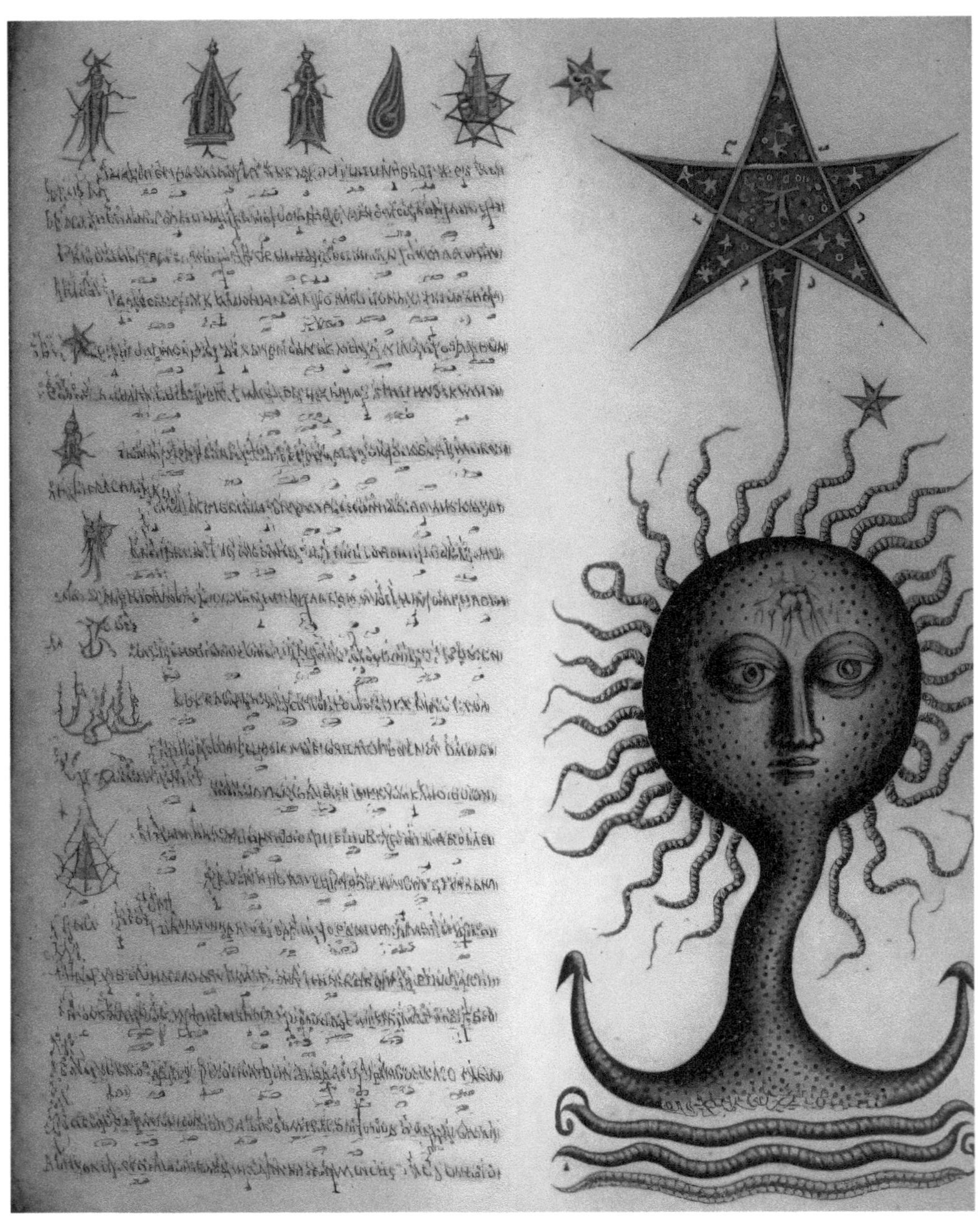

IV.30 Capricorn III ... a man holding a book and opening and closing it, and having before the book the tail of a fish. (Picatrix[†]2.XI§32)

/Oracle of DelphΛI

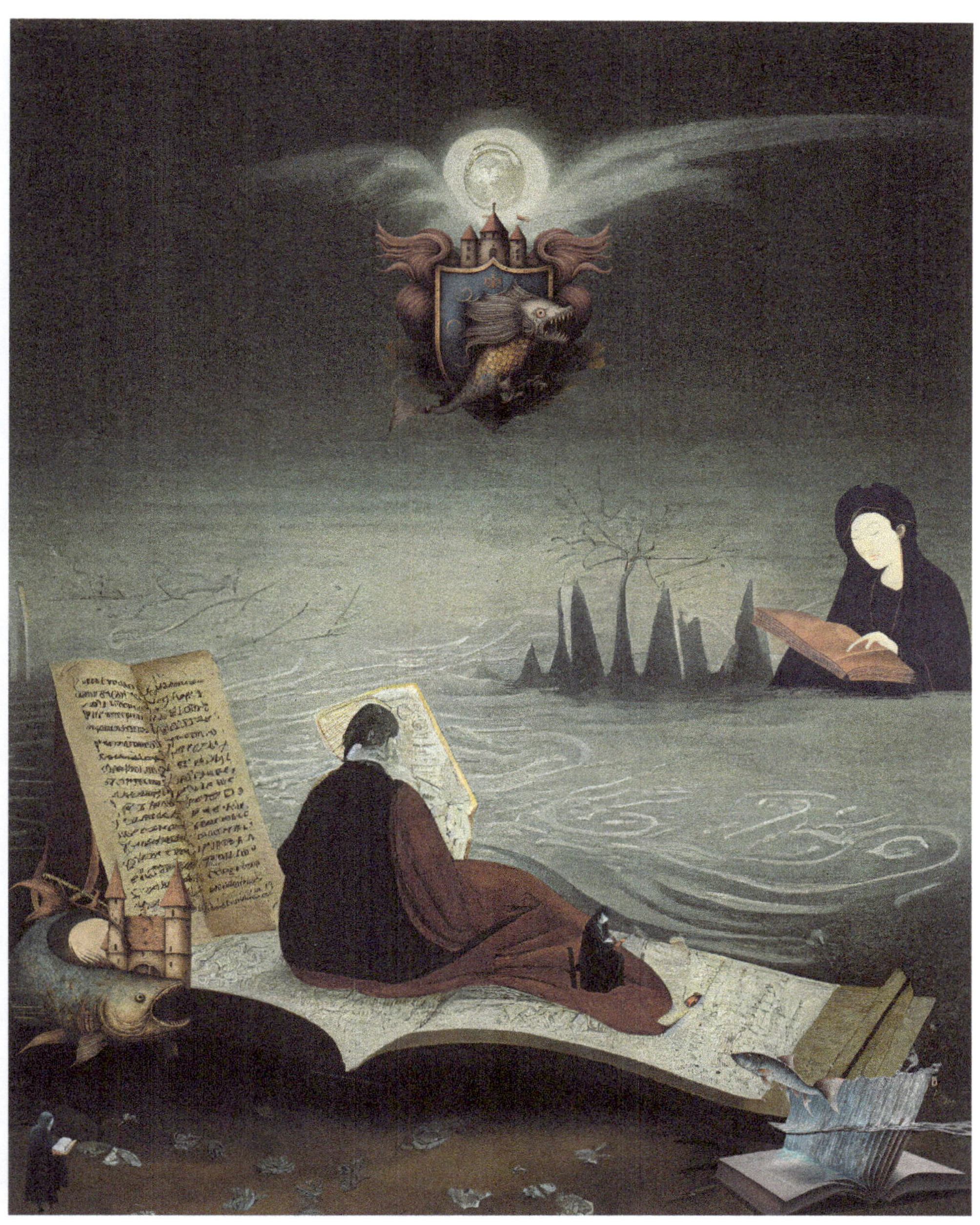

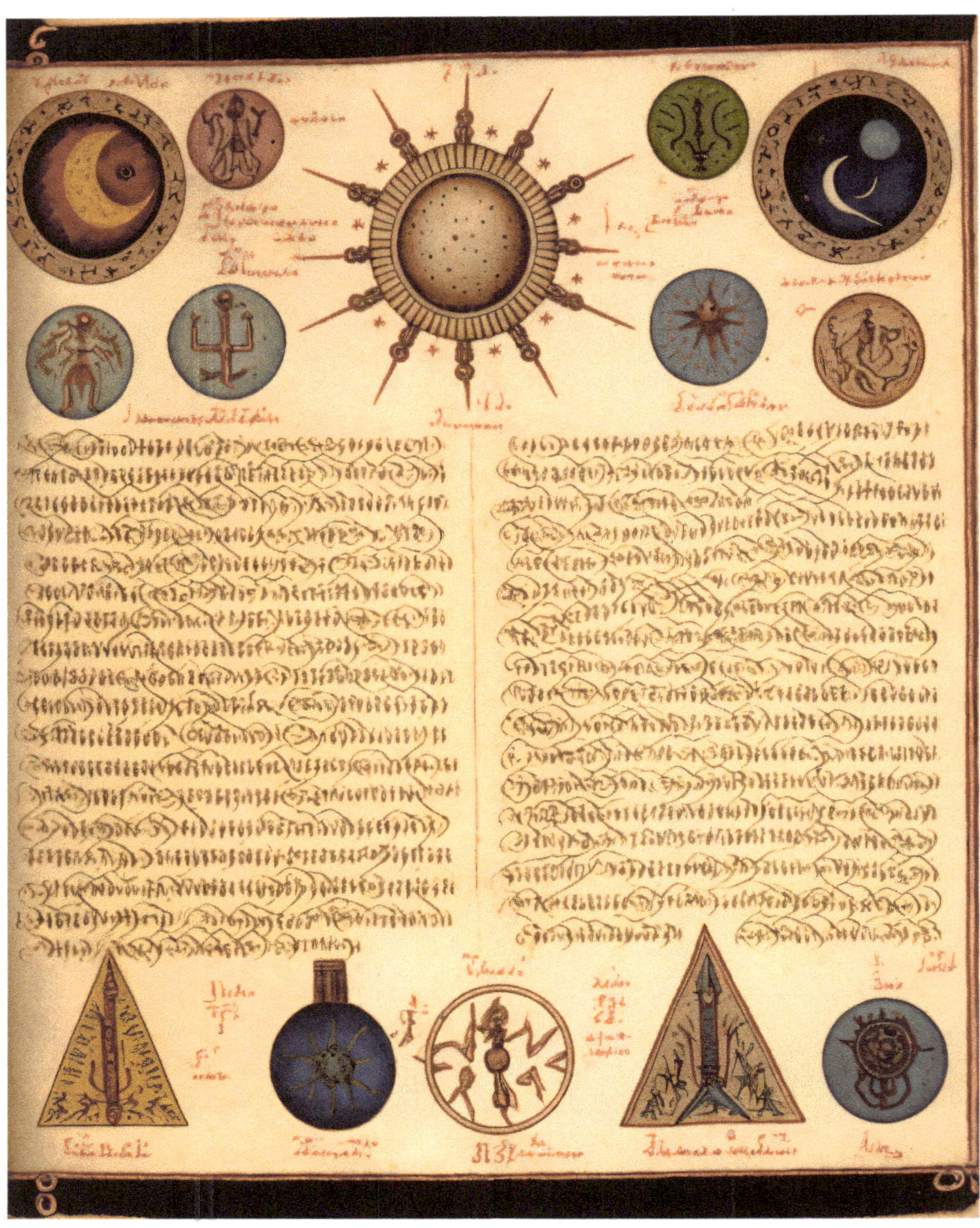

IV.31 Aquarius I ... a man who has his head cut short and who holds in his hand a peacock. (Picatrix†2.XI§33)

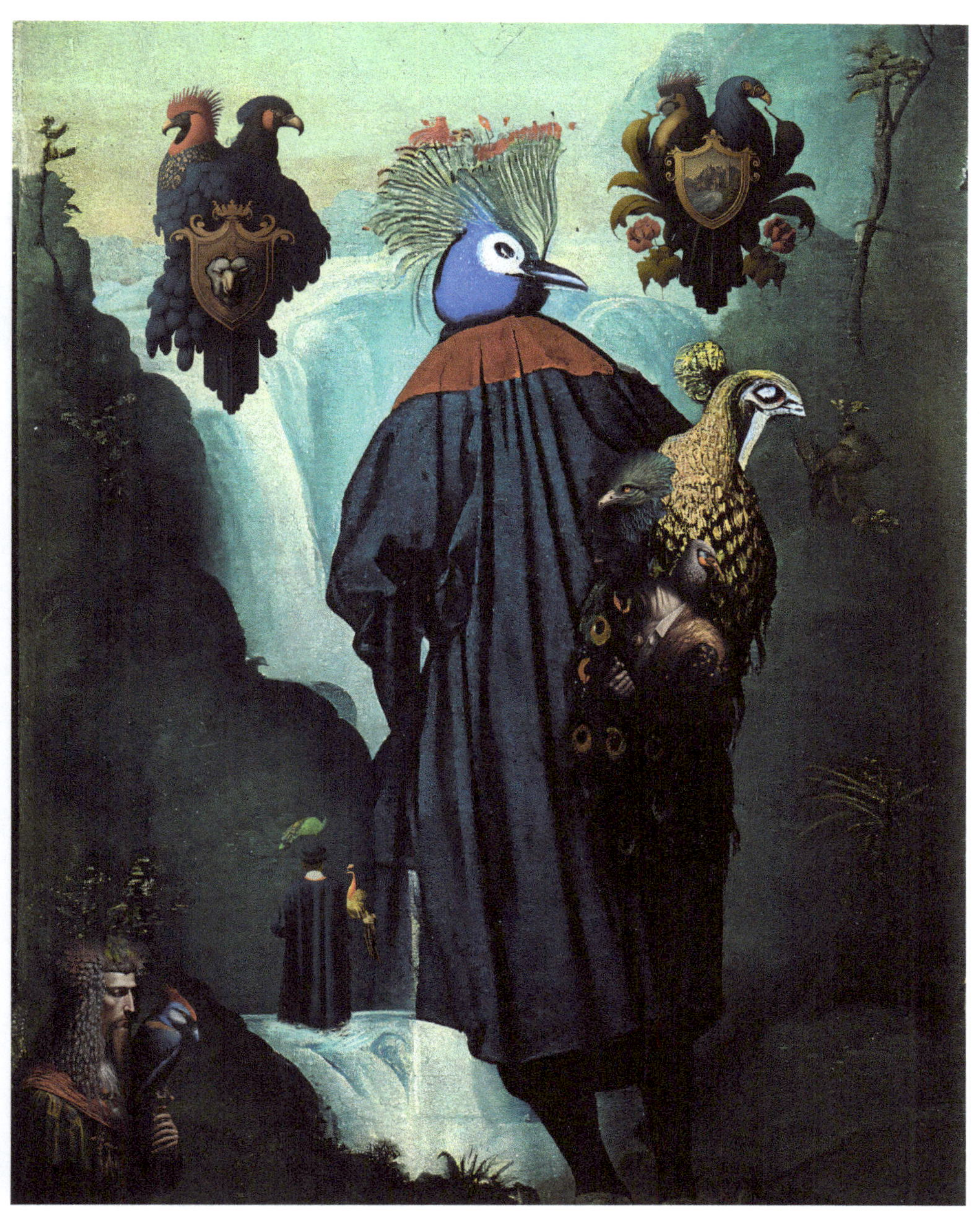

/169

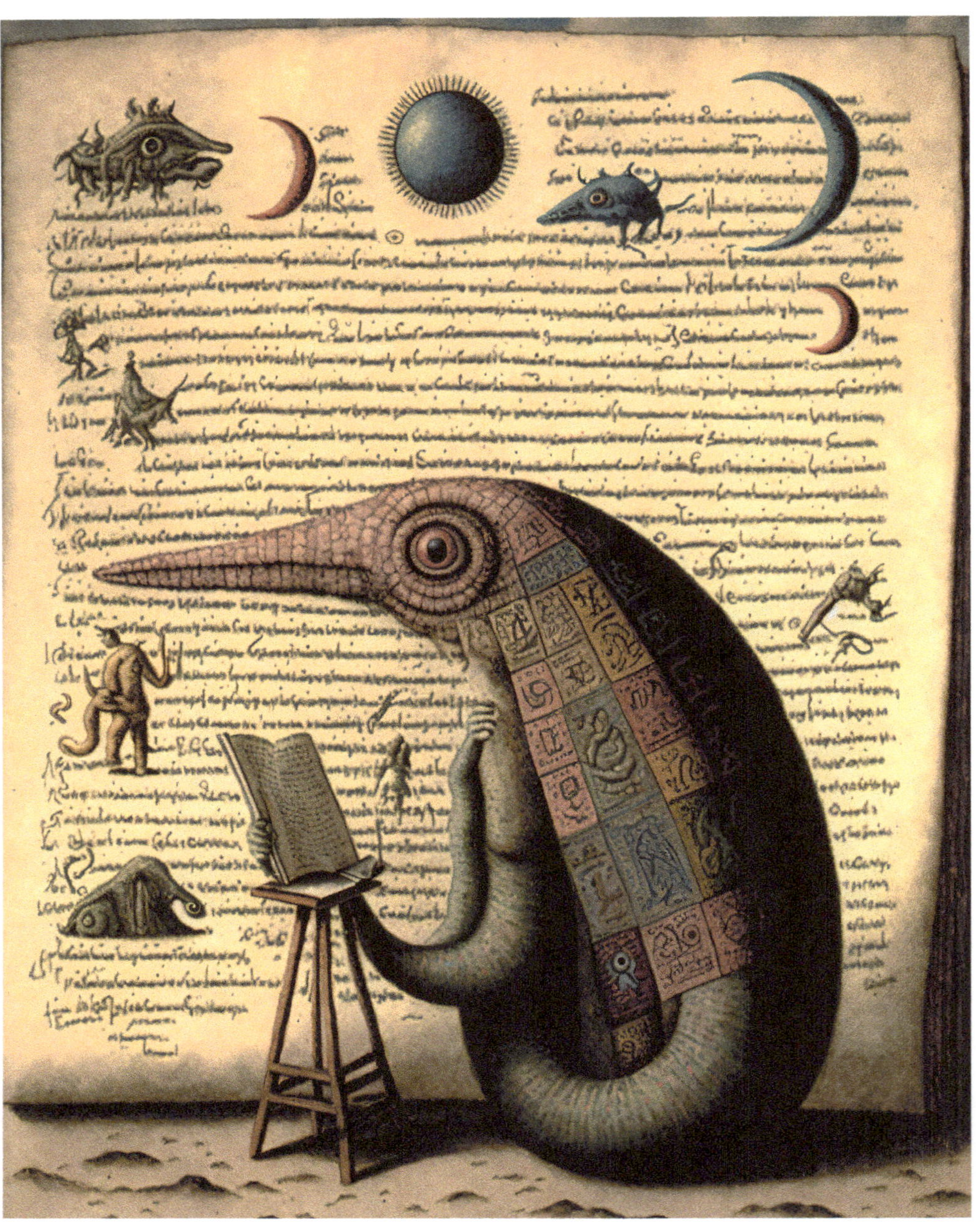

IV.32 Aquarius II ... a man similar to a king who permits himself much and abhors those he sees. (Picatrix‡2.XI§34)

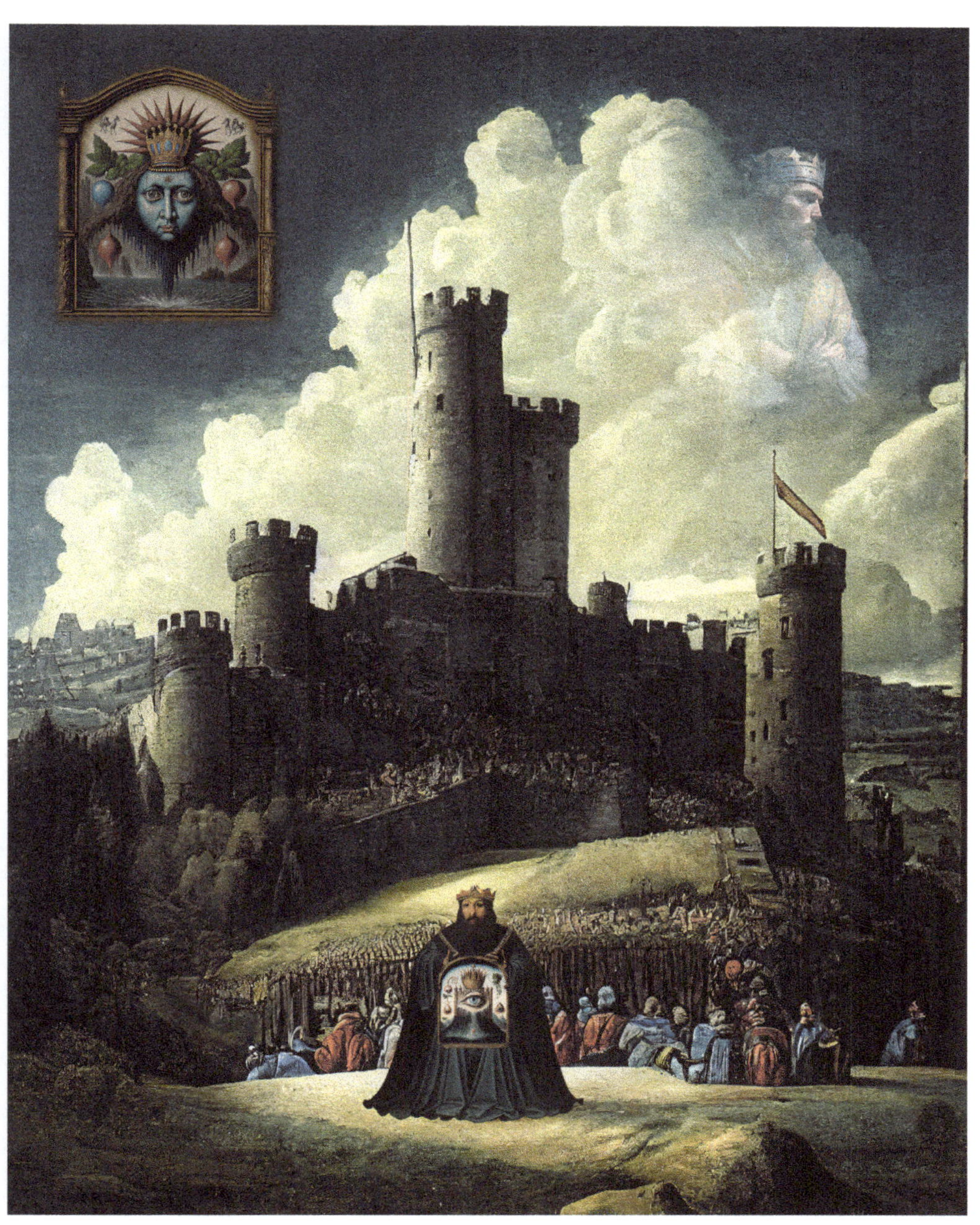

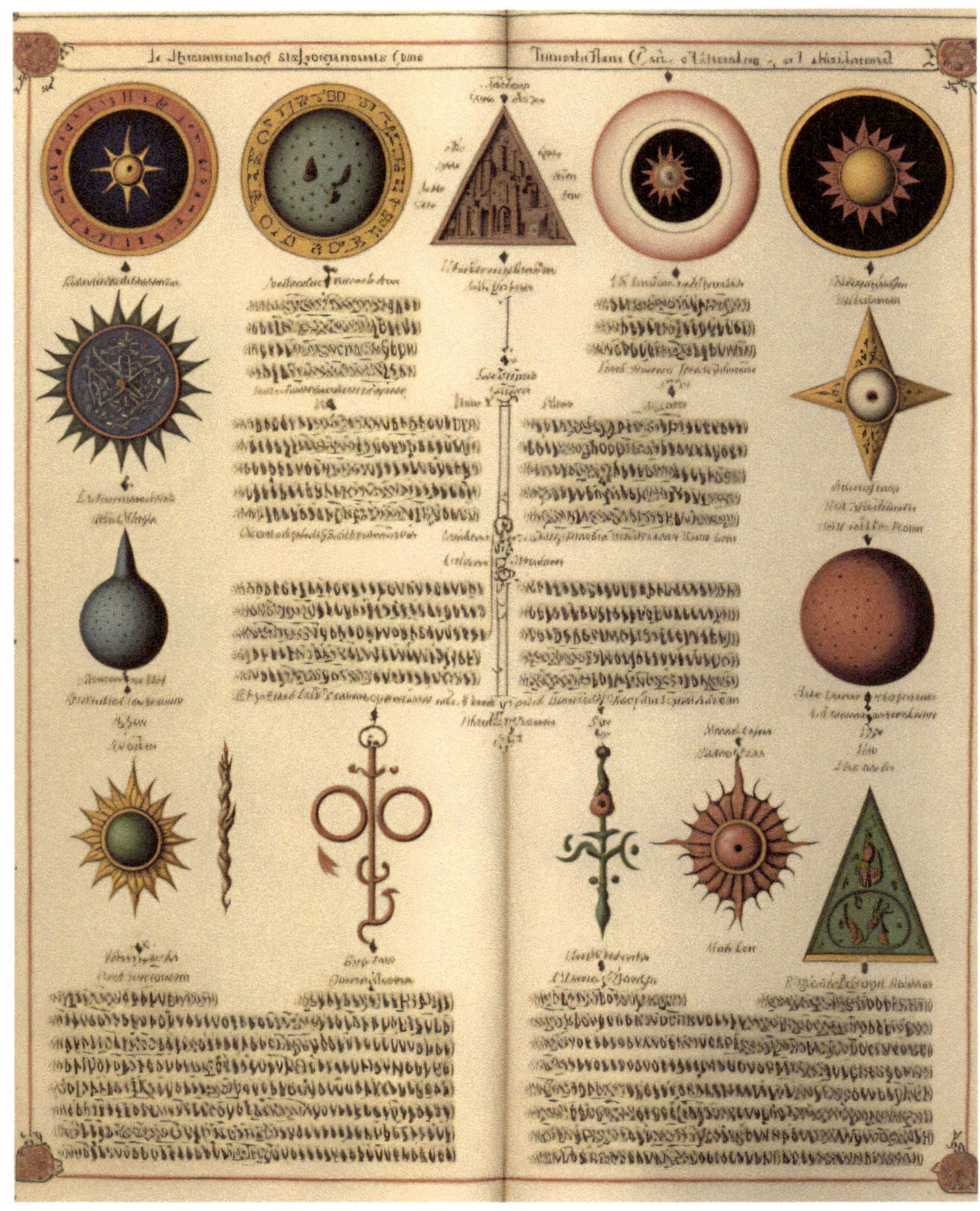

IV.33 Aquarius III ... a man with his head shortened and who has an old woman with him. (Picatrix†2.XI§35)

/Oracle of DelphΛI

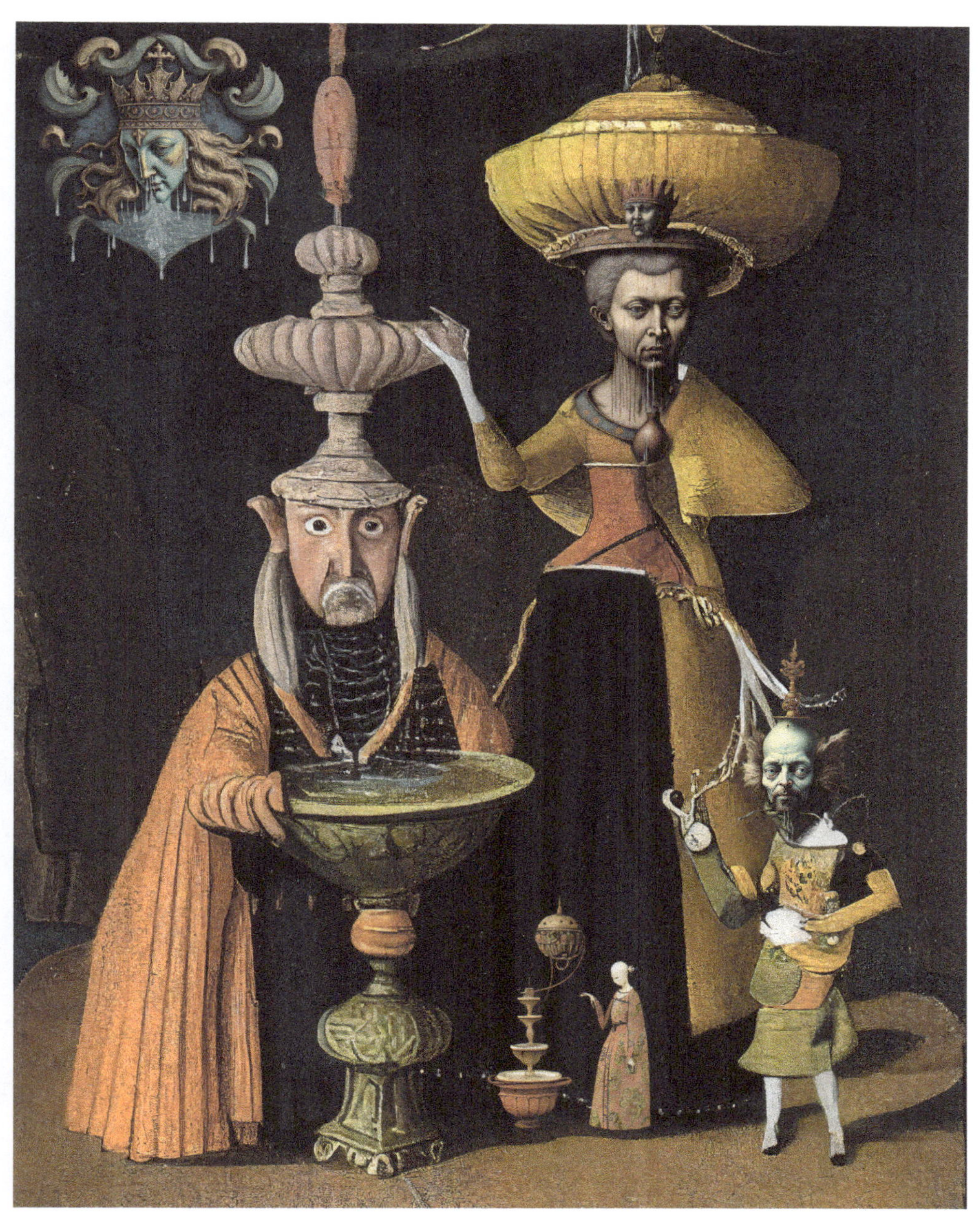

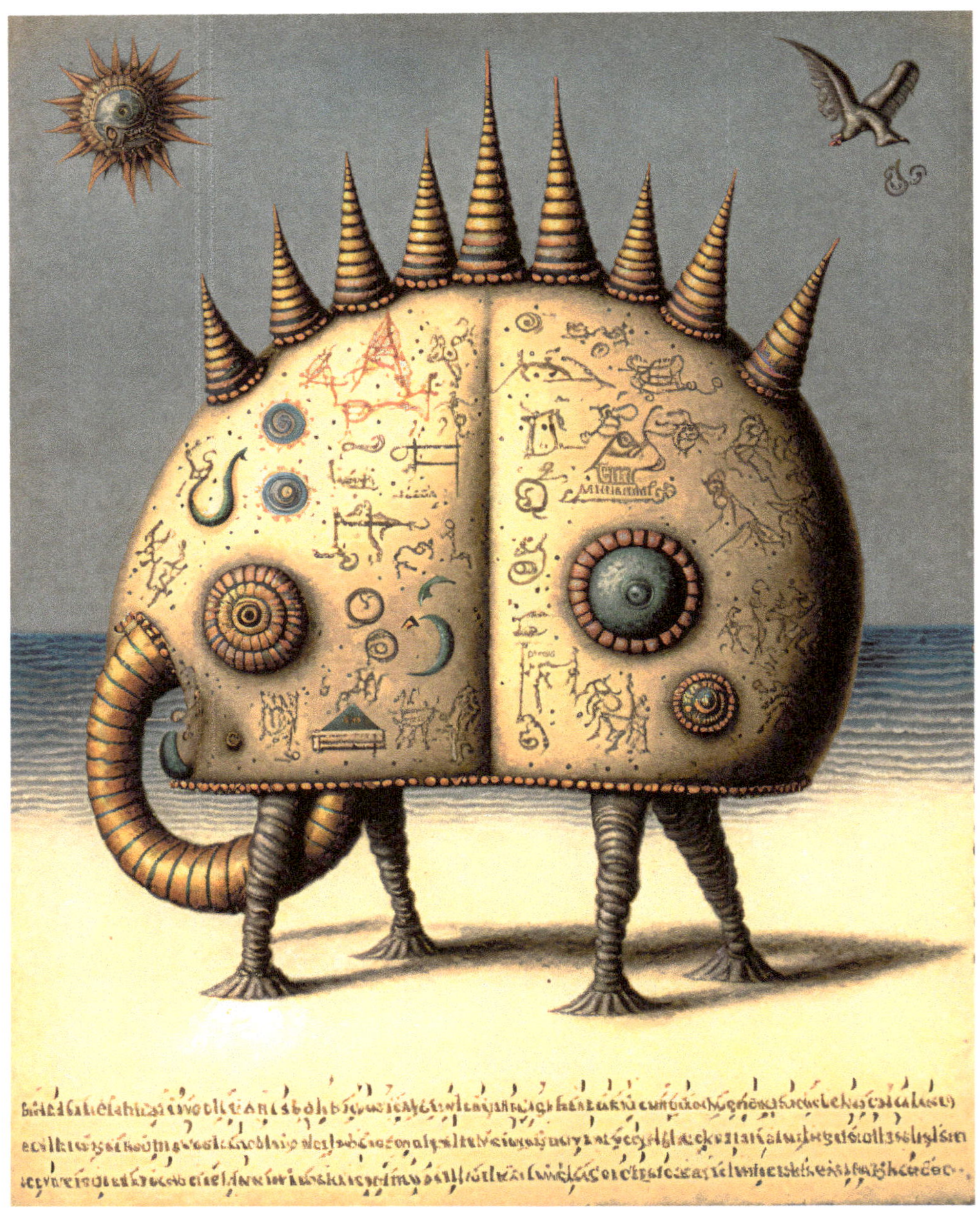

IV.34 Pisces I ... a man with two bodies, appearing as if he were greeting with his hands. (Picatrix‡2.XI§36)

/Oracle of DelphΛI

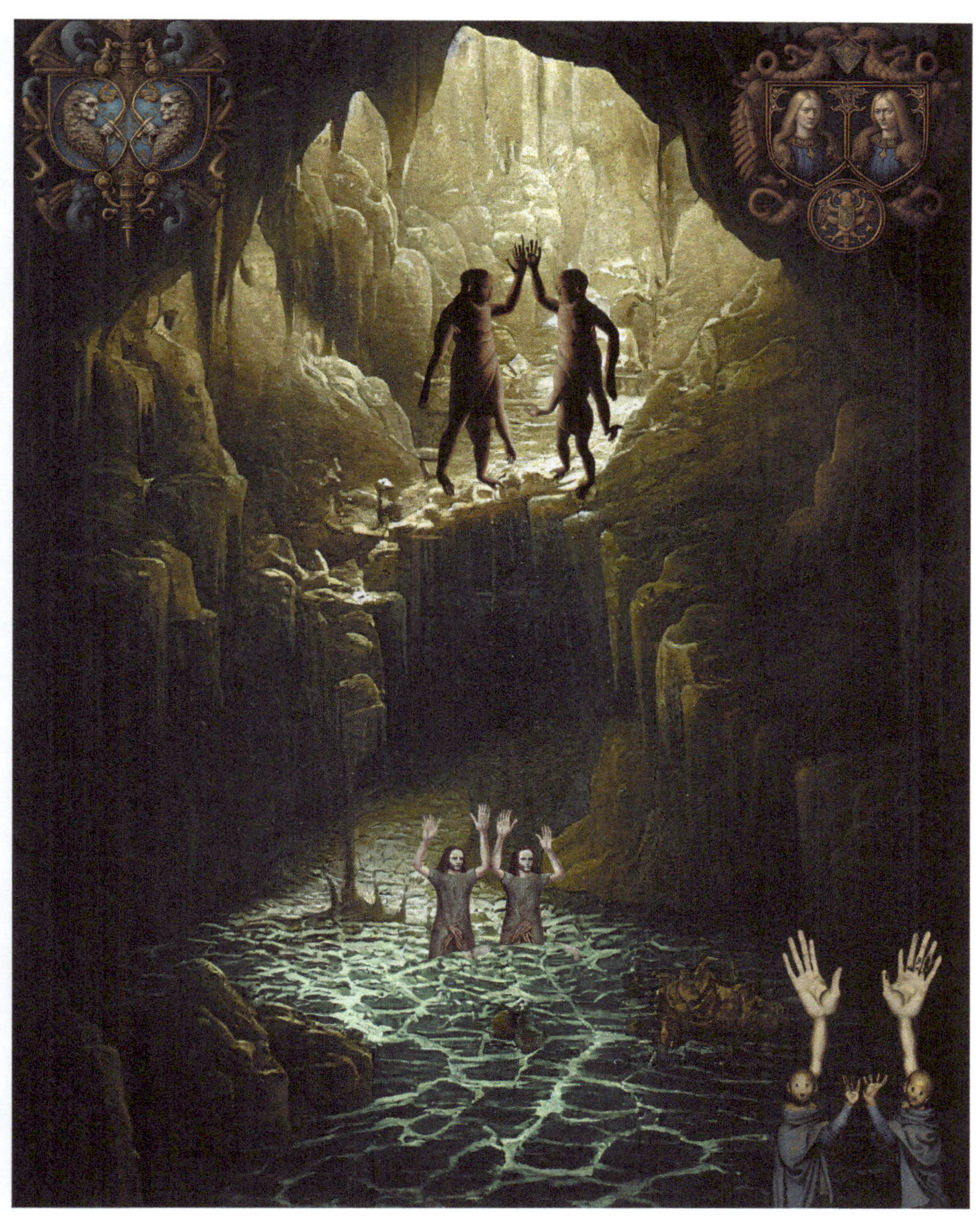

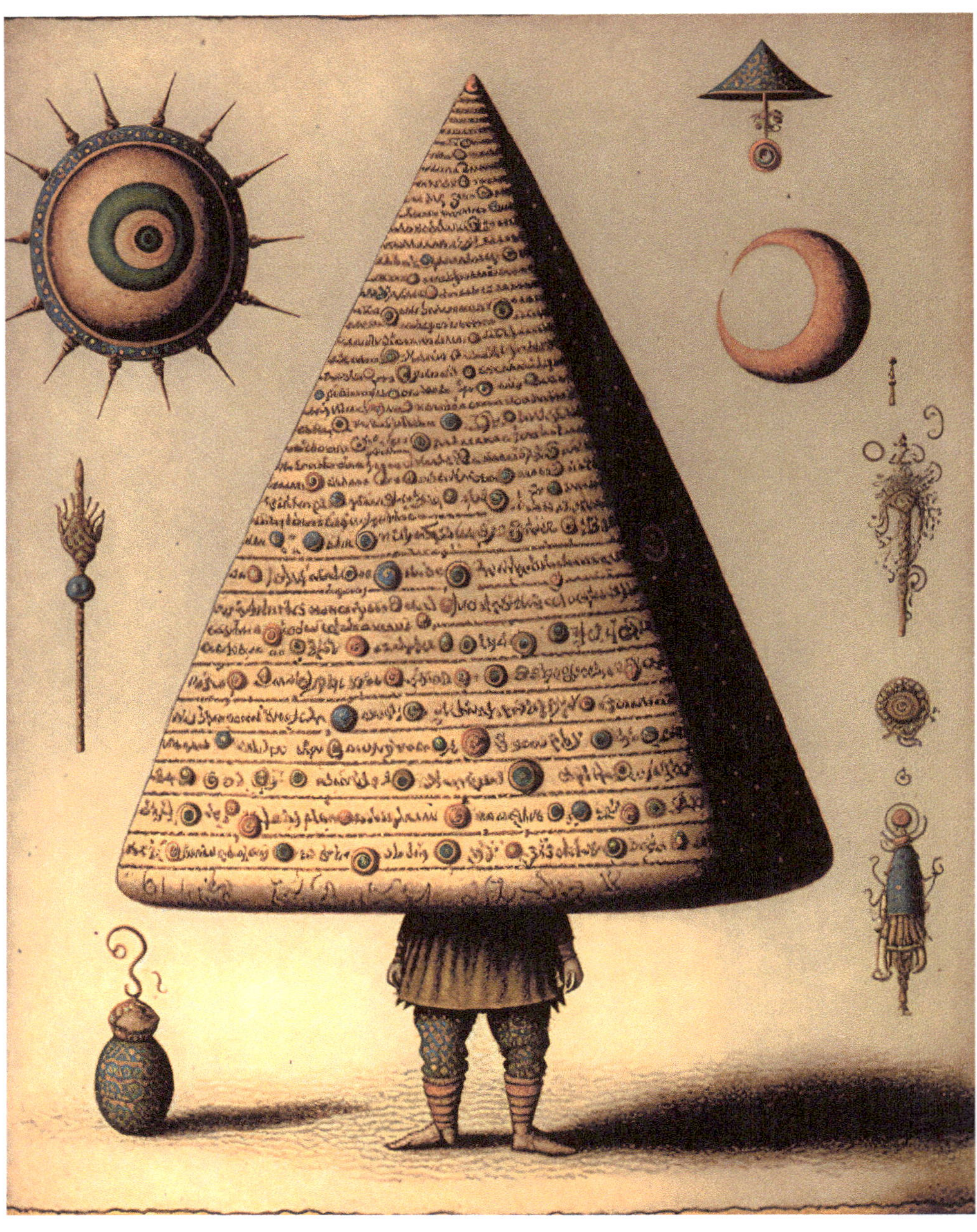

IV.35 Pisces II ... a man turned around backwards holding his head downwards, and his feet upwards lifted up on high, and in his hand a tray of something to be eaten. (Picatrix†2.XI§37)

/Oracle of DelphΛI

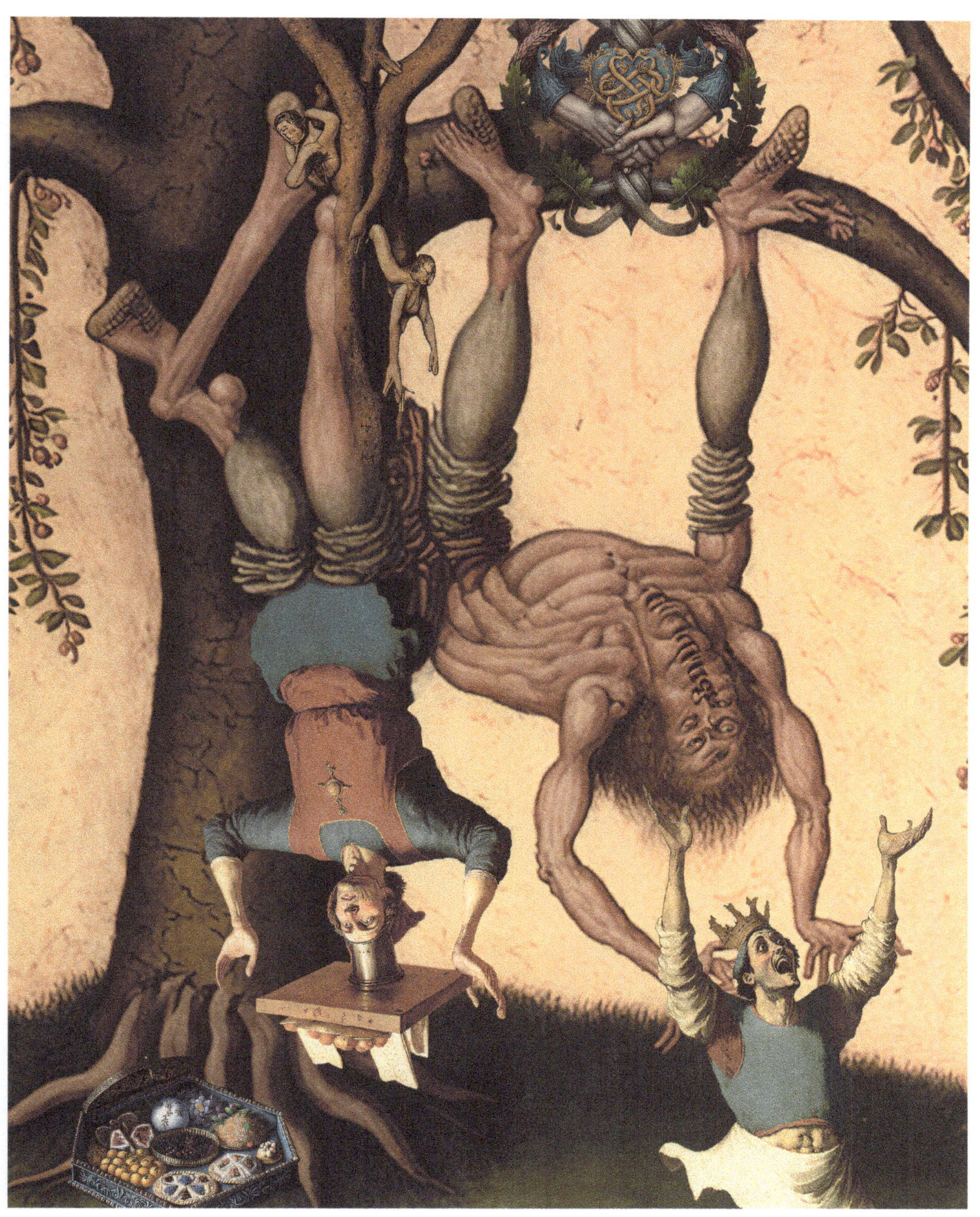

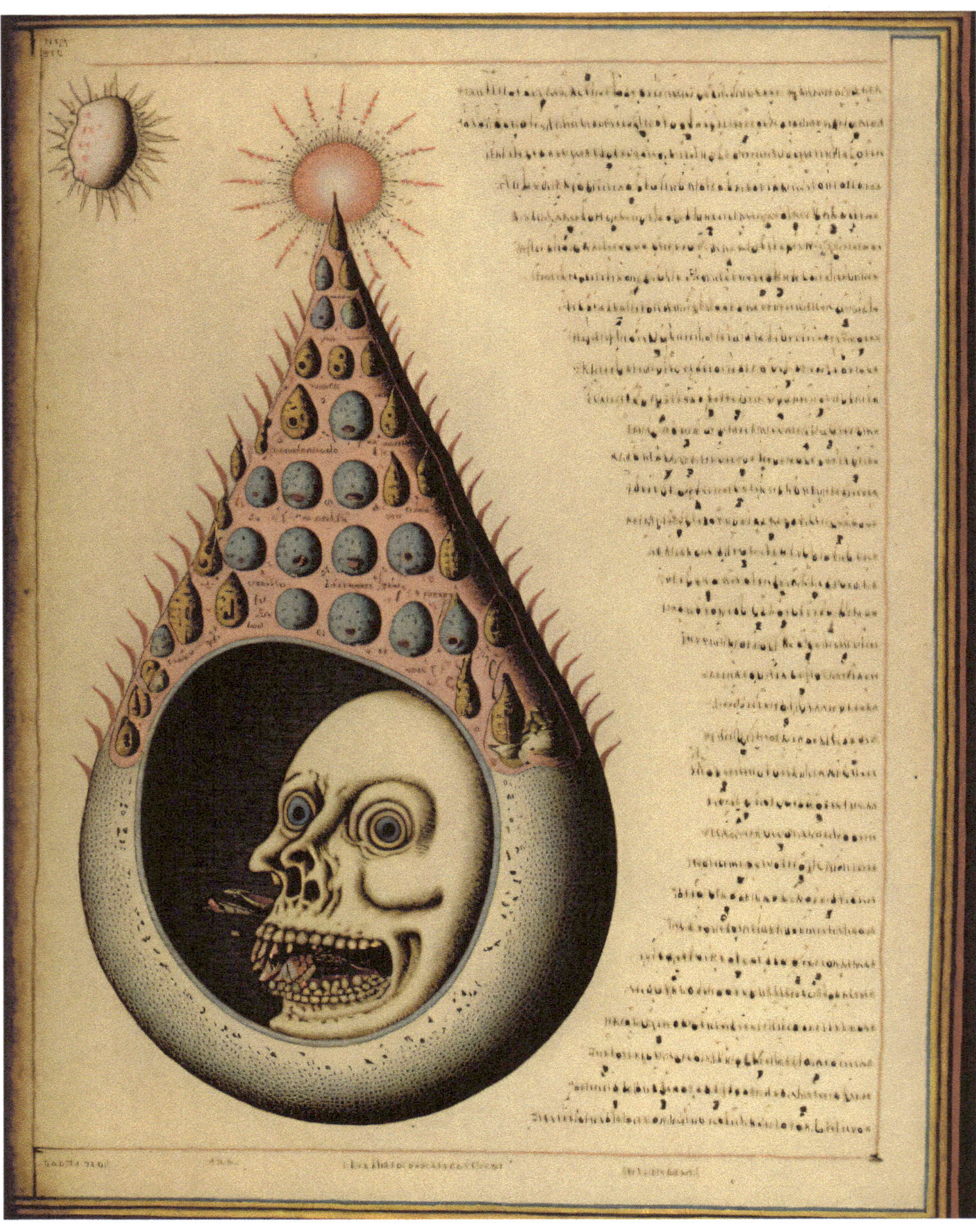

IV.36 Pisces III ... a gloomy man with evil thoughts, considering deceits and betrayals. In front of him there is a woman with an ass climbing atop her, and a bird in her hand. (Picatrix‡ 2.11§38)

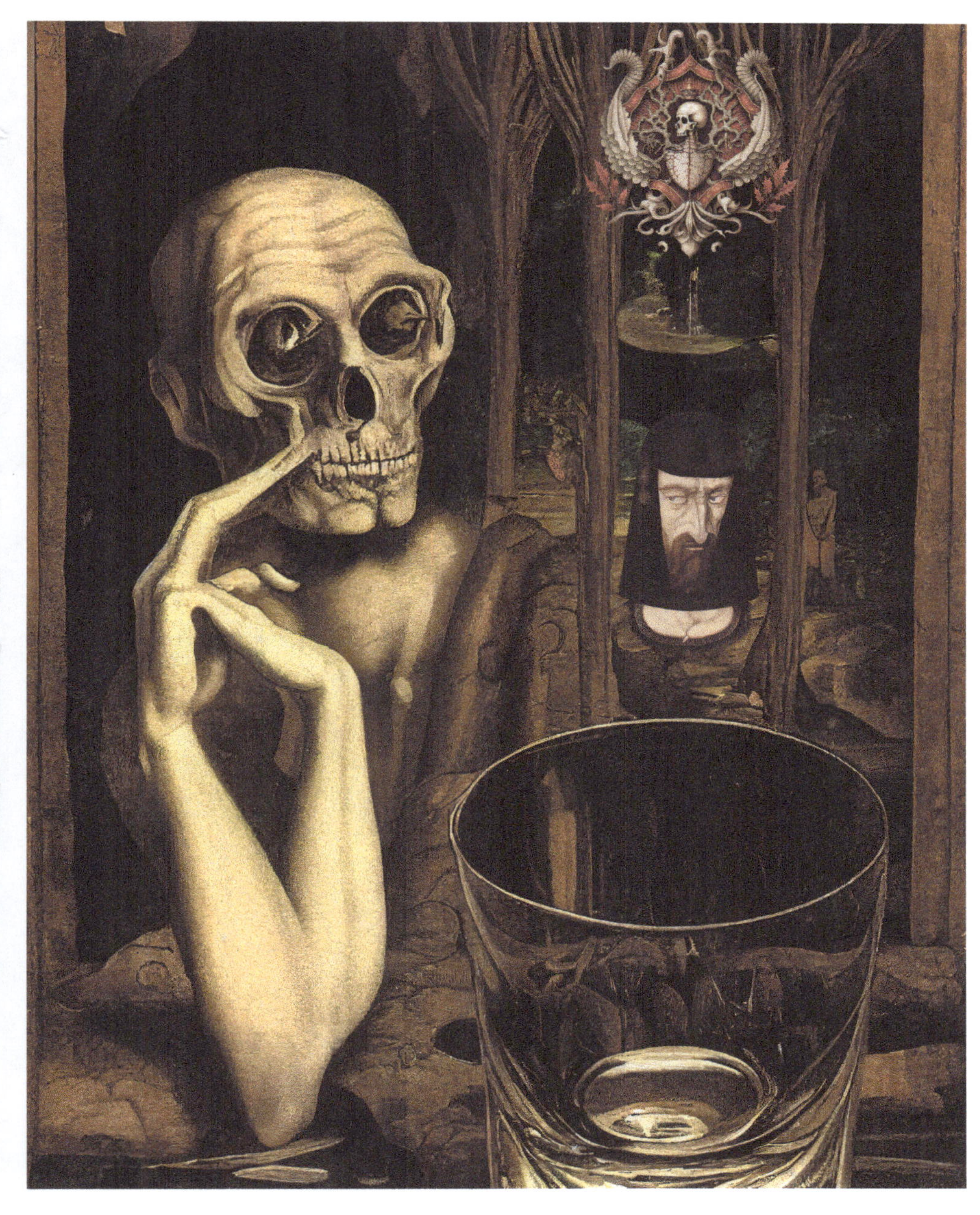

www.ingramcontent.com/pod-product-compliance
Lightning Source LLC
Chambersburg PA
CBHW050047040726

47599CB00015B/1841